ETERNITY

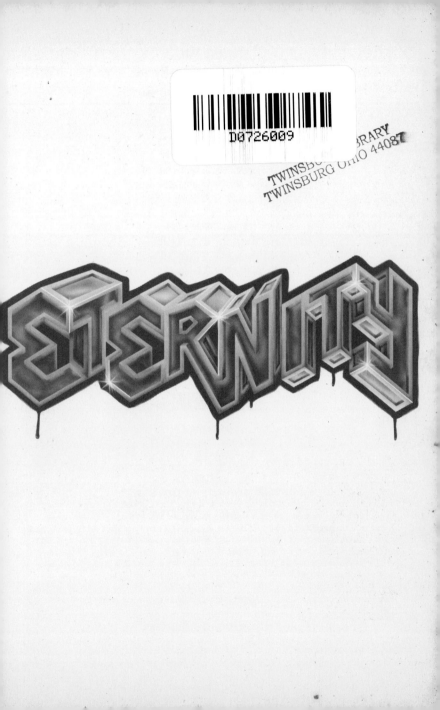

Eternity Vol. 3
written by Park Jin-Ryong
illustrated by Shin Yong-Gwan

Translation - Youngju Ryu
English Adaptation - Solina Wong
Copy Editor - Tim Beedle
Retouch and Lettering - Junemoon Studios
Production Artist - Vicente Rivera, Jr.
Cover Design - Anna Kernbaum

Editor - Rob Valois
Digital Imaging Manager - Chris Buford
Pre-Press Manager - Antonio DePietro
Production Managers - Jennifer Miller and Mutsumi Miyazaki
Art Director - Matt Alford
Managing Editor - Jill Freshney
VP of Production - Ron Klamert
Editor In Chief - Mike Kiley
President and C.O.O. - John Parker
Publisher and C.E.O. - Stuart Levy

A **TOKYOPOP** Manga

TOKYOPOP Inc.
5900 Wilshire Blvd. Suite 2000
Los Angeles, CA 90036

E-mail: info@TOKYOPOP.com
Come visit us online at www.TOKYOPOP.com

ISBN: 1-59182-964-X

First TOKYOPOP printing: January 2005
10 9 8 7 6 5 4 3 2 1
Printed in the USA

VOL. 3

STORY BY
PARK JIN-RYONG

ART BY
SHIN YONG-GWAN

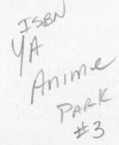

ISBN
YA
Anime
PARK
#3

HAMBURG // LONDON // LOS ANGELES // TOKYO

PREVIOUSLY IN

The spirits of millennia-old warriors have been reincarnated in the form of three disparate modern-day Korean teenagers. Their names are Gwanun, Jangbang and Yubin. Now a young shaman girl named Aram has arrived to unite them and guide them toward their mutual destiny. But another entity, far less friendly, has returned from the mists of time to affect the lives of the three boys. His name is JoJo, and he intends to lay waste to all those who have wronged him in the past. Preparing for the war they know will be coming, the heads of the six local youth gangs make plans to take down JoJo. But when they mistake Jangbang and Gwanun for JoJo's allies, this little turf war threatens to become all-out Armageddon.

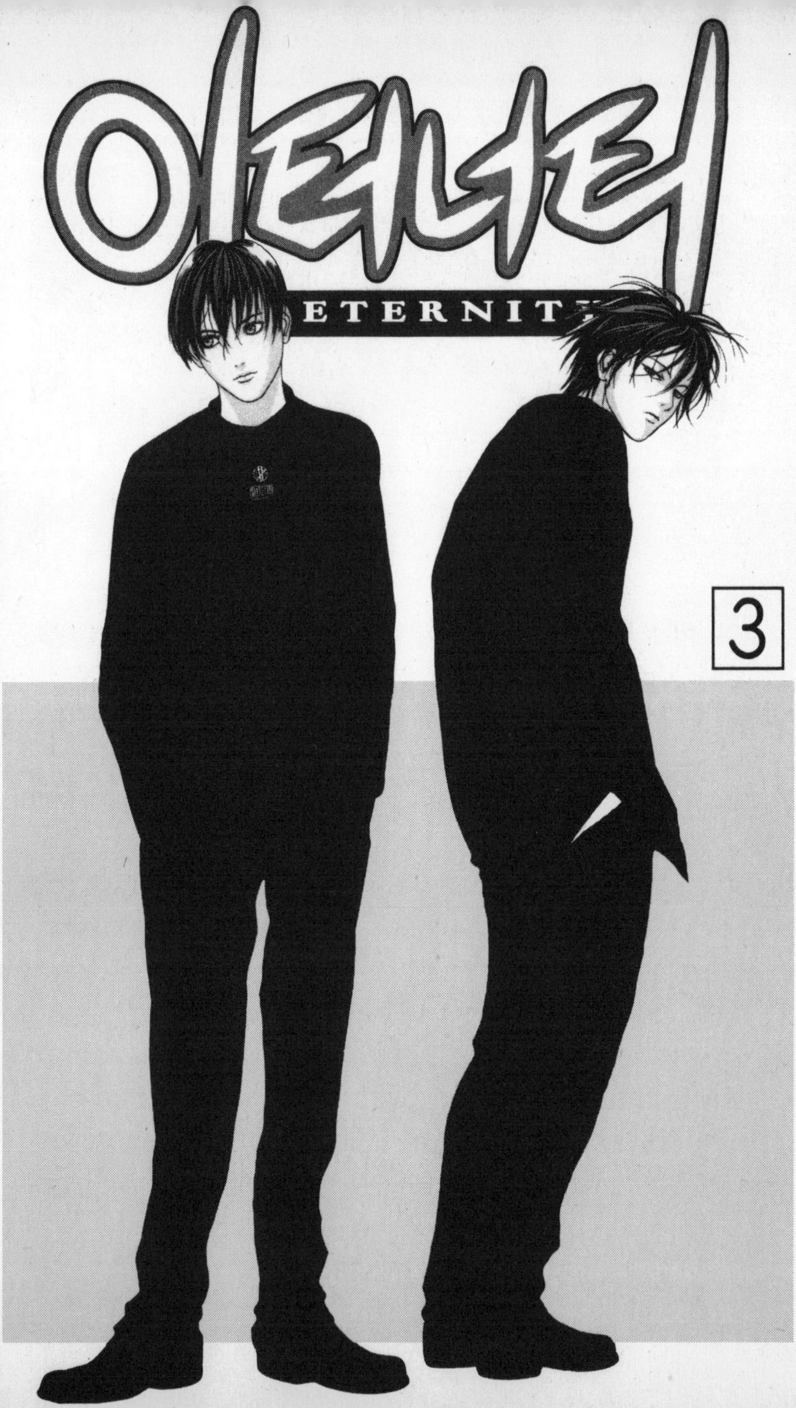
이터니티
ETERNITY
3

ETERNITY

#15. MOSA THE IMPERSONATOR ·········· 7

#16. MADEUNG MAKES HIS ENTRANCE ········ 31

#17. A BLOODY BATTLE ·········· 55

#18. RECONCILIATION ·········· 79

#19. THE POWER OF THE NAME JOJO 103

#20. A PICKPOCKET GIRL ········· 143

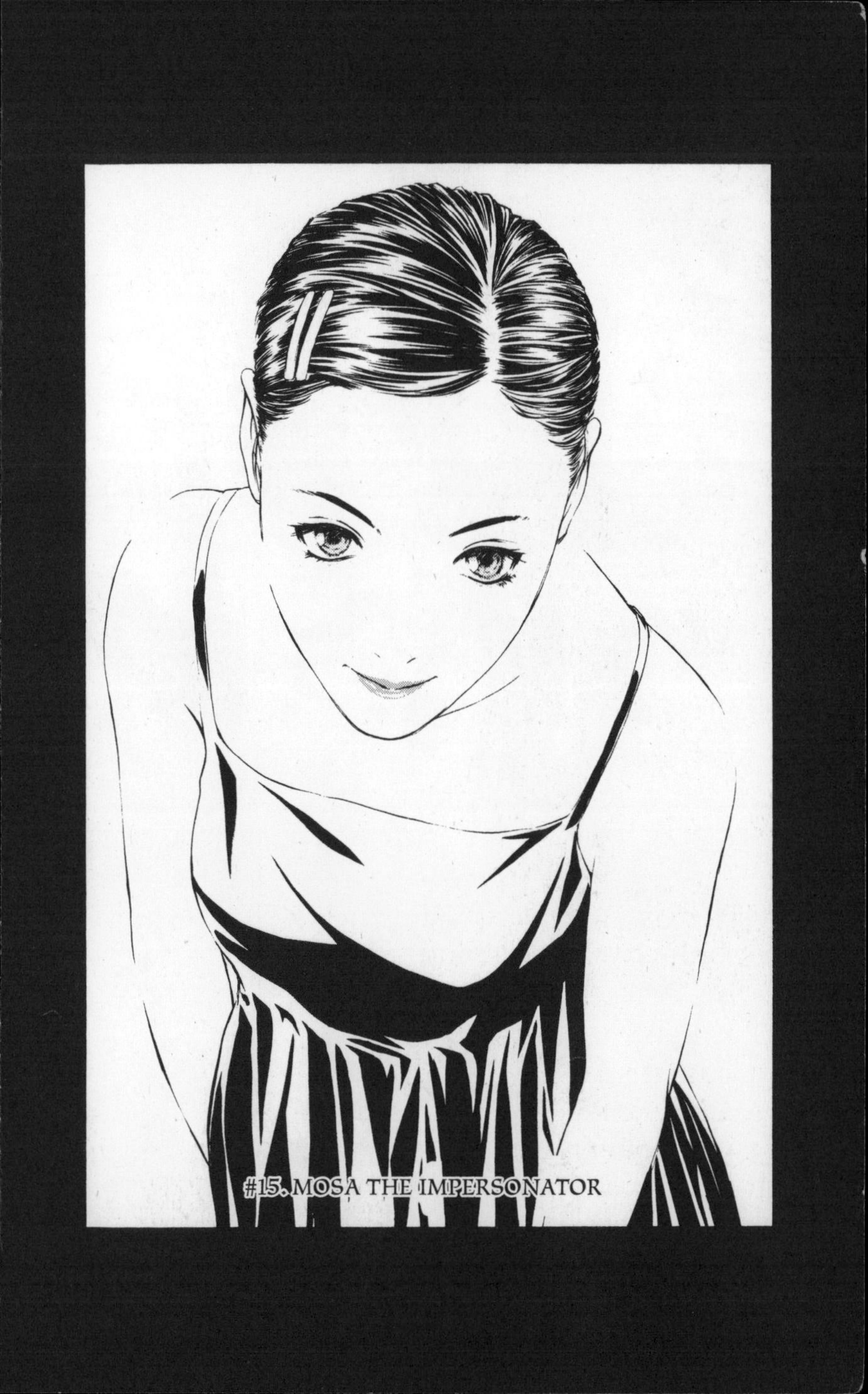
#15. MOSA THE IMPERSONATOR

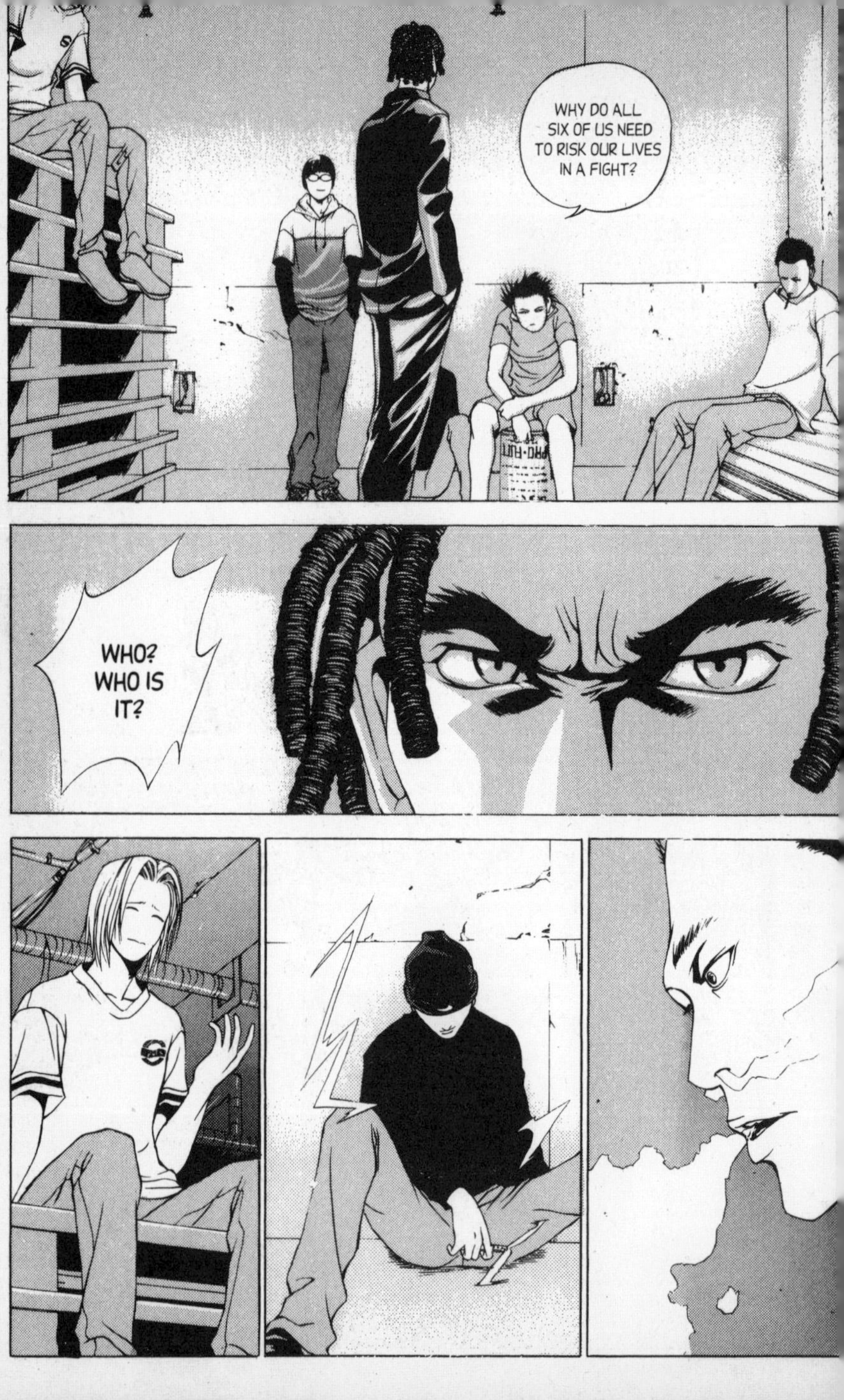
WHY DO ALL SIX OF US NEED TO RISK OUR LIVES IN A FIGHT?
WHO? WHO IS IT?

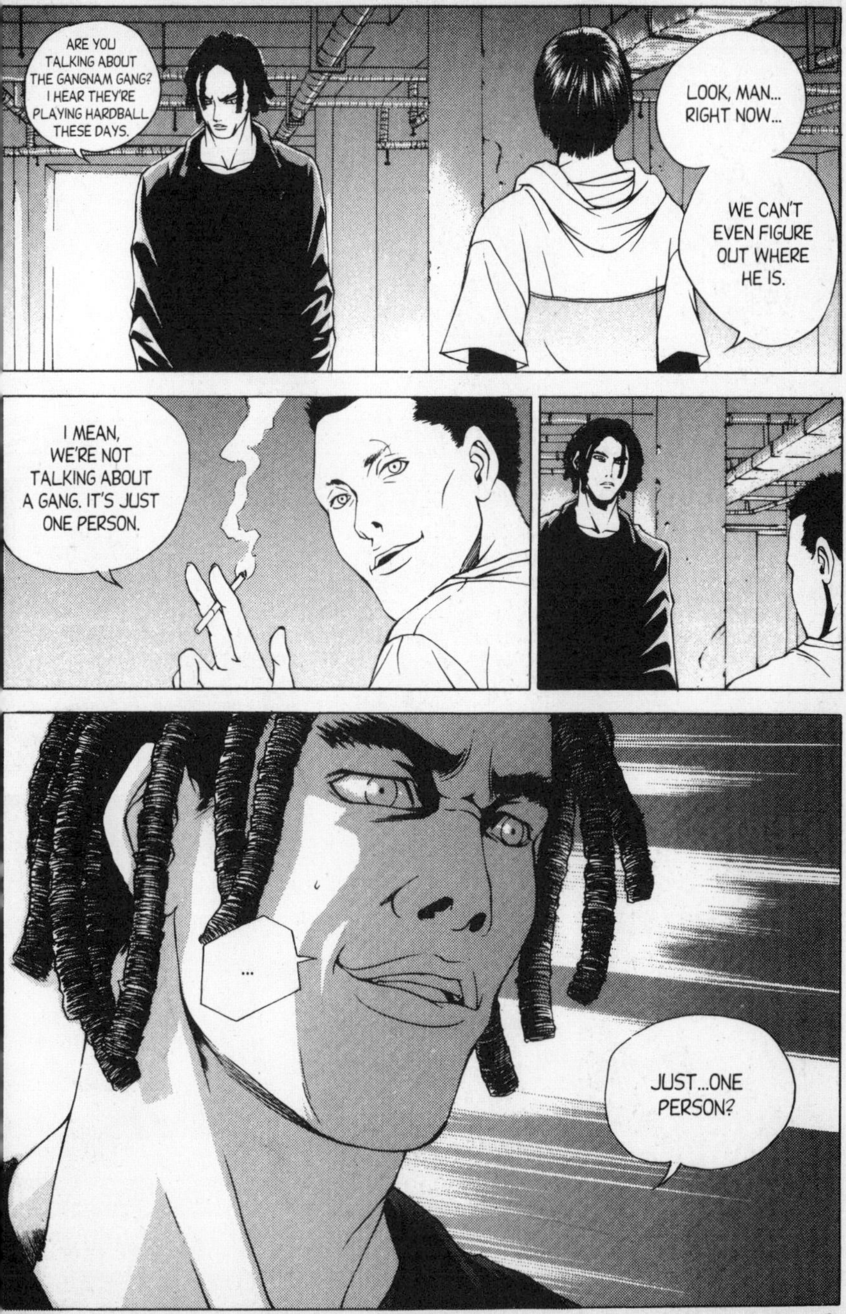
ARE YOU TALKING ABOUT THE GANGNAM GANG? I HEAR THEY'RE PLAYING HARDBALL THESE DAYS.
LOOK, MAN... RIGHT NOW...
WE CAN'T EVEN FIGURE OUT WHERE HE IS.
I MEAN, WE'RE NOT TALKING ABOUT A GANG. IT'S JUST ONE PERSON.
...
JUST...ONE PERSON?

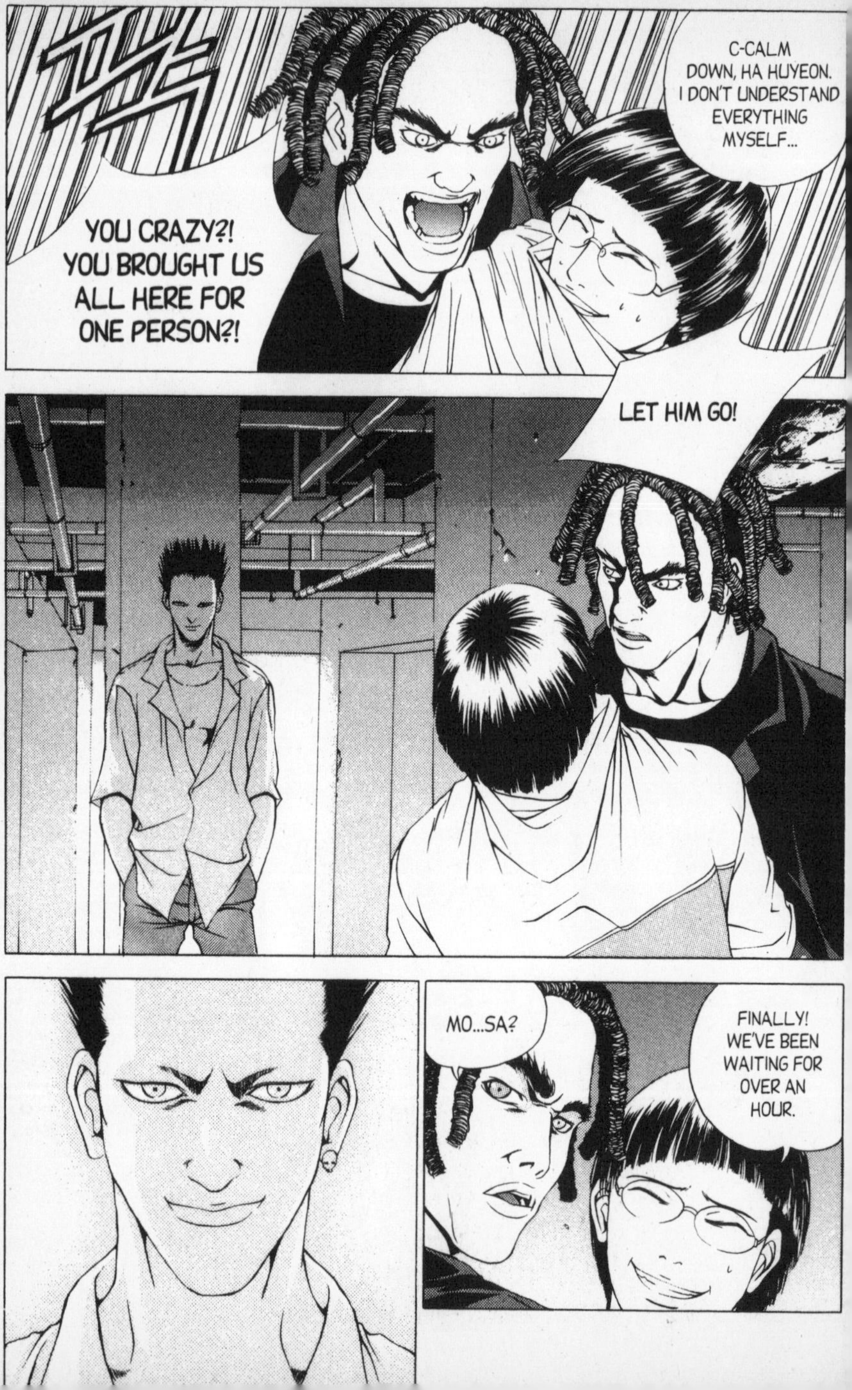
YOU CRAZY?! YOU BROUGHT US ALL HERE FOR ONE PERSON?!
C-CALM DOWN, HA HUYEON. I DON'T UNDERSTAND EVERYTHING MYSELF...
LET HIM GO!
MO...SA?
FINALLY! WE'VE BEEN WAITING FOR OVER AN HOUR.

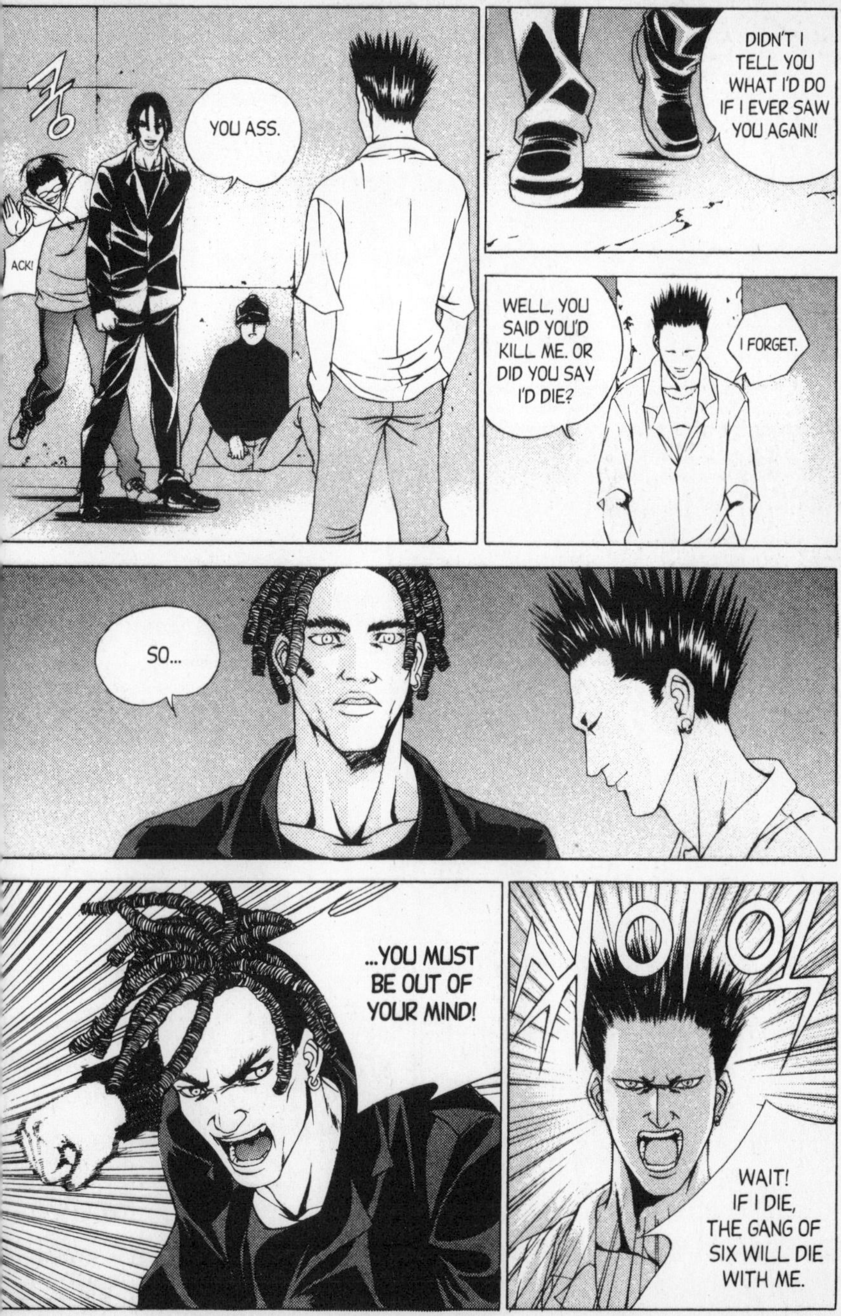
ACK!
YOU ASS.
DIDN'T I TELL YOU WHAT I'D DO IF I EVER SAW YOU AGAIN!
WELL, YOU SAID YOU'D KILL ME. OR DID YOU SAY I'D DIE?
I FORGET.
SO...
...YOU MUST BE OUT OF YOUR MIND!
WAIT! IF I DIE, THE GANG OF SIX WILL DIE WITH ME.

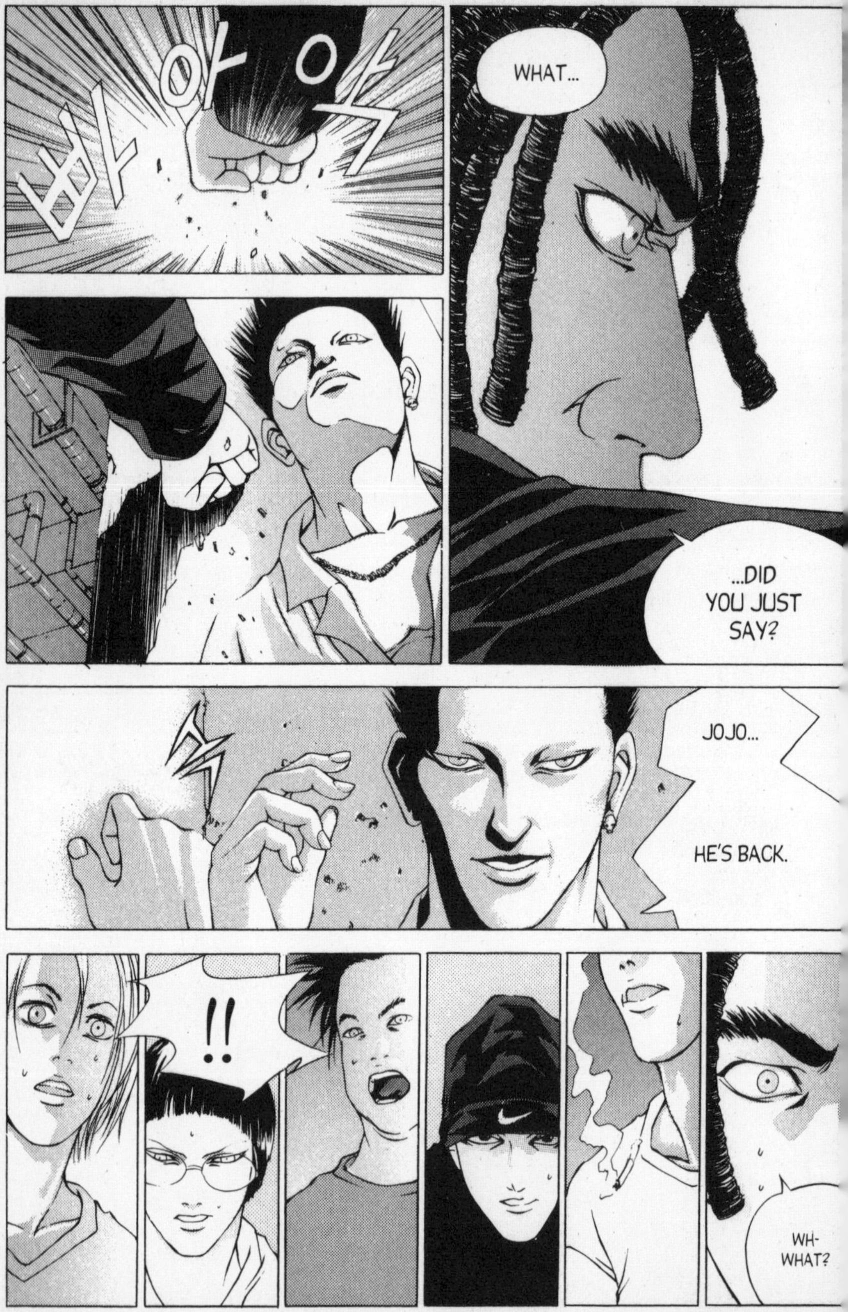
WHAT...
...DID YOU JUST SAY?
JOJO...
HE'S BACK.
!!
WH- WHAT?

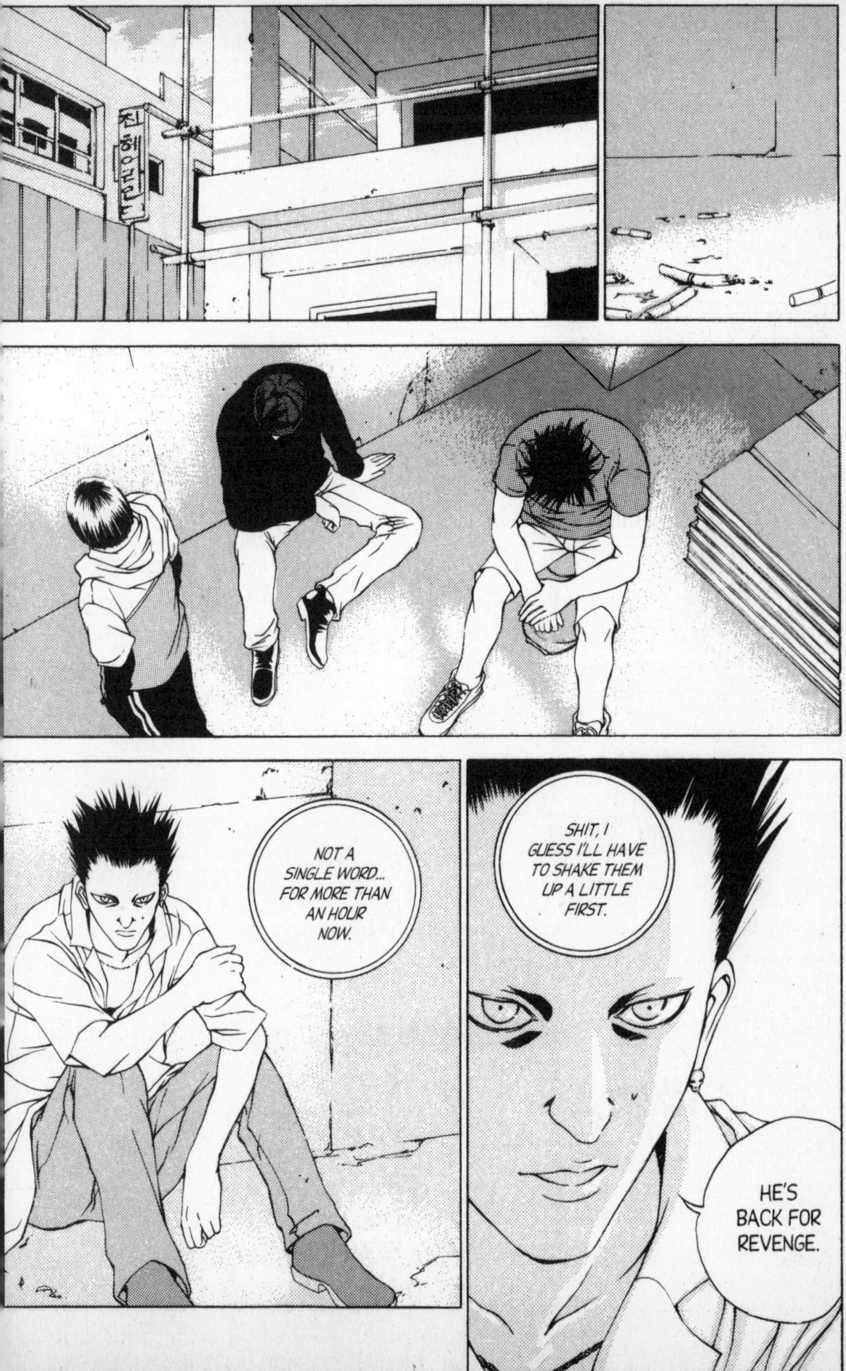
NOT A SINGLE WORD... FOR MORE THAN AN HOUR NOW.
SHIT, I GUESS I'LL HAVE TO SHAKE THEM UP A LITTLE FIRST.
HE'S BACK FOR REVENGE.

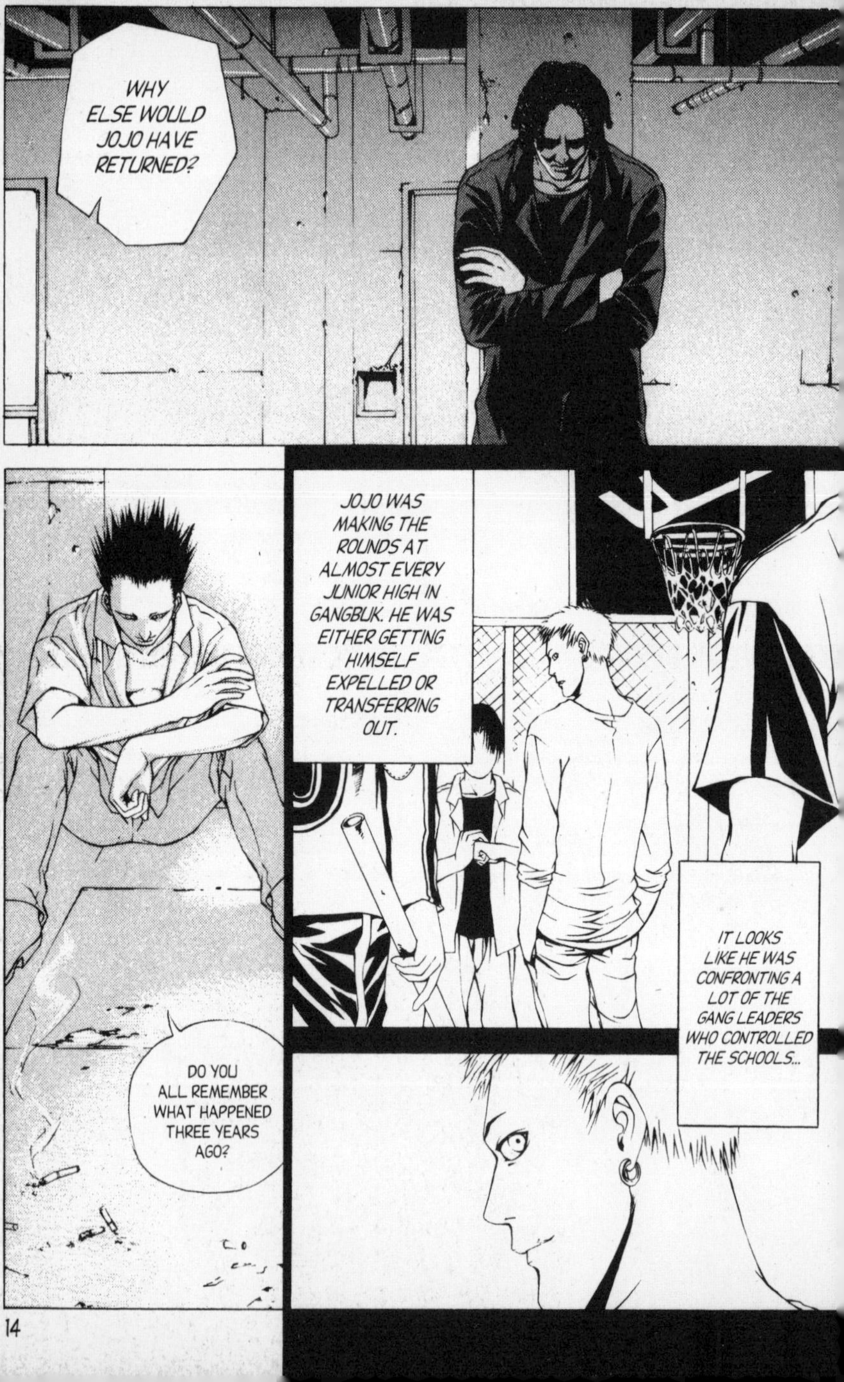
WHY ELSE WOULD JOJO HAVE RETURNED?
DO YOU ALL REMEMBER WHAT HAPPENED THREE YEARS AGO?
JOJO WAS MAKING THE ROUNDS AT ALMOST EVERY JUNIOR HIGH IN GANGBUK. HE WAS EITHER GETTING HIMSELF EXPELLED OR TRANSFERRING OUT.
IT LOOKS LIKE HE WAS CONFRONTING A LOT OF THE GANG LEADERS WHO CONTROLLED THE SCHOOLS...

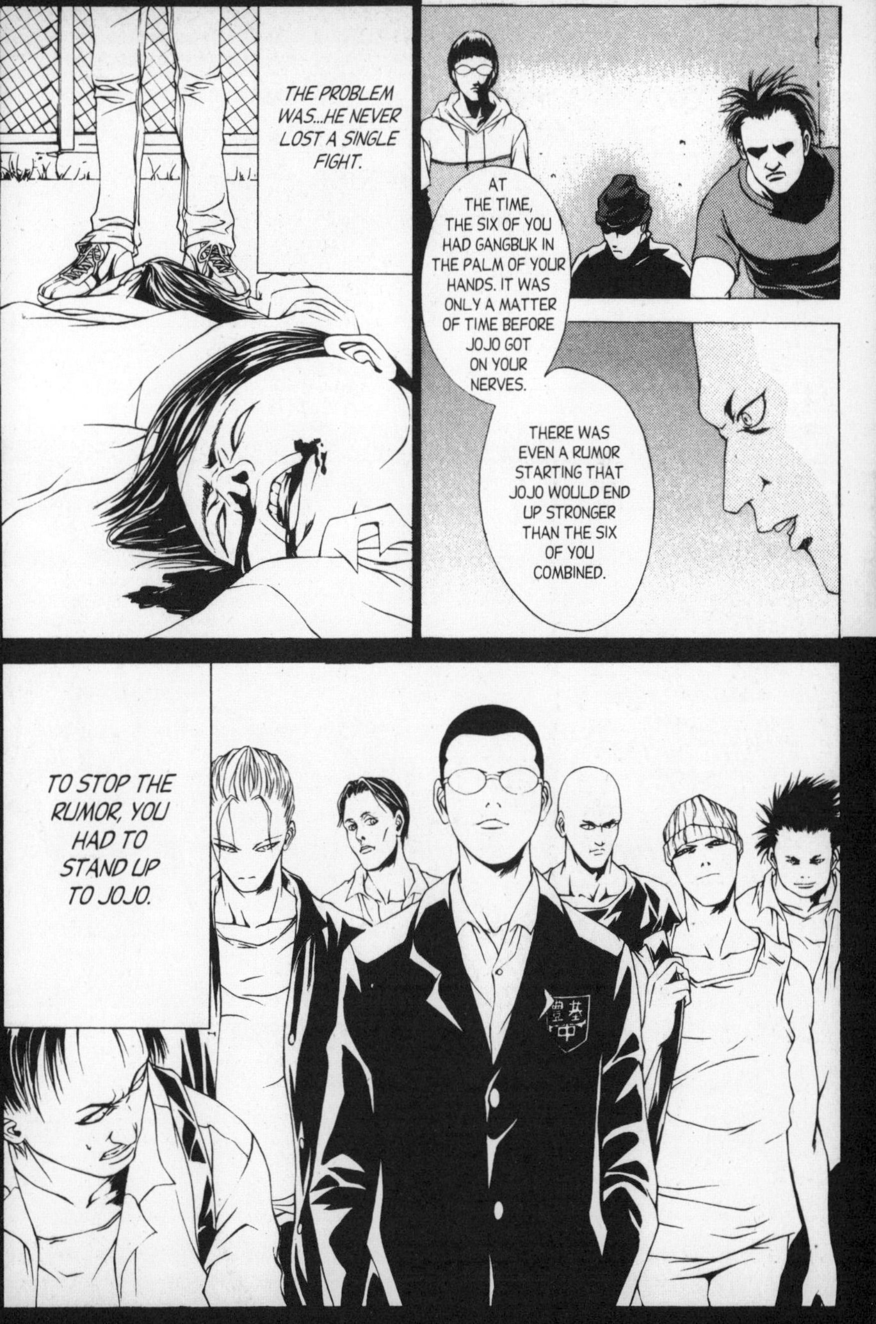
THE PROBLEM WAS...HE NEVER LOST A SINGLE FIGHT.
AT THE TIME, THE SIX OF YOU HAD GANGBUK IN THE PALM OF YOUR HANDS. IT WAS ONLY A MATTER OF TIME BEFORE JOJO GOT ON YOUR NERVES.
THERE WAS EVEN A RUMOR STARTING THAT JOJO WOULD END UP STRONGER THAN THE SIX OF YOU COMBINED.
TO STOP THE RUMOR, YOU HAD TO STAND UP TO JOJO.

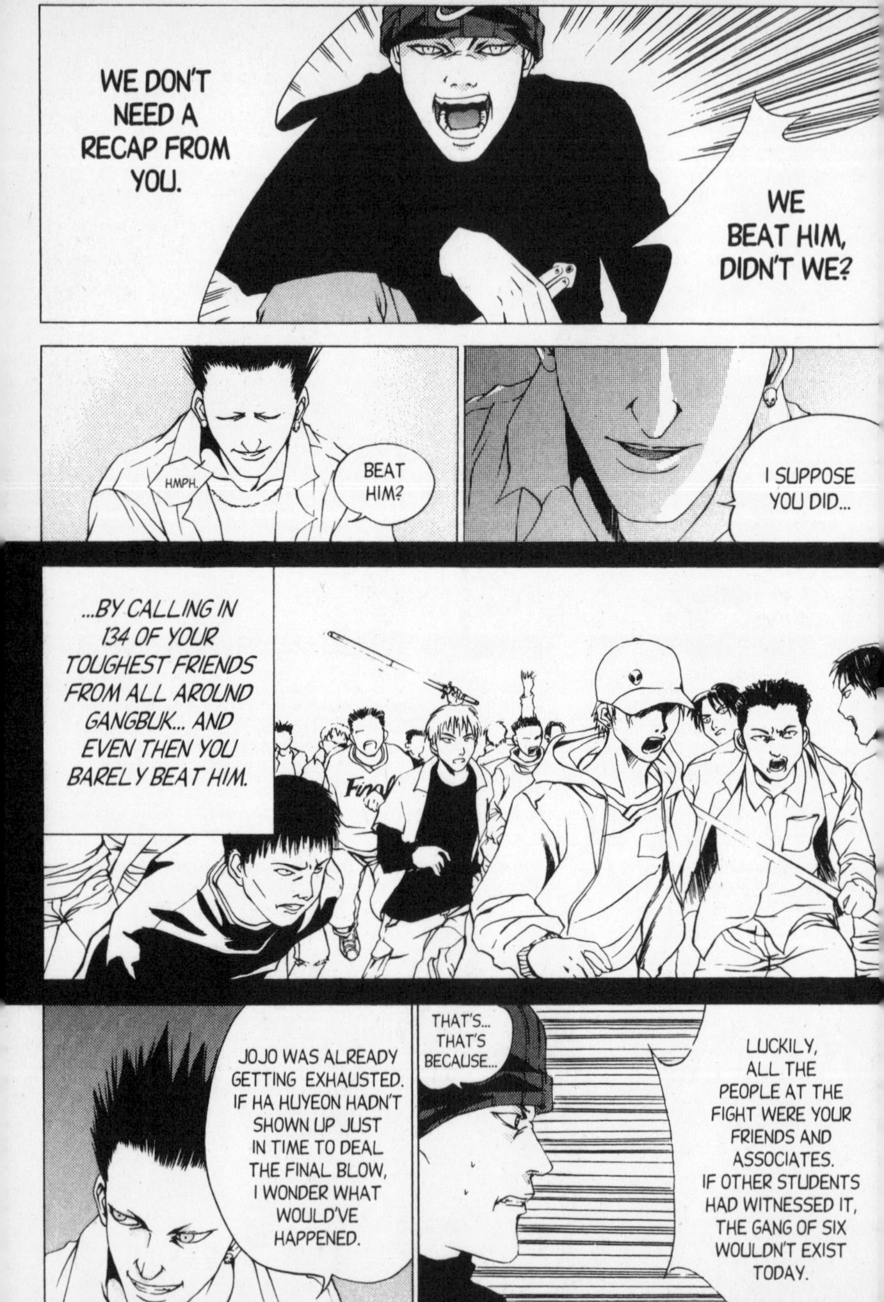
WE DON'T NEED A RECAP FROM YOU.
WE BEAT HIM, DIDN'T WE?
HMPH.
BEAT HIM?
I SUPPOSE YOU DID...
...BY CALLING IN 134 OF YOUR TOUGHEST FRIENDS FROM ALL AROUND GANGBUK... AND EVEN THEN YOU BARELY BEAT HIM.
JOJO WAS ALREADY GETTING EXHAUSTED. IF HA HUYEON HADN'T SHOWN UP JUST IN TIME TO DEAL THE FINAL BLOW, I WONDER WHAT WOULD'VE HAPPENED.
THAT'S... THAT'S BECAUSE...
LUCKILY, ALL THE PEOPLE AT THE FIGHT WERE YOUR FRIENDS AND ASSOCIATES. IF OTHER STUDENTS HAD WITNESSED IT, THE GANG OF SIX WOULDN'T EXIST TODAY.

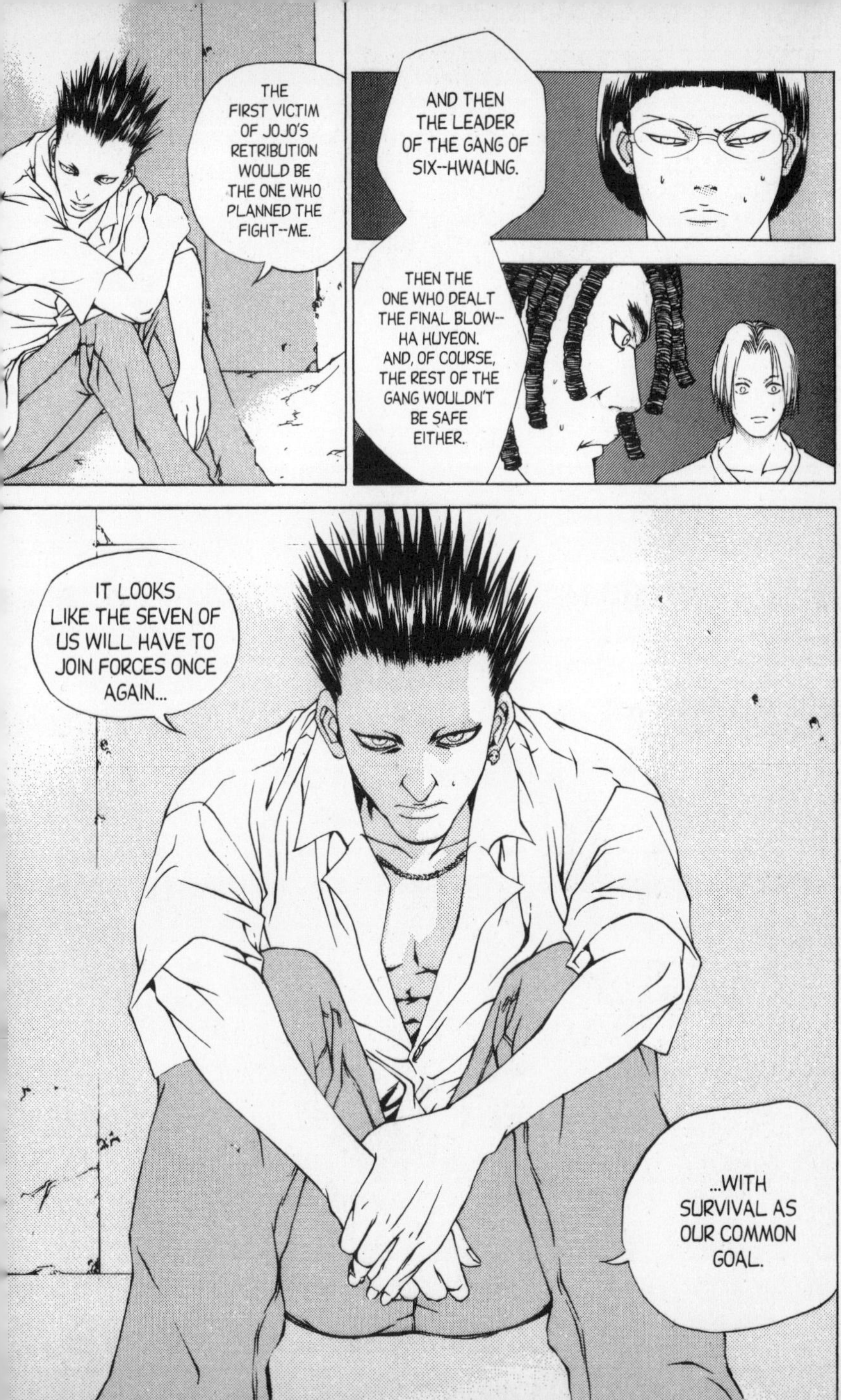
THE FIRST VICTIM OF JOJO'S RETRIBUTION WOULD BE THE ONE WHO PLANNED THE FIGHT--ME.
AND THEN THE LEADER OF THE GANG OF SIX--HWAUNG.
THEN THE ONE WHO DEALT THE FINAL BLOW--HA HUYEON. AND, OF COURSE, THE REST OF THE GANG WOULDN'T BE SAFE EITHER.
IT LOOKS LIKE THE SEVEN OF US WILL HAVE TO JOIN FORCES ONCE AGAIN...
...WITH SURVIVAL AS OUR COMMON GOAL.

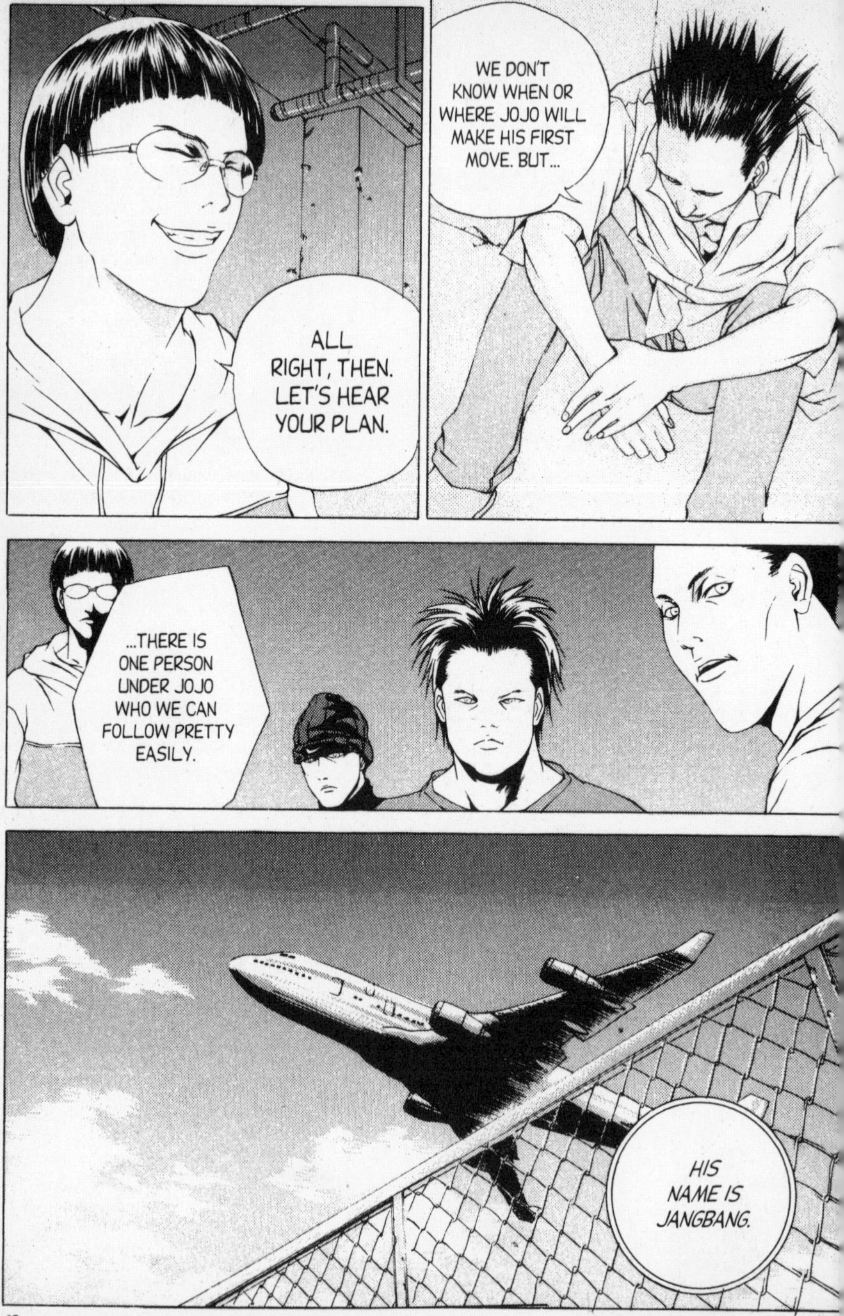
ALL RIGHT, THEN. LET'S HEAR YOUR PLAN.
WE DON'T KNOW WHEN OR WHERE JOJO WILL MAKE HIS FIRST MOVE. BUT...
...THERE IS ONE PERSON UNDER JOJO WHO WE CAN FOLLOW PRETTY EASILY.
HIS NAME IS JANGBANG.

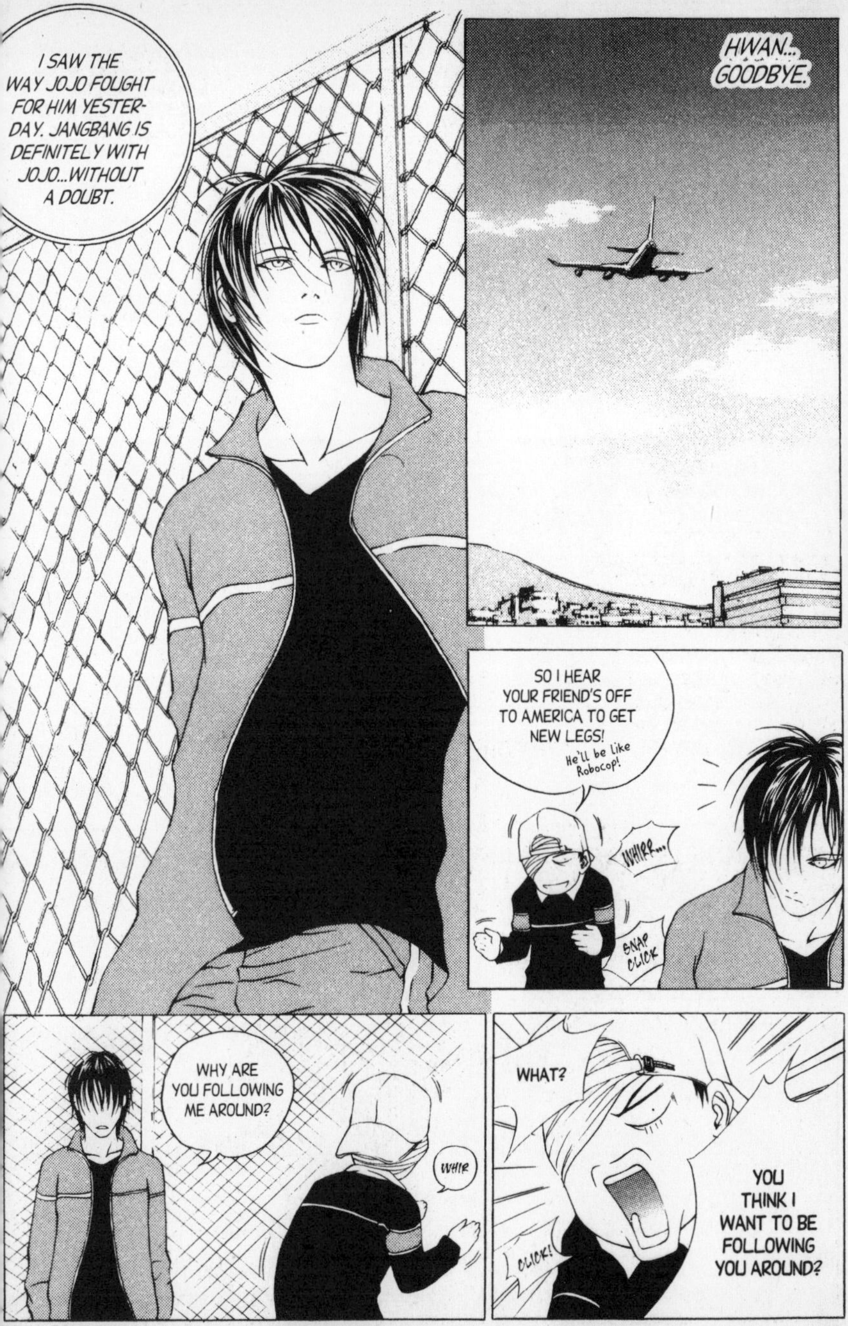
I SAW THE WAY JOJO FOUGHT FOR HIM YESTER-DAY. JANGBANG IS DEFINITELY WITH JOJO...WITHOUT A DOUBT.
HWAN... GOODBYE.
SO I HEAR YOUR FRIEND'S OFF TO AMERICA TO GET NEW LEGS!
He'll be like Robocop!
WHIRR...
SNAP CLICK
WHY ARE YOU FOLLOWING ME AROUND?
WHIR
WHAT?
YOU THINK I WANT TO BE FOLLOWING YOU AROUND?
CLICK!

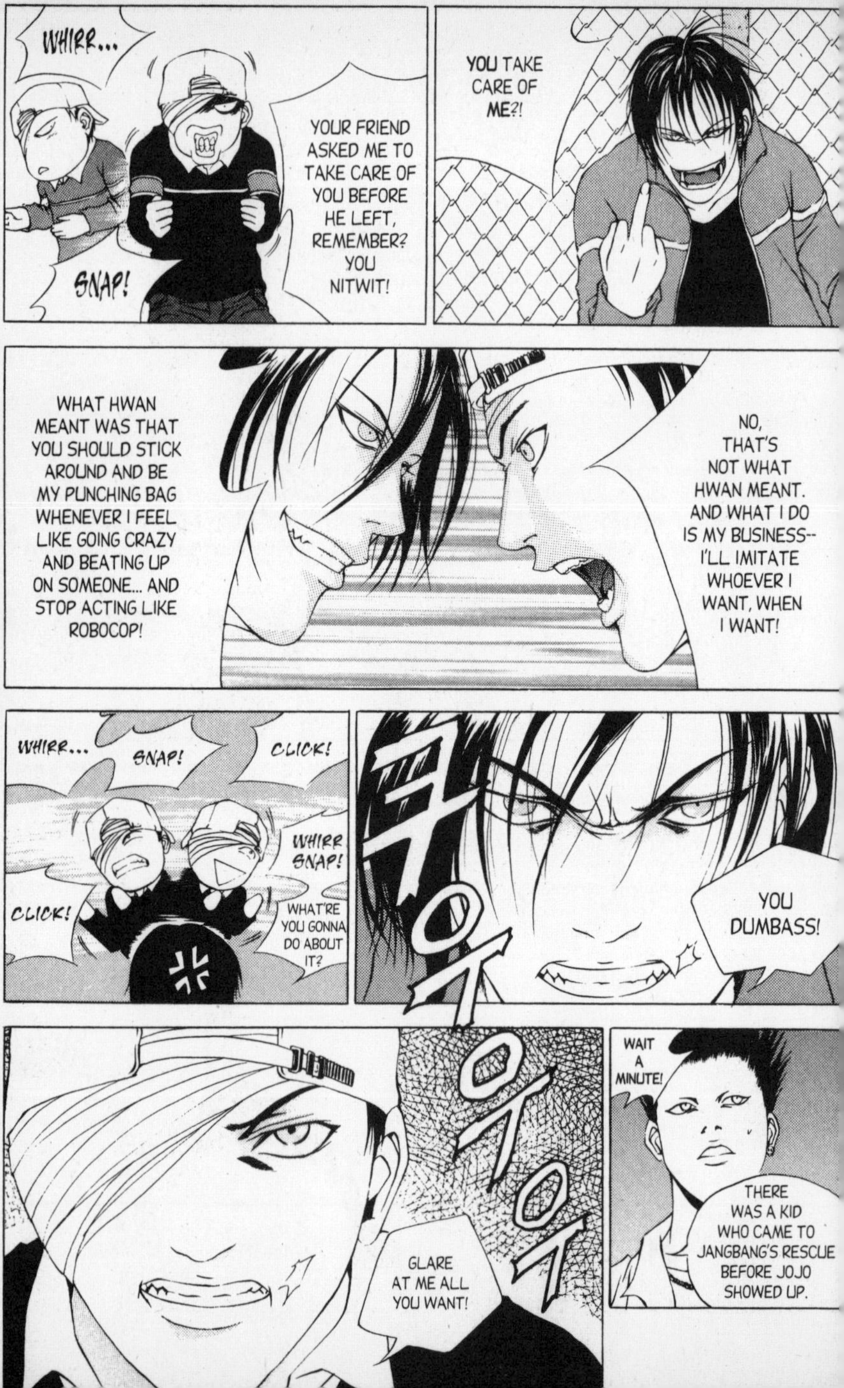
WHIRR...
SNAP!
YOUR FRIEND ASKED ME TO TAKE CARE OF YOU BEFORE HE LEFT, REMEMBER? YOU NITWIT!
YOU TAKE CARE OF ME?!
WHAT HWAN MEANT WAS THAT YOU SHOULD STICK AROUND AND BE MY PUNCHING BAG WHENEVER I FEEL LIKE GOING CRAZY AND BEATING UP ON SOMEONE... AND STOP ACTING LIKE ROBOCOP!
NO, THAT'S NOT WHAT HWAN MEANT. AND WHAT I DO IS MY BUSINESS-- I'LL IMITATE WHOEVER I WANT, WHEN I WANT!
WHIRR...
SNAP!
CLICK!
WHIRR SNAP!
CLICK!
WHAT'RE YOU GONNA DO ABOUT IT?
YOU DUMBASS!
GLARE AT ME ALL YOU WANT!
WAIT A MINUTE!
THERE WAS A KID WHO CAME TO JANGBANG'S RESCUE BEFORE JOJO SHOWED UP.

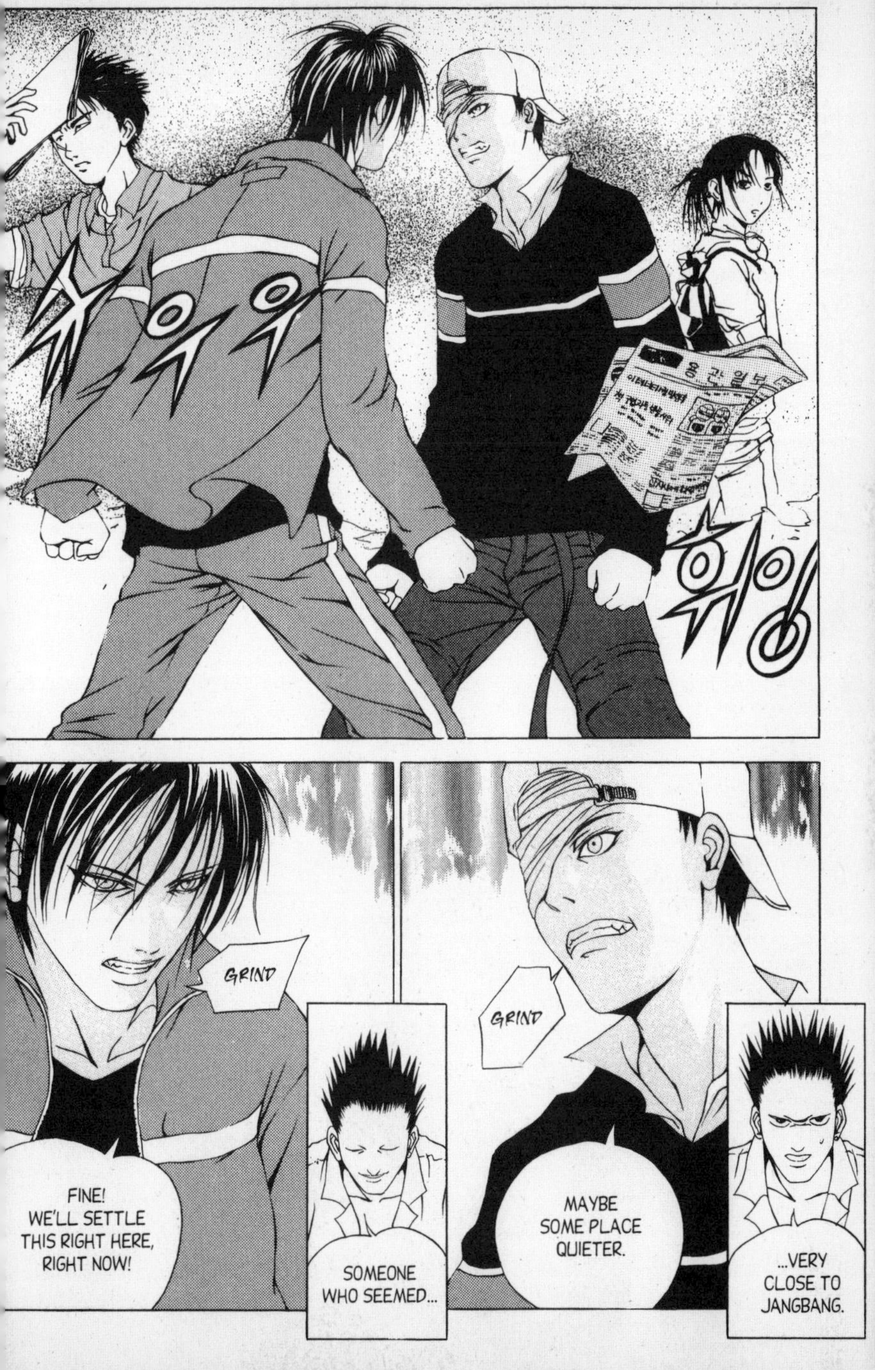
GRIND
FINE! WE'LL SETTLE THIS RIGHT HERE, RIGHT NOW!
SOMEONE WHO SEEMED...
GRIND
MAYBE SOME PLACE QUIETER.
...VERY CLOSE TO JANGBANG.

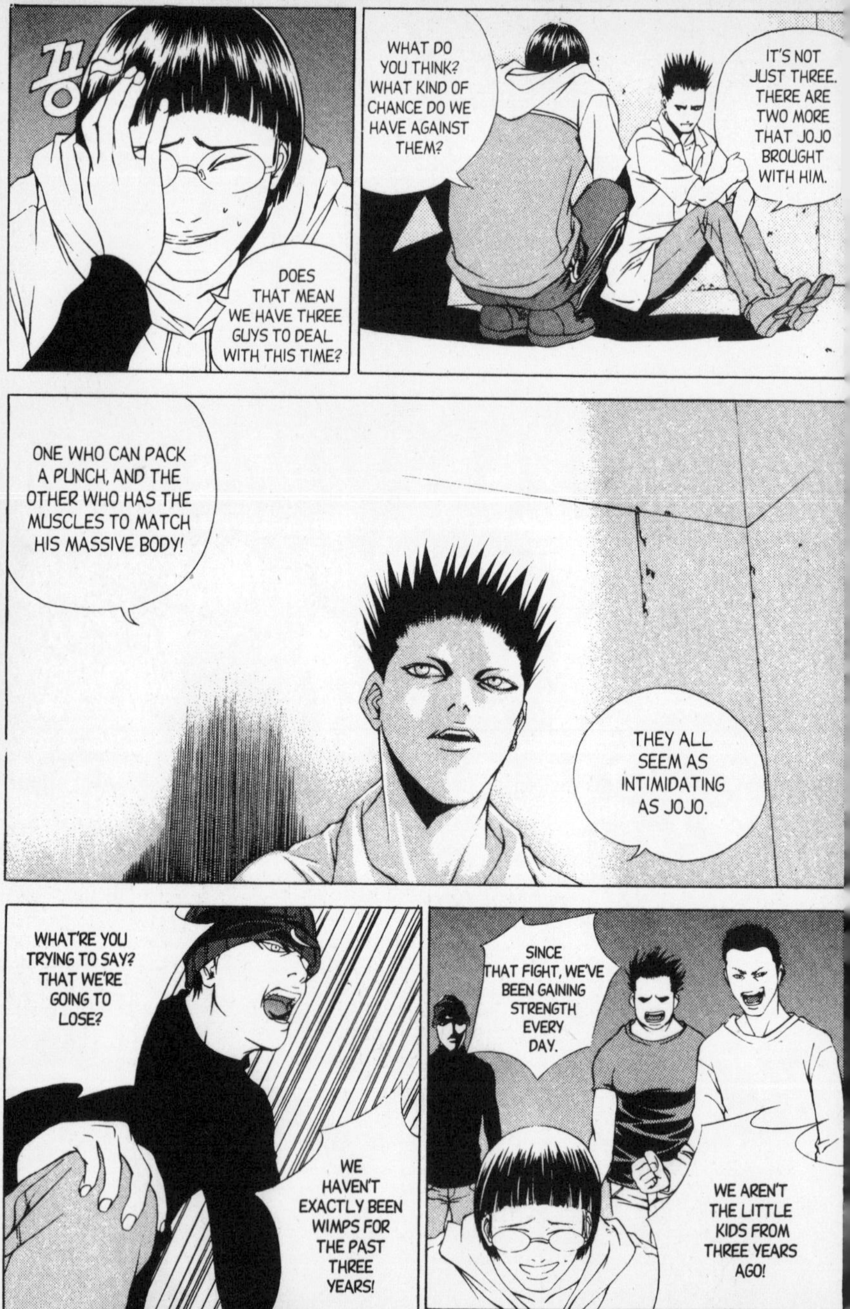
끙~
DOES THAT MEAN WE HAVE THREE GUYS TO DEAL WITH THIS TIME?
IT'S NOT JUST THREE. THERE ARE TWO MORE THAT JOJO BROUGHT WITH HIM.
WHAT DO YOU THINK? WHAT KIND OF CHANCE DO WE HAVE AGAINST THEM?
ONE WHO CAN PACK A PUNCH, AND THE OTHER WHO HAS THE MUSCLES TO MATCH HIS MASSIVE BODY!
THEY ALL SEEM AS INTIMIDATING AS JOJO.
WHAT'RE YOU TRYING TO SAY? THAT WE'RE GOING TO LOSE?
WE HAVEN'T EXACTLY BEEN WIMPS FOR THE PAST THREE YEARS!
SINCE THAT FIGHT, WE'VE BEEN GAINING STRENGTH EVERY DAY.
WE AREN'T THE LITTLE KIDS FROM THREE YEARS AGO!

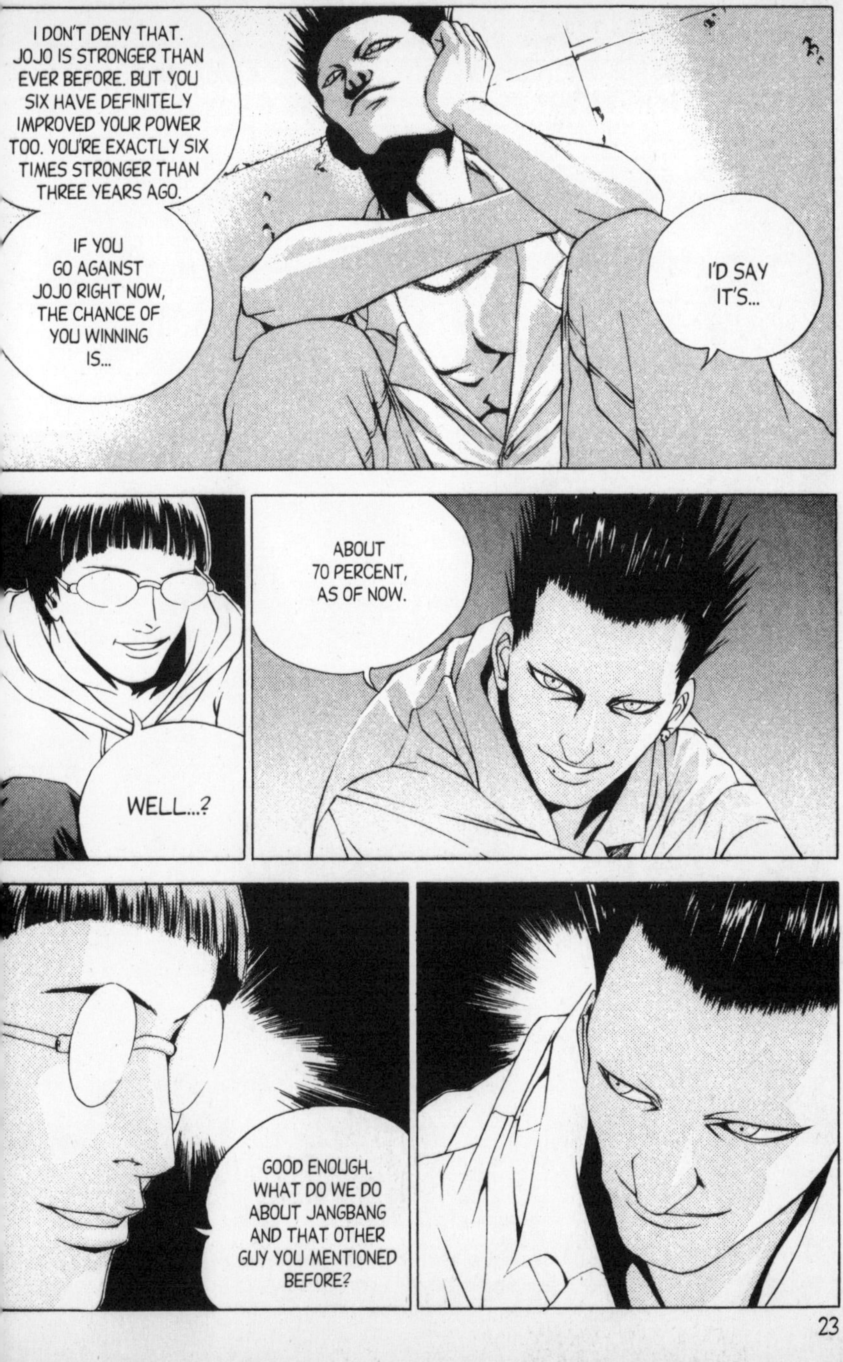
I DON'T DENY THAT. JOJO IS STRONGER THAN EVER BEFORE. BUT YOU SIX HAVE DEFINITELY IMPROVED YOUR POWER TOO. YOU'RE EXACTLY SIX TIMES STRONGER THAN THREE YEARS AGO.
IF YOU GO AGAINST JOJO RIGHT NOW, THE CHANCE OF YOU WINNING IS...
I'D SAY IT'S...
WELL...?
ABOUT 70 PERCENT, AS OF NOW.
GOOD ENOUGH. WHAT DO WE DO ABOUT JANGBANG AND THAT OTHER GUY YOU MENTIONED BEFORE?

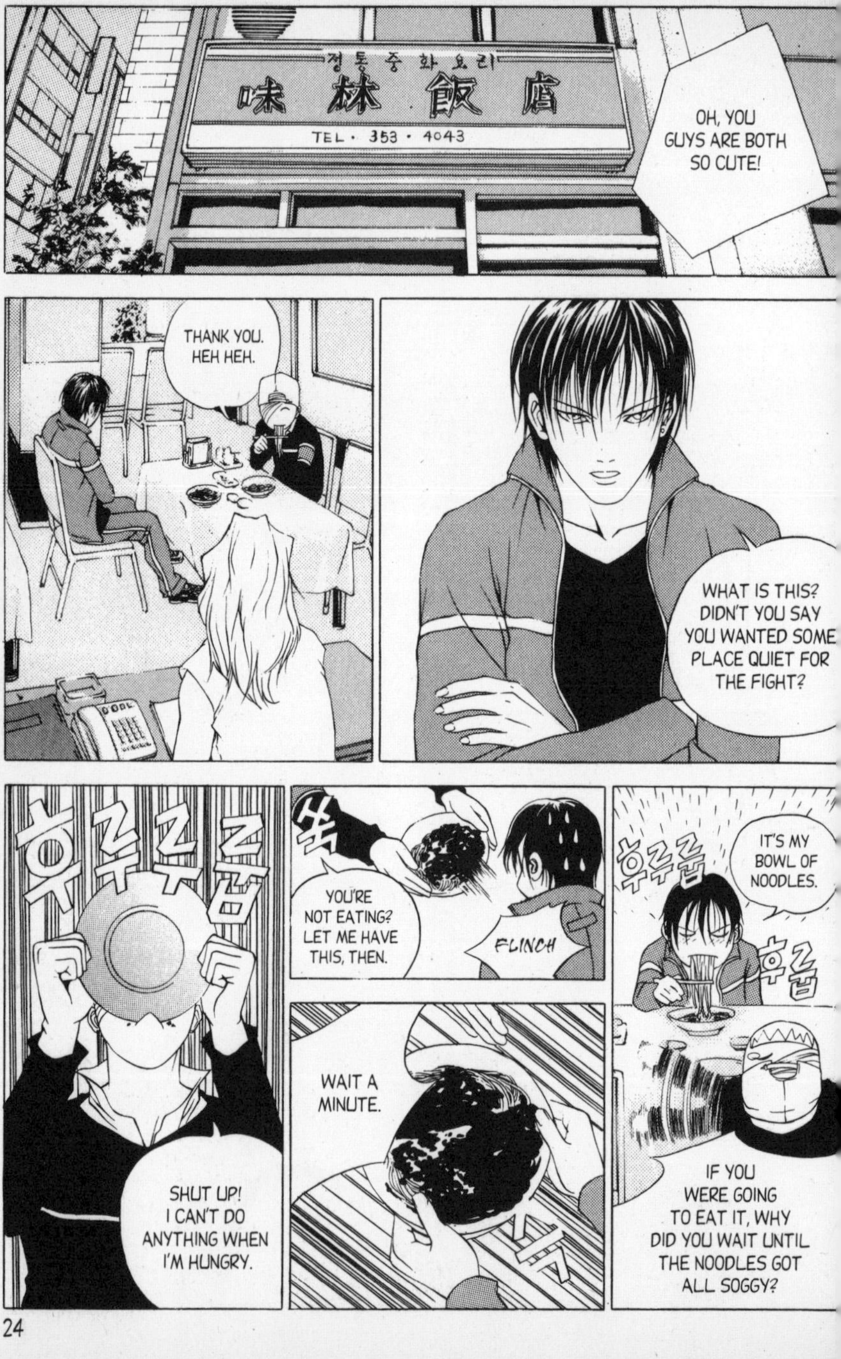
정통중화요리
味林飯店
TEL · 353 · 4043
OH, YOU GUYS ARE BOTH SO CUTE!
THANK YOU. HEH HEH.
WHAT IS THIS? DIDN'T YOU SAY YOU WANTED SOME PLACE QUIET FOR THE FIGHT?
YOU'RE NOT EATING? LET ME HAVE THIS, THEN.
FLINCH
IT'S MY BOWL OF NOODLES.
WAIT A MINUTE.
IF YOU WERE GOING TO EAT IT, WHY DID YOU WAIT UNTIL THE NOODLES GOT ALL SOGGY?
SHUT UP! I CAN'T DO ANYTHING WHEN I'M HUNGRY.

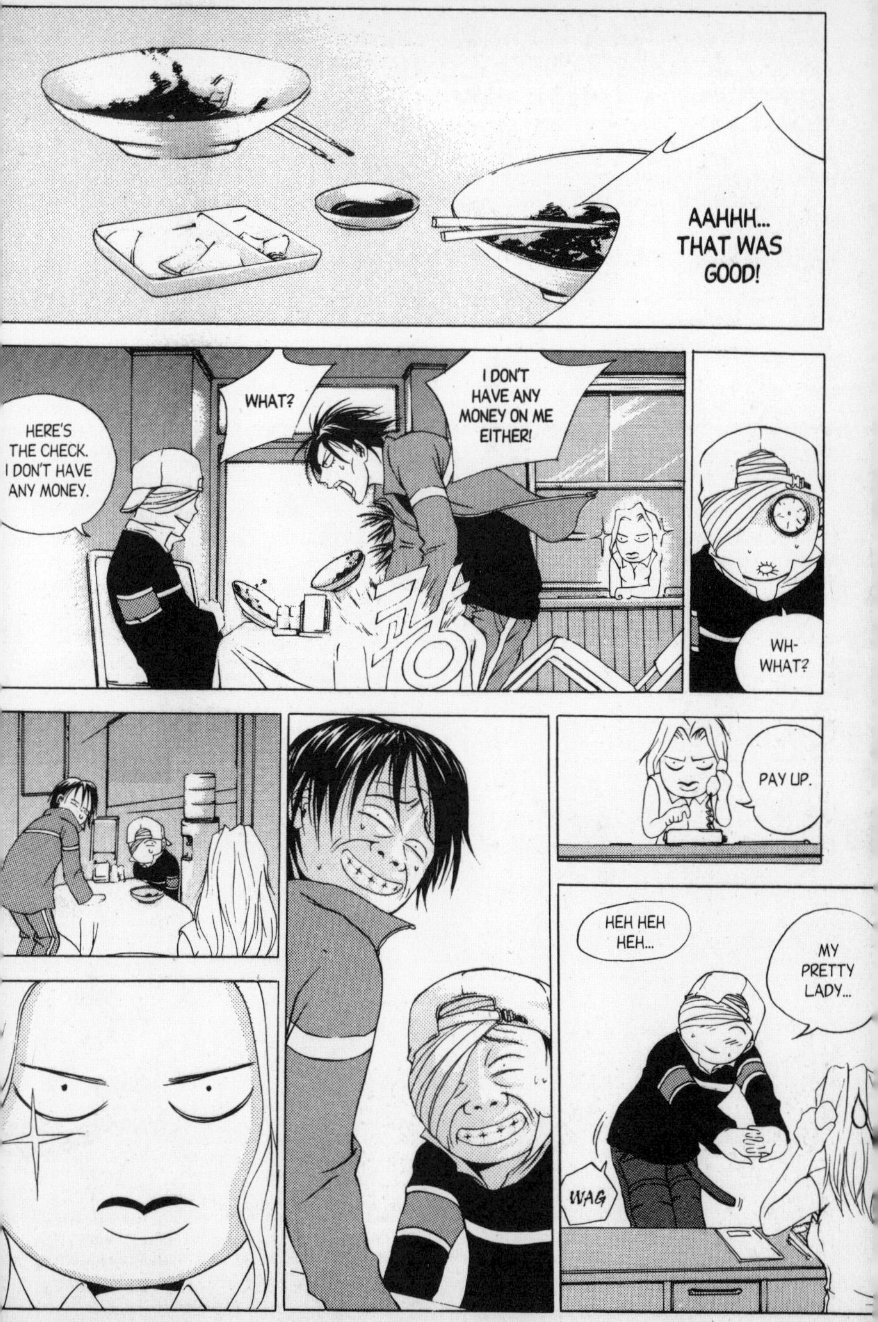
AAHHH... THAT WAS GOOD!
HERE'S THE CHECK. I DON'T HAVE ANY MONEY.
WHAT?
I DON'T HAVE ANY MONEY ON ME EITHER!
WH-WHAT?
PAY UP.
HEH HEH HEH...
MY PRETTY LADY...
WAG

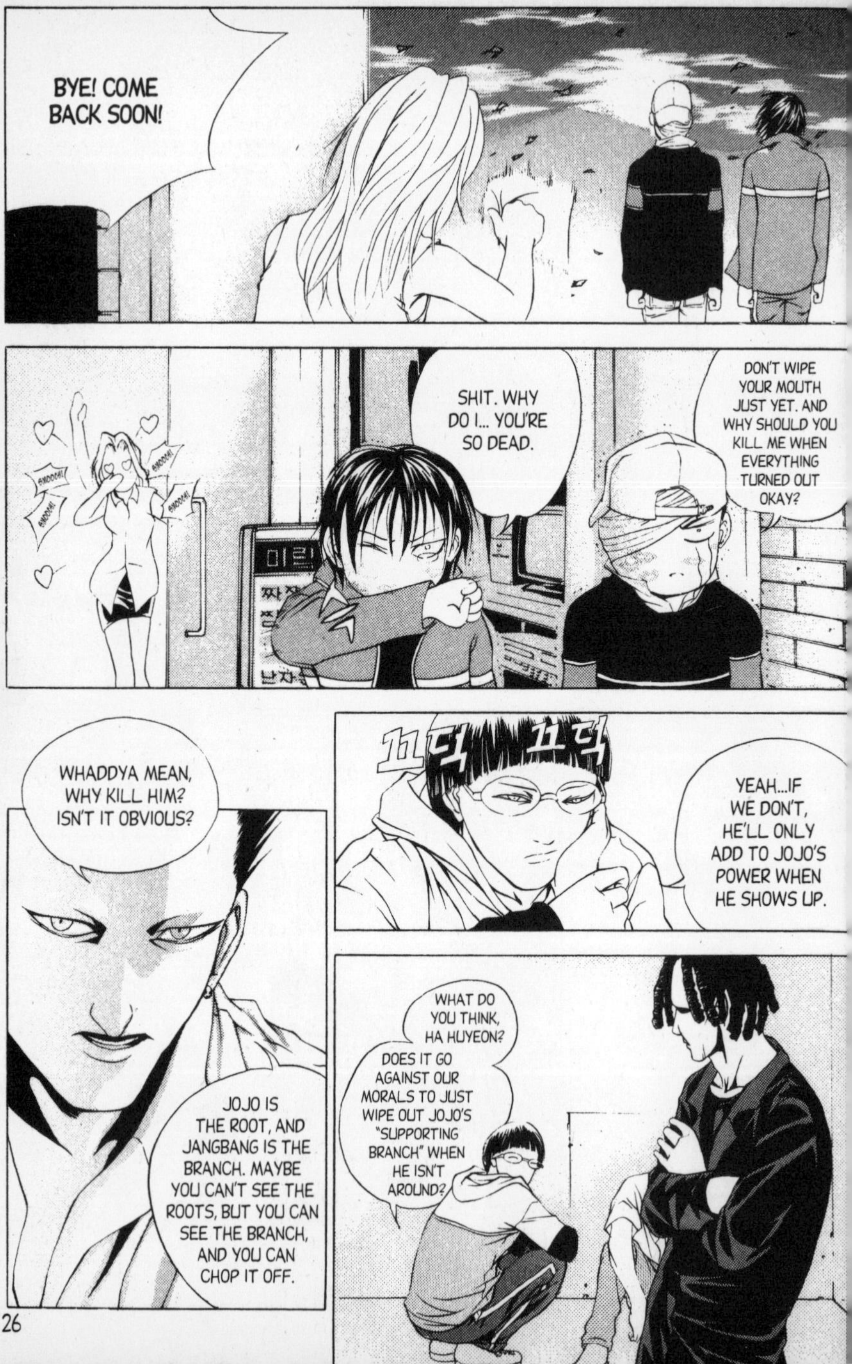
BYE! COME BACK SOON!
SHIT. WHY DO I... YOU'RE SO DEAD.
DON'T WIPE YOUR MOUTH JUST YET. AND WHY SHOULD YOU KILL ME WHEN EVERYTHING TURNED OUT OKAY?
WHADDYA MEAN, WHY KILL HIM? ISN'T IT OBVIOUS?
JOJO IS THE ROOT, AND JANGBANG IS THE BRANCH. MAYBE YOU CAN'T SEE THE ROOTS, BUT YOU CAN SEE THE BRANCH, AND YOU CAN CHOP IT OFF.
YEAH...IF WE DON'T, HE'LL ONLY ADD TO JOJO'S POWER WHEN HE SHOWS UP.
WHAT DO YOU THINK, HA HUYEON?
DOES IT GO AGAINST OUR MORALS TO JUST WIPE OUT JOJO'S "SUPPORTING BRANCH" WHEN HE ISN'T AROUND?

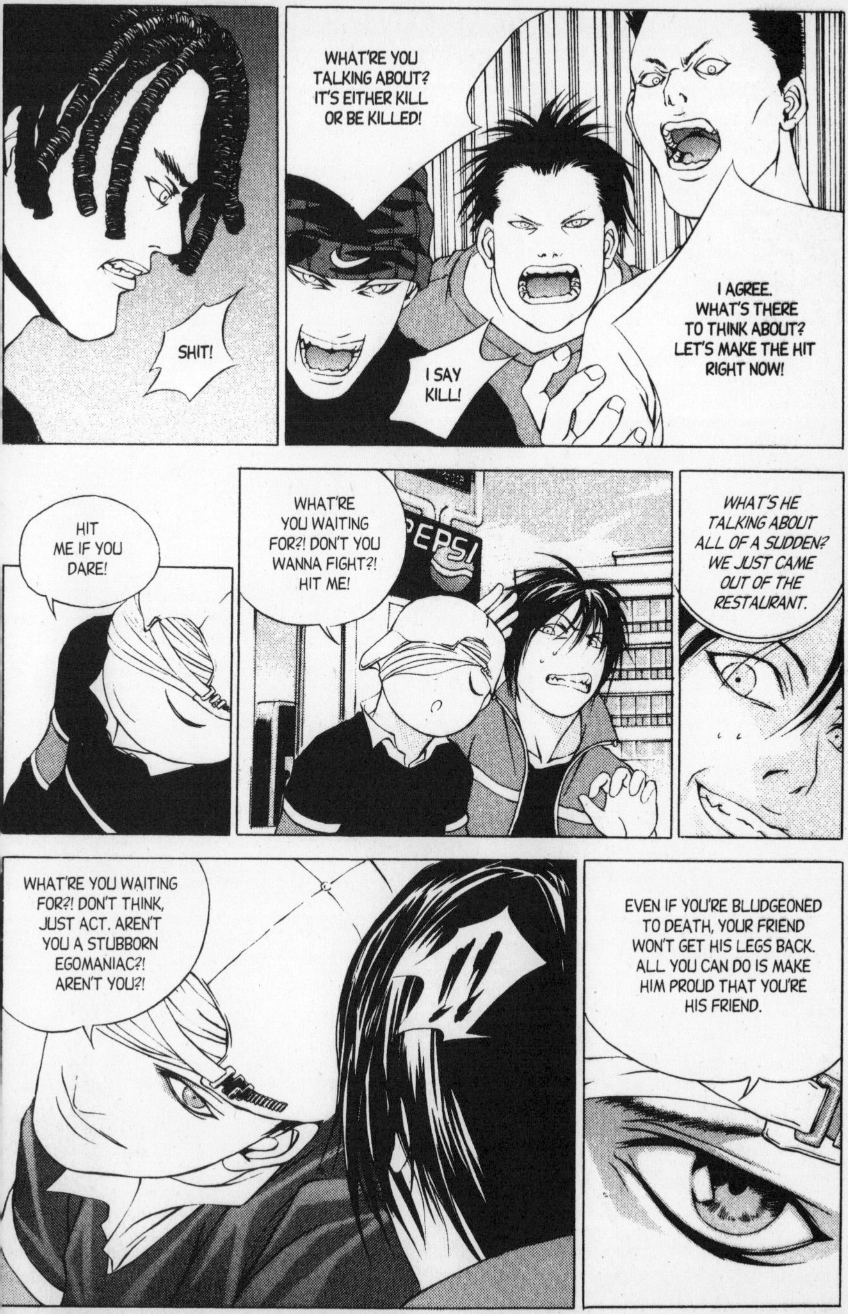
WHAT'RE YOU TALKING ABOUT? IT'S EITHER KILL OR BE KILLED!
I AGREE. WHAT'S THERE TO THINK ABOUT? LET'S MAKE THE HIT RIGHT NOW!
I SAY KILL!
SHIT!
WHAT'S HE TALKING ABOUT ALL OF A SUDDEN? WE JUST CAME OUT OF THE RESTAURANT.
WHAT'RE YOU WAITING FOR?! DON'T YOU WANNA FIGHT?! HIT ME!
PEPSI
HIT ME IF YOU DARE!
EVEN IF YOU'RE BLUDGEONED TO DEATH, YOUR FRIEND WON'T GET HIS LEGS BACK. ALL YOU CAN DO IS MAKE HIM PROUD THAT YOU'RE HIS FRIEND.
WHAT'RE YOU WAITING FOR?! DON'T THINK, JUST ACT. AREN'T YOU A STUBBORN EGOMANIAC?! AREN'T YOU?!

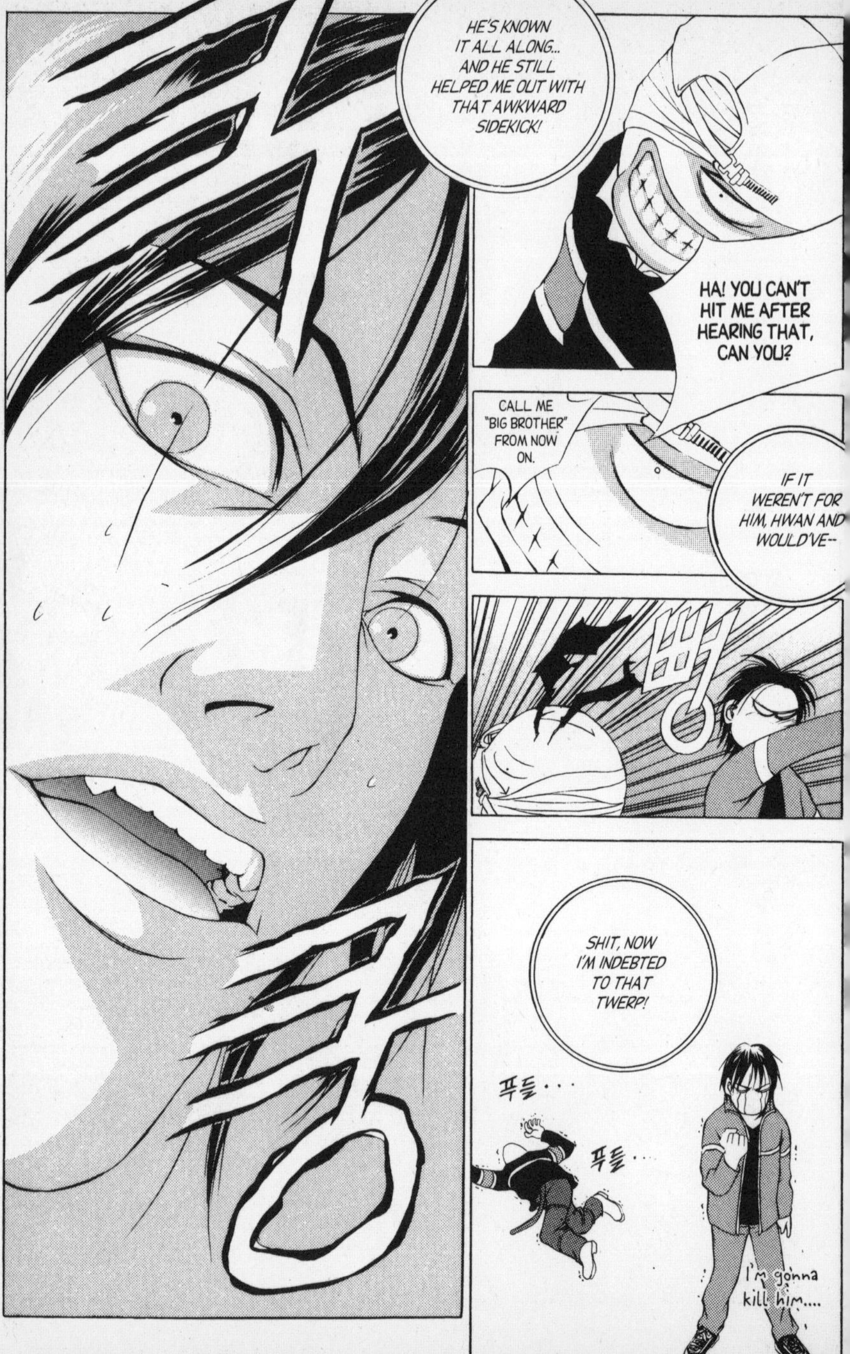
HE'S KNOWN IT ALL ALONG... AND HE STILL HELPED ME OUT WITH THAT AWKWARD SIDEKICK!
HA! YOU CAN'T HIT ME AFTER HEARING THAT, CAN YOU?
CALL ME "BIG BROTHER" FROM NOW ON.
IF IT WEREN'T FOR HIM, HWAN AND WOULD'VE--
SHIT, NOW I'M INDEBTED TO THAT TWERP!
푸들 . . .
푸들 . . .
I'm gonna kill him....

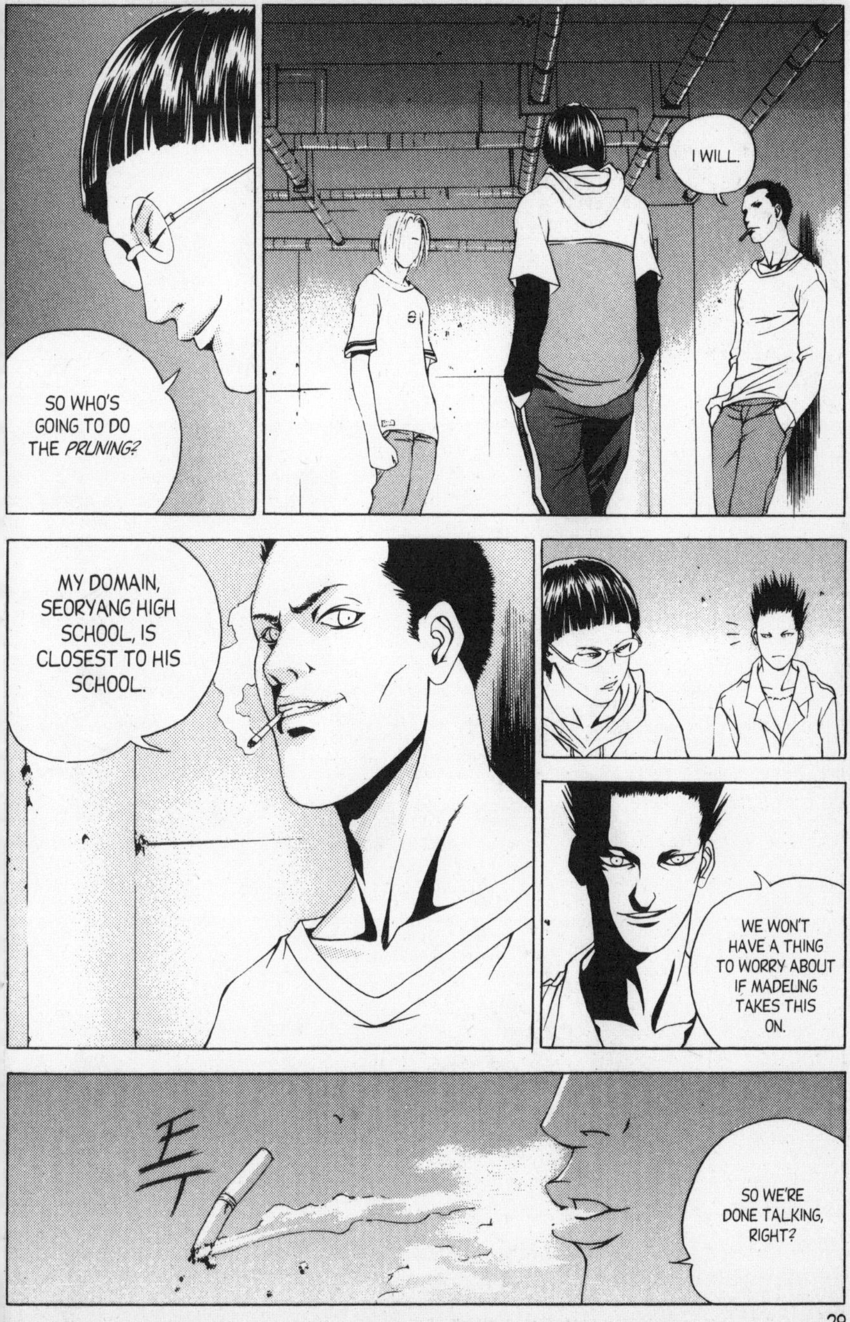
SO WHO'S GOING TO DO THE *PRUNING?*
I WILL.
MY DOMAIN, SEORYANG HIGH SCHOOL, IS CLOSEST TO HIS SCHOOL.
WE WON'T HAVE A THING TO WORRY ABOUT IF MADELING TAKES THIS ON.
SO WE'RE DONE TALKING, RIGHT?

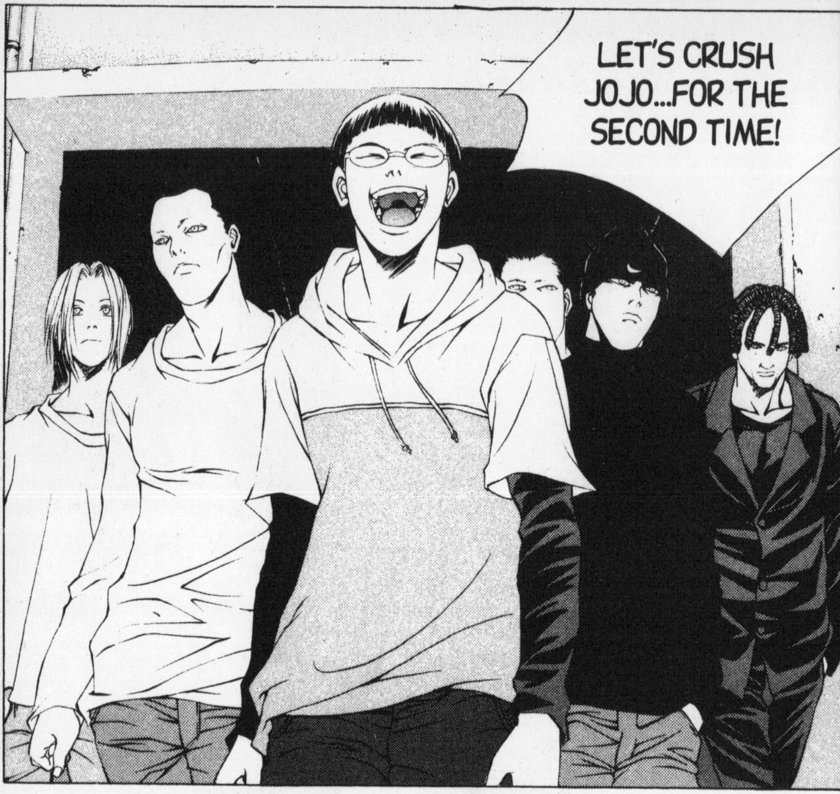
LET'S CRUSH JOJO...FOR THE SECOND TIME!
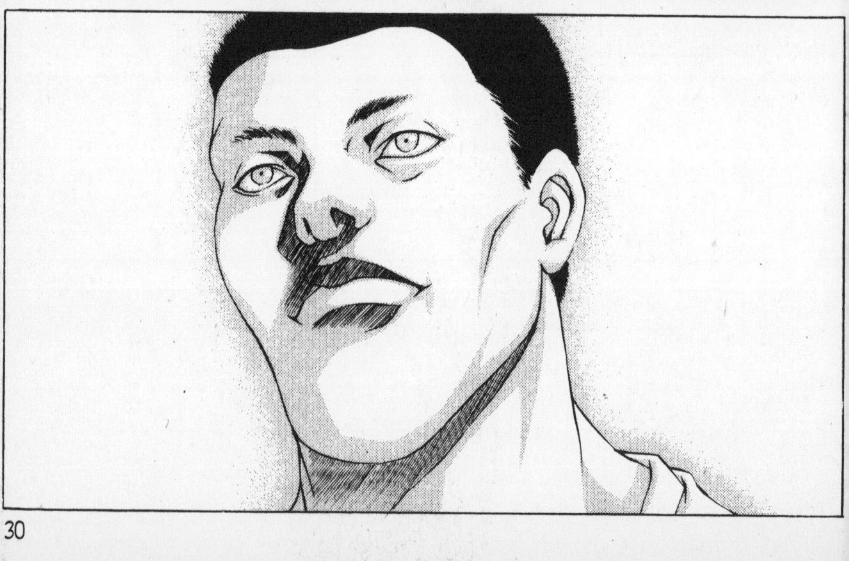

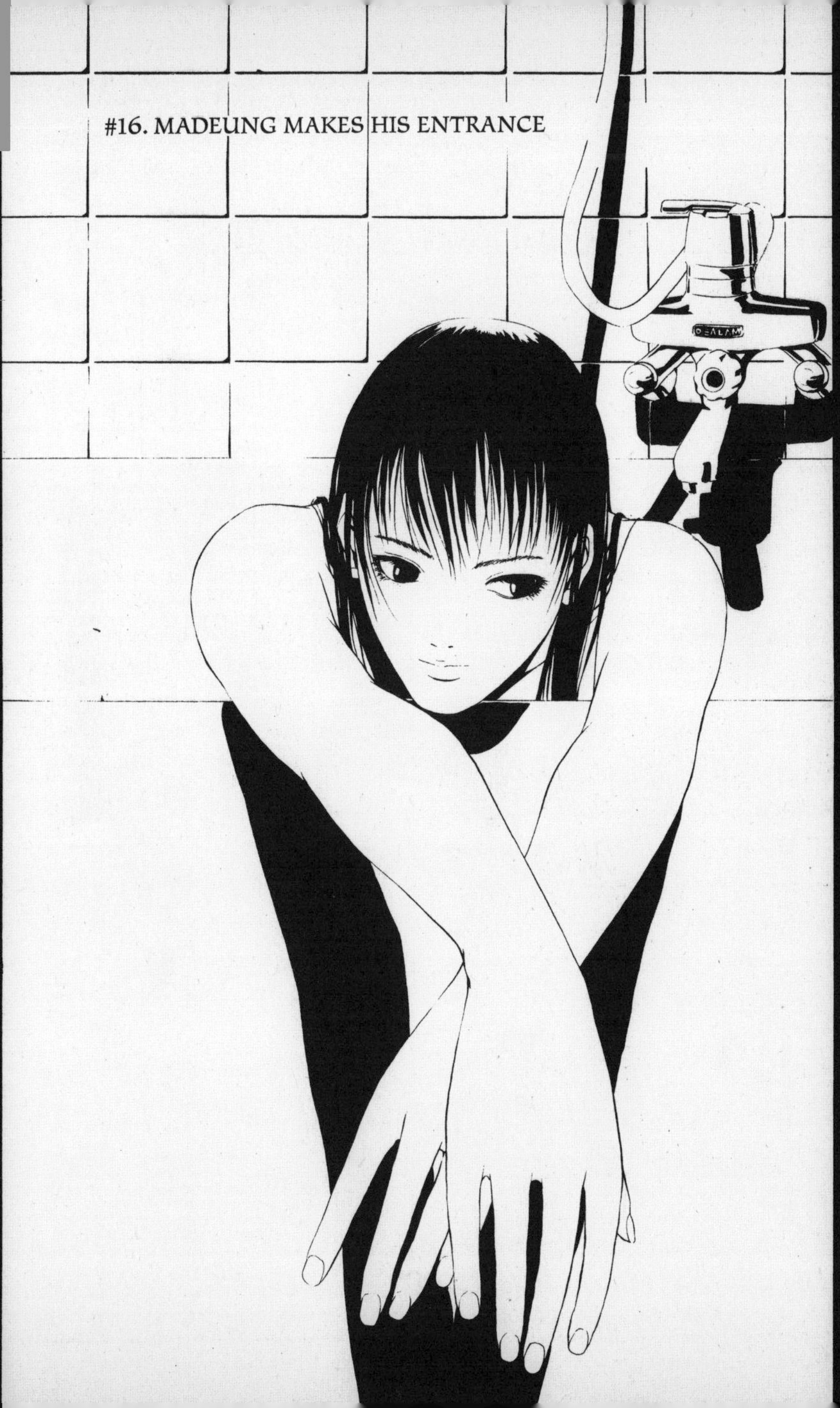
#16. MADEUNG MAKES HIS ENTRANCE
DEALAM

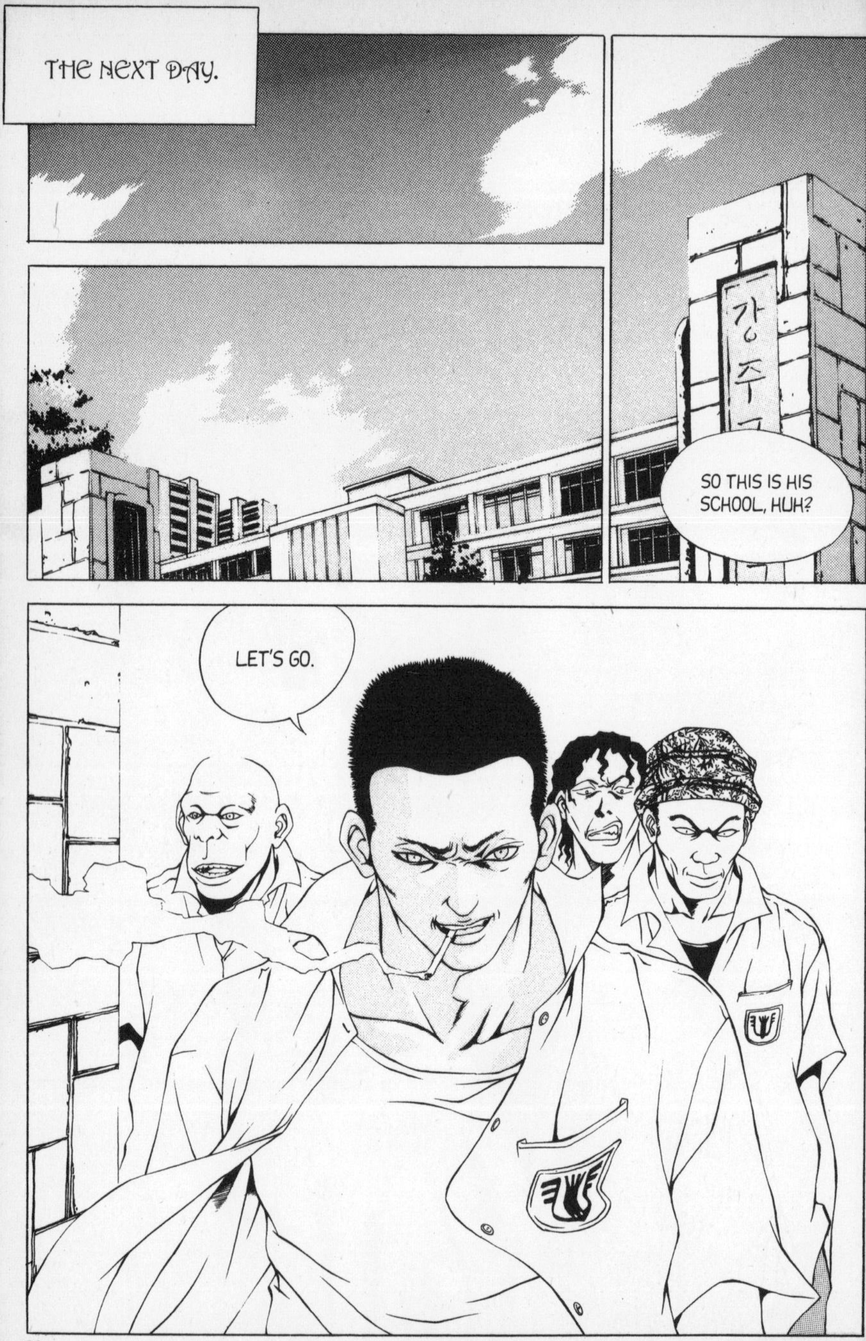
THE NEXT DAY.
SO THIS IS HIS SCHOOL, HUH?
LET'S GO.

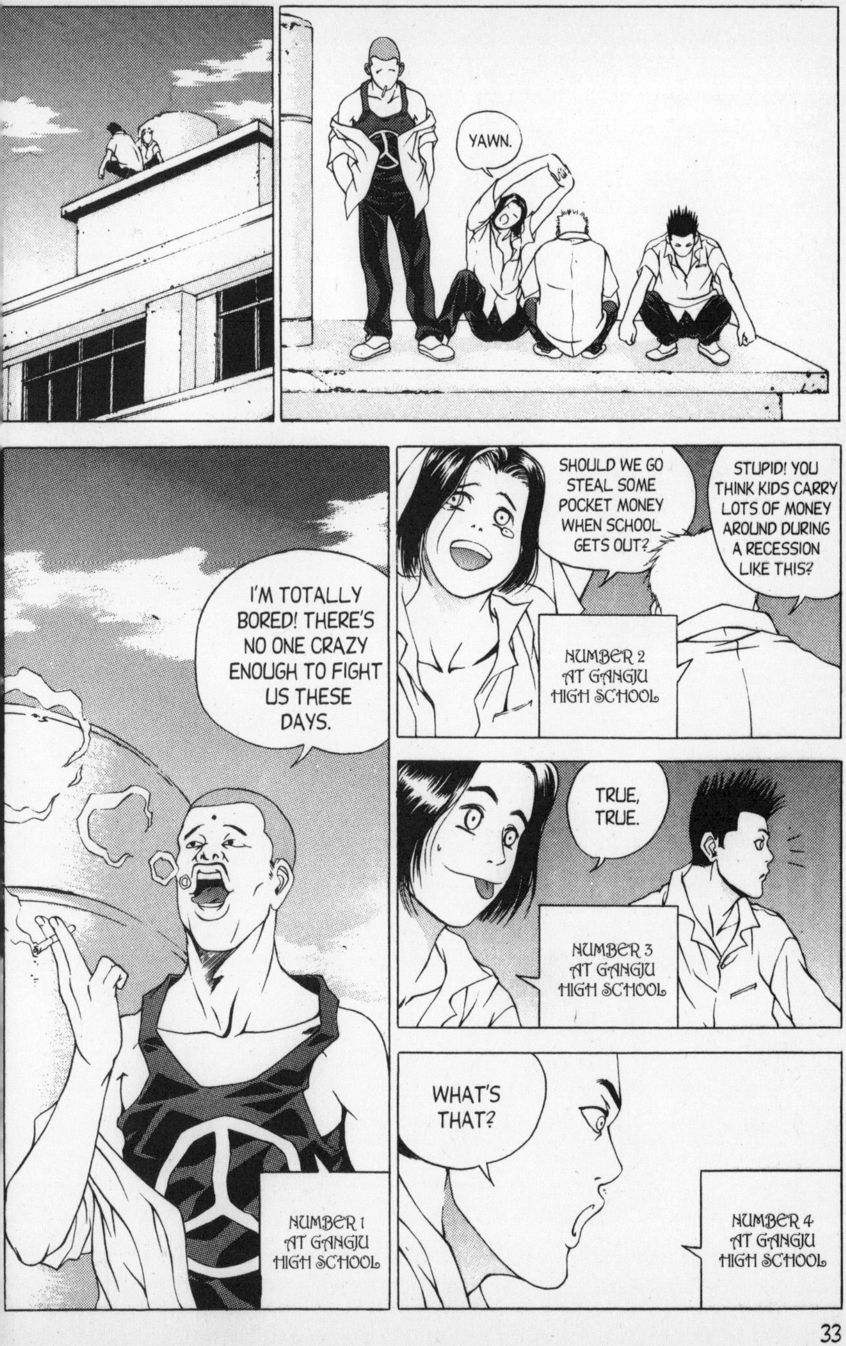
YAWN.
I'M TOTALLY BORED! THERE'S NO ONE CRAZY ENOUGH TO FIGHT US THESE DAYS.
NUMBER 1 AT GANGJU HIGH SCHOOL
SHOULD WE GO STEAL SOME POCKET MONEY WHEN SCHOOL GETS OUT?
STUPID! YOU THINK KIDS CARRY LOTS OF MONEY AROUND DURING A RECESSION LIKE THIS?
NUMBER 2 AT GANGJU HIGH SCHOOL
TRUE, TRUE.
NUMBER 3 AT GANGJU HIGH SCHOOL
WHAT'S THAT?
NUMBER 4 AT GANGJU HIGH SCHOOL

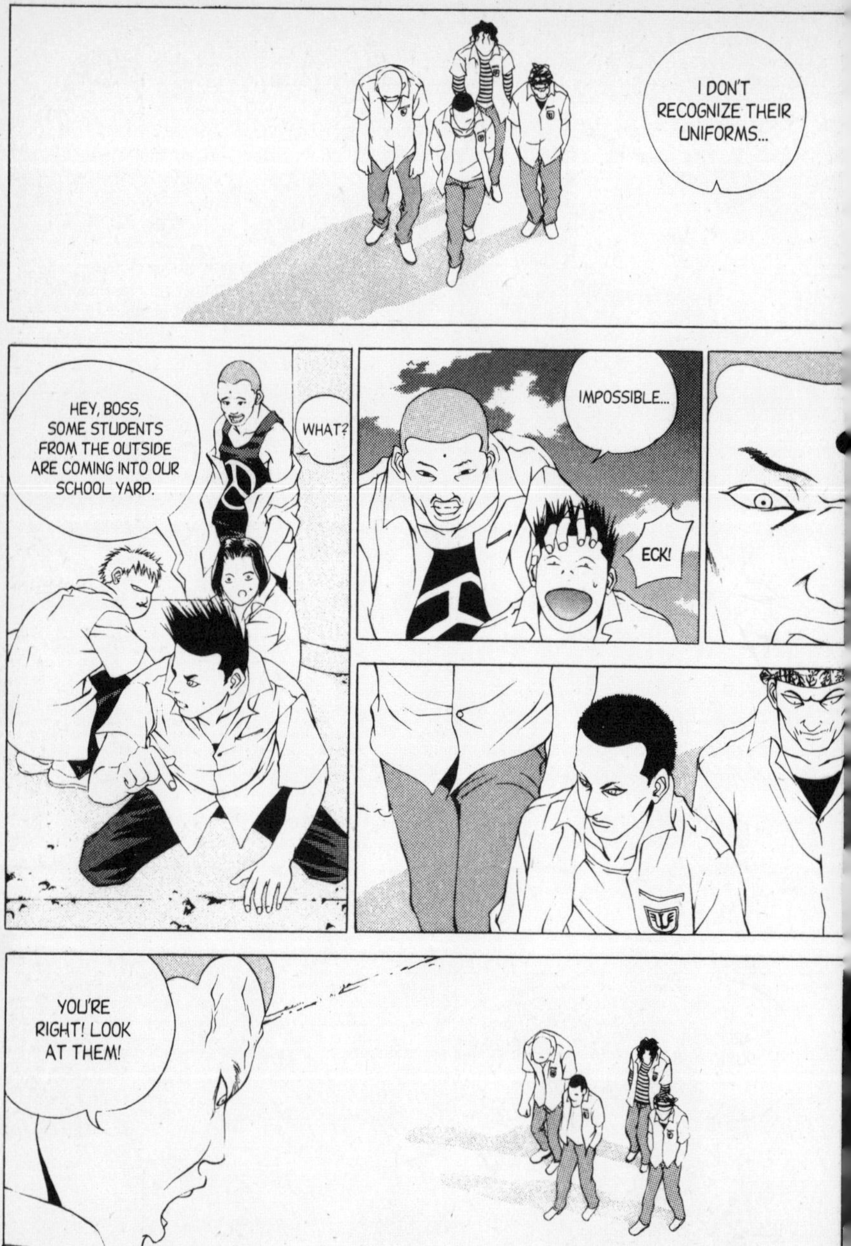
I DON'T RECOGNIZE THEIR UNIFORMS...
HEY, BOSS, SOME STUDENTS FROM THE OUTSIDE ARE COMING INTO OUR SCHOOL YARD.
WHAT?
IMPOSSIBLE...
ECK!
YOU'RE RIGHT! LOOK AT THEM!

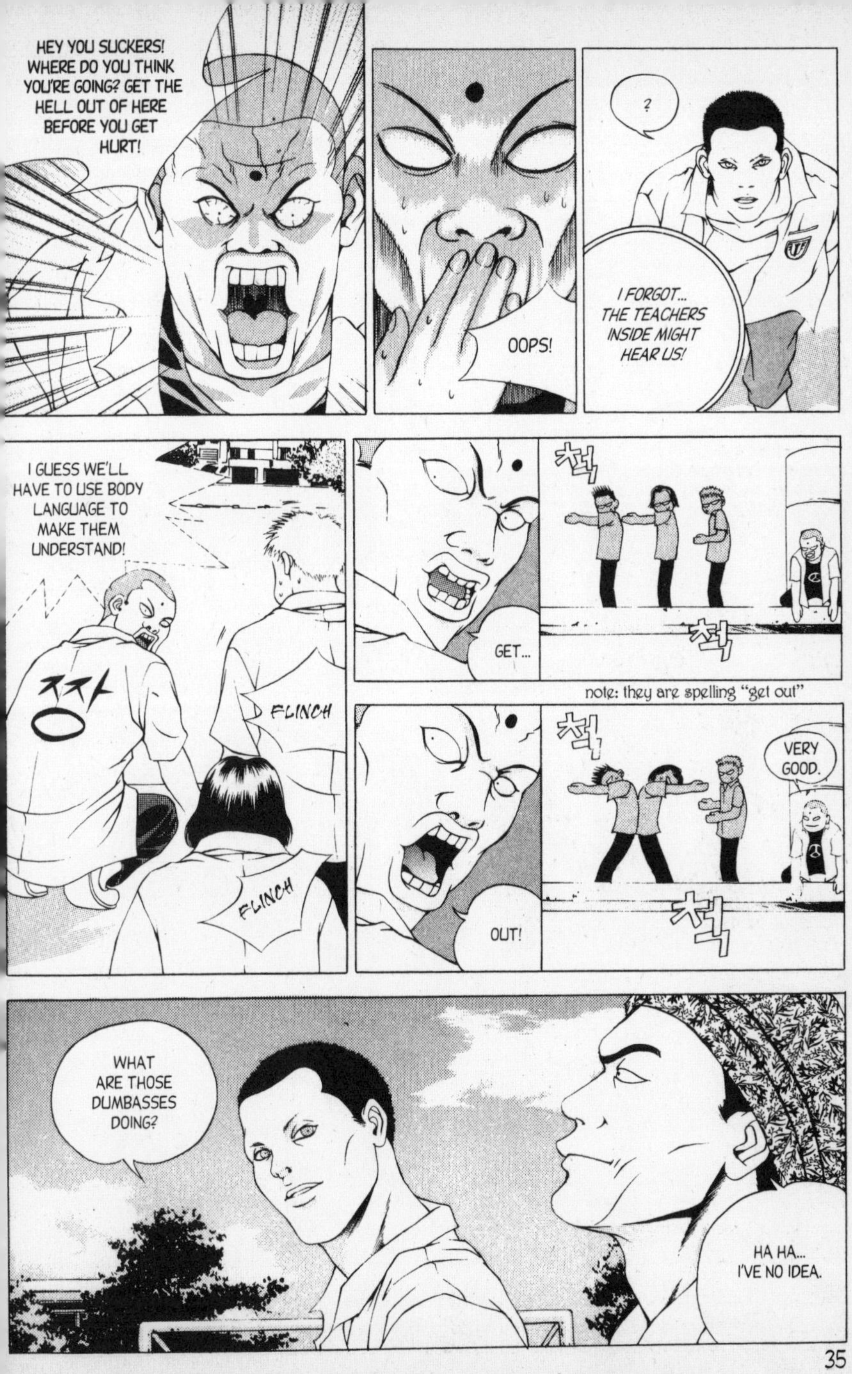
HEY YOU SUCKERS! WHERE DO YOU THINK YOU'RE GOING? GET THE HELL OUT OF HERE BEFORE YOU GET HURT!
OOPS!
?
I FORGOT... THE TEACHERS INSIDE MIGHT HEAR US!
I GUESS WE'LL HAVE TO USE BODY LANGUAGE TO MAKE THEM UNDERSTAND!
FLINCH
FLINCH
GET...
척
척
note: they are spelling "get out"
OUT!
척
VERY GOOD.
척
WHAT ARE THOSE DUMBASSES DOING?
HA HA... I'VE NO IDEA.

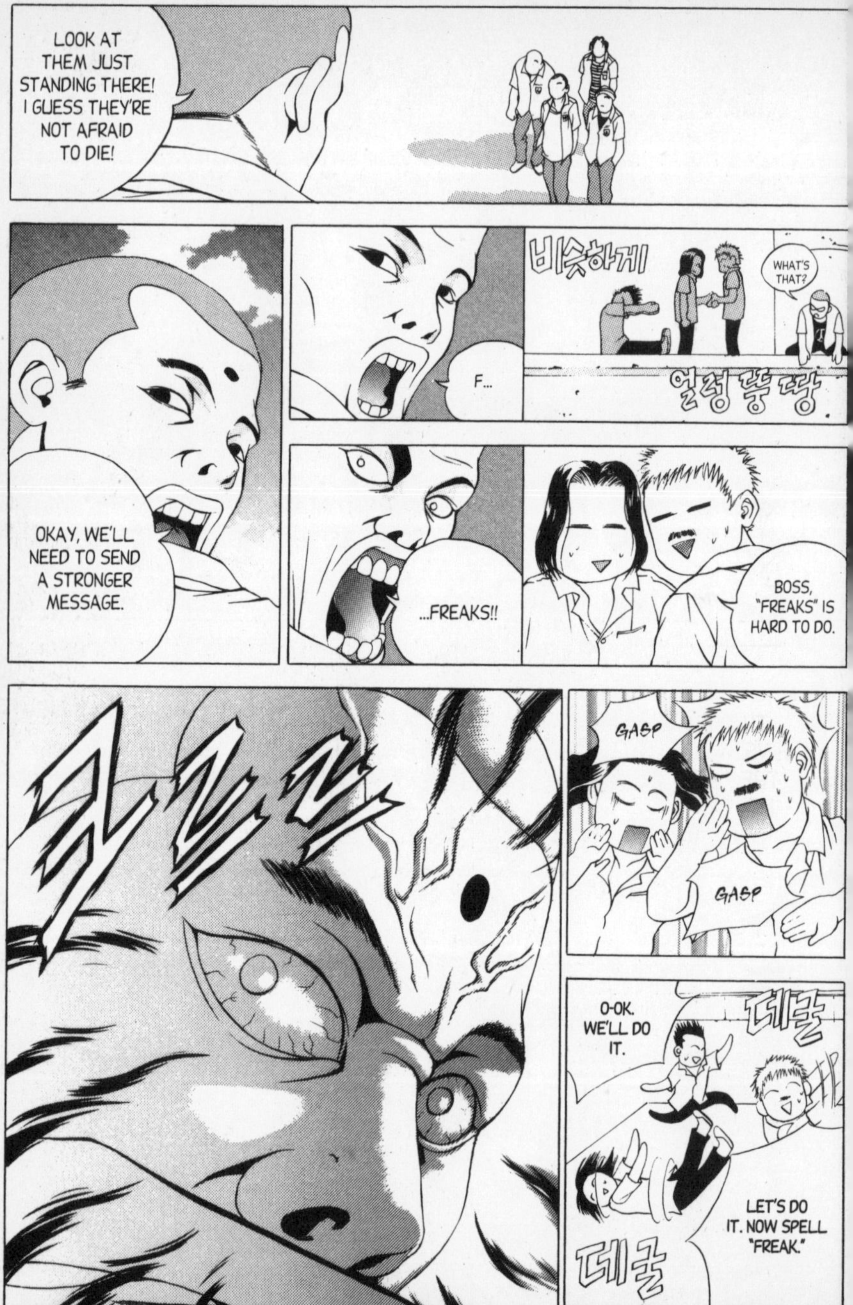
LOOK AT THEM JUST STANDING THERE! I GUESS THEY'RE NOT AFRAID TO DIE!
OKAY, WE'LL NEED TO SEND A STRONGER MESSAGE.
F...
비슷하게
얼렁뚱땅
WHAT'S THAT?
...FREAKS!!
BOSS, "FREAKS" IS HARD TO DO.
GASP
GASP
O-OK. WE'LL DO IT.
데굴
LET'S DO IT. NOW SPELL "FREAK."
데굴

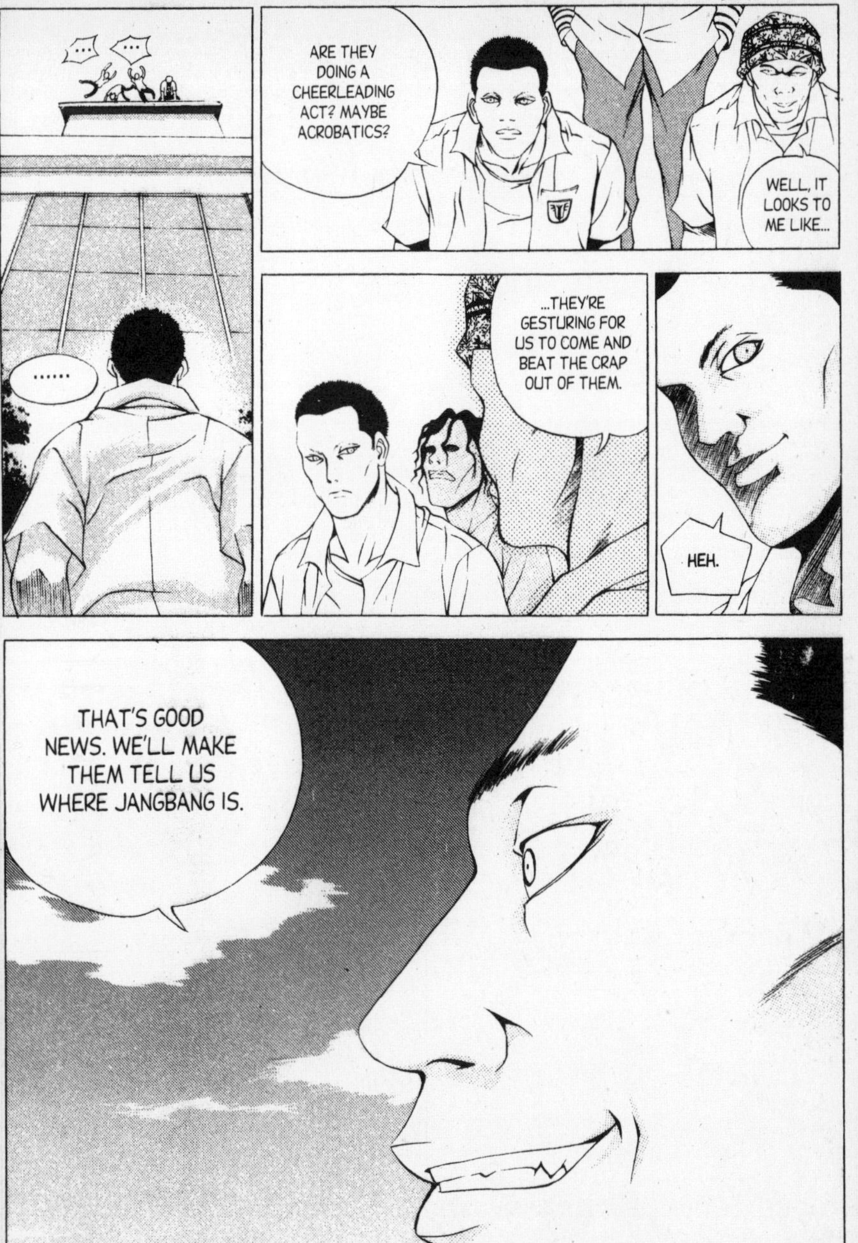
...
...
......
ARE THEY DOING A CHEERLEADING ACT? MAYBE ACROBATICS?
WELL, IT LOOKS TO ME LIKE...
...THEY'RE GESTURING FOR US TO COME AND BEAT THE CRAP OUT OF THEM.
HEH.
THAT'S GOOD NEWS. WE'LL MAKE THEM TELL US WHERE JANGBANG IS.

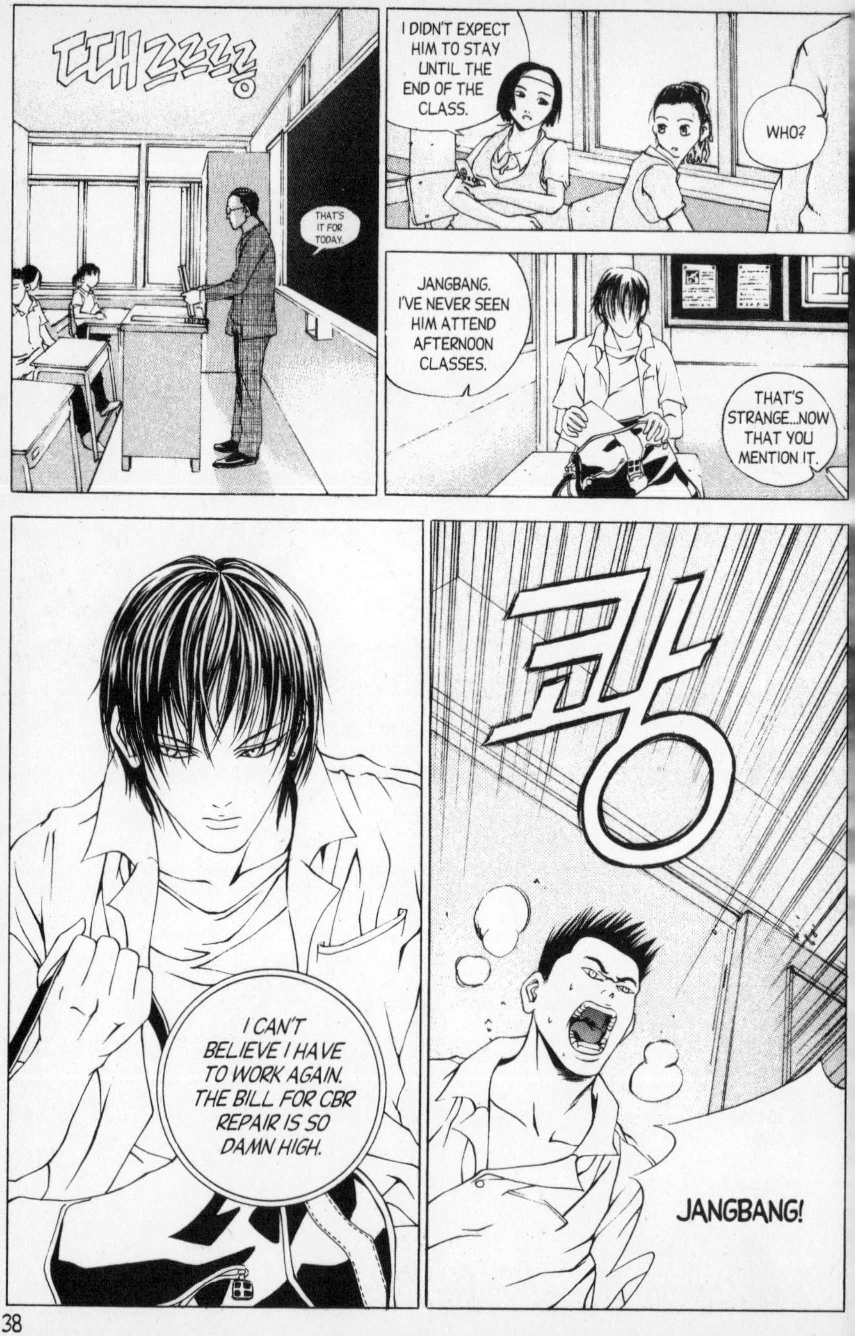
THAT'S IT FOR TODAY.
I DIDN'T EXPECT HIM TO STAY UNTIL THE END OF THE CLASS.
WHO?
JANGBANG. I'VE NEVER SEEN HIM ATTEND AFTERNOON CLASSES.
THAT'S STRANGE...NOW THAT YOU MENTION IT.
I CAN'T BELIEVE I HAVE TO WORK AGAIN. THE BILL FOR CBR REPAIR IS SO DAMN HIGH.
쾅
JANGBANG!

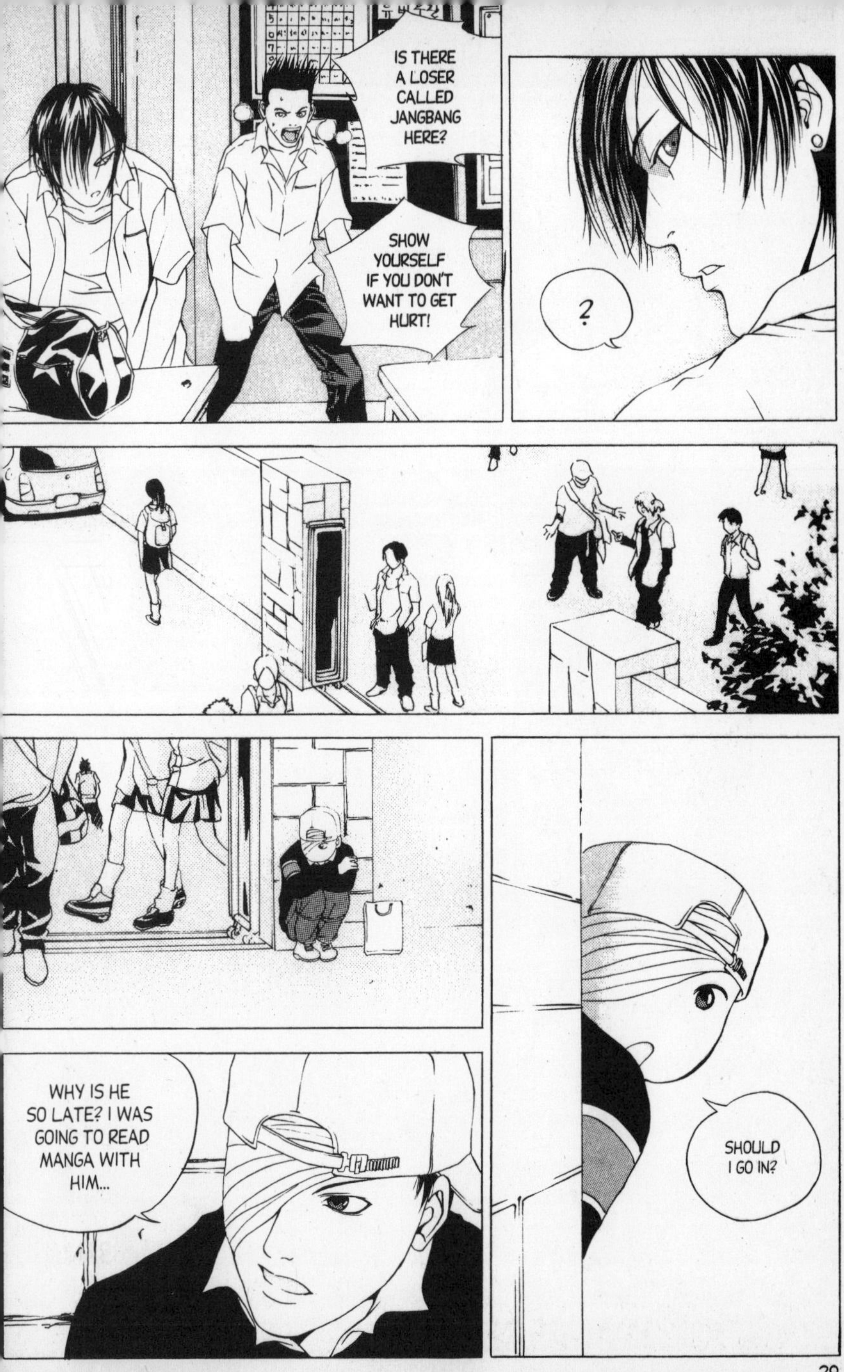
IS THERE A LOSER CALLED JANGBANG HERE?
SHOW YOURSELF IF YOU DON'T WANT TO GET HURT!
?
WHY IS HE SO LATE? I WAS GOING TO READ MANGA WITH HIM...
SHOULD I GO IN?

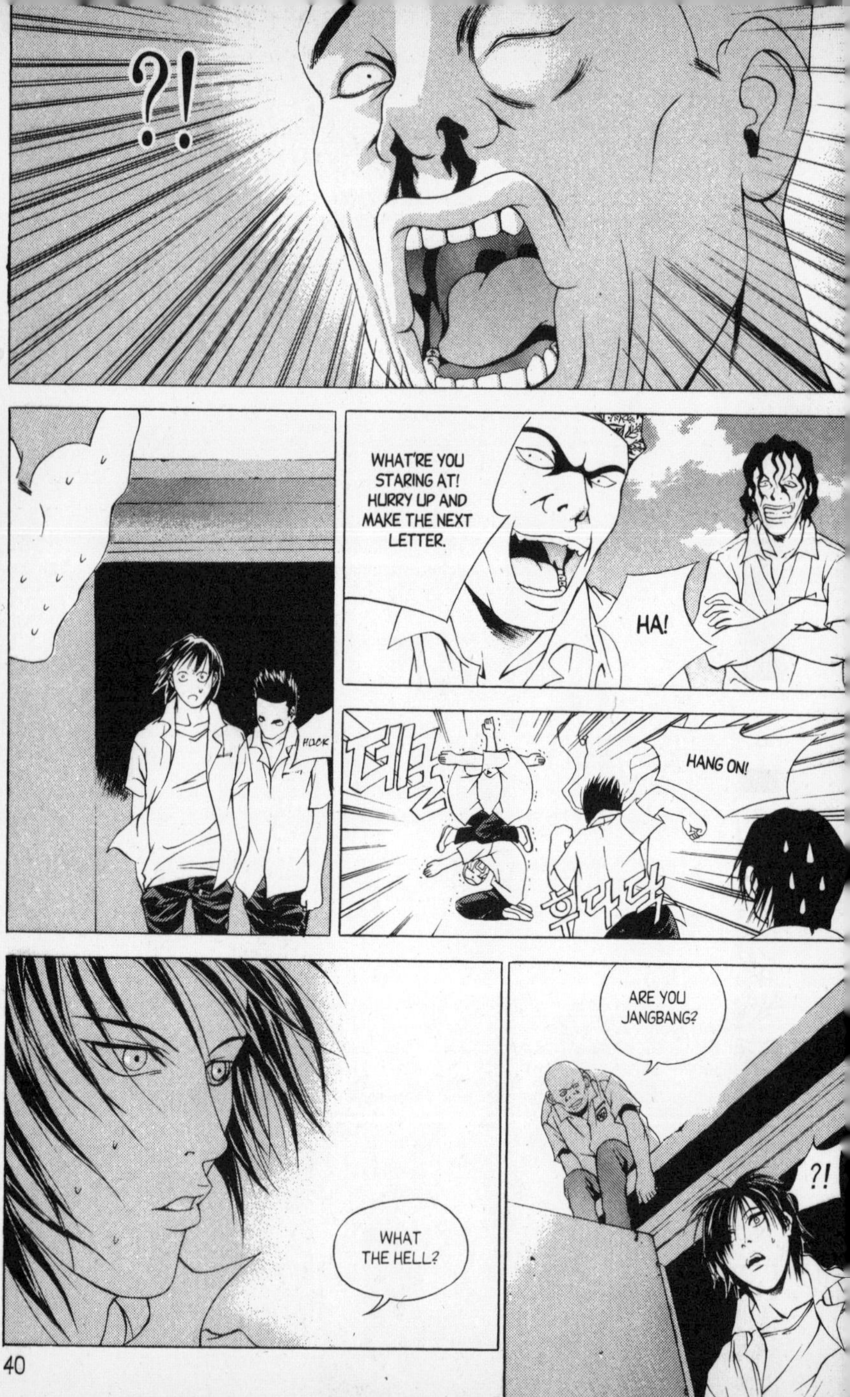
?!
HOCK
WHAT'RE YOU STARING AT! HURRY UP AND MAKE THE NEXT LETTER.
HA!
데굴
HANG ON!
후다닥
WHAT THE HELL?
ARE YOU JANGBANG?
?!

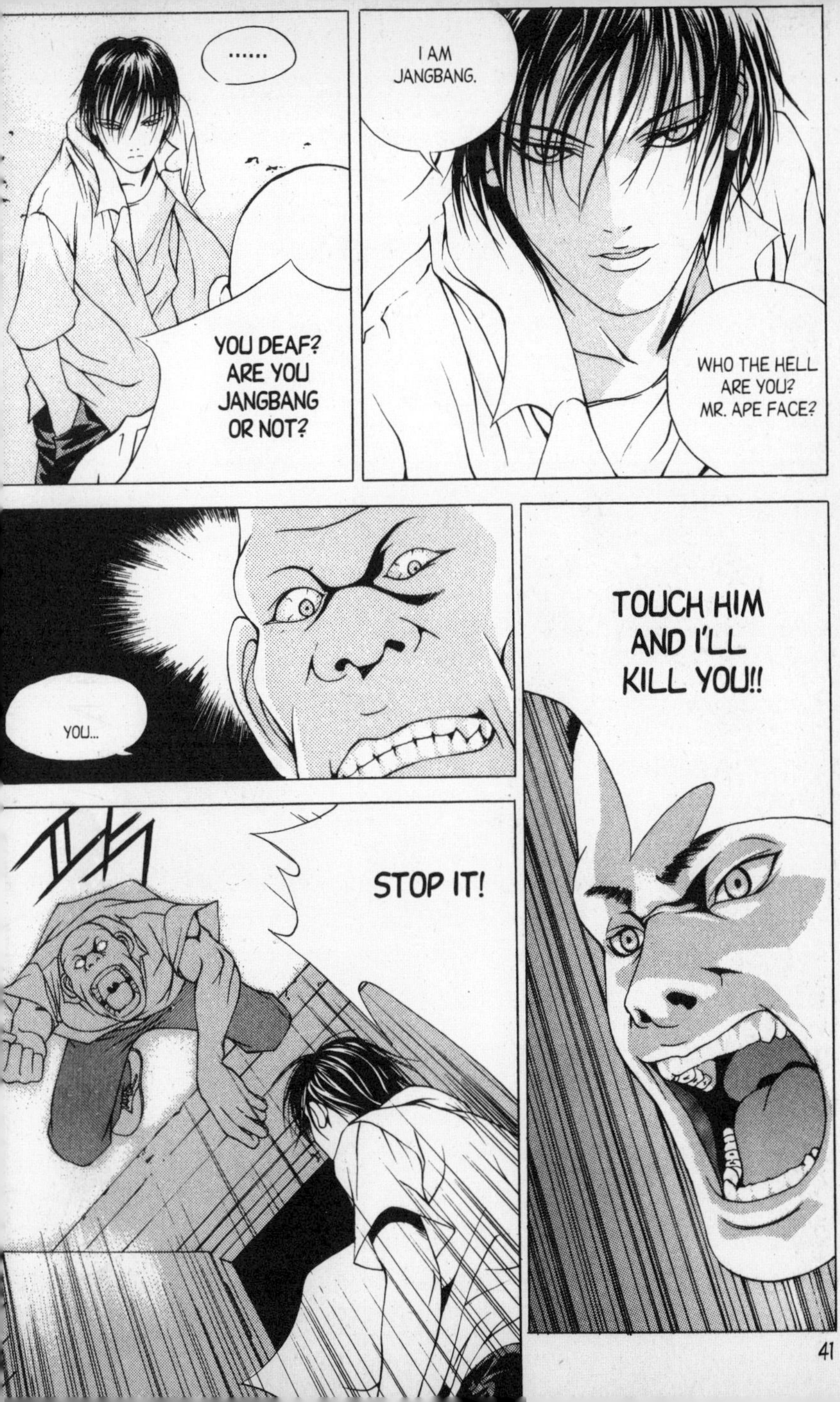
......
YOU DEAF? ARE YOU JANGBANG OR NOT?
I AM JANGBANG.
WHO THE HELL ARE YOU? MR. APE FACE?
YOU...
STOP IT!
TOUCH HIM AND I'LL KILL YOU!!

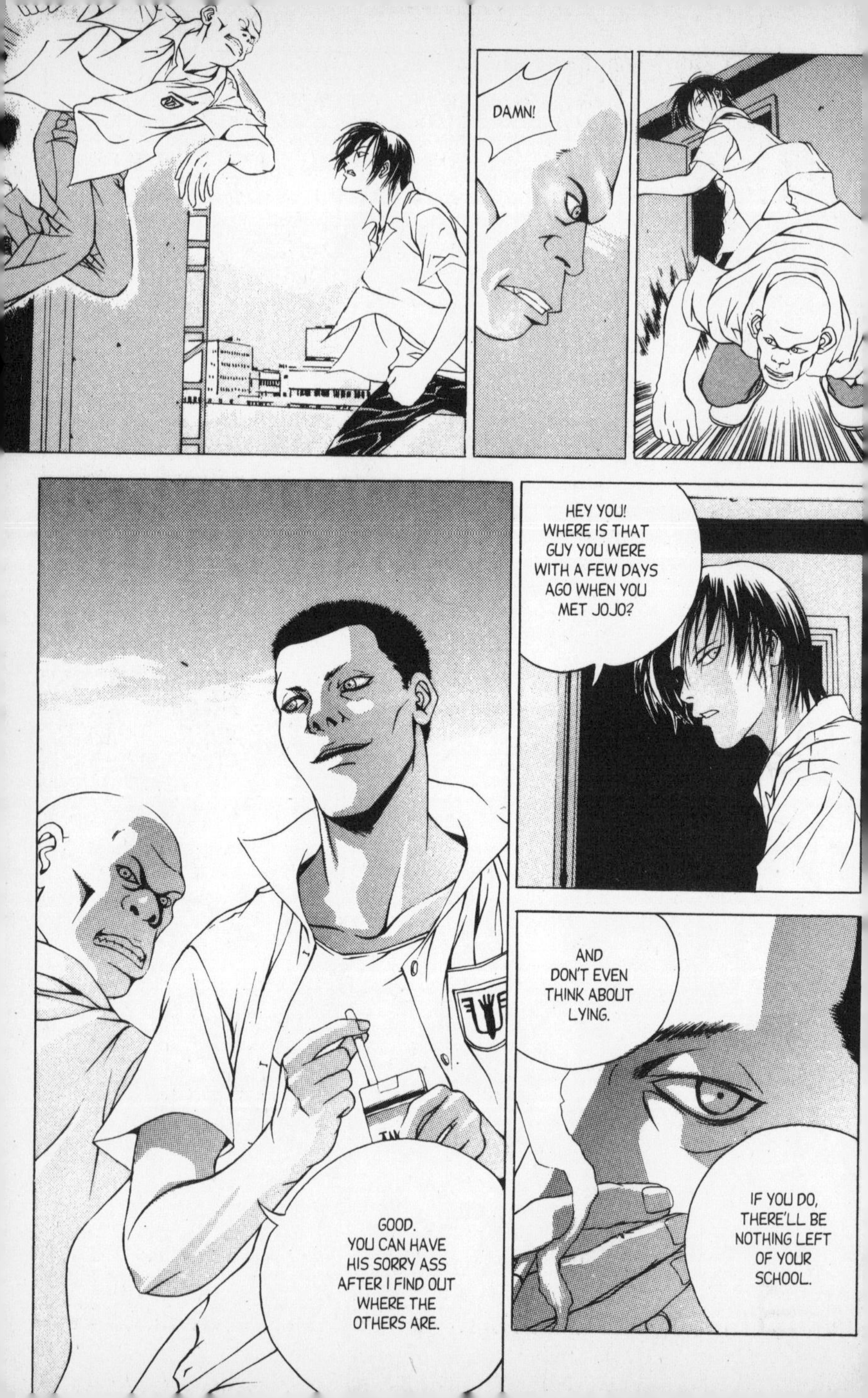
DAMN!
HEY YOU! WHERE IS THAT GUY YOU WERE WITH A FEW DAYS AGO WHEN YOU MET JOJO?
AND DON'T EVEN THINK ABOUT LYING.
IF YOU DO, THERE'LL BE NOTHING LEFT OF YOUR SCHOOL.
GOOD. YOU CAN HAVE HIS SORRY ASS AFTER I FIND OUT WHERE THE OTHERS ARE.

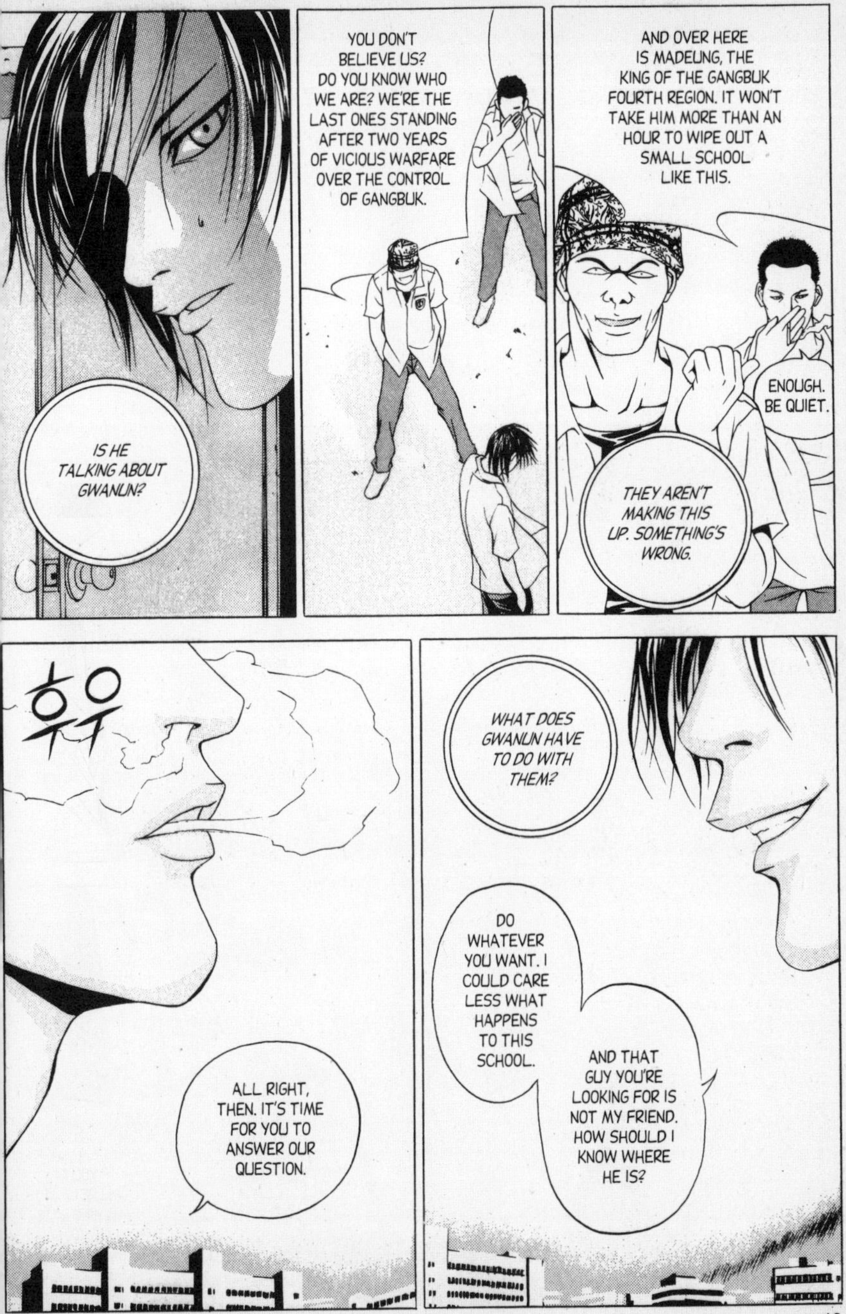
IS HE TALKING ABOUT GWANUN?
YOU DON'T BELIEVE US? DO YOU KNOW WHO WE ARE? WE'RE THE LAST ONES STANDING AFTER TWO YEARS OF VICIOUS WARFARE OVER THE CONTROL OF GANGBUK.
AND OVER HERE IS MADEUNG, THE KING OF THE GANGBUK FOURTH REGION. IT WON'T TAKE HIM MORE THAN AN HOUR TO WIPE OUT A SMALL SCHOOL LIKE THIS.
ENOUGH. BE QUIET.
THEY AREN'T MAKING THIS UP. SOMETHING'S WRONG.
후우
ALL RIGHT, THEN. IT'S TIME FOR YOU TO ANSWER OUR QUESTION.
WHAT DOES GWANUN HAVE TO DO WITH THEM?
DO WHATEVER YOU WANT. I COULD CARE LESS WHAT HAPPENS TO THIS SCHOOL.
AND THAT GUY YOU'RE LOOKING FOR IS NOT MY FRIEND. HOW SHOULD I KNOW WHERE HE IS?

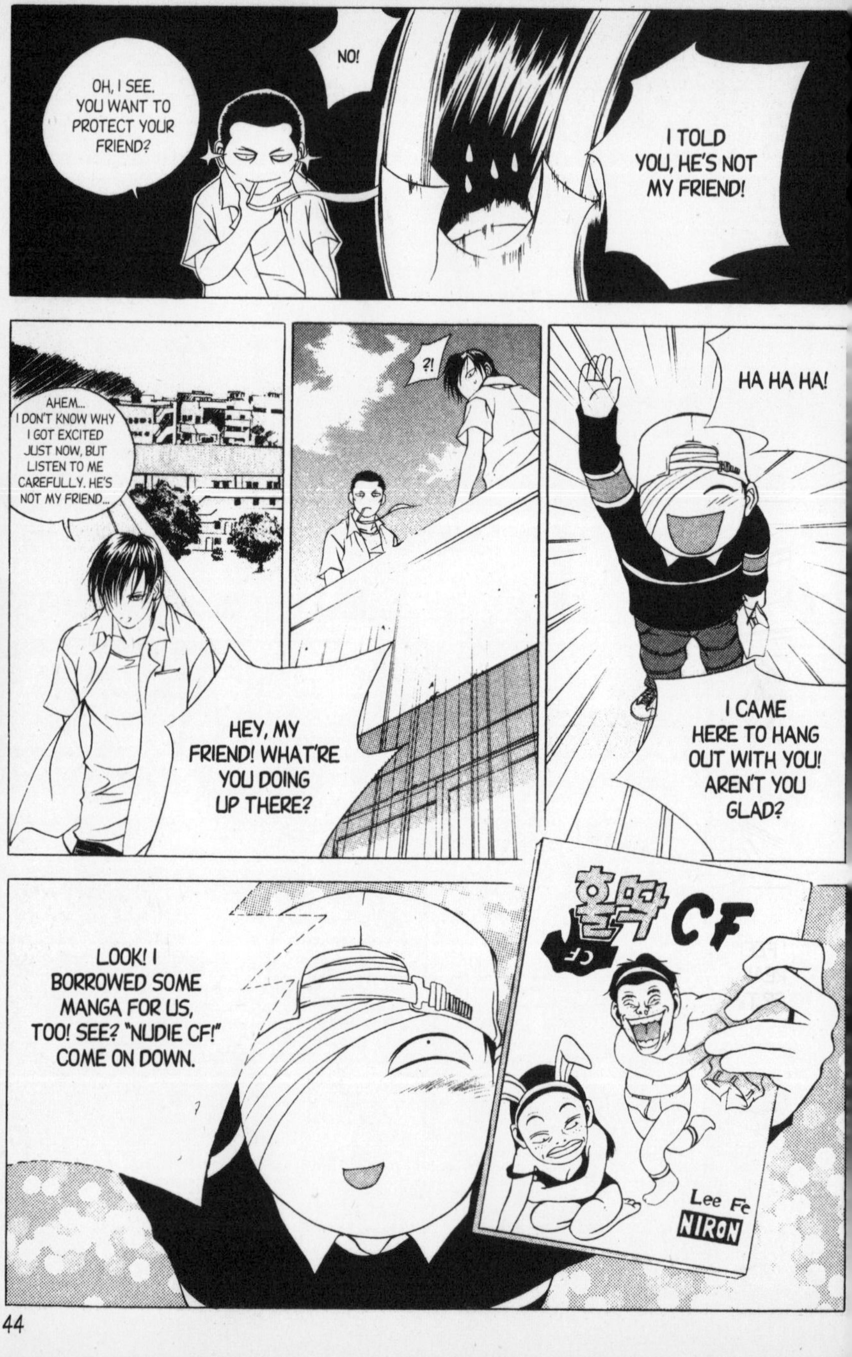
OH, I SEE. YOU WANT TO PROTECT YOUR FRIEND?
NO!
I TOLD YOU, HE'S NOT MY FRIEND!
AHEM... I DON'T KNOW WHY I GOT EXCITED JUST NOW, BUT LISTEN TO ME CAREFULLY. HE'S NOT MY FRIEND...
?!
HEY, MY FRIEND! WHAT'RE YOU DOING UP THERE?
HA HA HA!
I CAME HERE TO HANG OUT WITH YOU! AREN'T YOU GLAD?
LOOK! I BORROWED SOME MANGA FOR US, TOO! SEE? "NUDIE CF!" COME ON DOWN.
홀딱 CF
CF
Lee Fe
NIRON

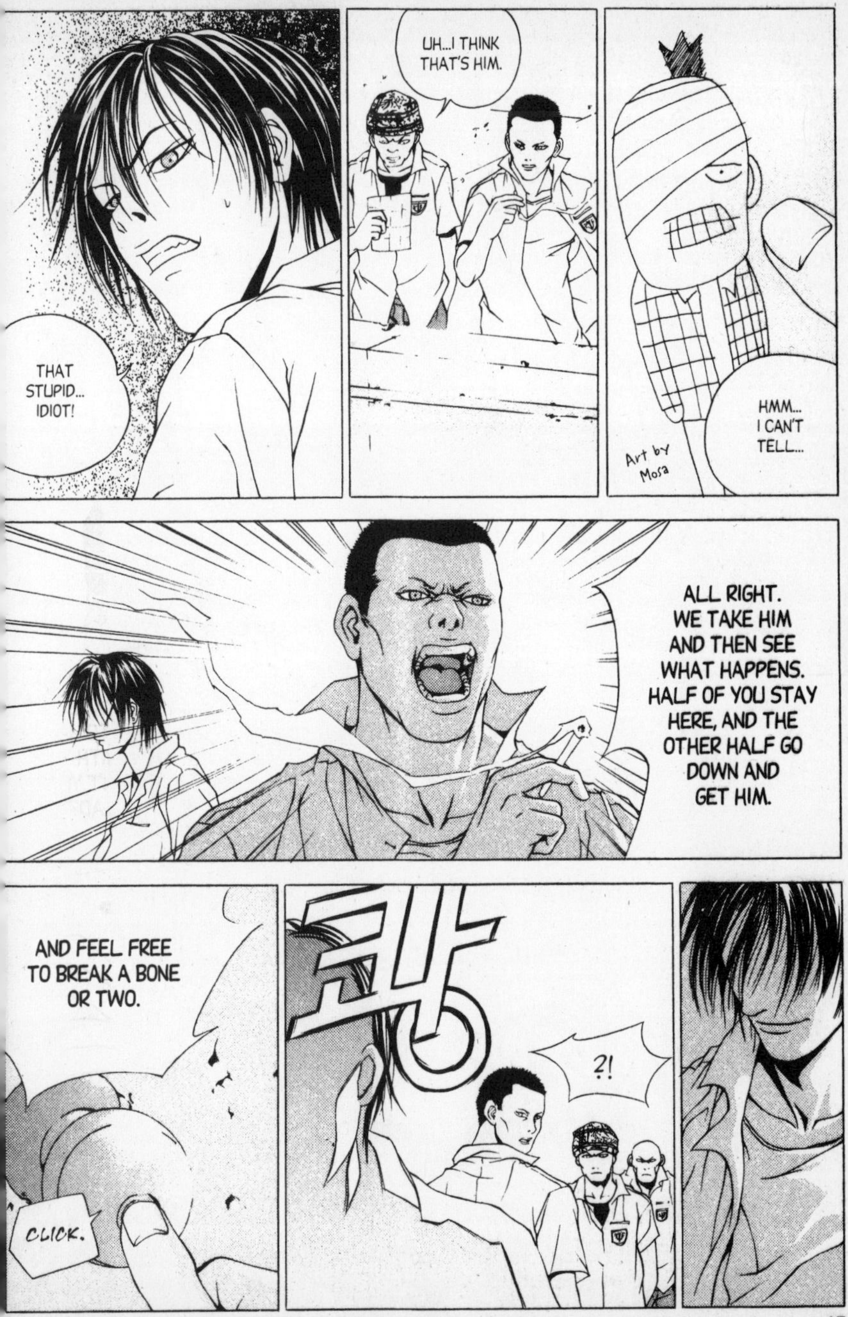
THAT STUPID... IDIOT!
UH...I THINK THAT'S HIM.
HMM... I CAN'T TELL...
Art by Mosa
ALL RIGHT. WE TAKE HIM AND THEN SEE WHAT HAPPENS. HALF OF YOU STAY HERE, AND THE OTHER HALF GO DOWN AND GET HIM.
AND FEEL FREE TO BREAK A BONE OR TWO.
CLICK.
?!

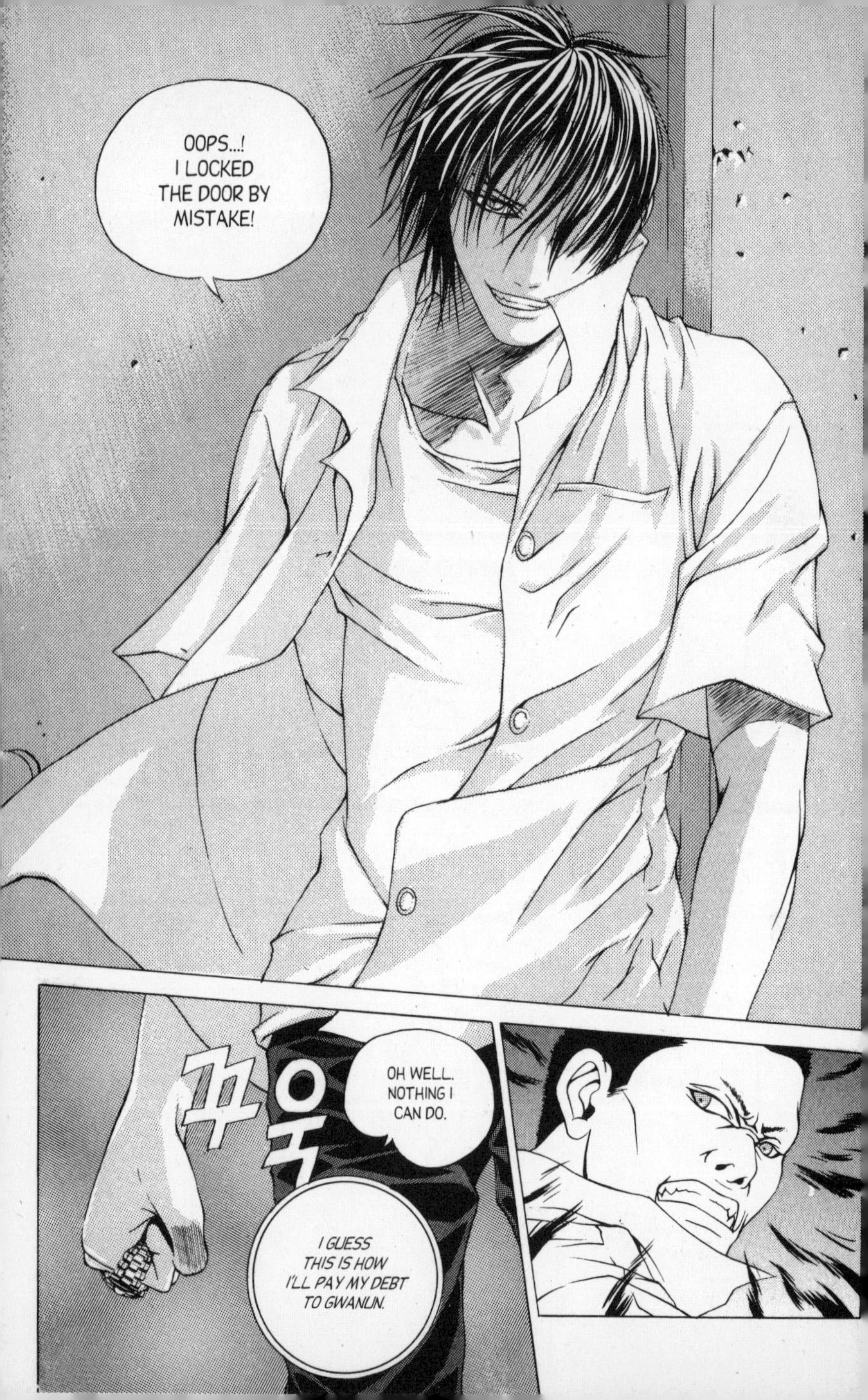
OOPS...! I LOCKED THE DOOR BY MISTAKE!
OH WELL. NOTHING I CAN DO.
I GUESS THIS IS HOW I'LL PAY MY DEBT TO GWANUN.

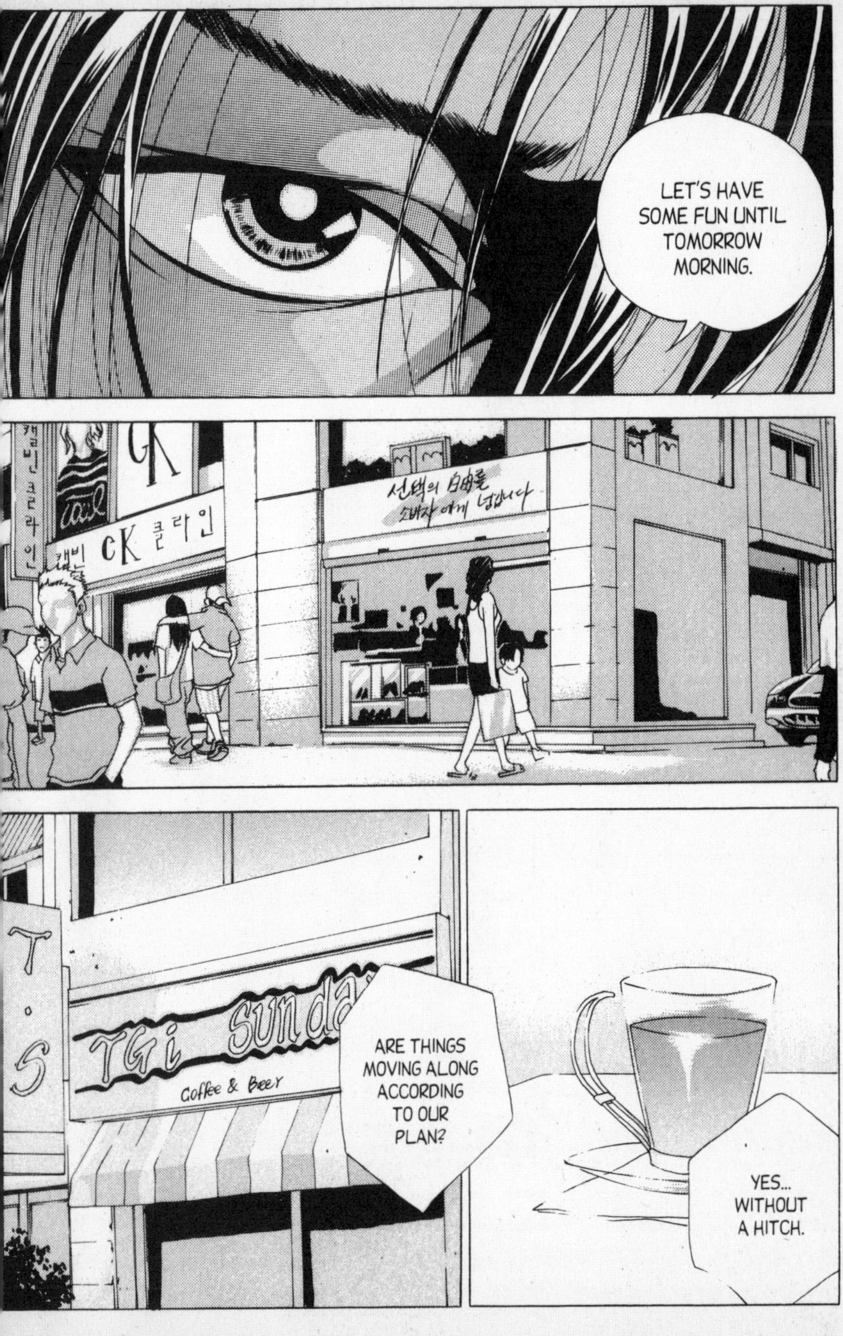
LET'S HAVE SOME FUN UNTIL TOMORROW MORNING.
캘빈 CK 클라인
Coffee & Beer
ARE THINGS MOVING ALONG ACCORDING TO OUR PLAN?
YES... WITHOUT A HITCH.

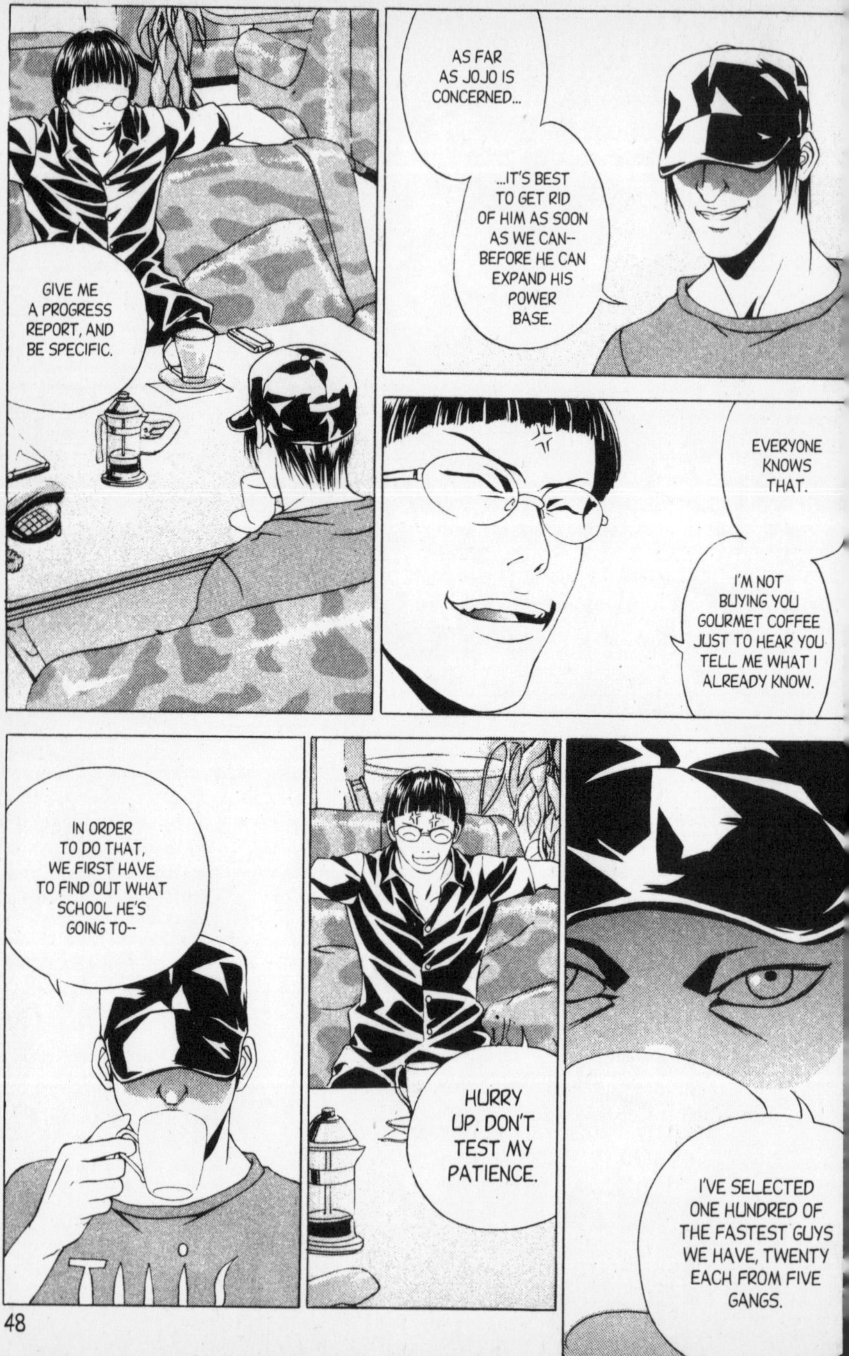
GIVE ME A PROGRESS REPORT, AND BE SPECIFIC.
AS FAR AS JOJO IS CONCERNED...
...IT'S BEST TO GET RID OF HIM AS SOON AS WE CAN-- BEFORE HE CAN EXPAND HIS POWER BASE.
EVERYONE KNOWS THAT.
I'M NOT BUYING YOU GOURMET COFFEE JUST TO HEAR YOU TELL ME WHAT I ALREADY KNOW.
IN ORDER TO DO THAT, WE FIRST HAVE TO FIND OUT WHAT SCHOOL HE'S GOING TO--
HURRY UP. DON'T TEST MY PATIENCE.
I'VE SELECTED ONE HUNDRED OF THE FASTEST GUYS WE HAVE, TWENTY EACH FROM FIVE GANGS.

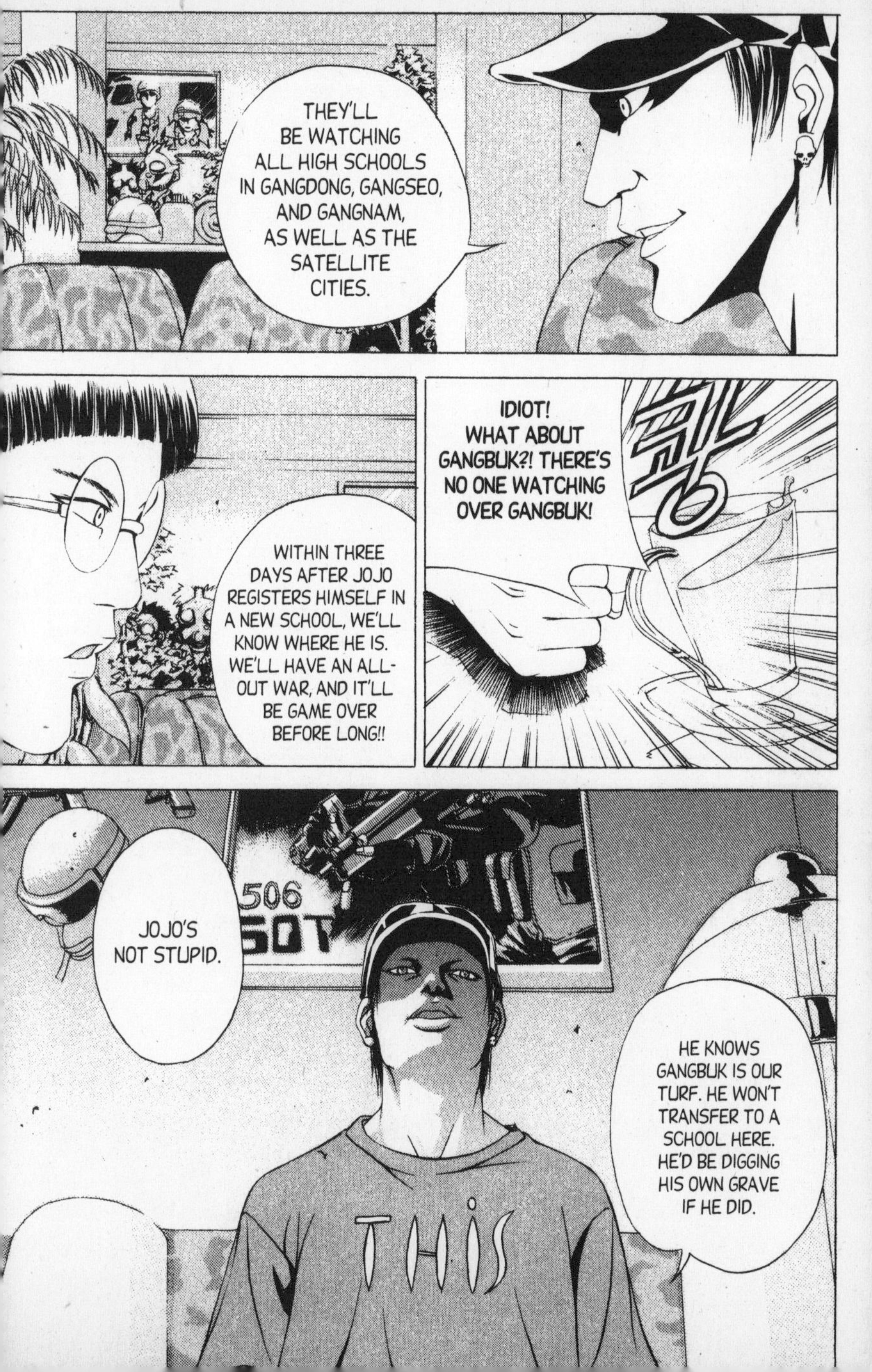
THEY'LL BE WATCHING ALL HIGH SCHOOLS IN GANGDONG, GANGSEO, AND GANGNAM, AS WELL AS THE SATELLITE CITIES.
WITHIN THREE DAYS AFTER JOJO REGISTERS HIMSELF IN A NEW SCHOOL, WE'LL KNOW WHERE HE IS. WE'LL HAVE AN ALL-OUT WAR, AND IT'LL BE GAME OVER BEFORE LONG!!
IDIOT! WHAT ABOUT GANGBUK?! THERE'S NO ONE WATCHING OVER GANGBUK!
쾅
506
SOT
JOJO'S NOT STUPID.
THIS
HE KNOWS GANGBUK IS OUR TURF. HE WON'T TRANSFER TO A SCHOOL HERE. HE'D BE DIGGING HIS OWN GRAVE IF HE DID.

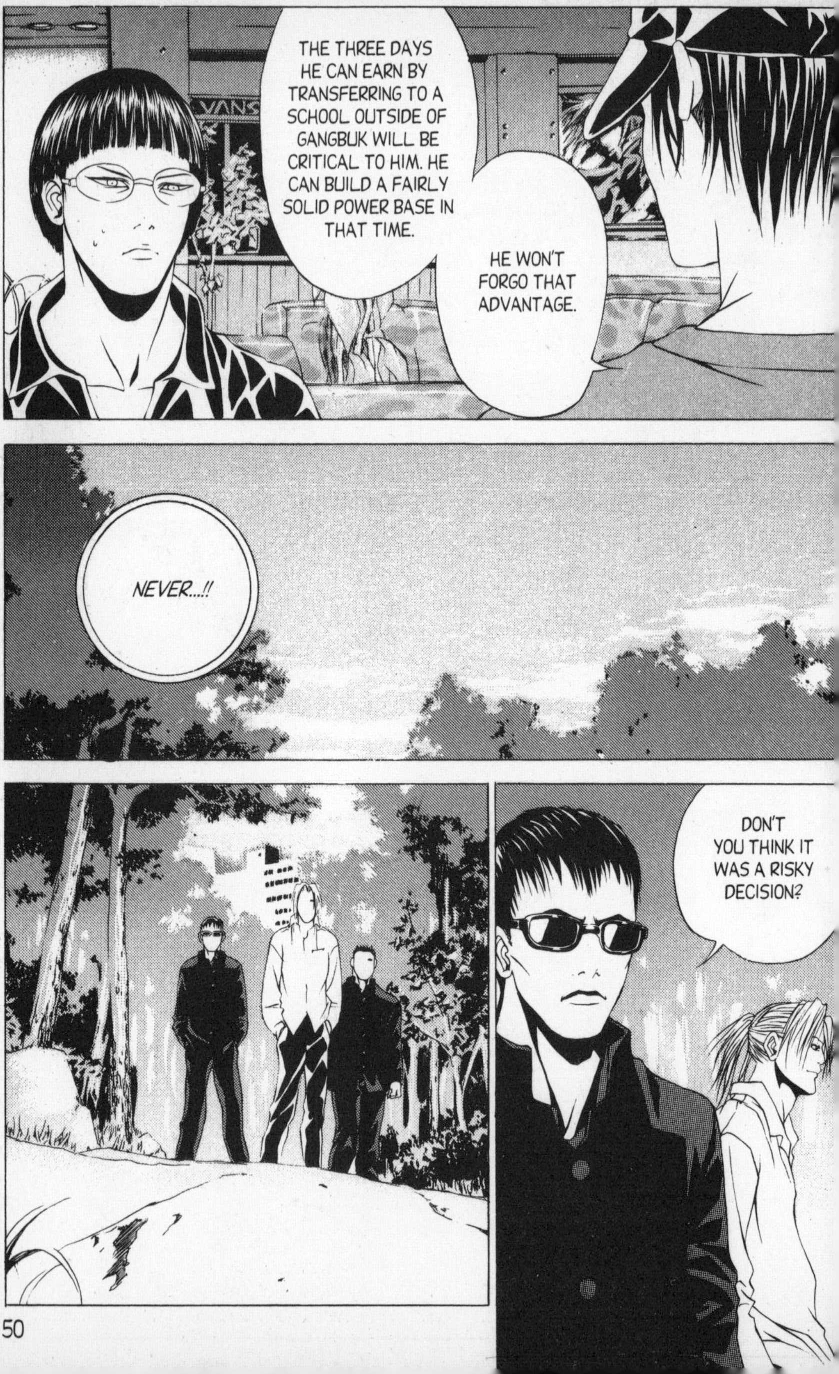
THE THREE DAYS HE CAN EARN BY TRANSFERRING TO A SCHOOL OUTSIDE OF GANGBUK WILL BE CRITICAL TO HIM. HE CAN BUILD A FAIRLY SOLID POWER BASE IN THAT TIME.
HE WON'T FORGO THAT ADVANTAGE.
NEVER...!!
DON'T YOU THINK IT WAS A RISKY DECISION?

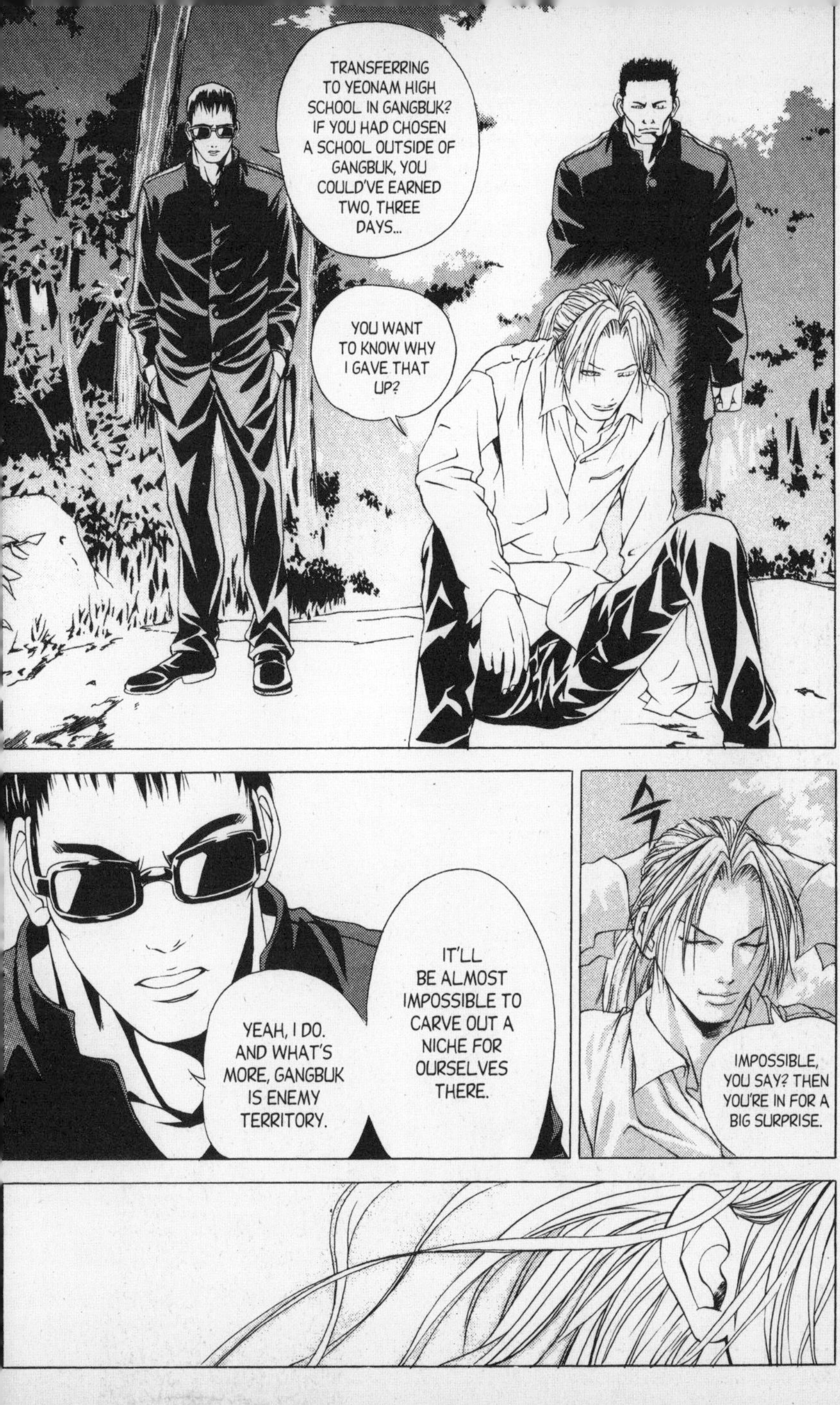
TRANSFERRING TO YEONAM HIGH SCHOOL IN GANGBUK? IF YOU HAD CHOSEN A SCHOOL OUTSIDE OF GANGBUK, YOU COULD'VE EARNED TWO, THREE DAYS...
YOU WANT TO KNOW WHY I GAVE THAT UP?
YEAH, I DO. AND WHAT'S MORE, GANGBUK IS ENEMY TERRITORY.
IT'LL BE ALMOST IMPOSSIBLE TO CARVE OUT A NICHE FOR OURSELVES THERE.
IMPOSSIBLE, YOU SAY? THEN YOU'RE IN FOR A BIG SURPRISE.

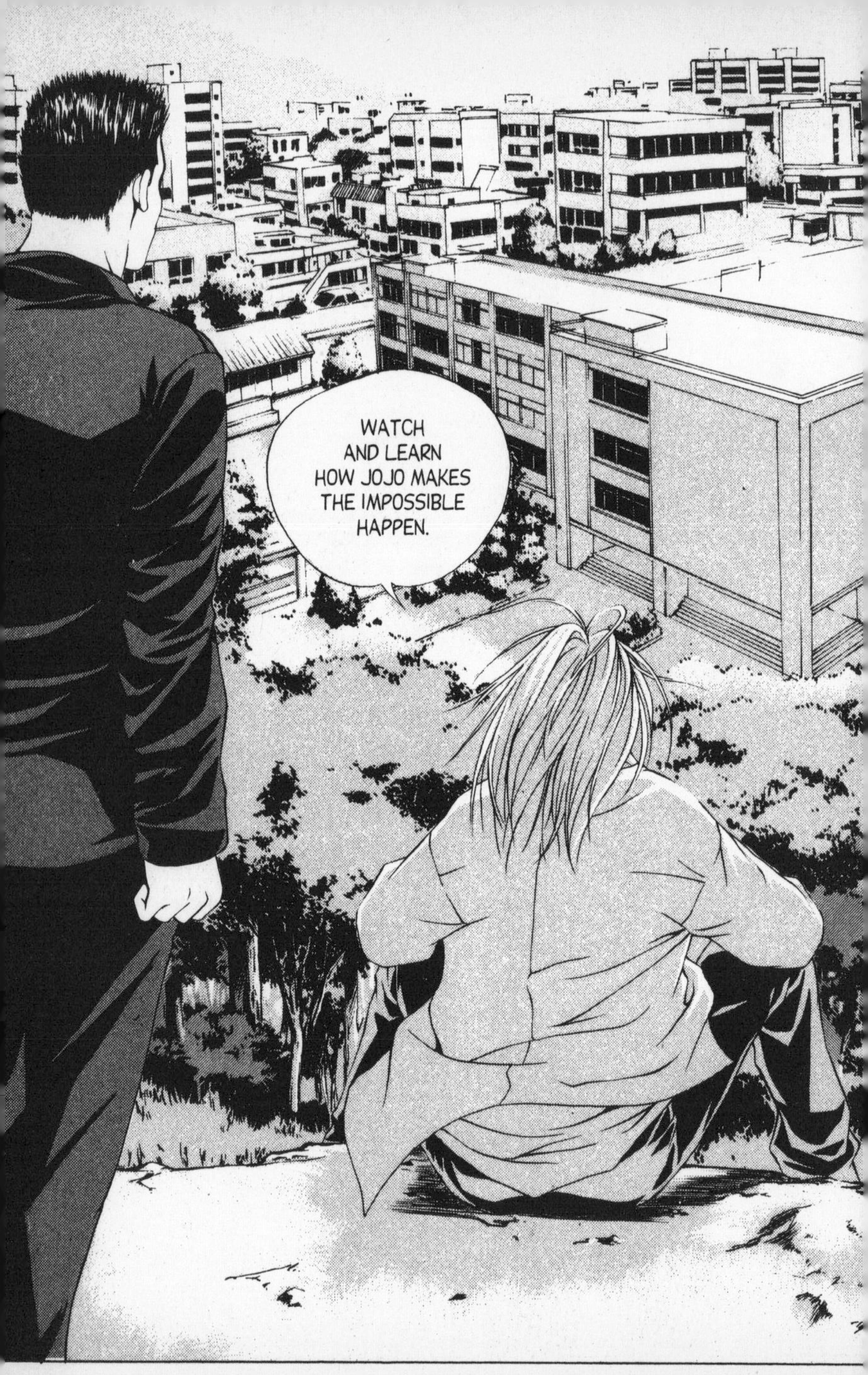
WATCH AND LEARN HOW JOJO MAKES THE IMPOSSIBLE HAPPEN.

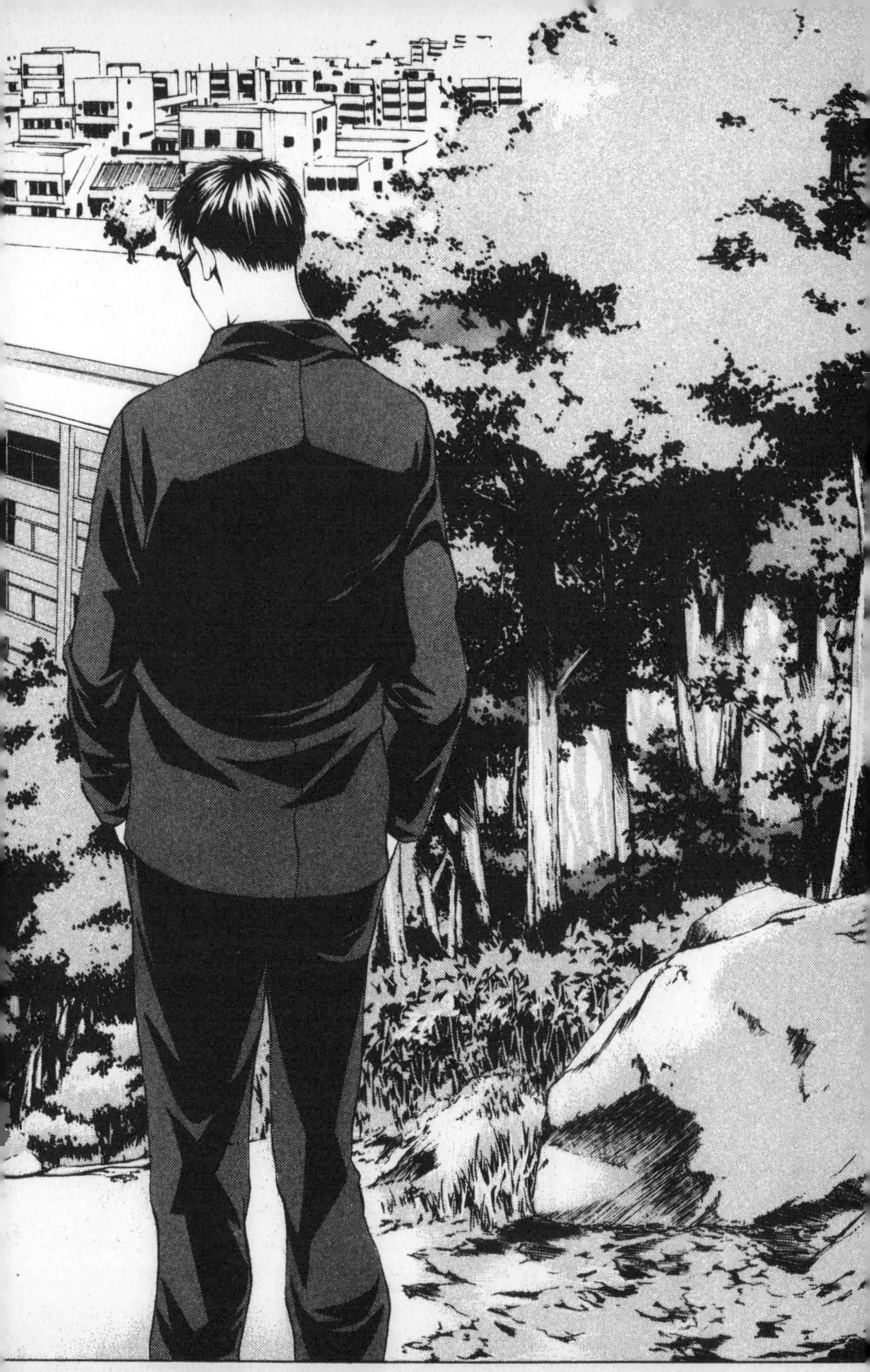

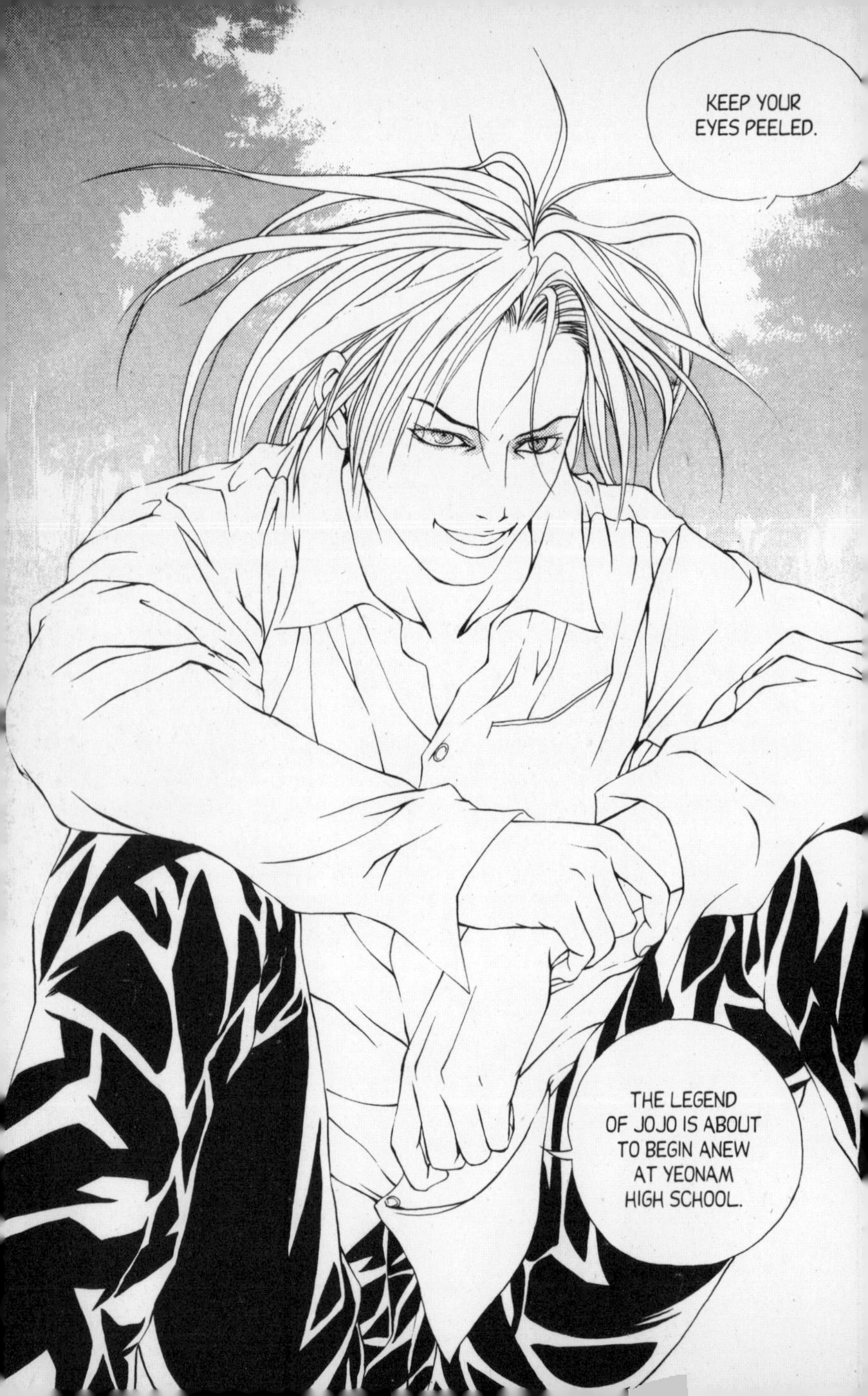
KEEP YOUR EYES PEELED.
THE LEGEND OF JOJO IS ABOUT TO BEGIN ANEW AT YEONAM HIGH SCHOOL.

#17 A BLOODY BATTLE

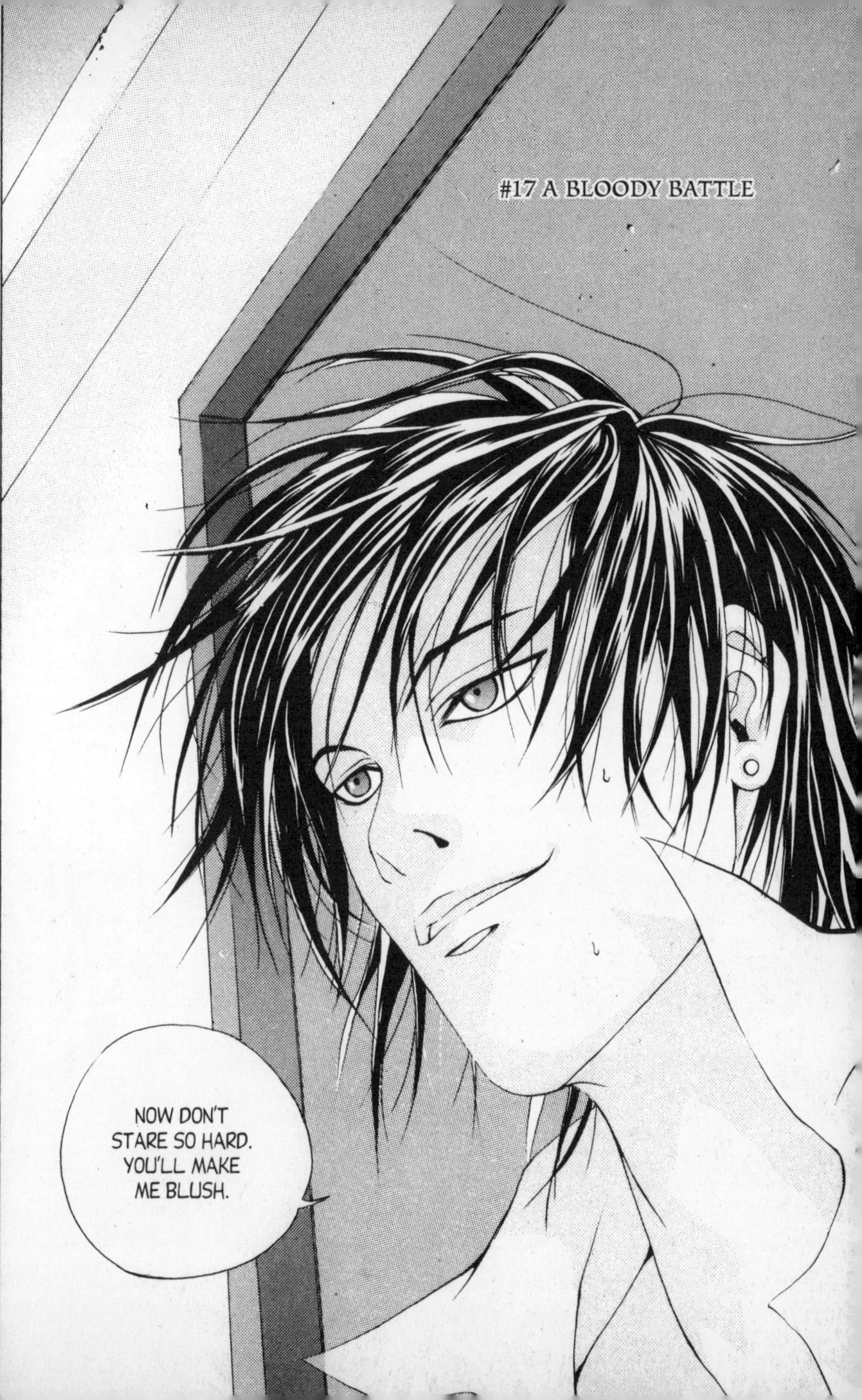
NOW DON'T STARE SO HARD. YOU'LL MAKE ME BLUSH.

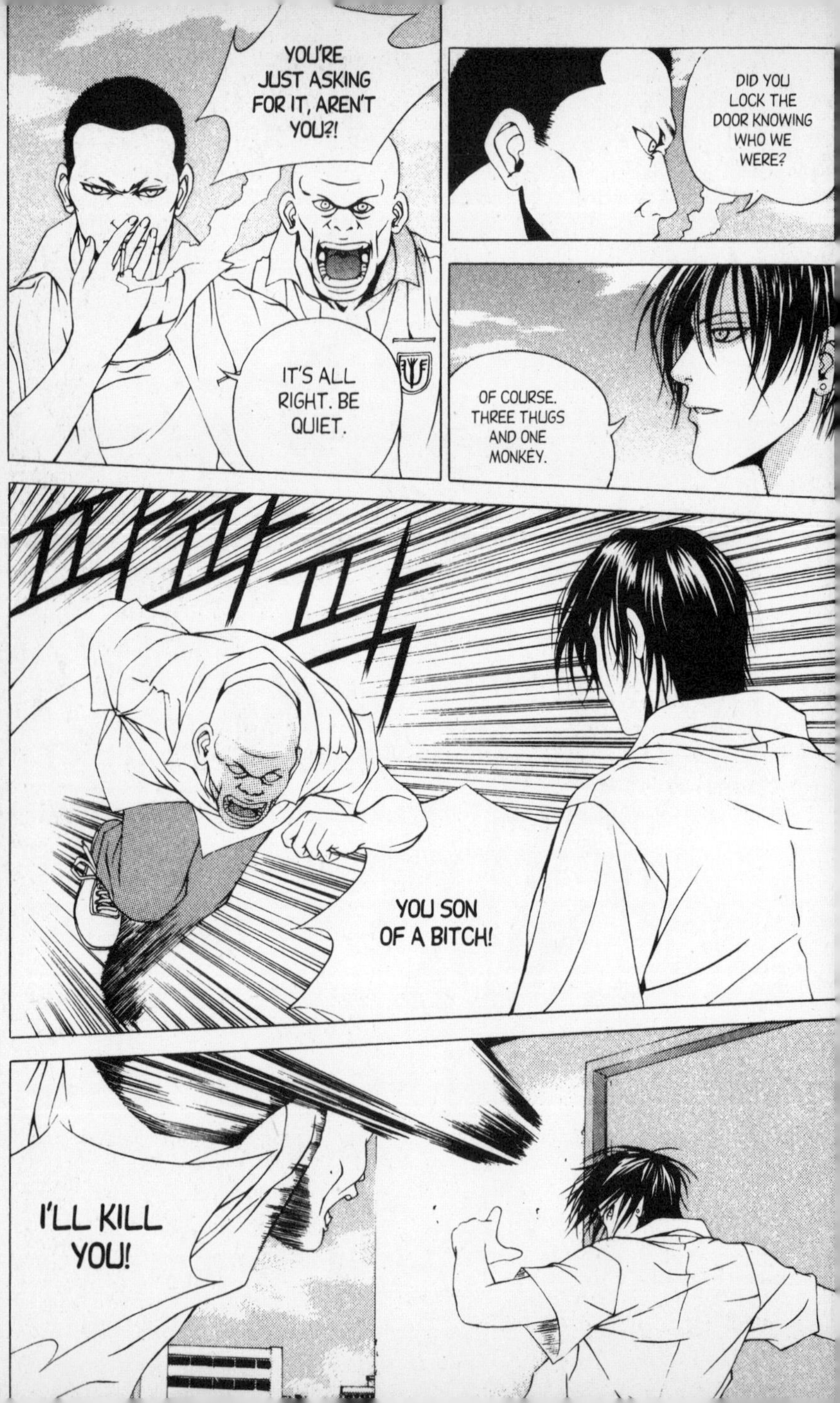
DID YOU LOCK THE DOOR KNOWING WHO WE WERE?
OF COURSE. THREE THUGS AND ONE MONKEY.
YOU'RE JUST ASKING FOR IT, AREN'T YOU?!
IT'S ALL RIGHT. BE QUIET.
YOU SON OF A BITCH!
I'LL KILL YOU!

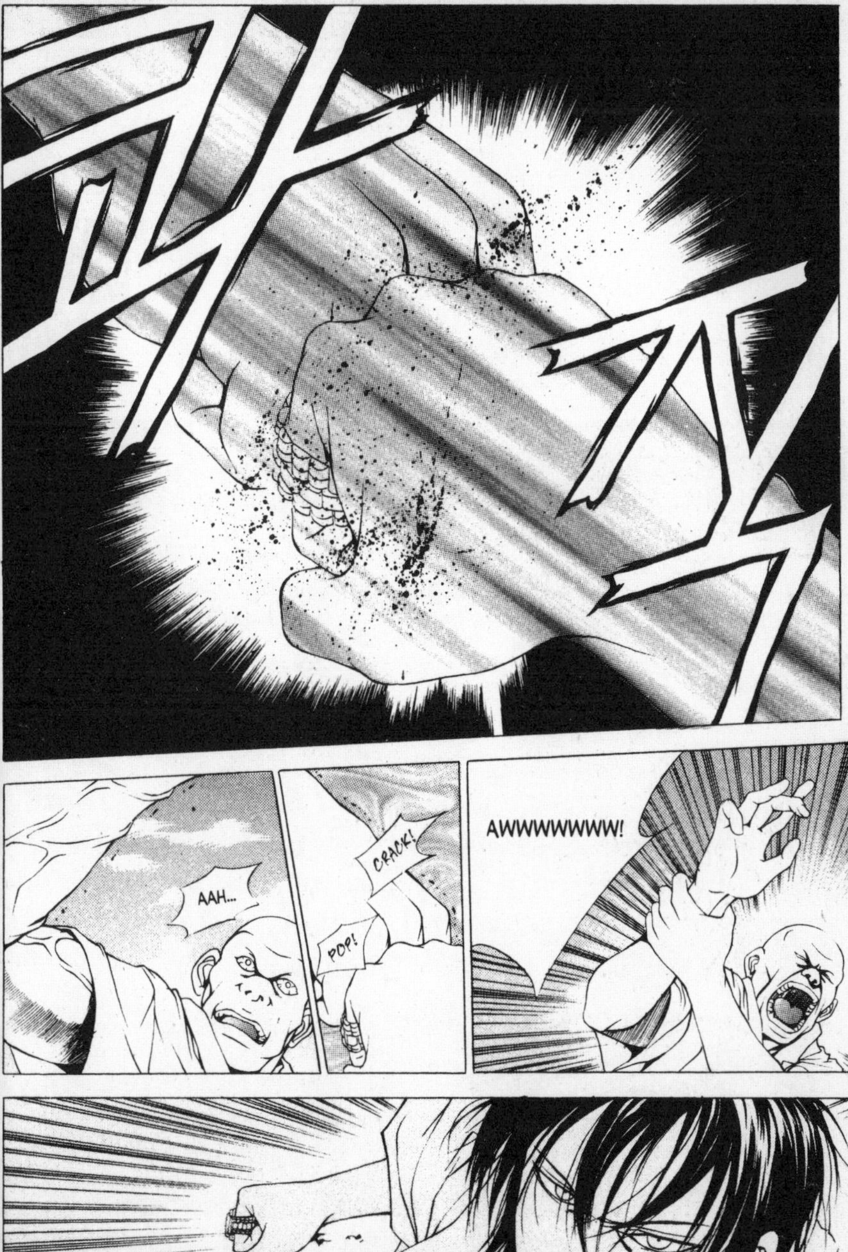
AWWWWWWWW!
CRACK!
POP!
AAH...

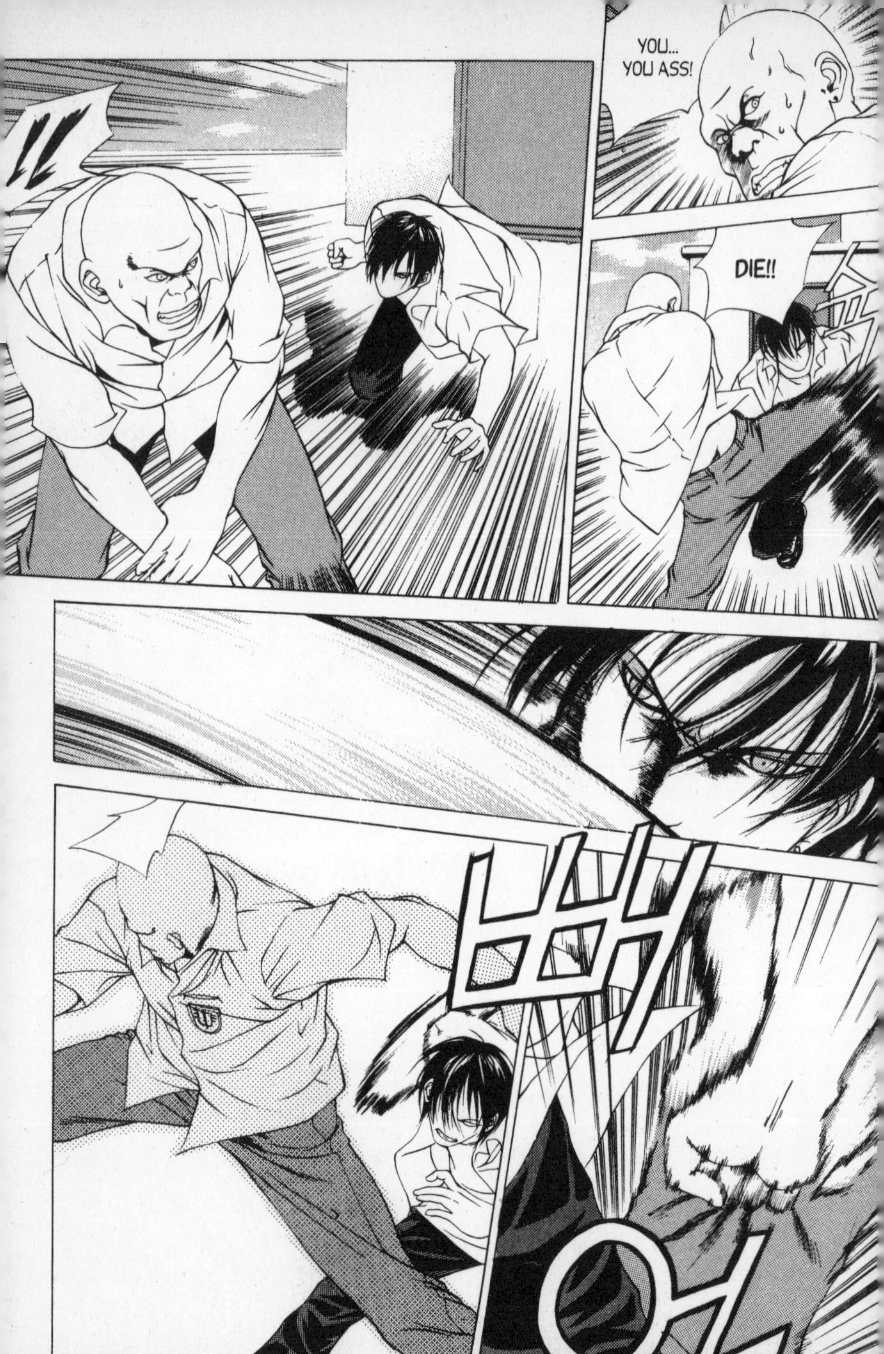
YOU... YOU ASS!
DIE!!
!!

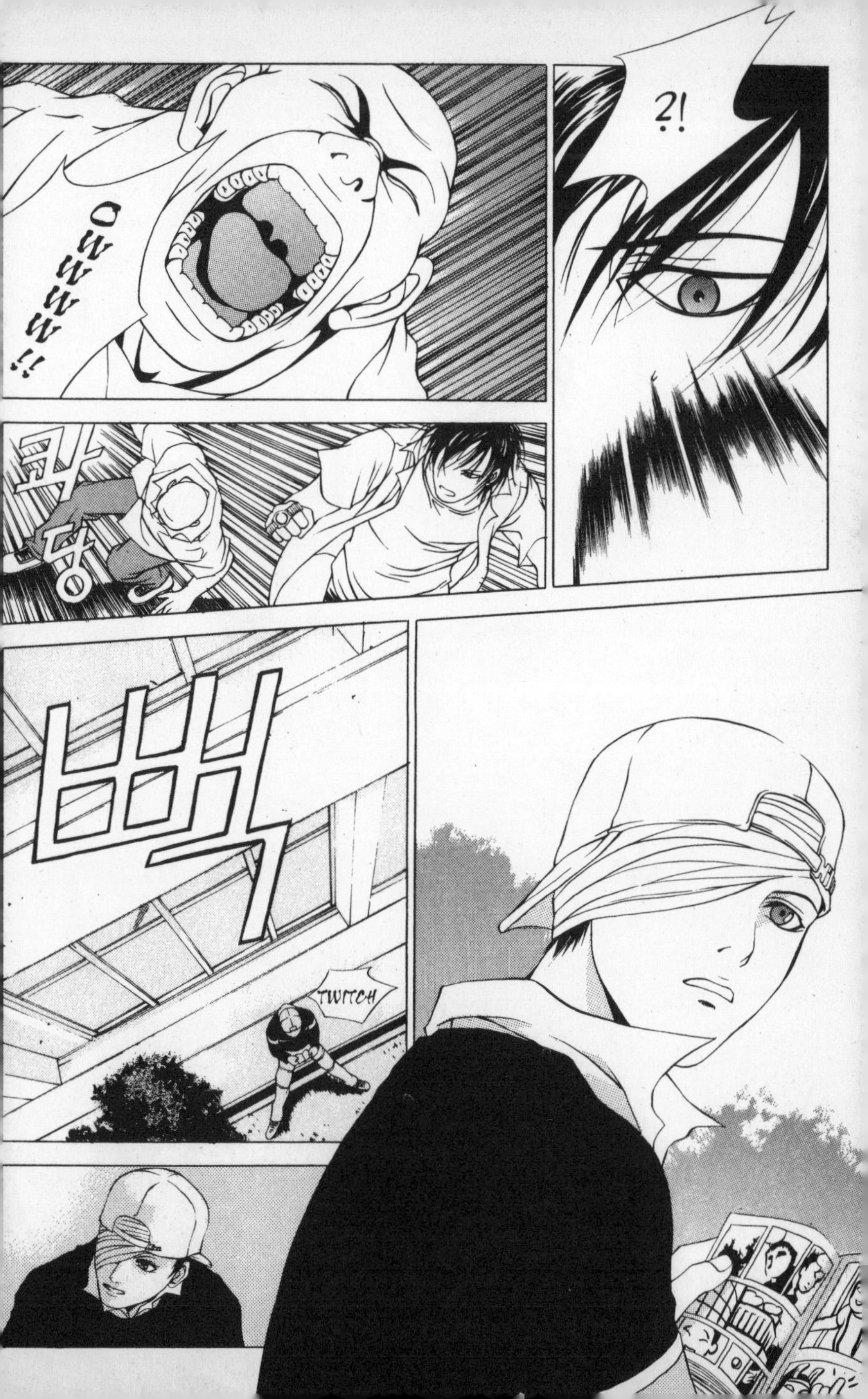
?!
OWWWW!!
TWITCH

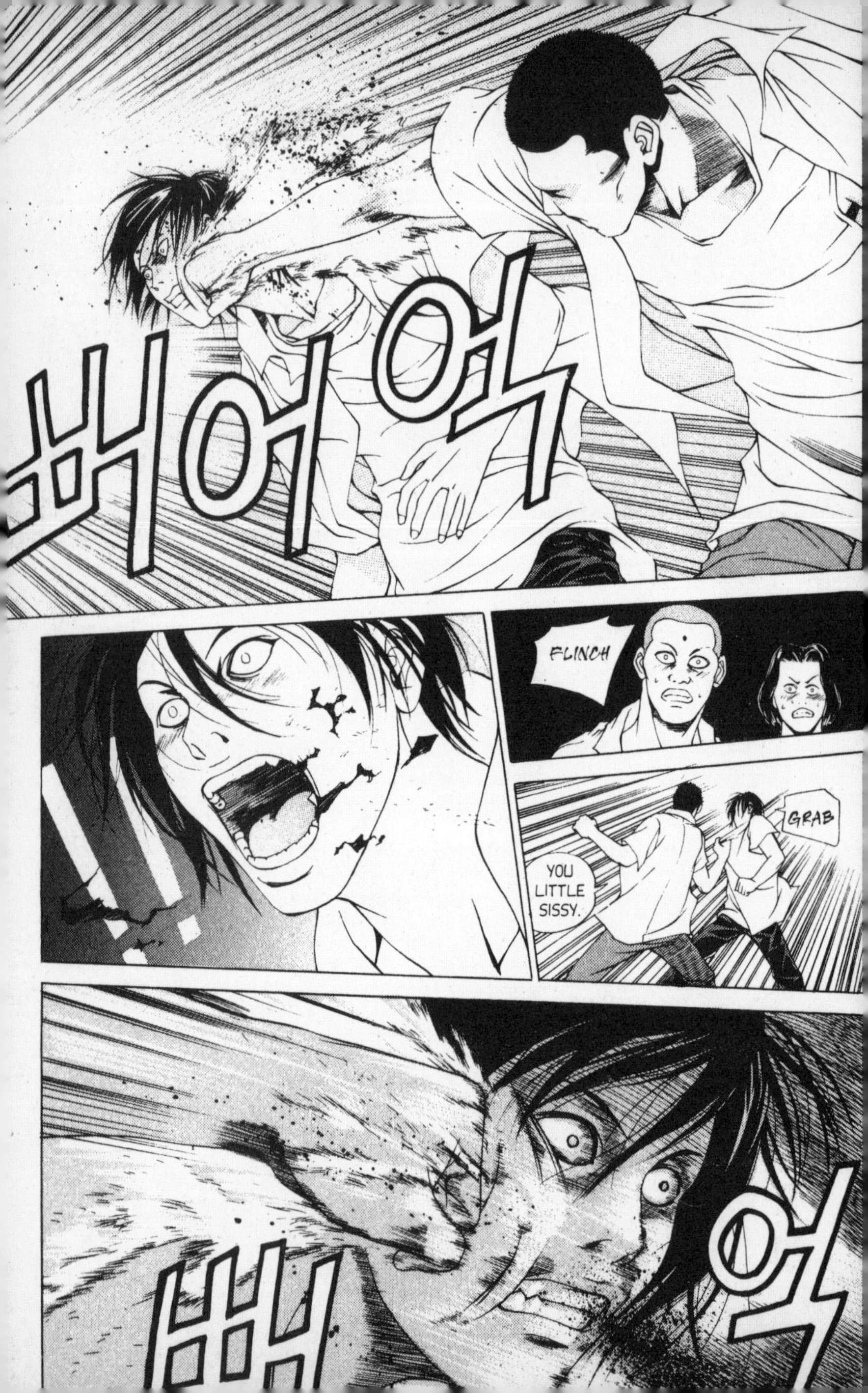
FLINCH
GRAB
YOU LITTLE SISSY.

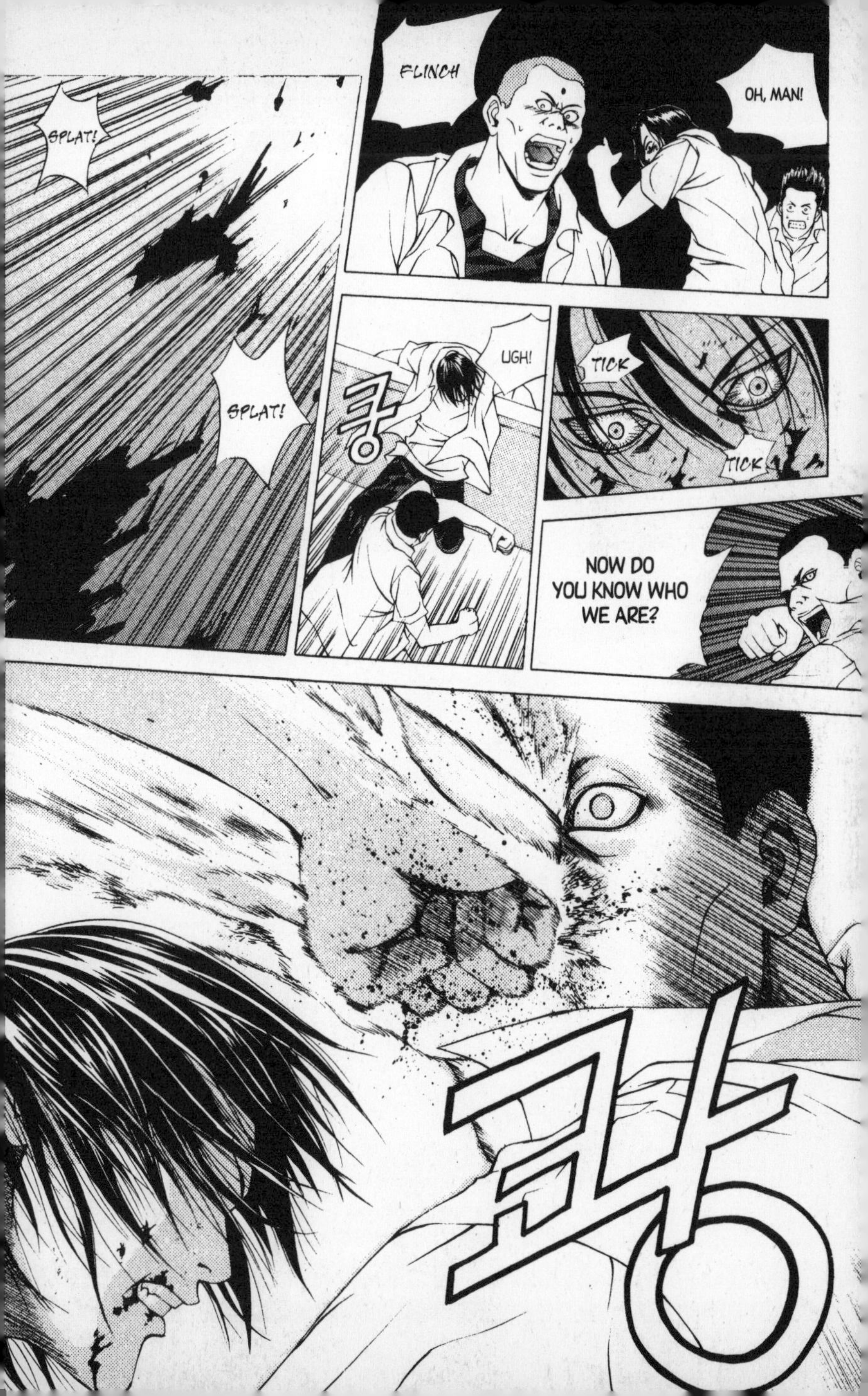
OH, MAN!
FLINCH
TICK
TICK
UGH!
NOW DO YOU KNOW WHO WE ARE?
SPLAT!
SPLAT!

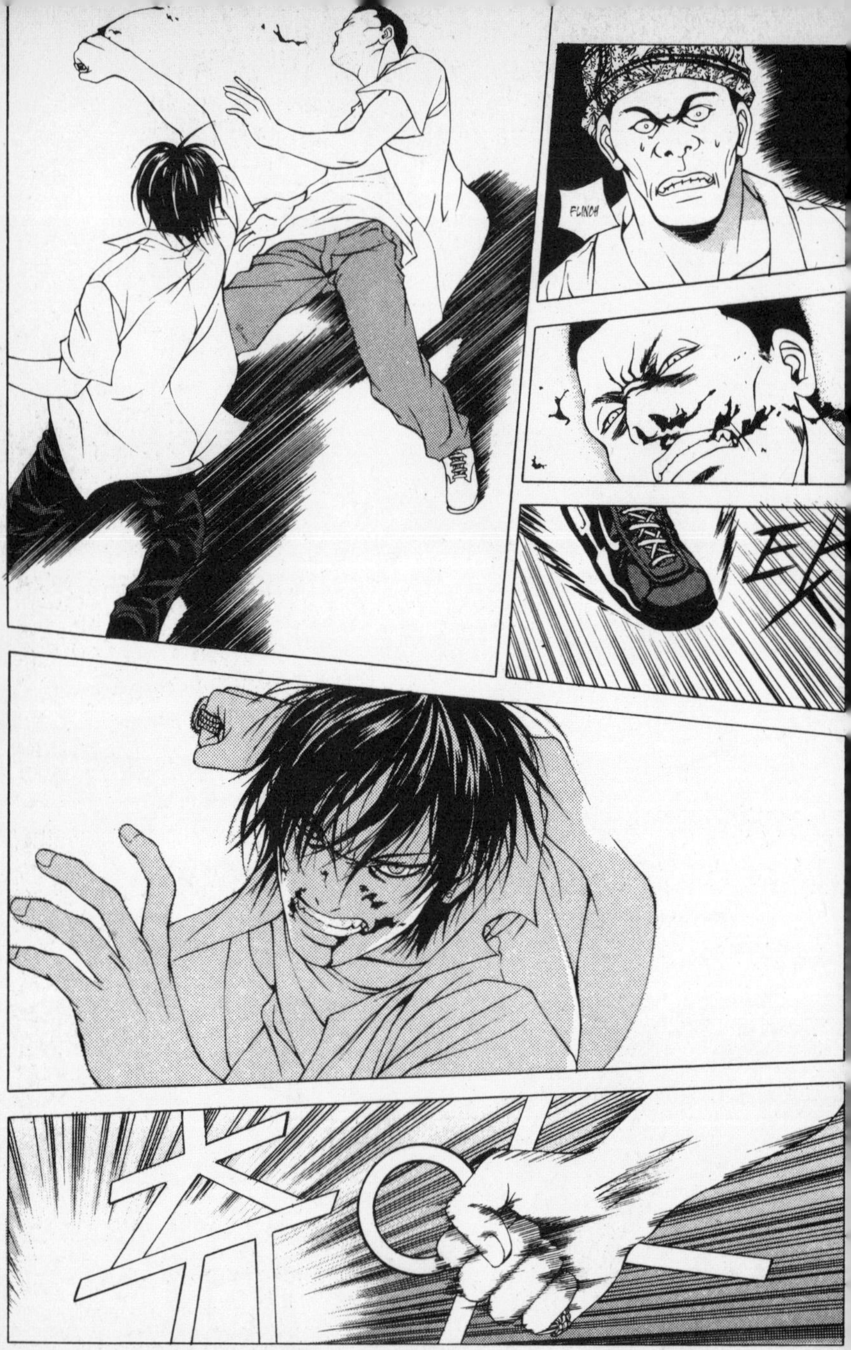
FLINCH
EK

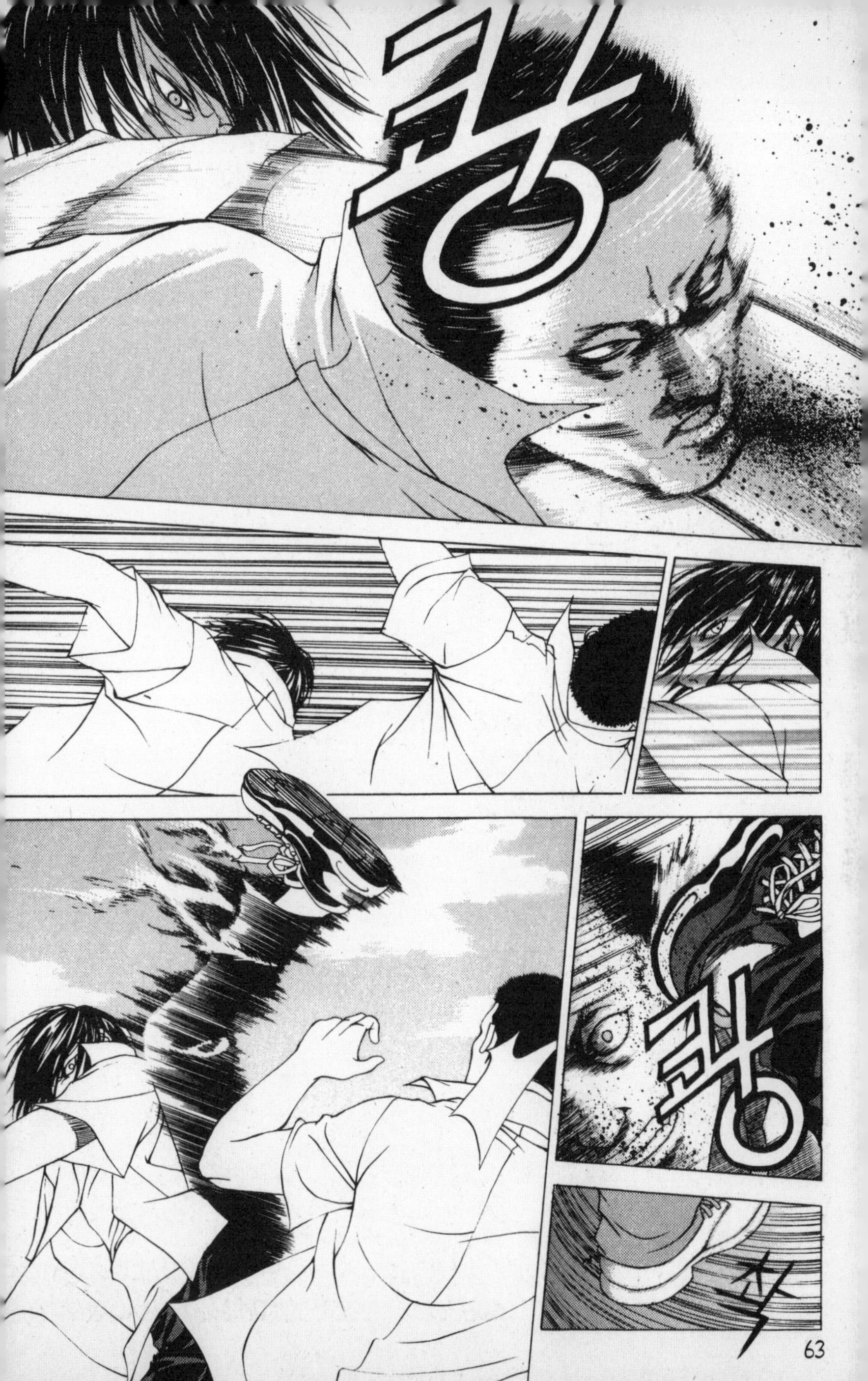

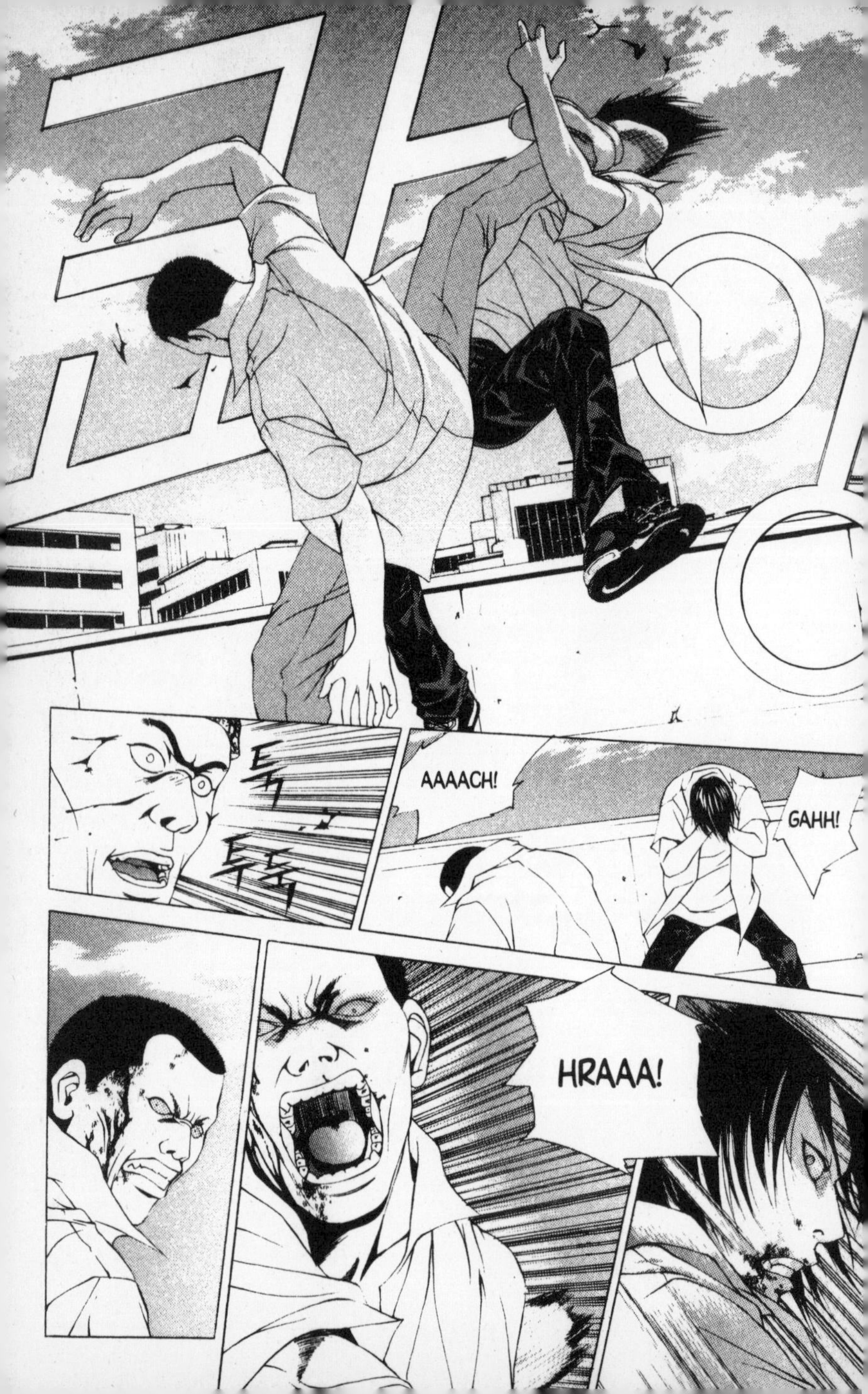
AAAACH!
GAHH!
HRAAA!

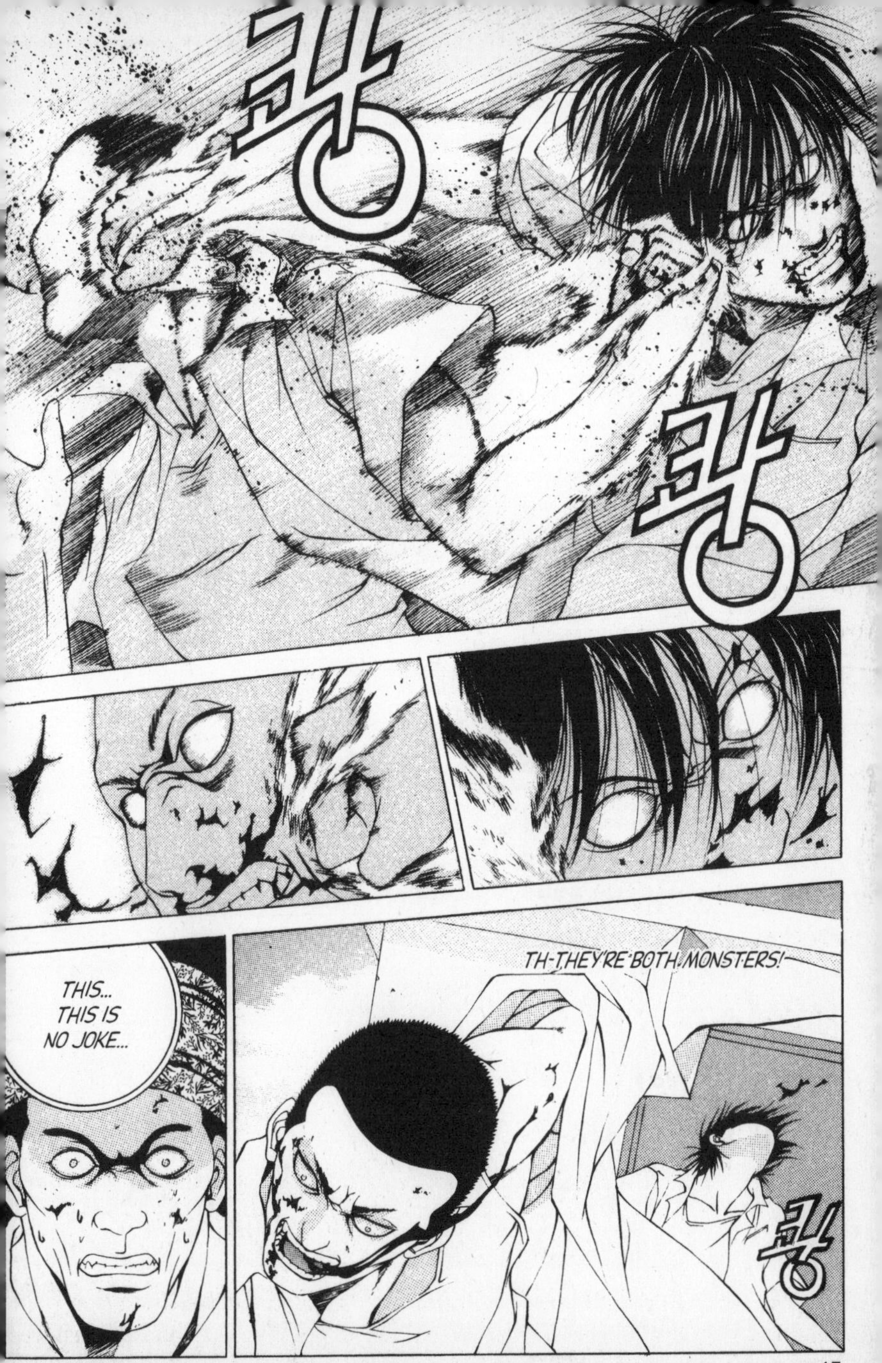
쾅
쾅
TH-THEY'RE BOTH MONSTERS!
쿵
THIS... THIS IS NO JOKE...

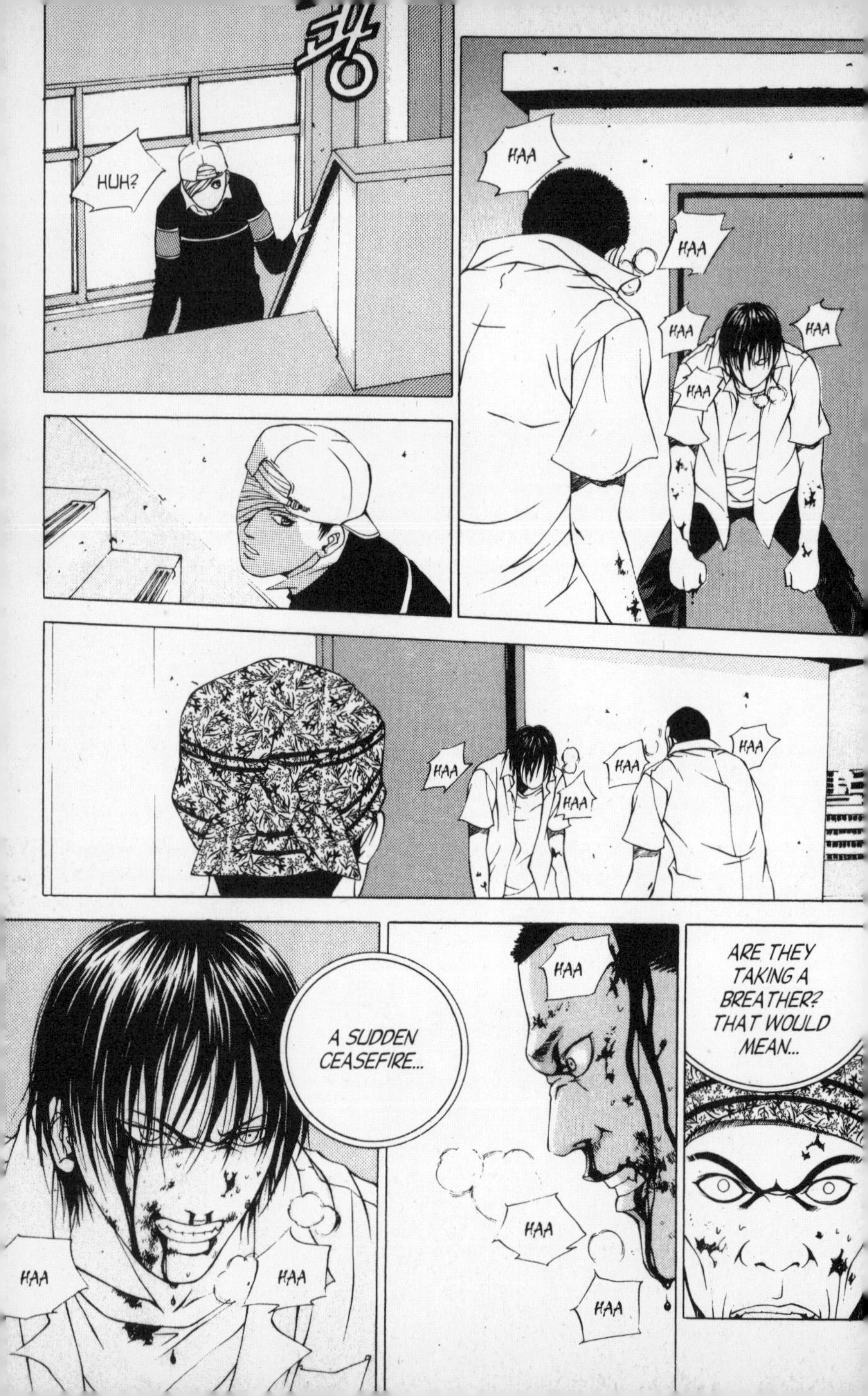
HAA
HAA
HAA
HAA
HAA
HUH?
HAA
HAA
HAA!
HAA
ARE THEY TAKING A BREATHER? THAT WOULD MEAN...
HAA
HAA
HAA
A SUDDEN CEASEFIRE...
HAA
HAA

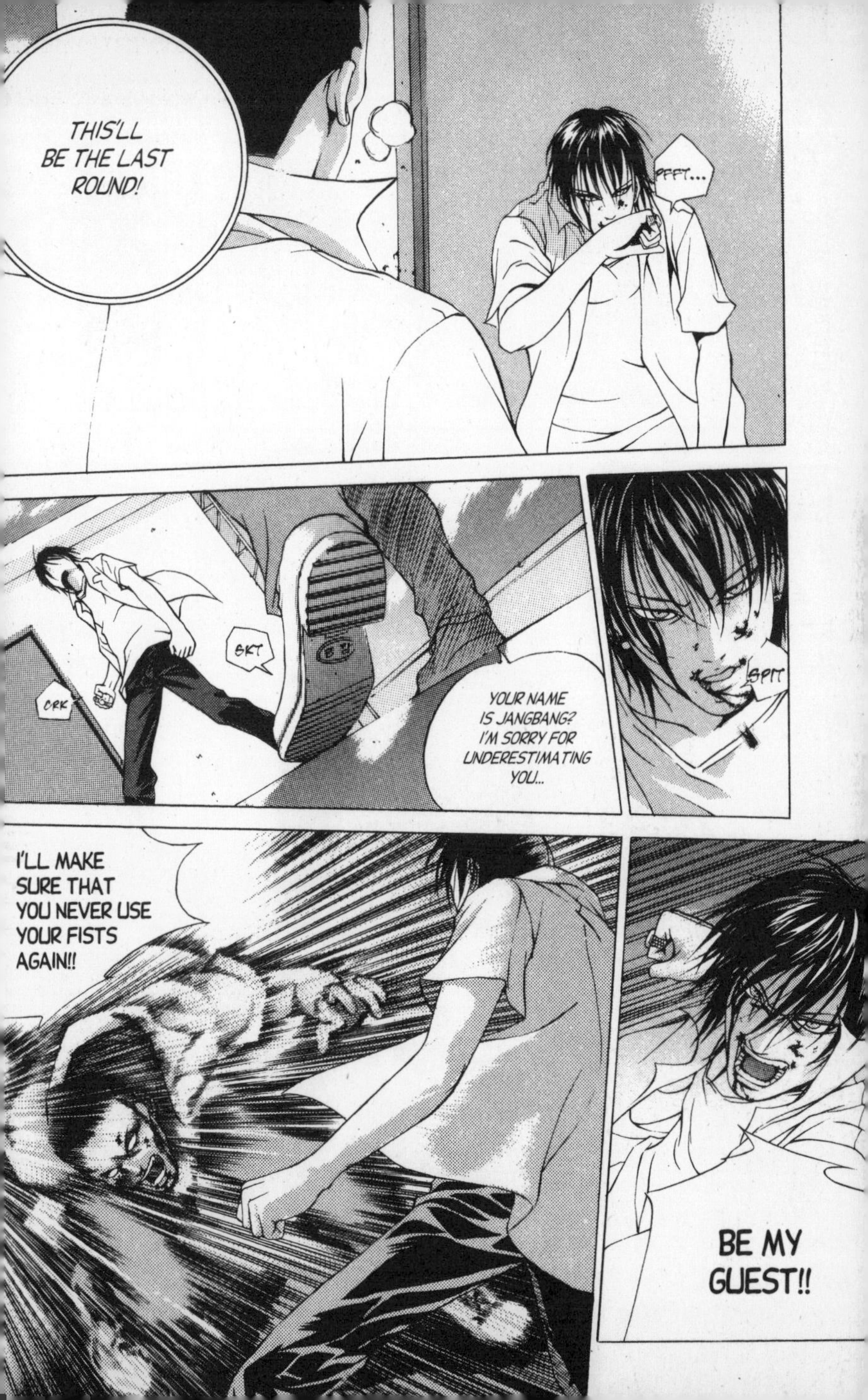
THIS'LL BE THE LAST ROUND!
PFFT...
CRK
SKT
YOUR NAME IS JANGBANG? I'M SORRY FOR UNDERESTIMATING YOU...
SPIT
I'LL MAKE SURE THAT YOU NEVER USE YOUR FISTS AGAIN!!
BE MY GUEST!!

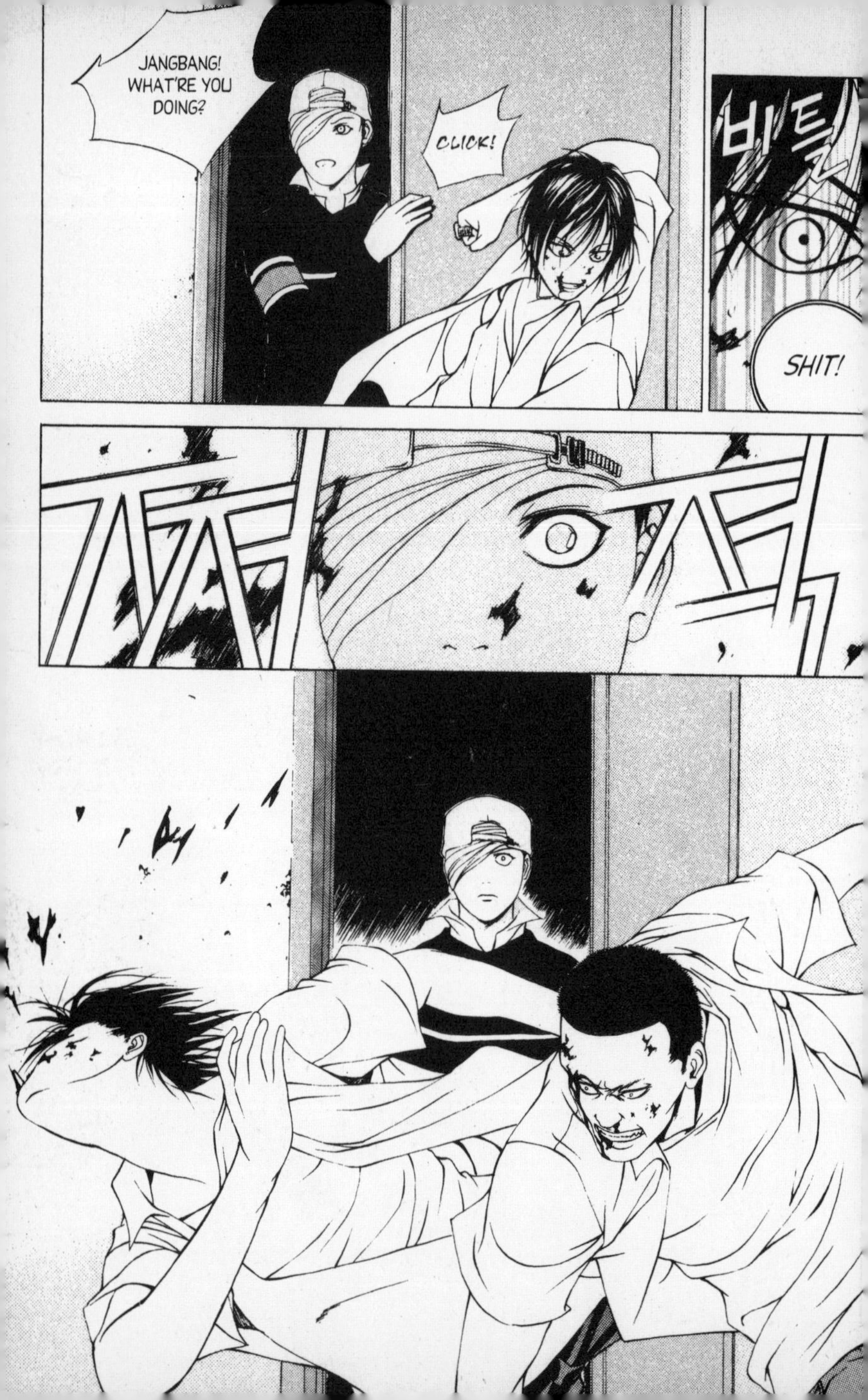
JANGBANG! WHAT'RE YOU DOING?
CLICK!
비틀
SHIT!

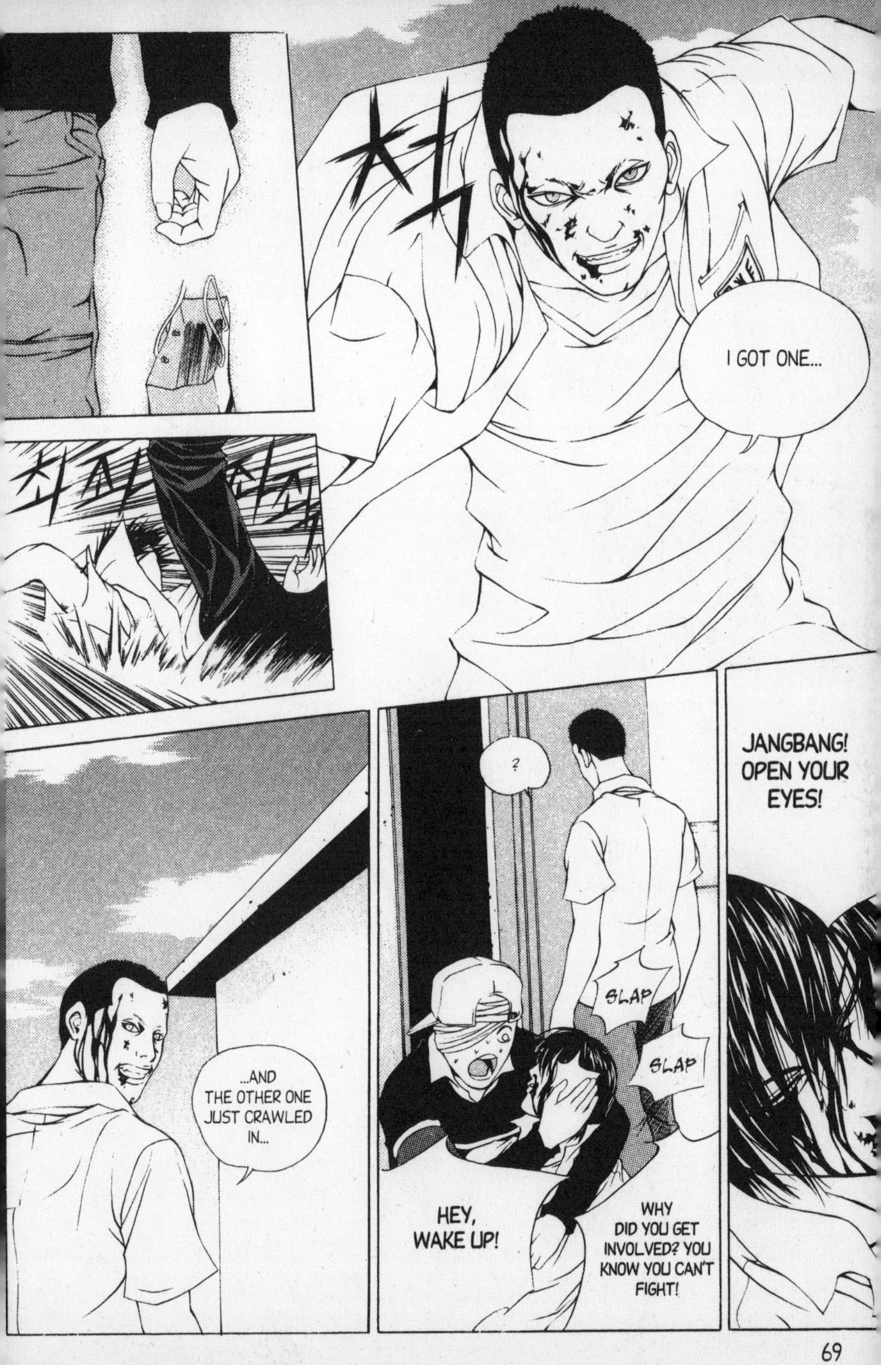
I GOT ONE...
...AND THE OTHER ONE JUST CRAWLED IN...
?
SLAP
SLAP
HEY, WAKE UP!
WHY DID YOU GET INVOLVED? YOU KNOW YOU CAN'T FIGHT!
JANGBANG! OPEN YOUR EYES!

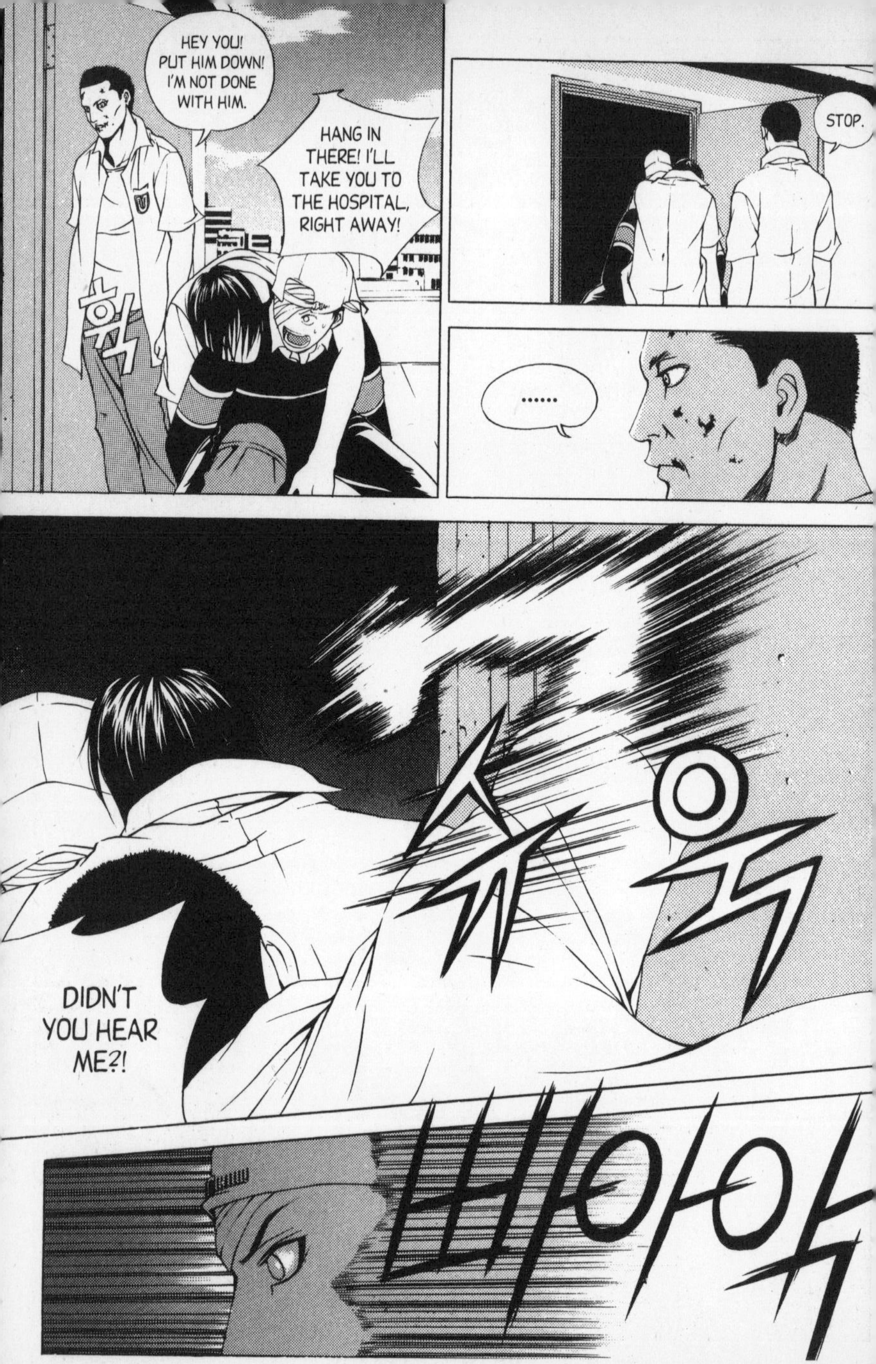
HEY YOU! PUT HIM DOWN! I'M NOT DONE WITH HIM.
HANG IN THERE! I'LL TAKE YOU TO THE HOSPITAL, RIGHT AWAY!
STOP.
......
DIDN'T YOU HEAR ME?!

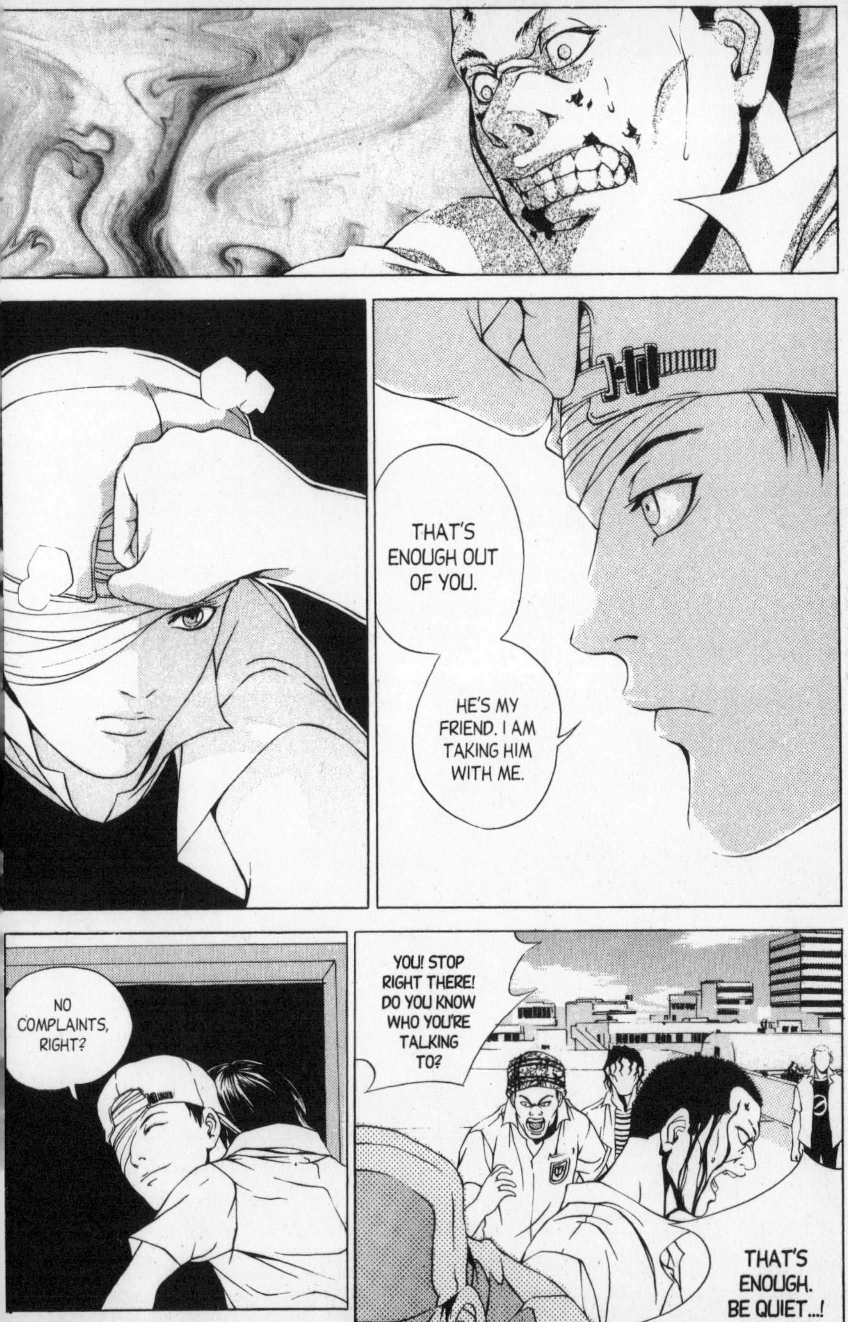
THAT'S ENOUGH OUT OF YOU.
HE'S MY FRIEND. I AM TAKING HIM WITH ME.
YOU! STOP RIGHT THERE! DO YOU KNOW WHO YOU'RE TALKING TO?
THAT'S ENOUGH. BE QUIET...!
NO COMPLAINTS, RIGHT?

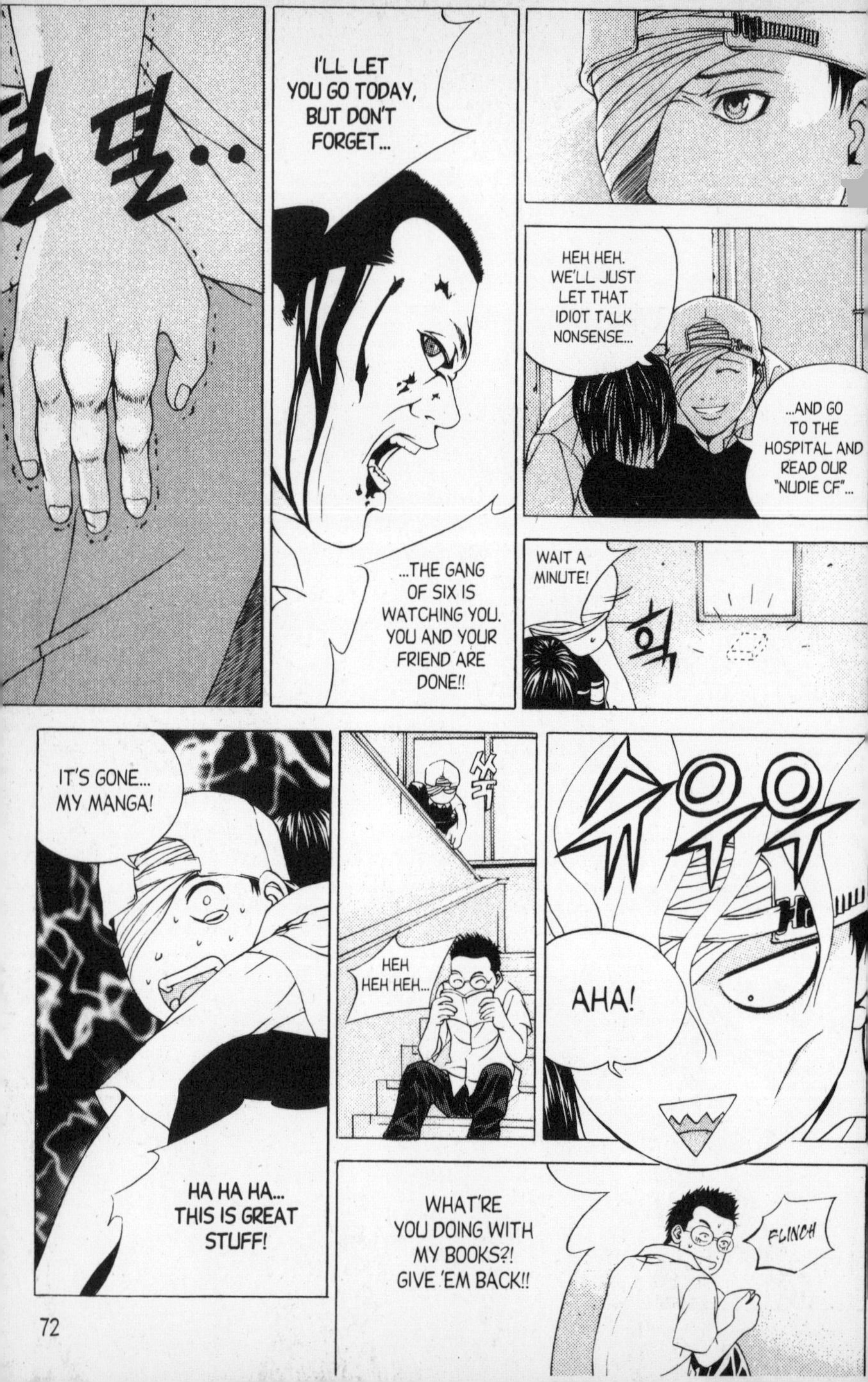
I'LL LET YOU GO TODAY, BUT DON'T FORGET...
...THE GANG OF SIX IS WATCHING YOU. YOU AND YOUR FRIEND ARE DONE!!
HEH HEH. WE'LL JUST LET THAT IDIOT TALK NONSENSE...
...AND GO TO THE HOSPITAL AND READ OUR "NUDIE CF"...
WAIT A MINUTE!
헉
IT'S GONE... MY MANGA!
HA HA HA... THIS IS GREAT STUFF!
HEH HEH HEH...
AHA!
WHAT'RE YOU DOING WITH MY BOOKS?! GIVE 'EM BACK!!
FLINCH

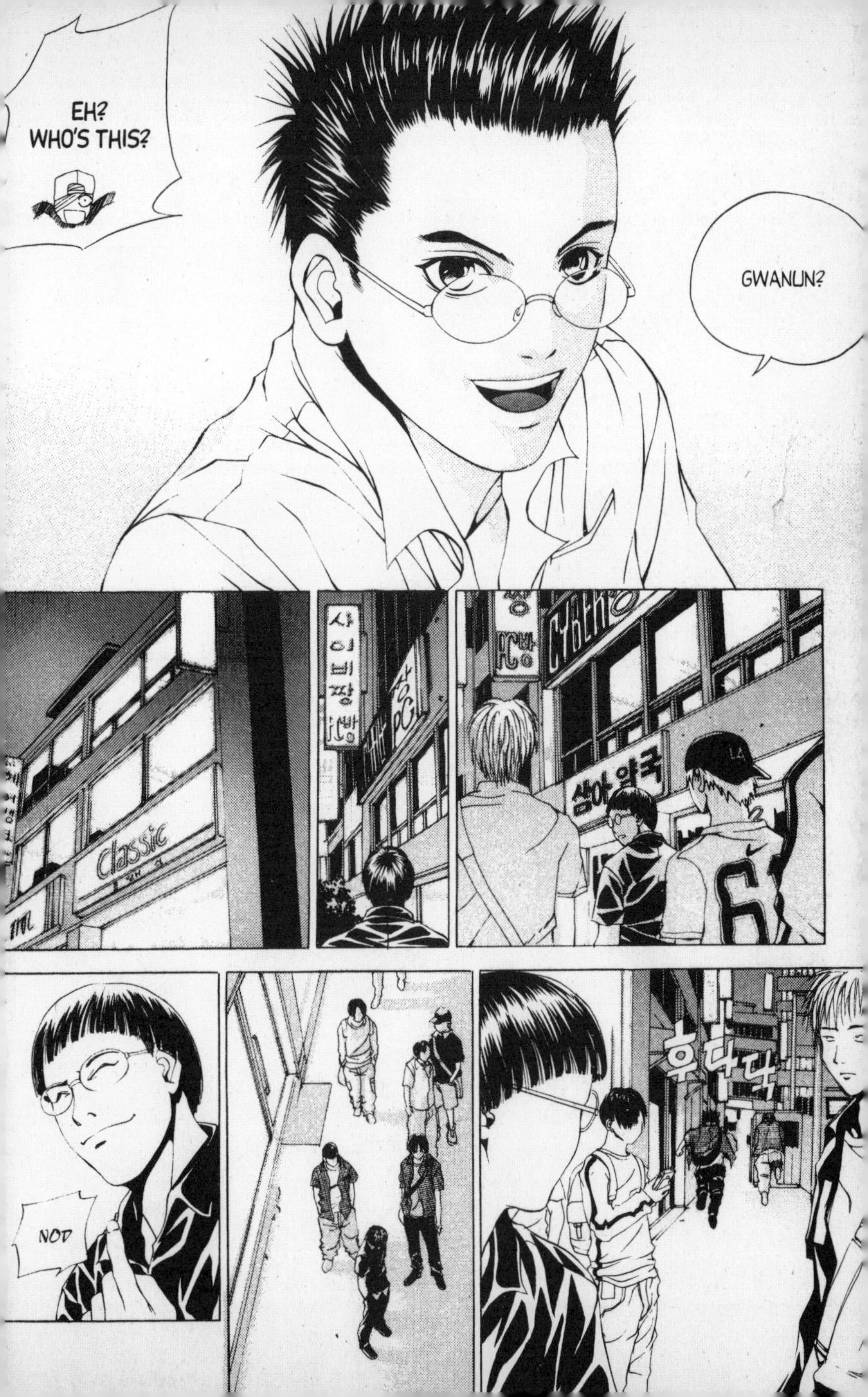
EH? WHO'S THIS?
GWANUN?
Classic
사이버짱 PC방
삼아 약국
NOD
후다닥

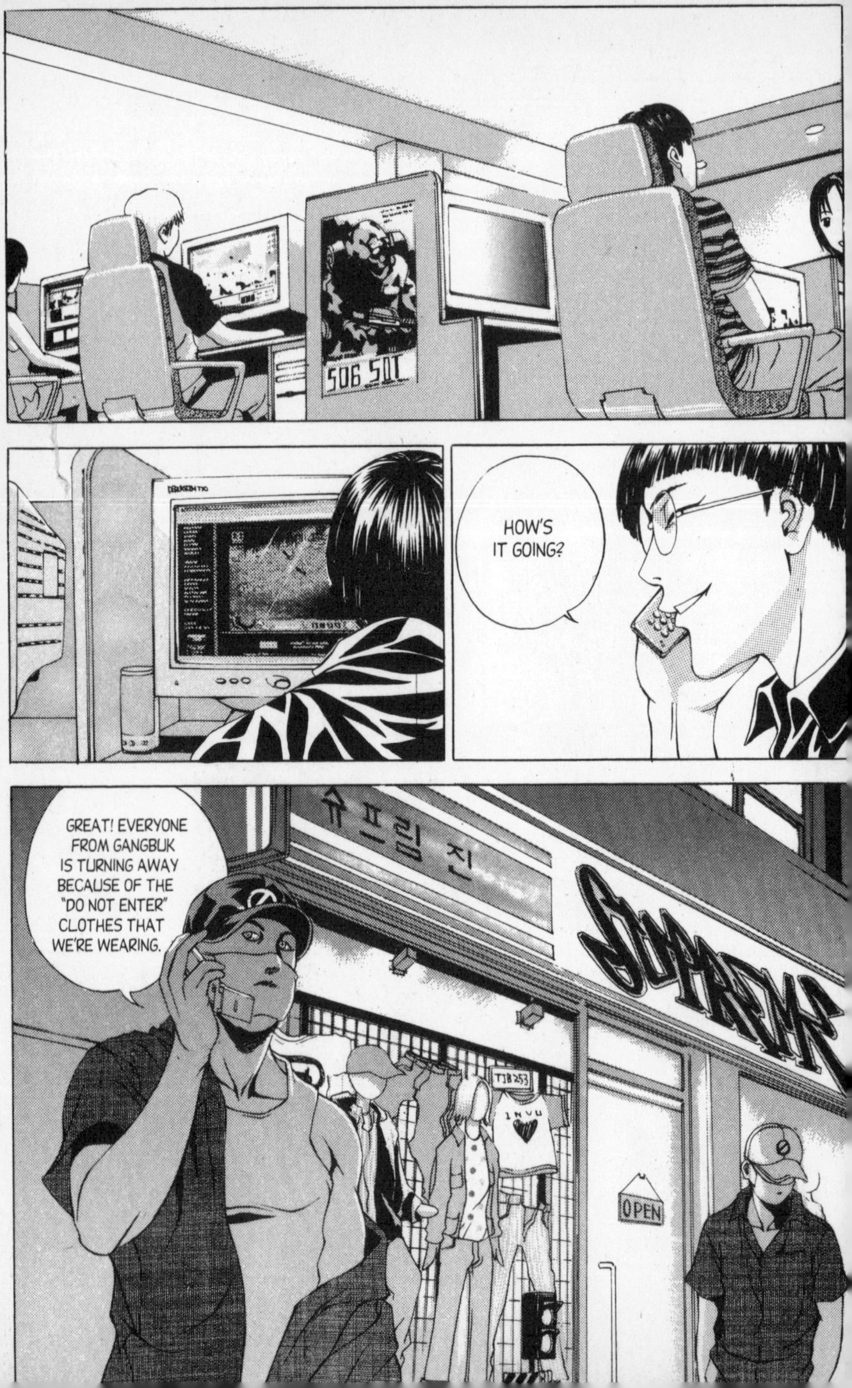
HOW'S IT GOING?
GREAT! EVERYONE FROM GANGBUK IS TURNING AWAY BECAUSE OF THE "DO NOT ENTER" CLOTHES THAT WE'RE WEARING.
슈프림 진
OPEN

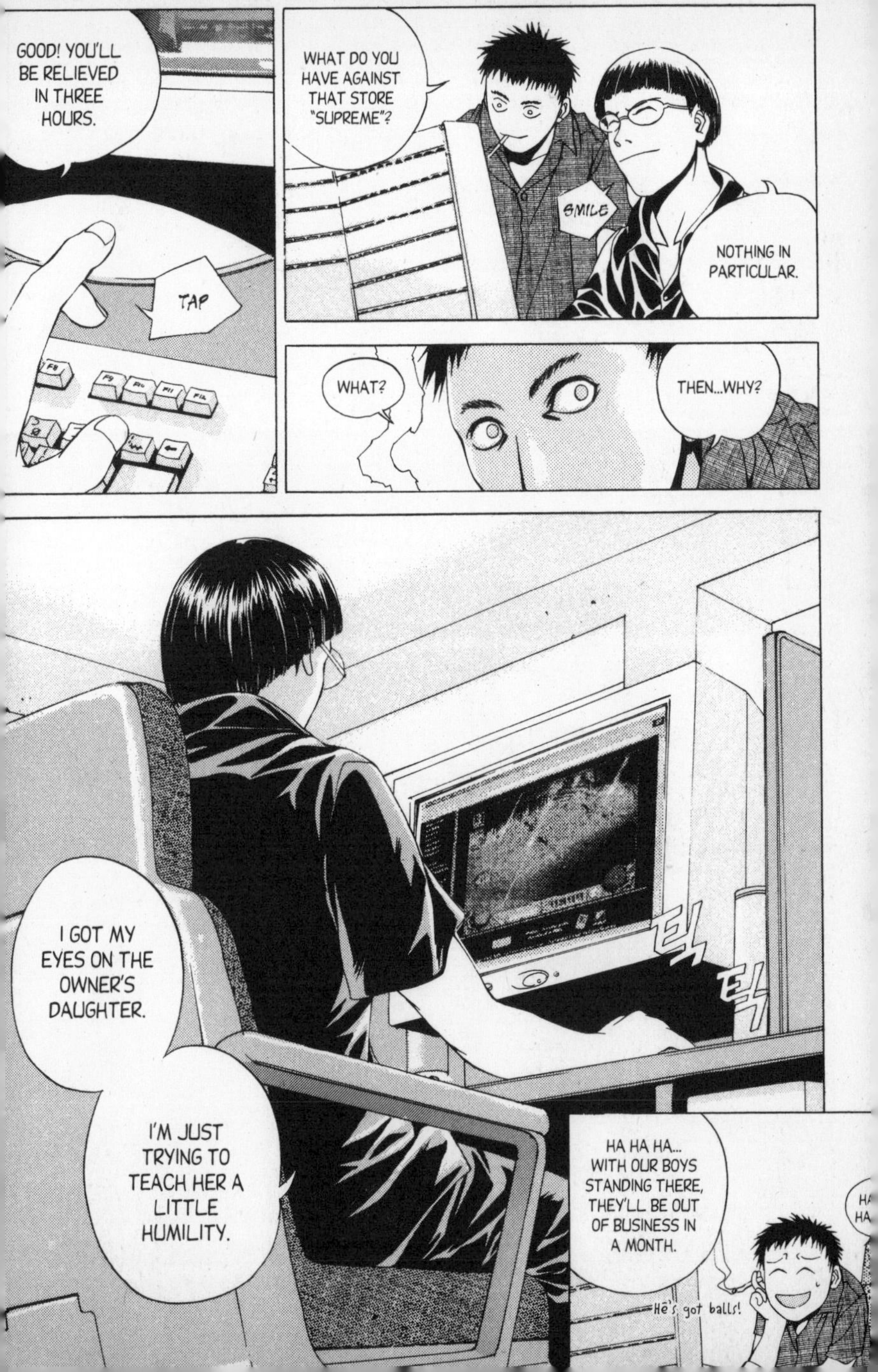
GOOD! YOU'LL BE RELIEVED IN THREE HOURS.
TAP
WHAT DO YOU HAVE AGAINST THAT STORE "SUPREME"?
SMILE
NOTHING IN PARTICULAR.
WHAT?
THEN...WHY?
I GOT MY EYES ON THE OWNER'S DAUGHTER.
I'M JUST TRYING TO TEACH HER A LITTLE HUMILITY.
턱
턱
HA HA HA... WITH OUR BOYS STANDING THERE, THEY'LL BE OUT OF BUSINESS IN A MONTH.
He's got balls!
HA HA

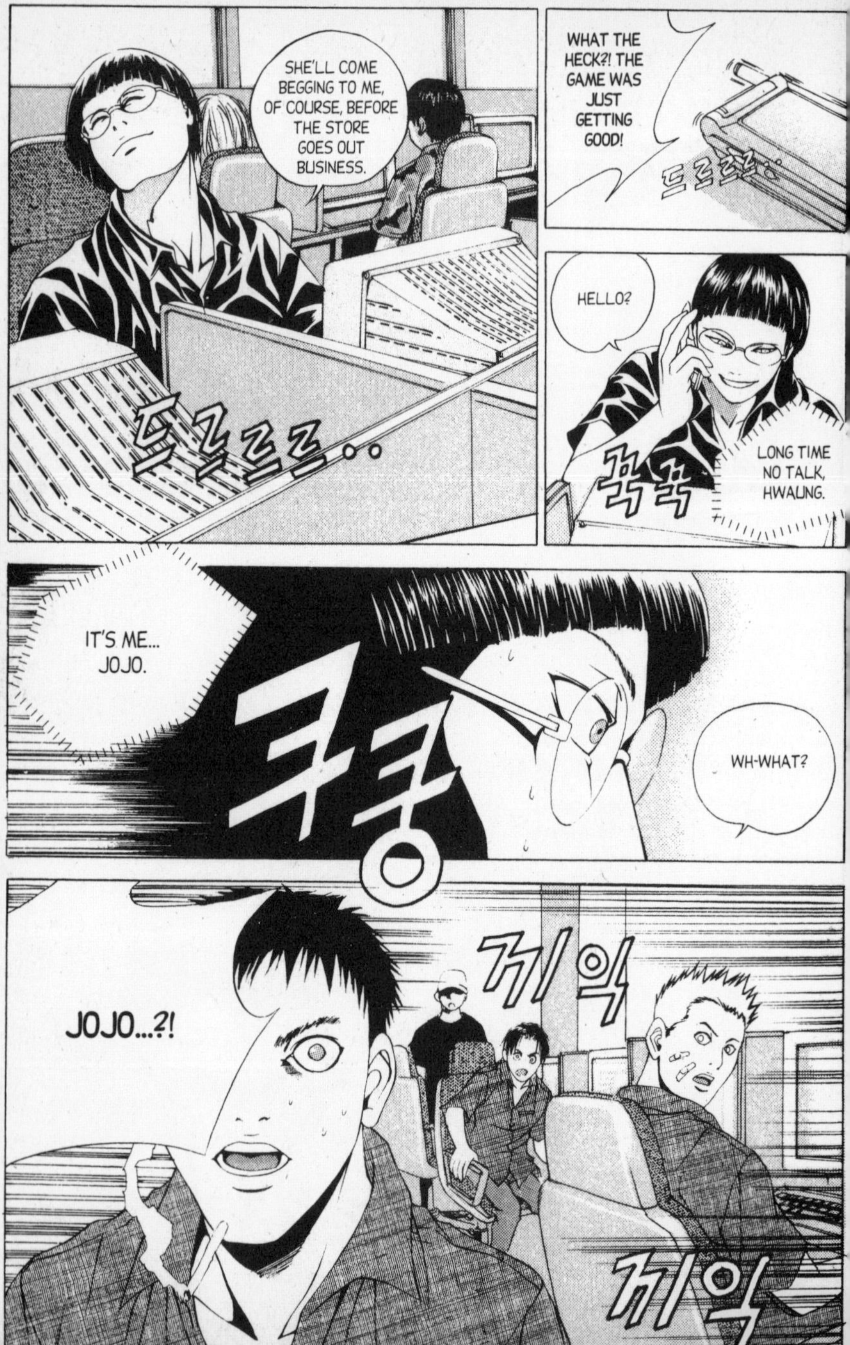
SHE'LL COME BEGGING TO ME, OF COURSE, BEFORE THE STORE GOES OUT BUSINESS.
드르르르..
WHAT THE HECK?! THE GAME WAS JUST GETTING GOOD!
드르르르..
HELLO?
LONG TIME NO TALK, HWAUNG.
IT'S ME... JOJO.
쿠궁
WH-WHAT?
JOJO...?!
끼익
끼익

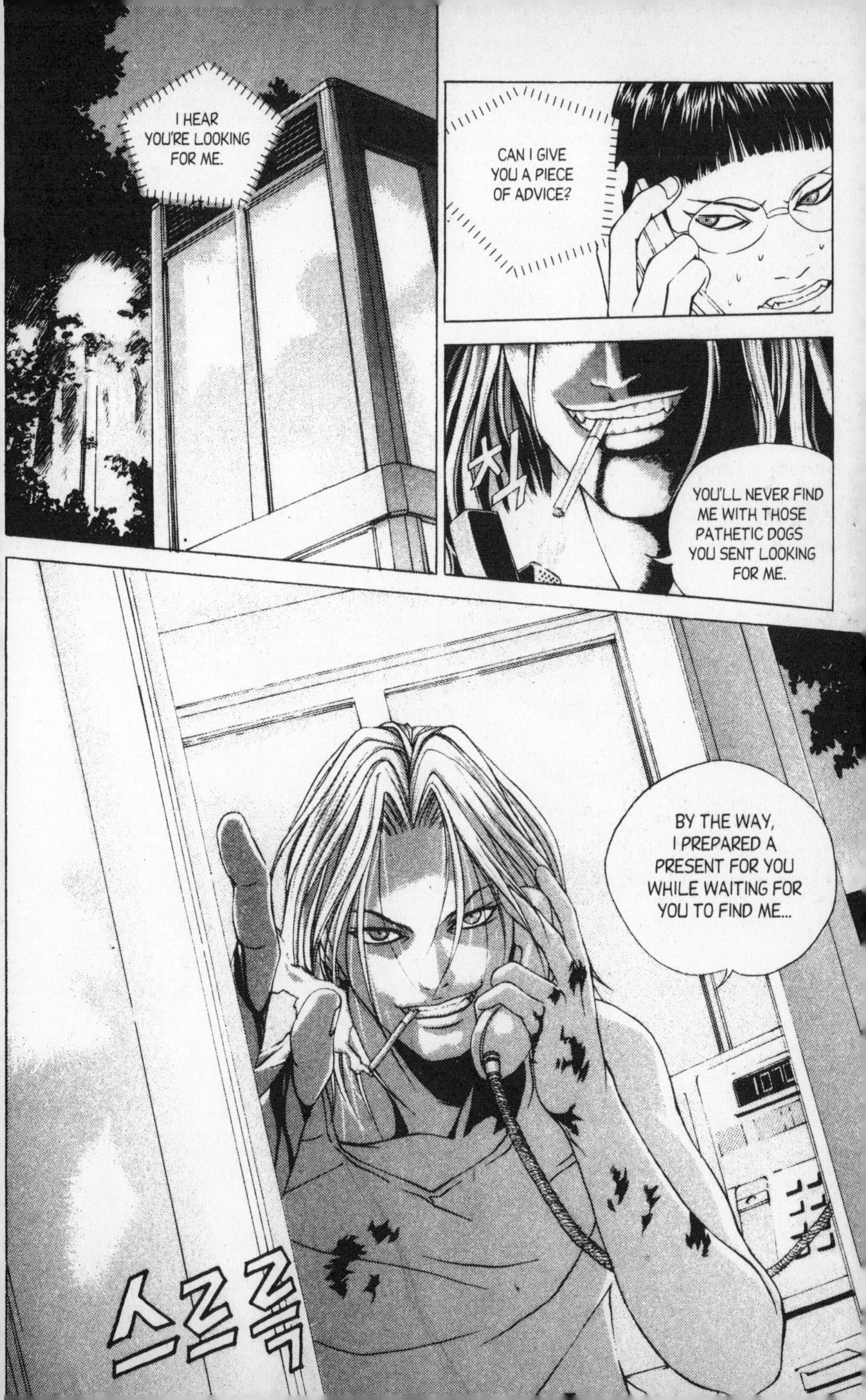
I HEAR YOU'RE LOOKING FOR ME.
CAN I GIVE YOU A PIECE OF ADVICE?
YOU'LL NEVER FIND ME WITH THOSE PATHETIC DOGS YOU SENT LOOKING FOR ME.
BY THE WAY, I PREPARED A PRESENT FOR YOU WHILE WAITING FOR YOU TO FIND ME...
스르륵

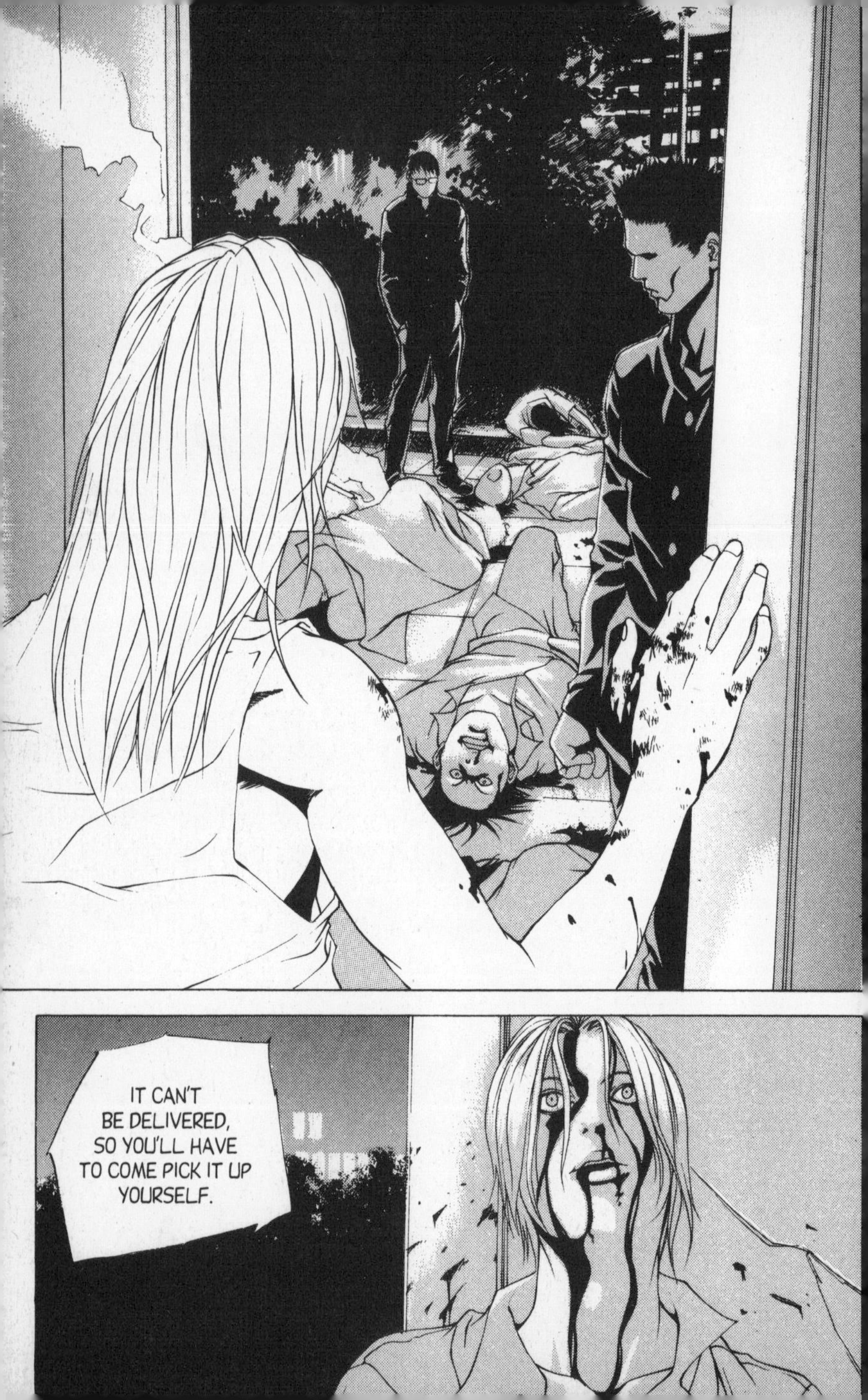
IT CAN'T BE DELIVERED, SO YOU'LL HAVE TO COME PICK IT UP YOURSELF.

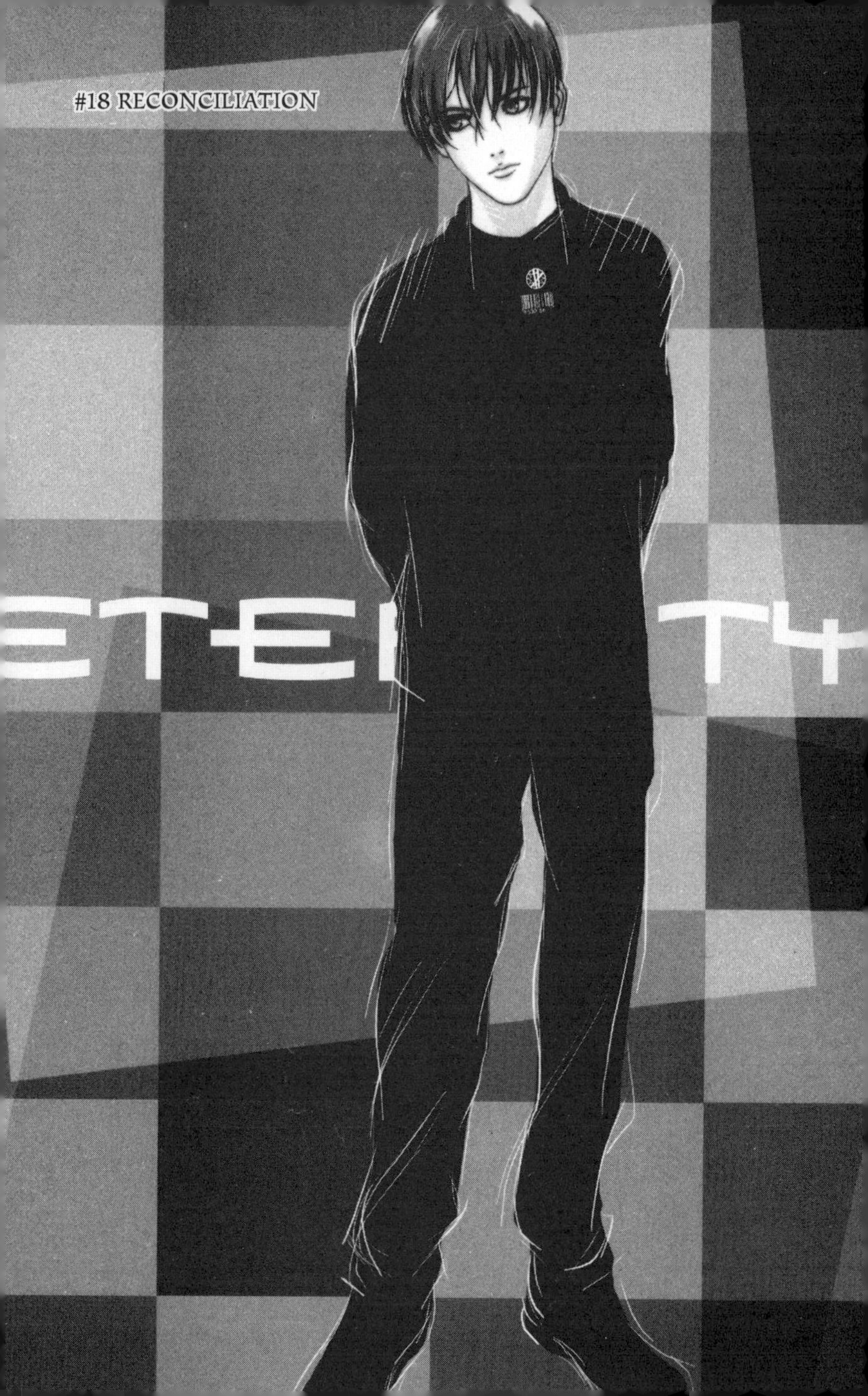
#18 RECONCILIATION

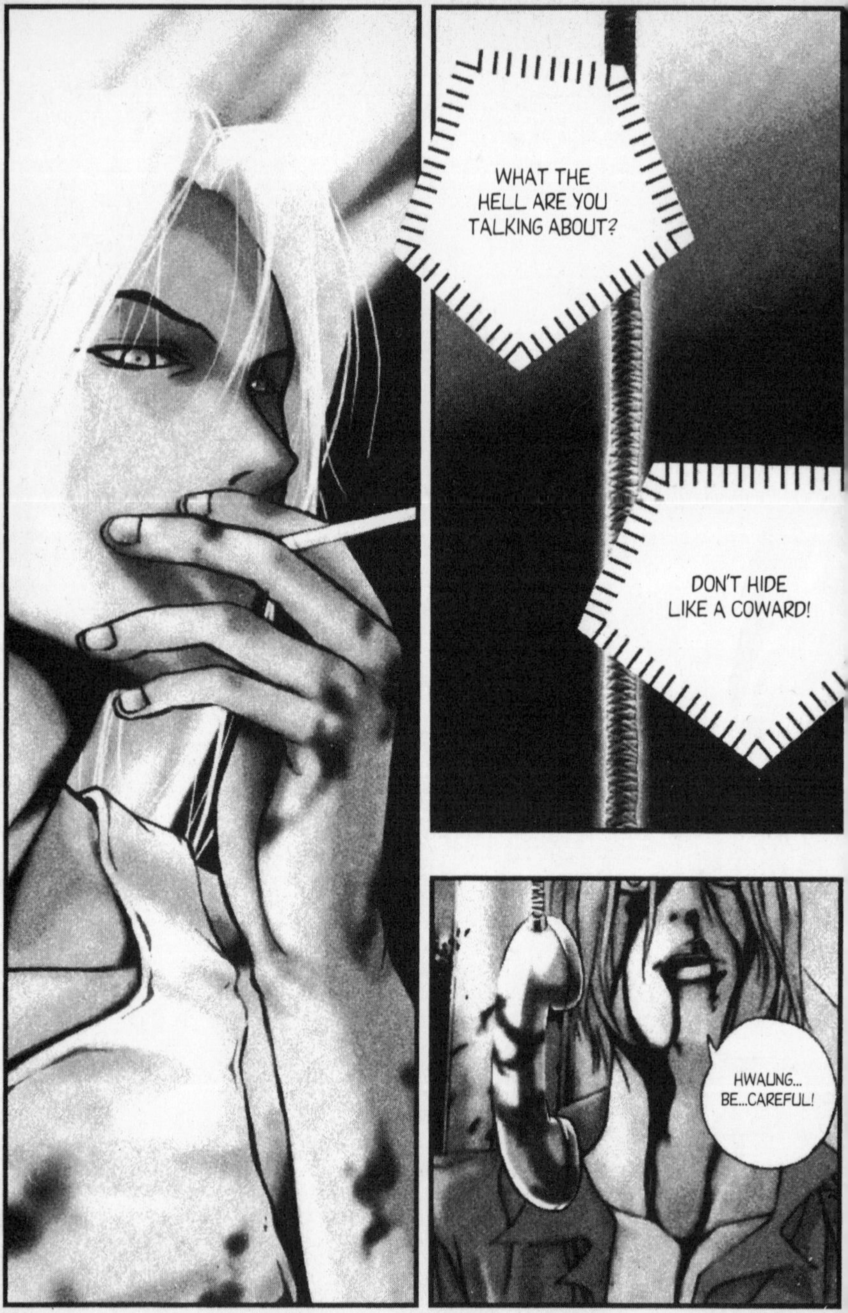
WHAT THE HELL ARE YOU TALKING ABOUT?
DON'T HIDE LIKE A COWARD!
HWAUNG... BE...CAREFUL!

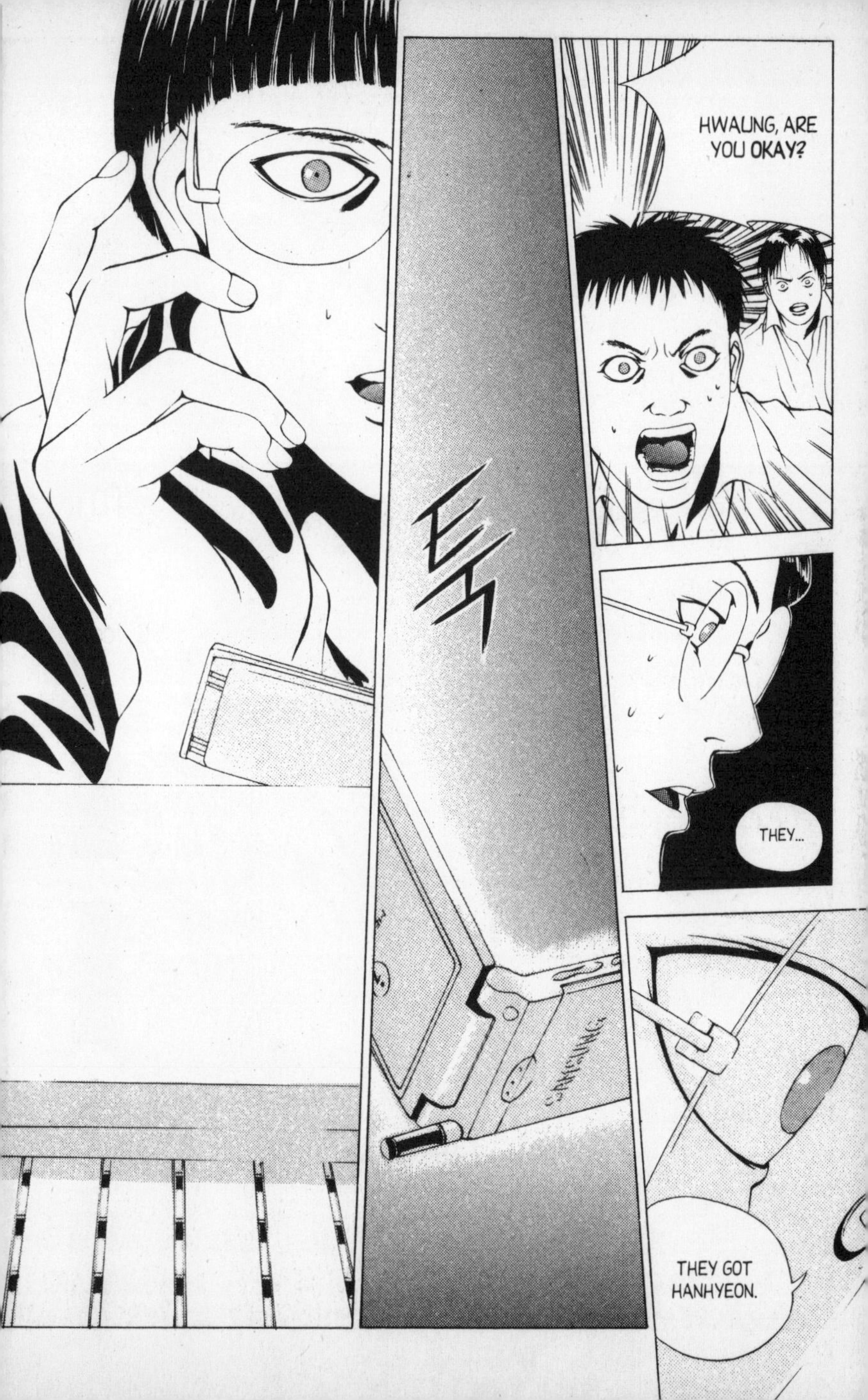
HWAUNG, ARE YOU OKAY?
THEY...
THEY GOT HANHYEON.

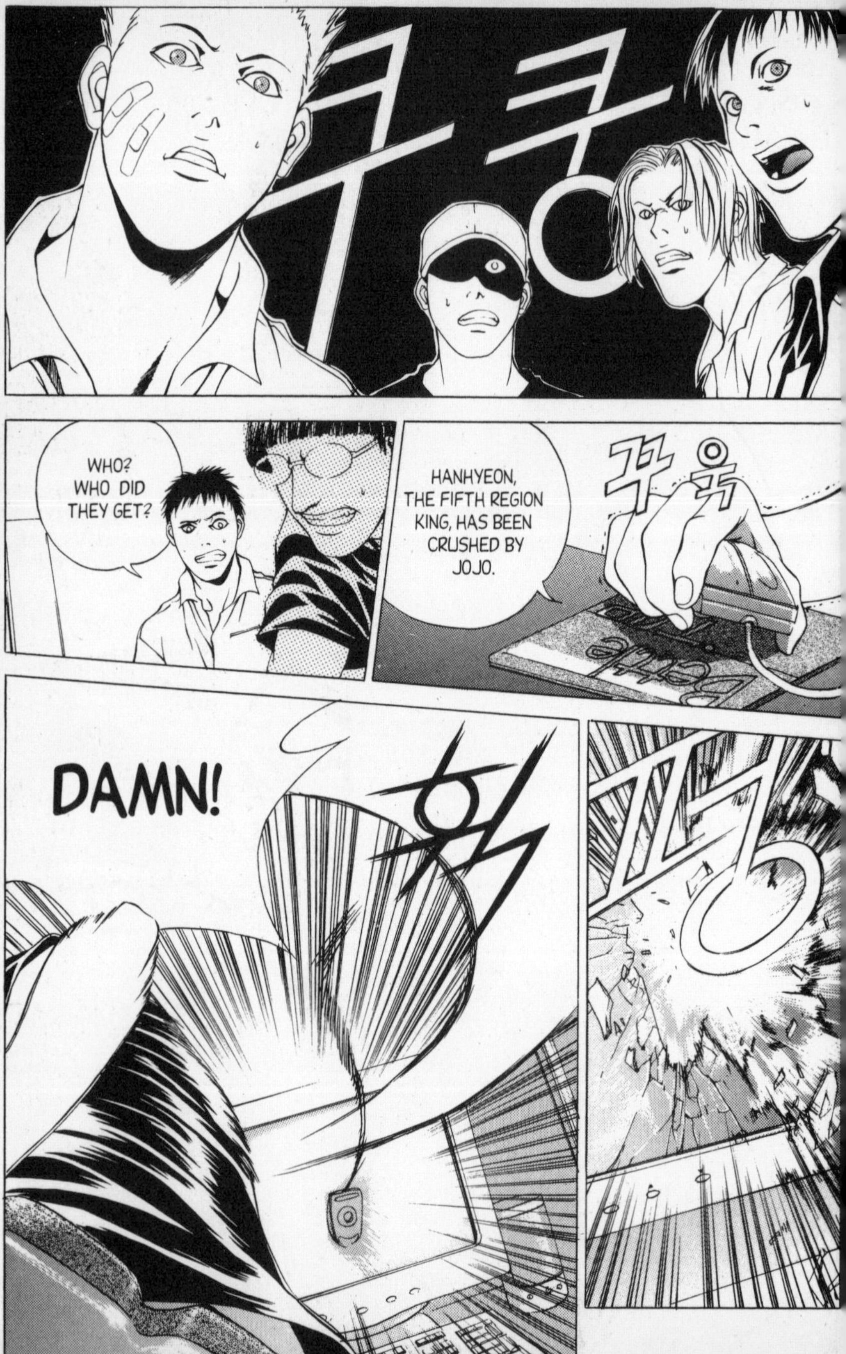
WHO? WHO DID THEY GET?
HANHYEON, THE FIFTH REGION KING, HAS BEEN CRUSHED BY JOJO.
DAMN!

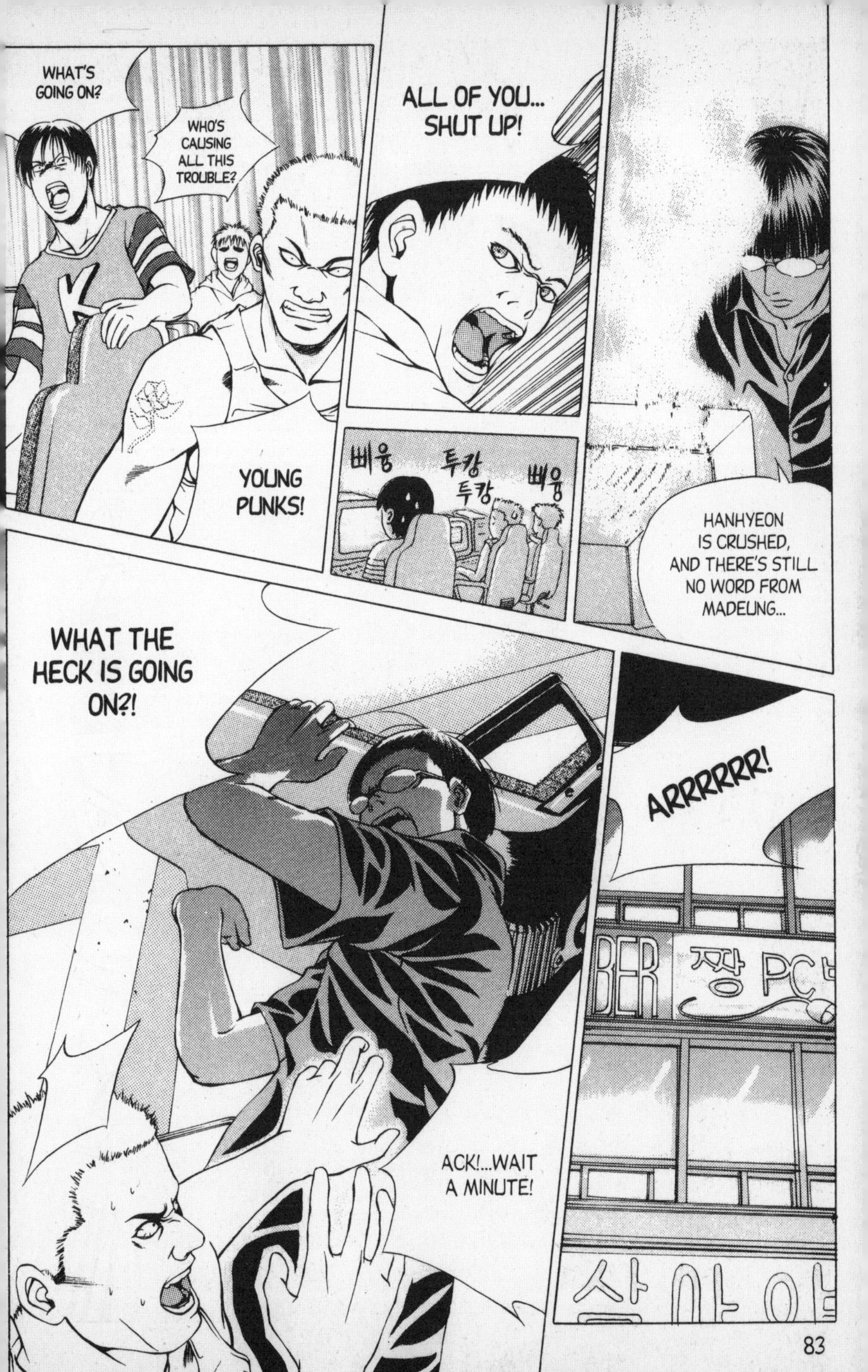
WHAT'S GOING ON?
WHO'S CAUSING ALL THIS TROUBLE?
YOUNG PUNKS!
ALL OF YOU... SHUT UP!
삐융
투캉
투캉
삐융
HANHYEON IS CRUSHED, AND THERE'S STILL NO WORD FROM MADEUNG...
WHAT THE HECK IS GOING ON?!
ACK!...WAIT A MINUTE!
ARRRRRR!
BER
짱 PC

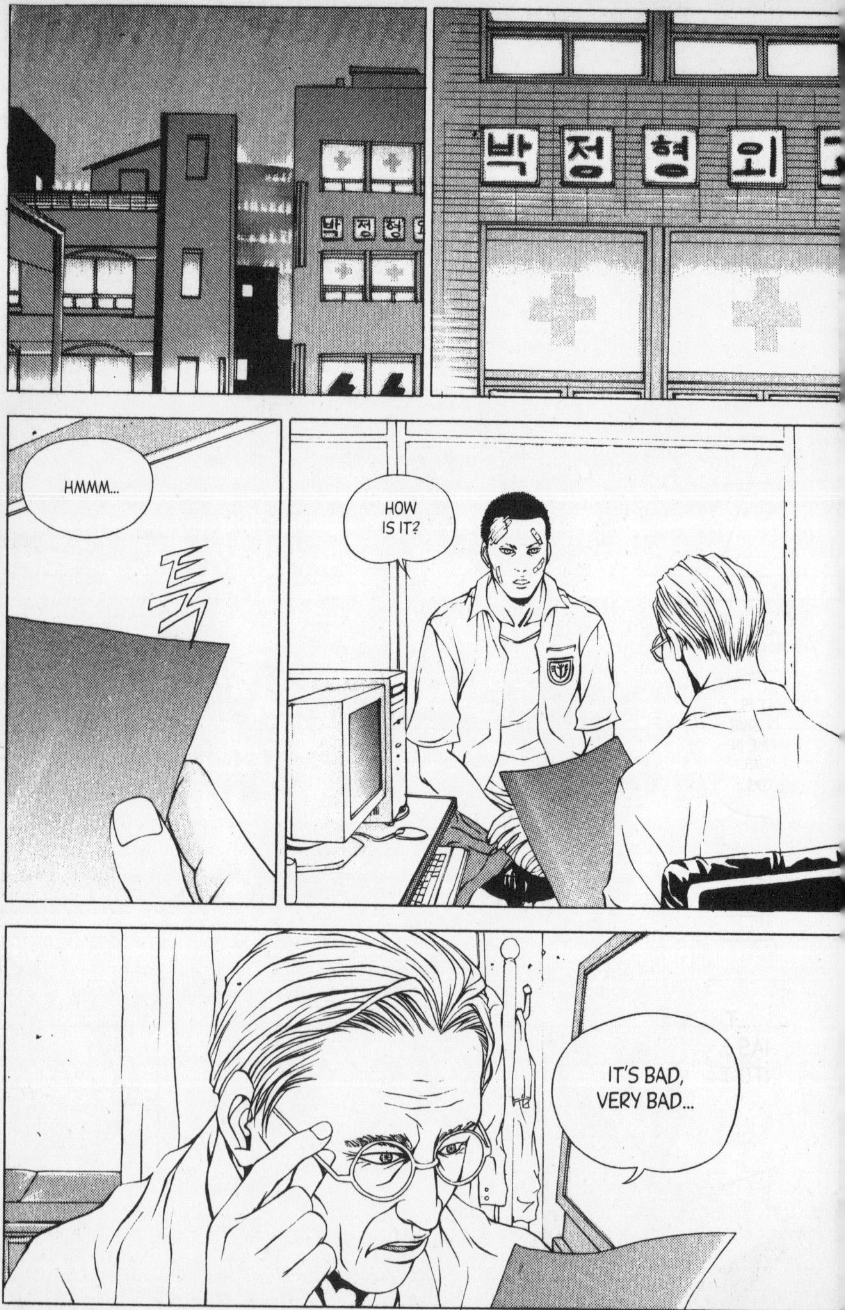
박정형외
박정형외
HMMM...
툭
HOW IS IT?
IT'S BAD, VERY BAD...

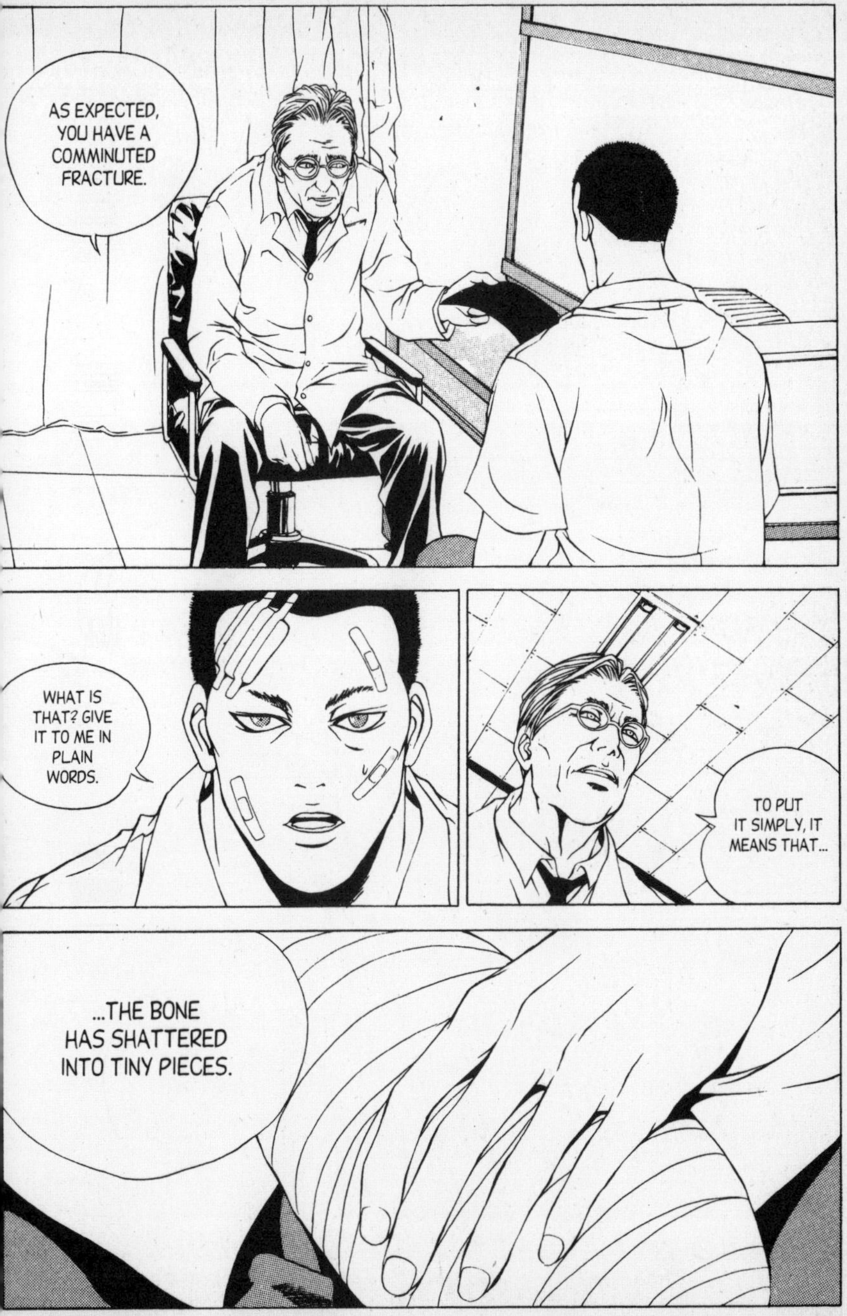
AS EXPECTED, YOU HAVE A COMMINUTED FRACTURE.
WHAT IS THAT? GIVE IT TO ME IN PLAIN WORDS.
TO PUT IT SIMPLY, IT MEANS THAT...
...THE BONE HAS SHATTERED INTO TINY PIECES.

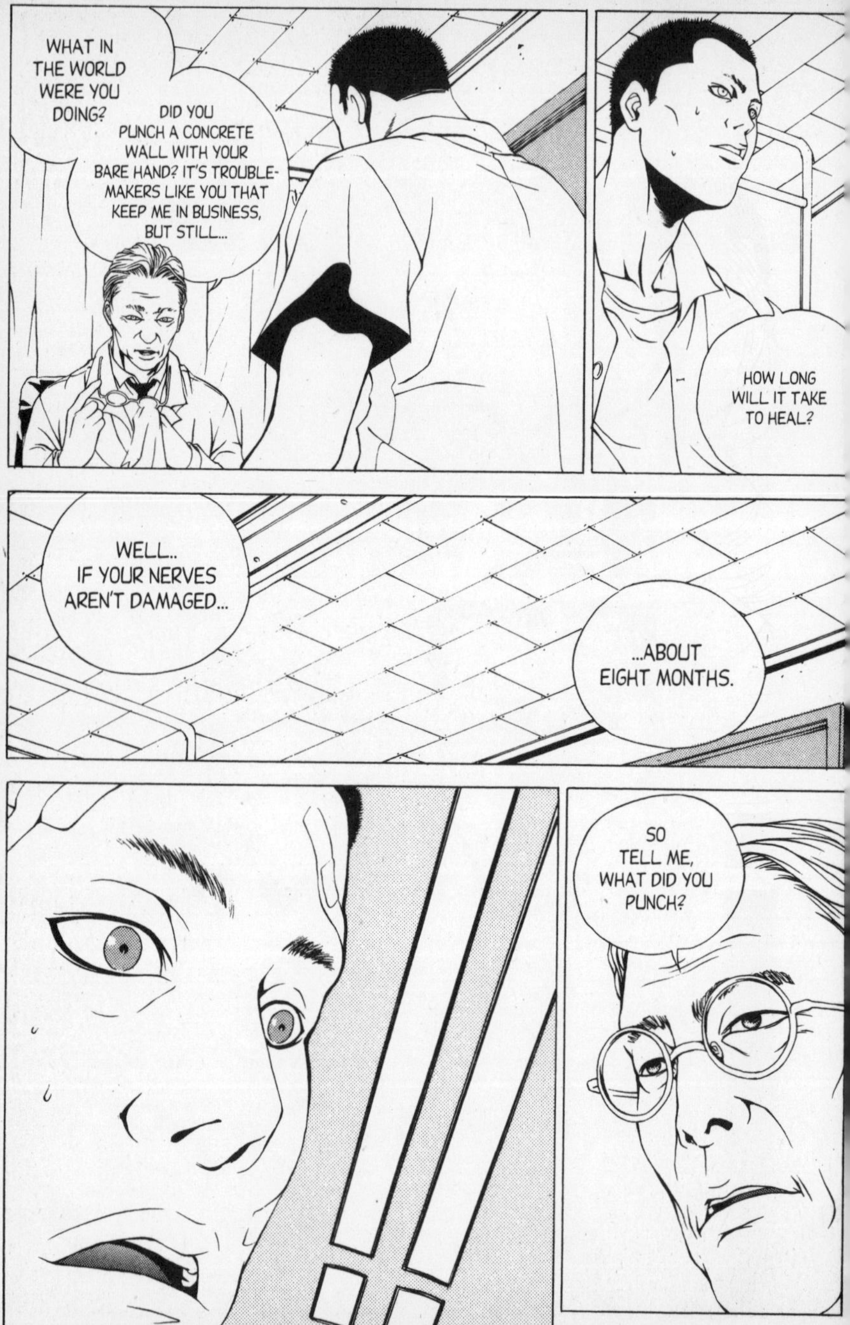
WHAT IN THE WORLD WERE YOU DOING?
DID YOU PUNCH A CONCRETE WALL WITH YOUR BARE HAND? IT'S TROUBLE-MAKERS LIKE YOU THAT KEEP ME IN BUSINESS, BUT STILL...
HOW LONG WILL IT TAKE TO HEAL?
WELL.. IF YOUR NERVES AREN'T DAMAGED...
...ABOUT EIGHT MONTHS.
SO TELL ME, WHAT DID YOU PUNCH?

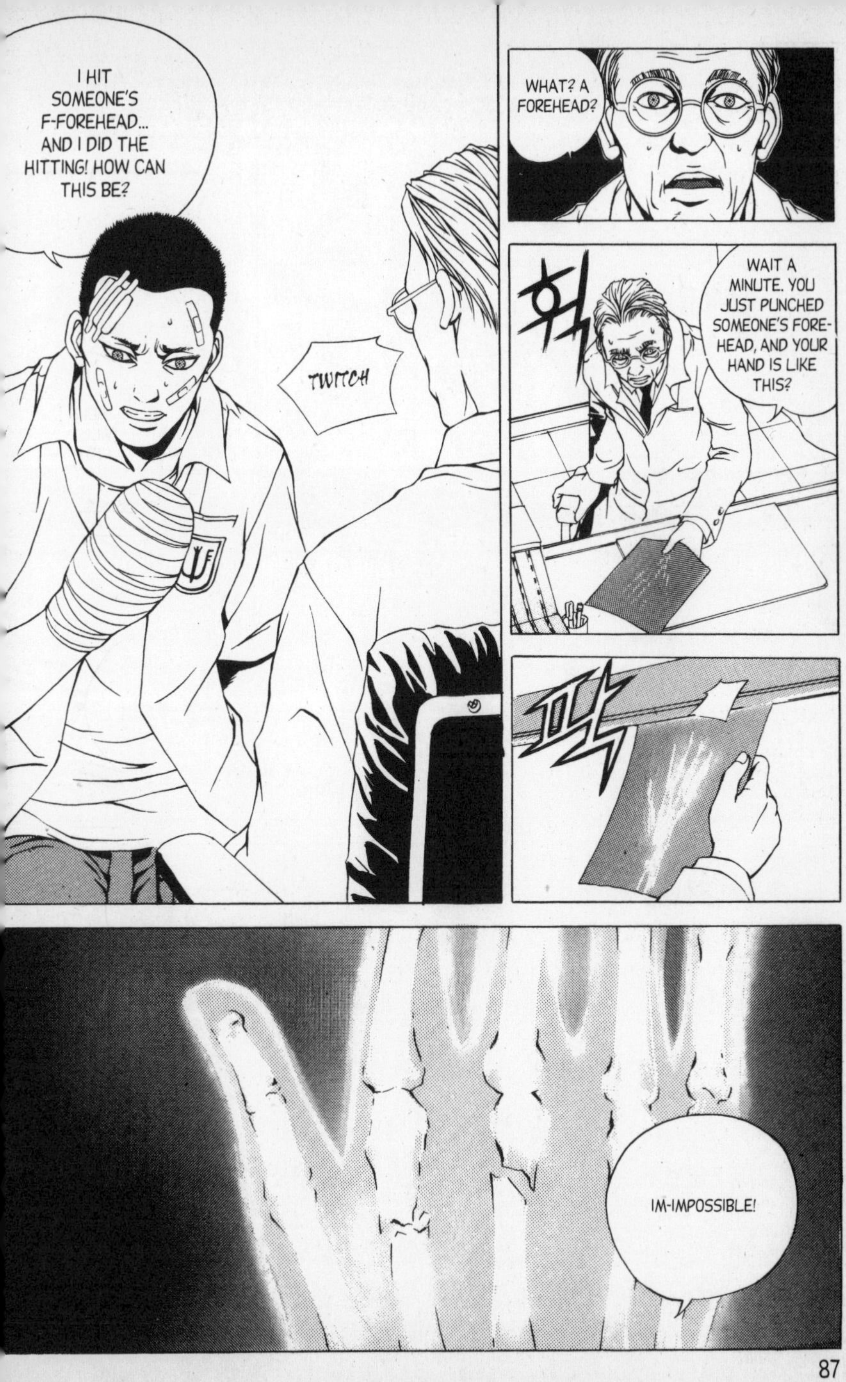
I HIT SOMEONE'S F-FOREHEAD... AND I DID THE HITTING! HOW CAN THIS BE?
TWITCH
WHAT? A FOREHEAD?
WAIT A MINUTE. YOU JUST PUNCHED SOMEONE'S FORE-HEAD, AND YOUR HAND IS LIKE THIS?
IM-IMPOSSIBLE!

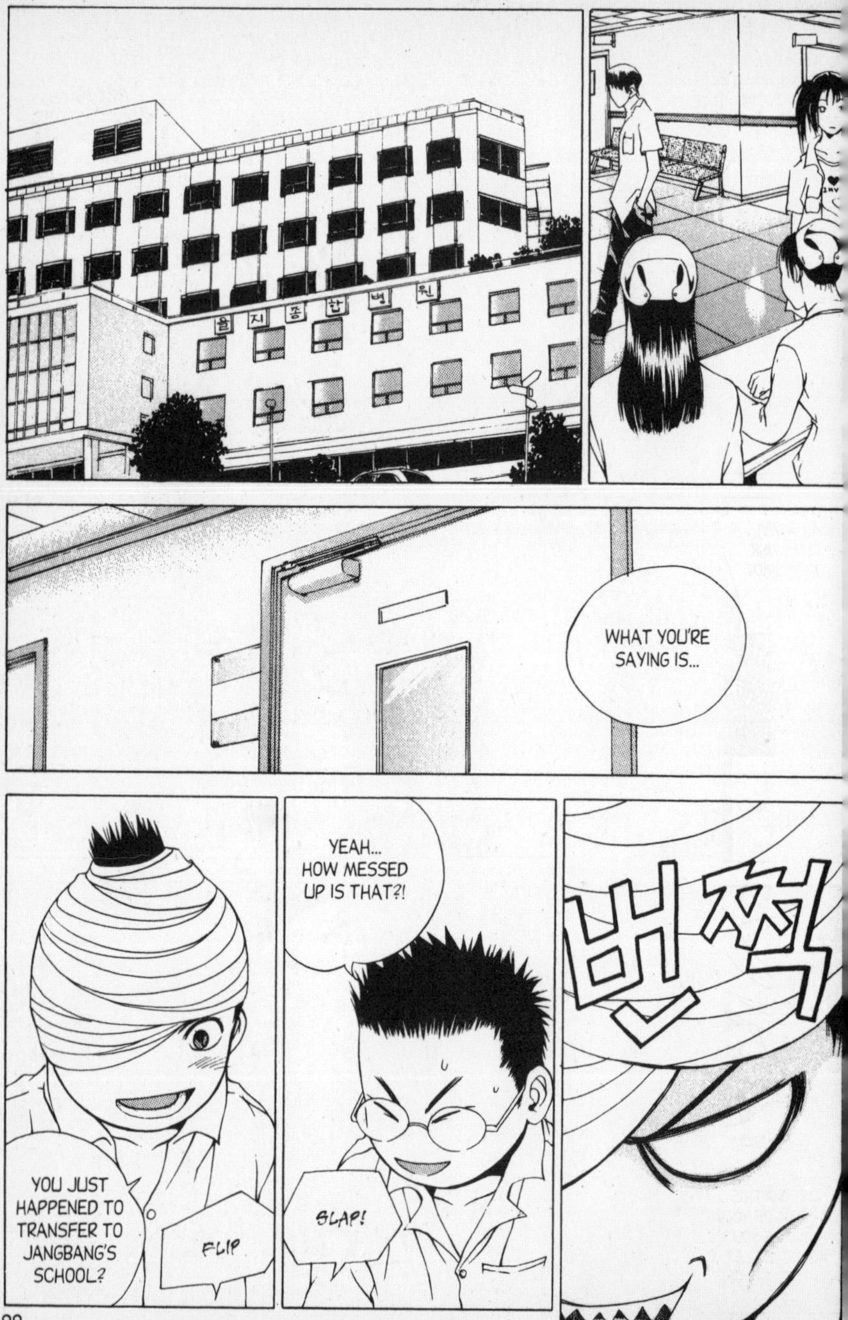
을지종합병원
WHAT YOU'RE SAYING IS...
YOU JUST HAPPENED TO TRANSFER TO JANGBANG'S SCHOOL?
FLIP
YEAH... HOW MESSED UP IS THAT?!
SLAP!
번쩍

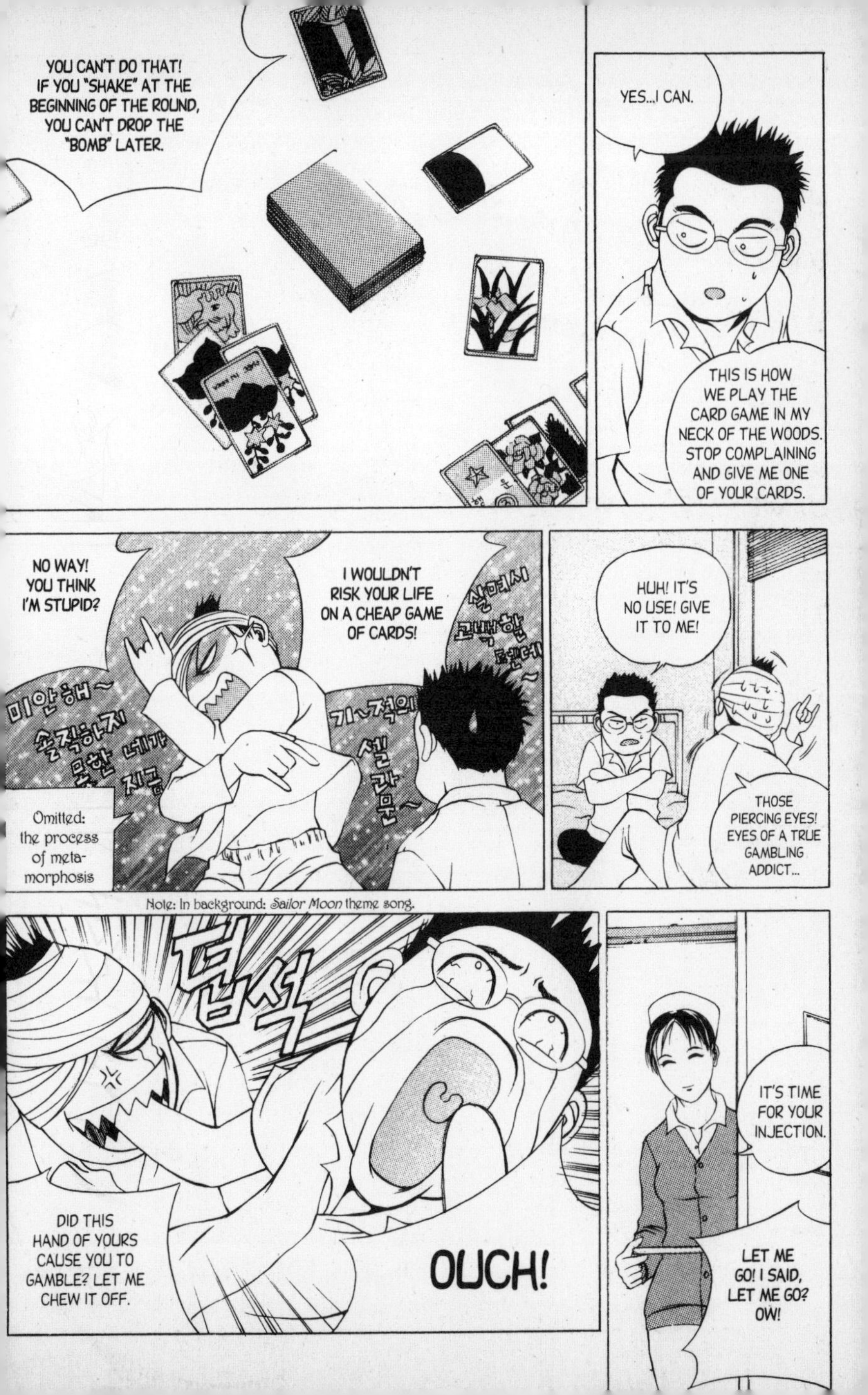
YOU CAN'T DO THAT! IF YOU "SHAKE" AT THE BEGINNING OF THE ROUND, YOU CAN'T DROP THE "BOMB" LATER.
YES...I CAN.
THIS IS HOW WE PLAY THE CARD GAME IN MY NECK OF THE WOODS. STOP COMPLAINING AND GIVE ME ONE OF YOUR CARDS.
NO WAY! YOU THINK I'M STUPID?
I WOULDN'T RISK YOUR LIFE ON A CHEAP GAME OF CARDS!
미안해~
솔직하지 못한
Omitted: the process of meta-morphosis
HUH! IT'S NO USE! GIVE IT TO ME!
THOSE PIERCING EYES! EYES OF A TRUE GAMBLING ADDICT...
Note: In background: Sailor Moon theme song.
덥석
DID THIS HAND OF YOURS CAUSE YOU TO GAMBLE? LET ME CHEW IT OFF.
OUCH!
IT'S TIME FOR YOUR INJECTION.
LET ME GO! I SAID, LET ME GO? OW!

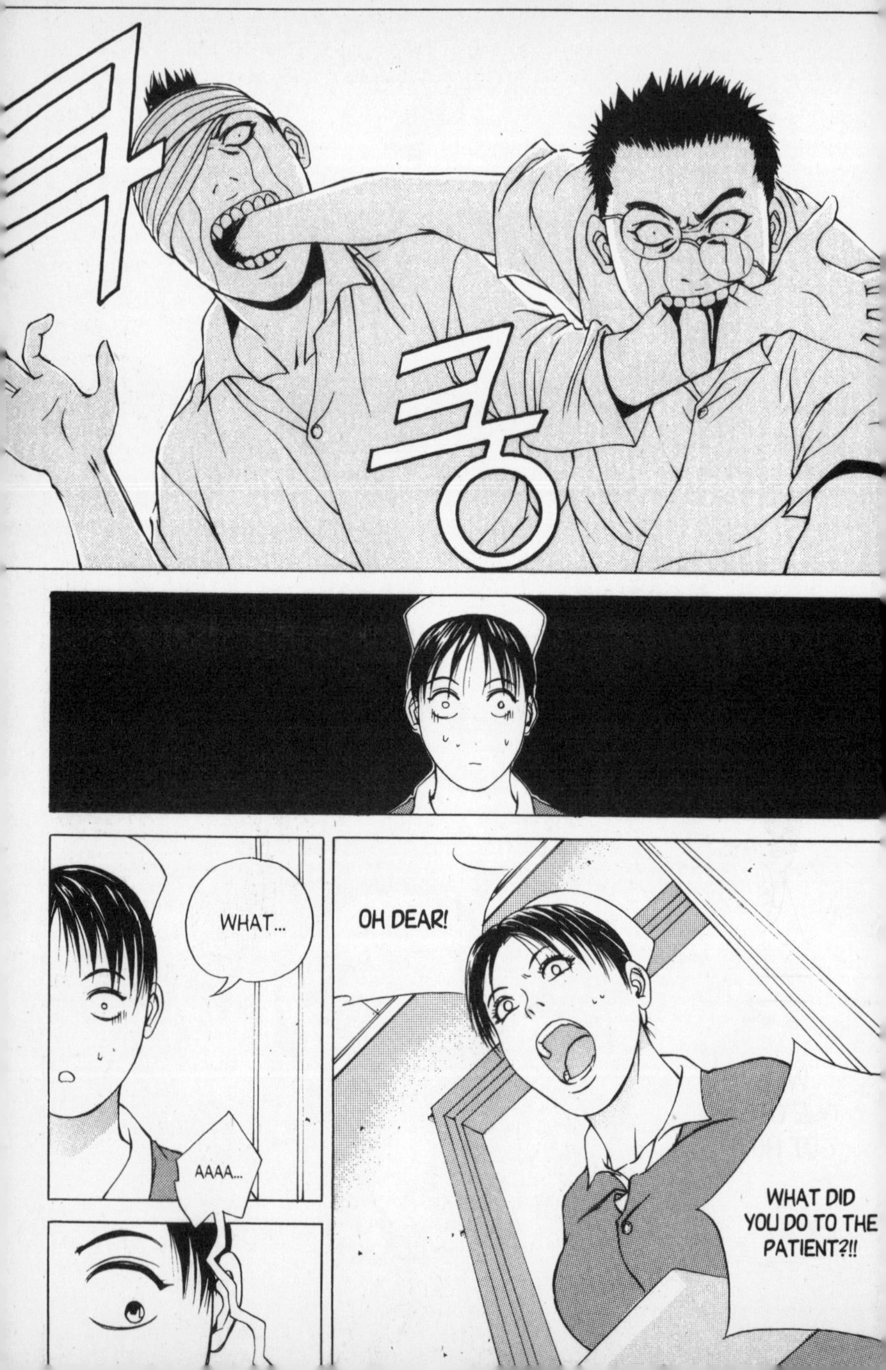
OH DEAR!
WHAT DID YOU DO TO THE PATIENT?!!
WHAT...
AAAA...

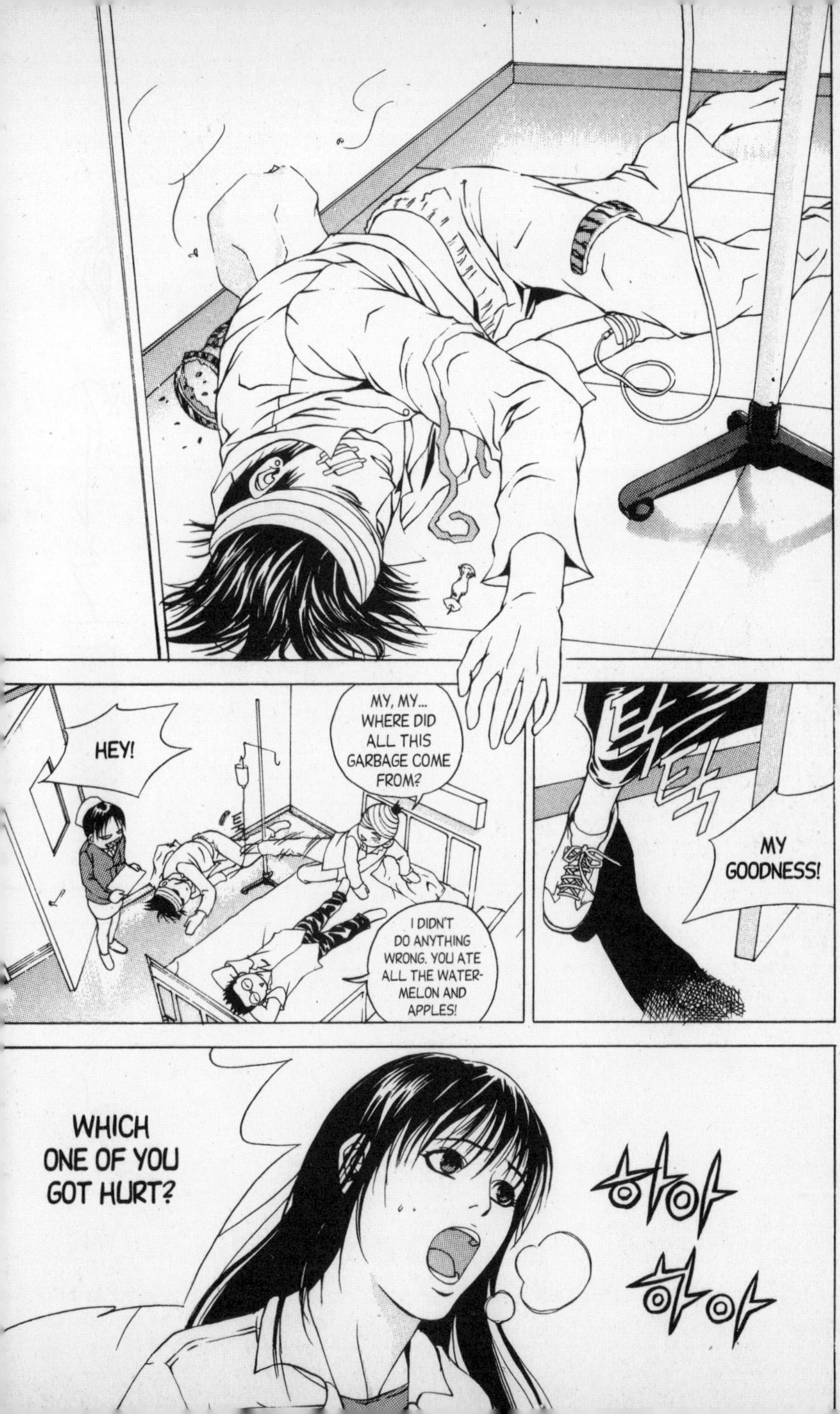
HEY!
MY, MY... WHERE DID ALL THIS GARBAGE COME FROM?
I DIDN'T DO ANYTHING WRONG. YOU ATE ALL THE WATER-MELON AND APPLES!
탁
탁
MY GOODNESS!
WHICH ONE OF YOU GOT HURT?
하아
하아

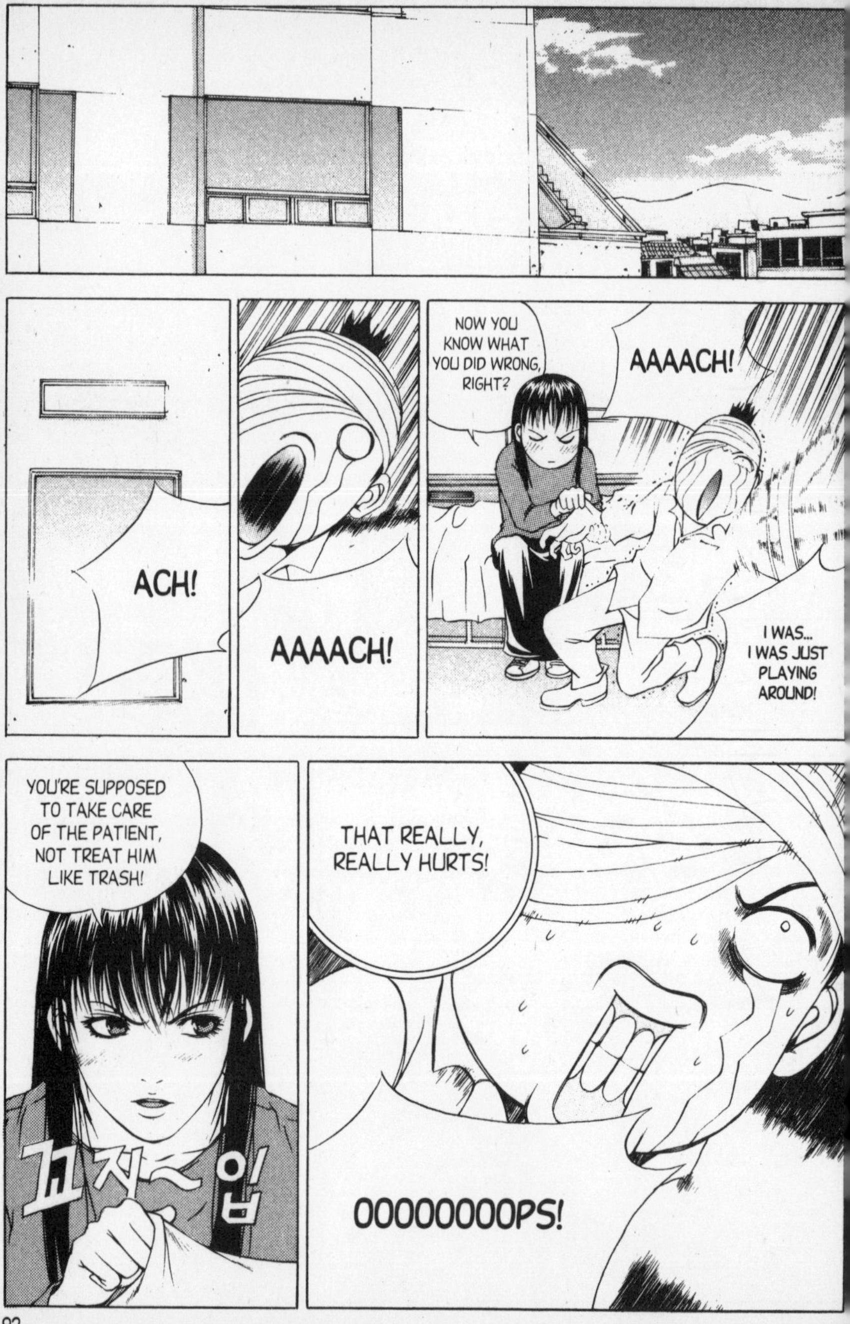
ACH!
AAAACH!
NOW YOU KNOW WHAT YOU DID WRONG, RIGHT?
AAAACH!
I WAS... I WAS JUST PLAYING AROUND!
YOU'RE SUPPOSED TO TAKE CARE OF THE PATIENT, NOT TREAT HIM LIKE TRASH!
THAT REALLY, REALLY HURTS!
OOOOOOOOPS!

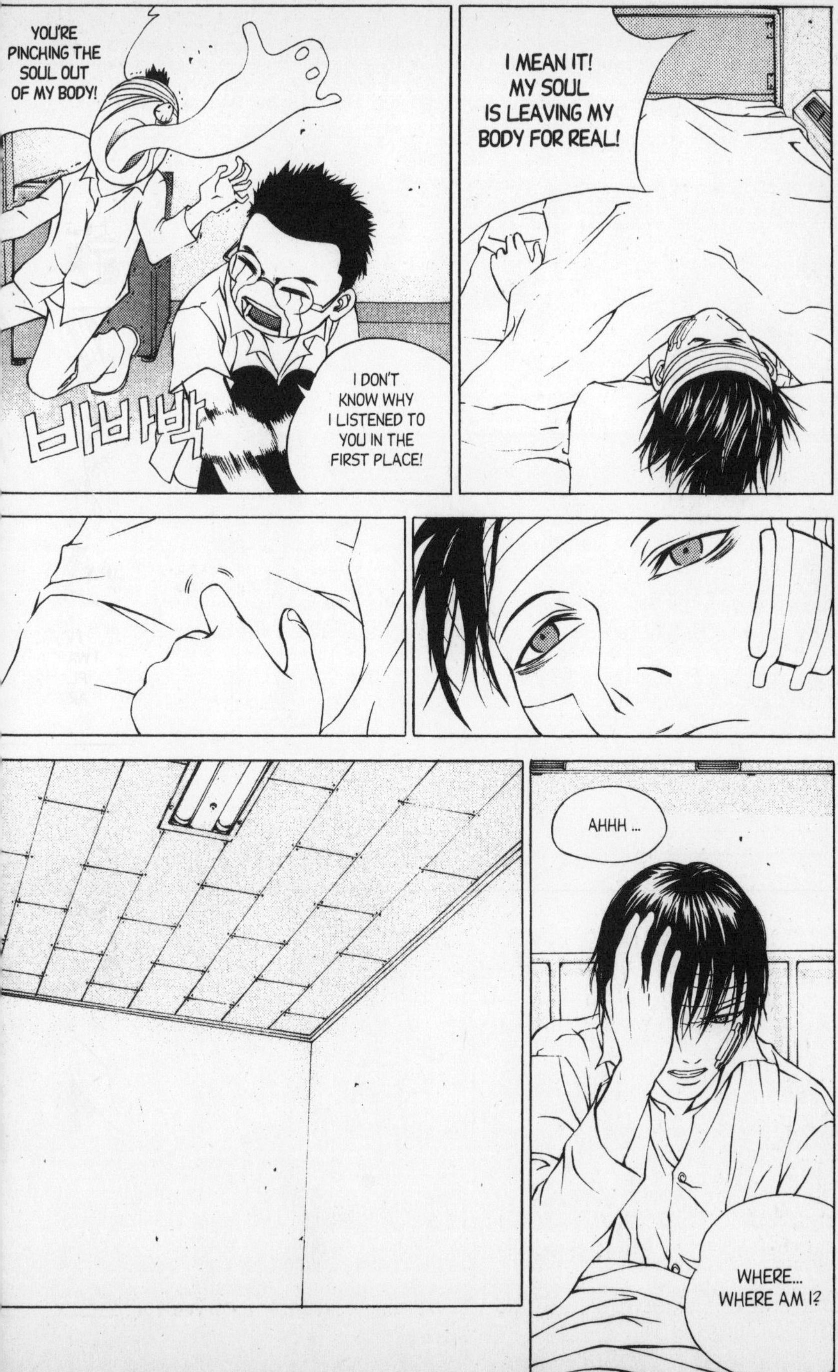
YOU'RE PINCHING THE SOUL OUT OF MY BODY!
바바박
I DON'T KNOW WHY I LISTENED TO YOU IN THE FIRST PLACE!
I MEAN IT! MY SOUL IS LEAVING MY BODY FOR REAL!
AHHH ...
WHERE... WHERE AM I?

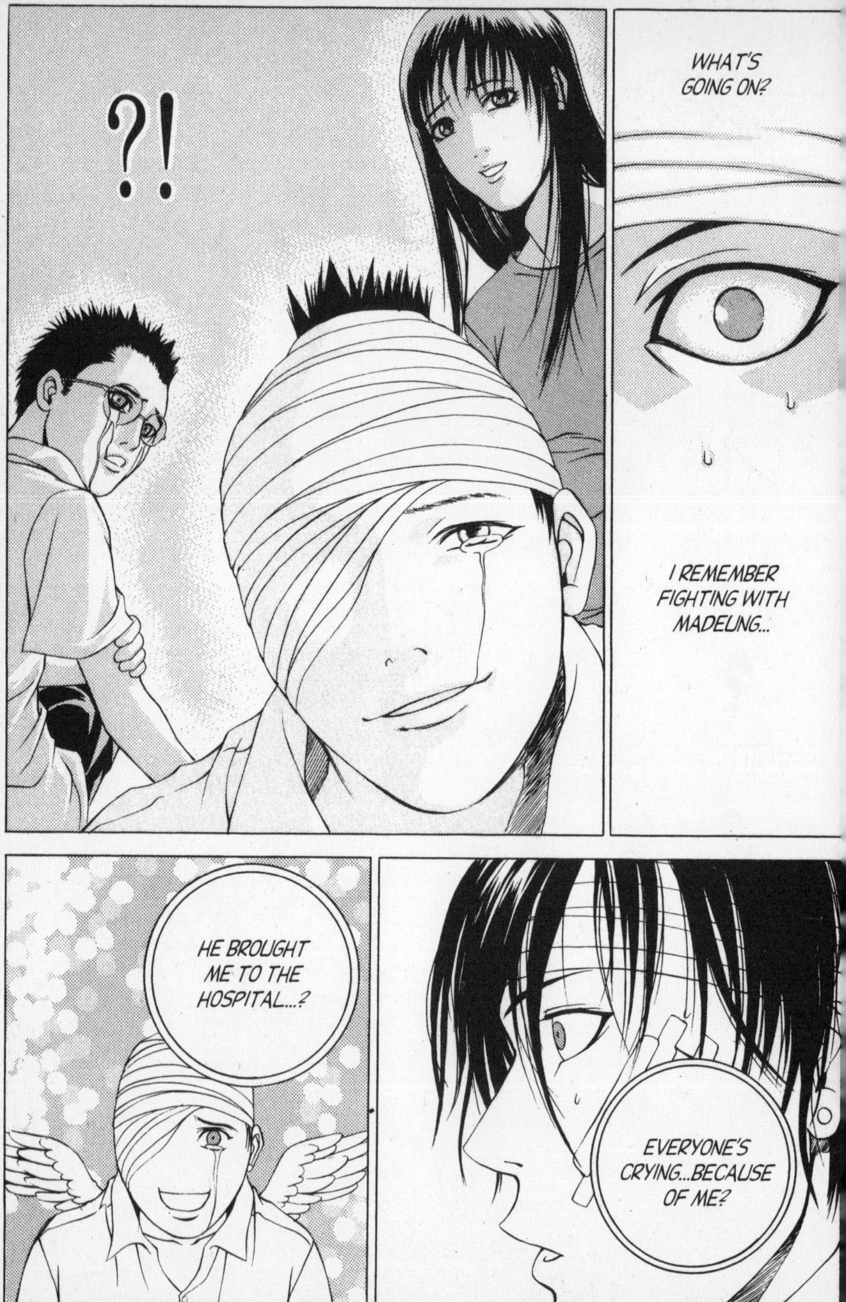
WHAT'S GOING ON?
I REMEMBER FIGHTING WITH MADELUNG...
?!
EVERYONE'S CRYING...BECAUSE OF ME?
HE BROUGHT ME TO THE HOSPITAL...?

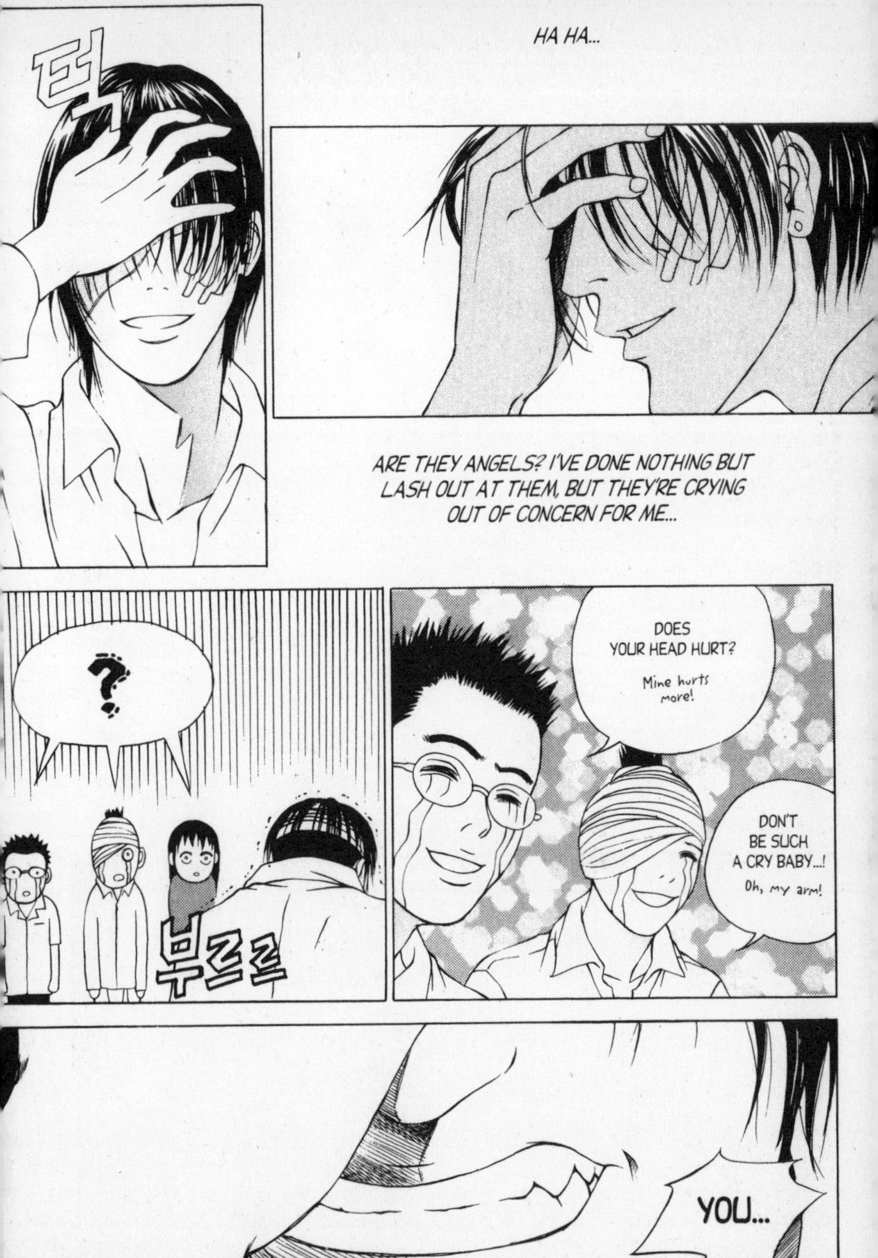
턱
HA HA...
ARE THEY ANGELS? I'VE DONE NOTHING BUT LASH OUT AT THEM, BUT THEY'RE CRYING OUT OF CONCERN FOR ME...
?
부르르
DOES YOUR HEAD HURT?
Mine hurts more!
DON'T BE SUCH A CRY BABY...!
Oh, my arm!
YOU...

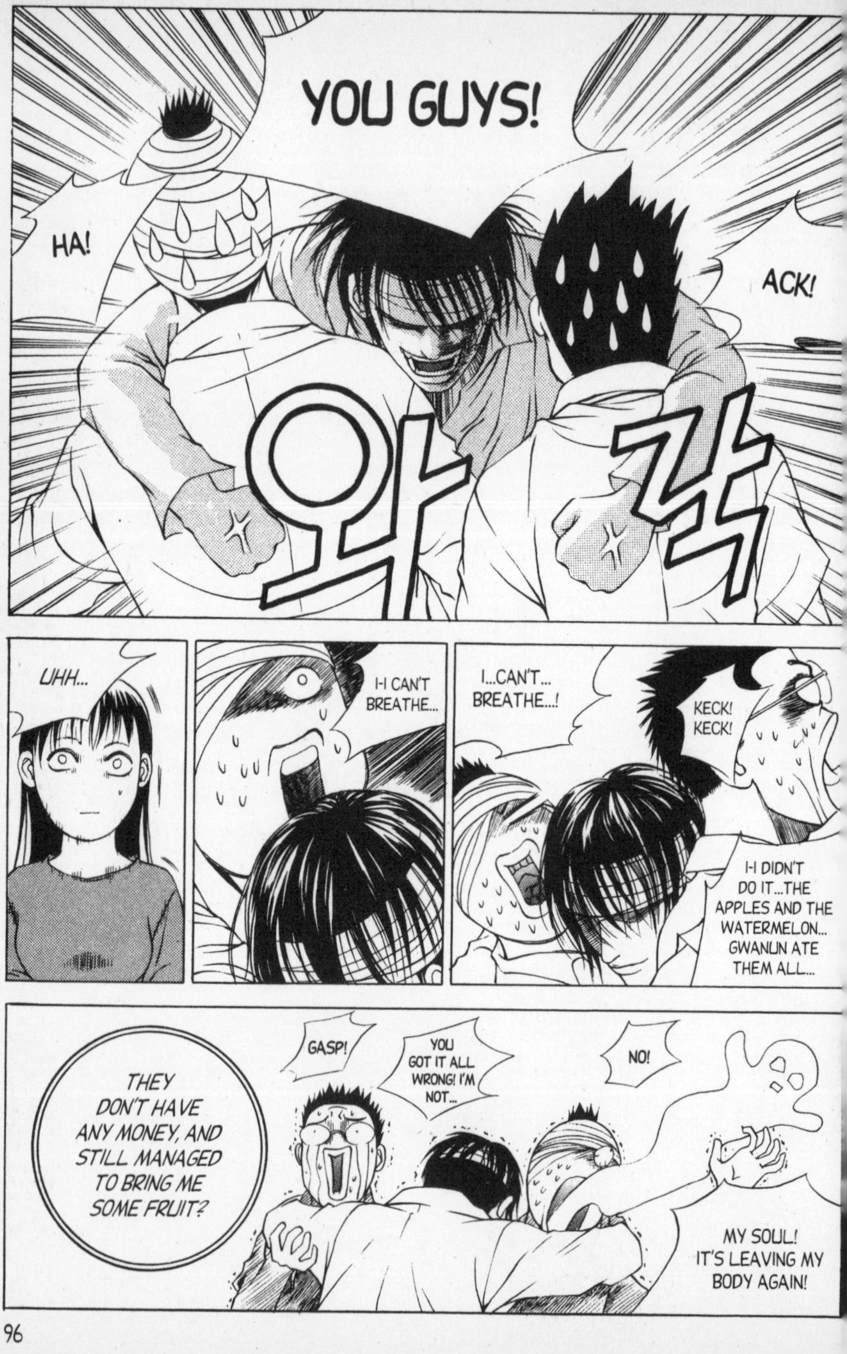
YOU GUYS!
HA!
ACK!
와락
UHH...
I-I CAN'T BREATHE...
I...CAN'T... BREATHE...!
KECK! KECK!
I-I DIDN'T DO IT...THE APPLES AND THE WATERMELON... GWANUN ATE THEM ALL...
THEY DON'T HAVE ANY MONEY, AND STILL MANAGED TO BRING ME SOME FRUIT?
GASP!
YOU GOT IT ALL WRONG! I'M NOT...
NO!
MY SOUL! IT'S LEAVING MY BODY AGAIN!

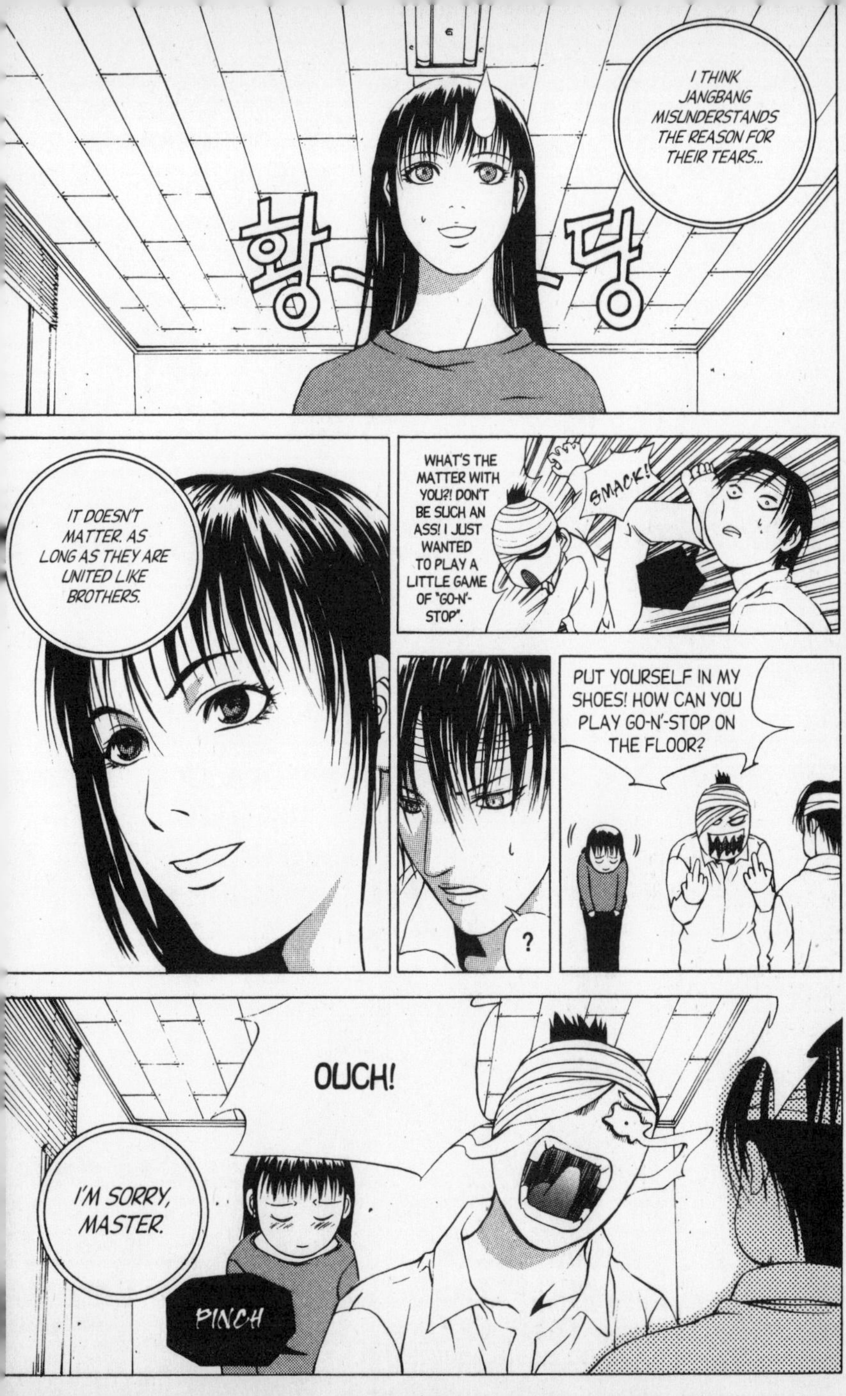
황
당
I THINK JANGBANG MISUNDERSTANDS THE REASON FOR THEIR TEARS...
IT DOESN'T MATTER. AS LONG AS THEY ARE UNITED LIKE BROTHERS.
WHAT'S THE MATTER WITH YOU?! DON'T BE SUCH AN ASS! I JUST WANTED TO PLAY A LITTLE GAME OF "GO-N'-STOP".
SMACK!!
?
PUT YOURSELF IN MY SHOES! HOW CAN YOU PLAY GO-N'-STOP ON THE FLOOR?
OUCH!
I'M SORRY, MASTER.
PINCH

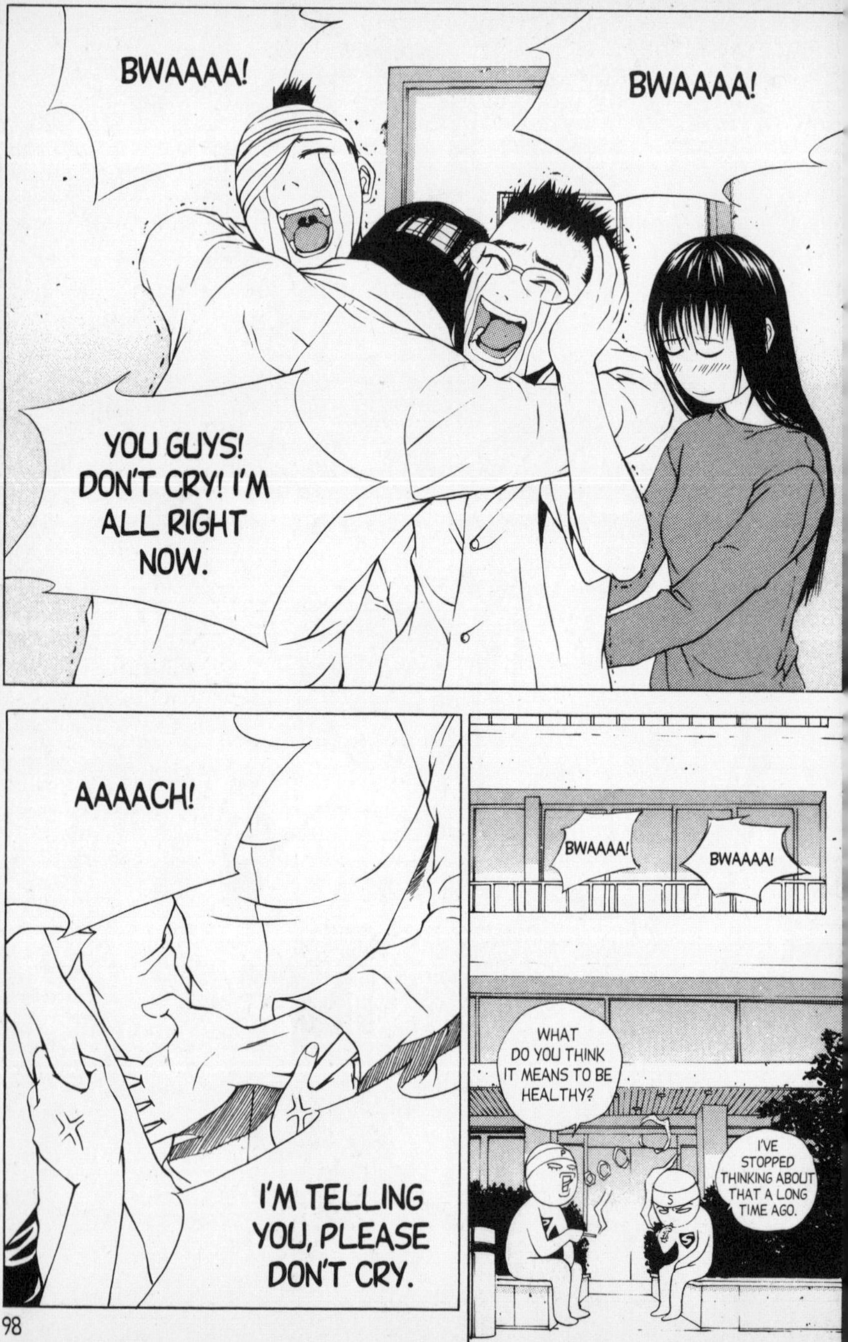
BWAAAA!
BWAAAA!
YOU GUYS! DON'T CRY! I'M ALL RIGHT NOW.
AAAACH!
I'M TELLING YOU, PLEASE DON'T CRY.
BWAAAA!
BWAAAA!
WHAT DO YOU THINK IT MEANS TO BE HEALTHY?
I'VE STOPPED THINKING ABOUT THAT A LONG TIME AGO.

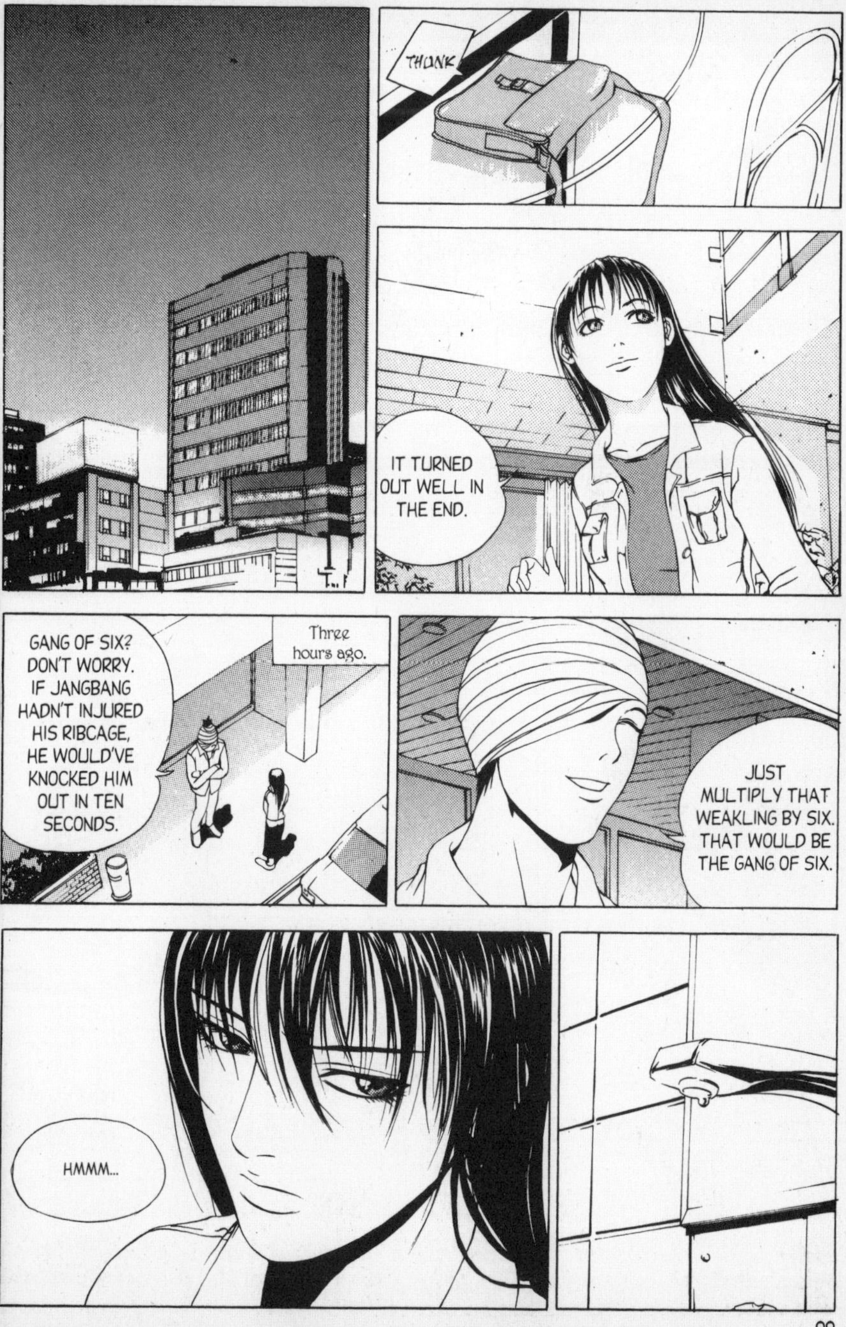
THUNK
IT TURNED OUT WELL IN THE END.
Three hours ago.
GANG OF SIX? DON'T WORRY. IF JANGBANG HADN'T INJURED HIS RIBCAGE, HE WOULD'VE KNOCKED HIM OUT IN TEN SECONDS.
JUST MULTIPLY THAT WEAKLING BY SIX. THAT WOULD BE THE GANG OF SIX.
HMMM...

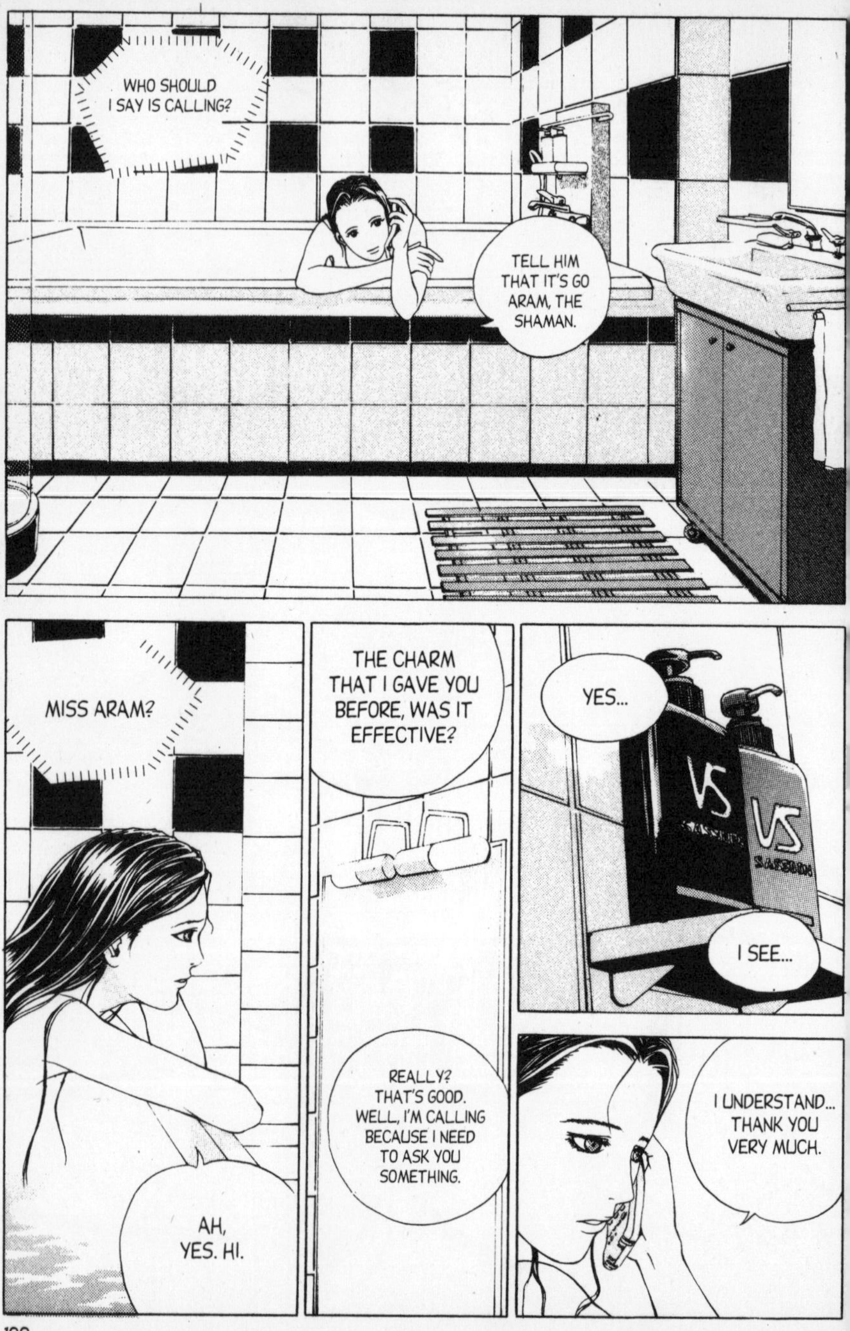
WHO SHOULD I SAY IS CALLING?
TELL HIM THAT IT'S GO ARAM, THE SHAMAN.
MISS ARAM?
AH, YES. HI.
THE CHARM THAT I GAVE YOU BEFORE, WAS IT EFFECTIVE?
REALLY? THAT'S GOOD. WELL, I'M CALLING BECAUSE I NEED TO ASK YOU SOMETHING.
YES...
I SEE...
I UNDERSTAND... THANK YOU VERY MUCH.

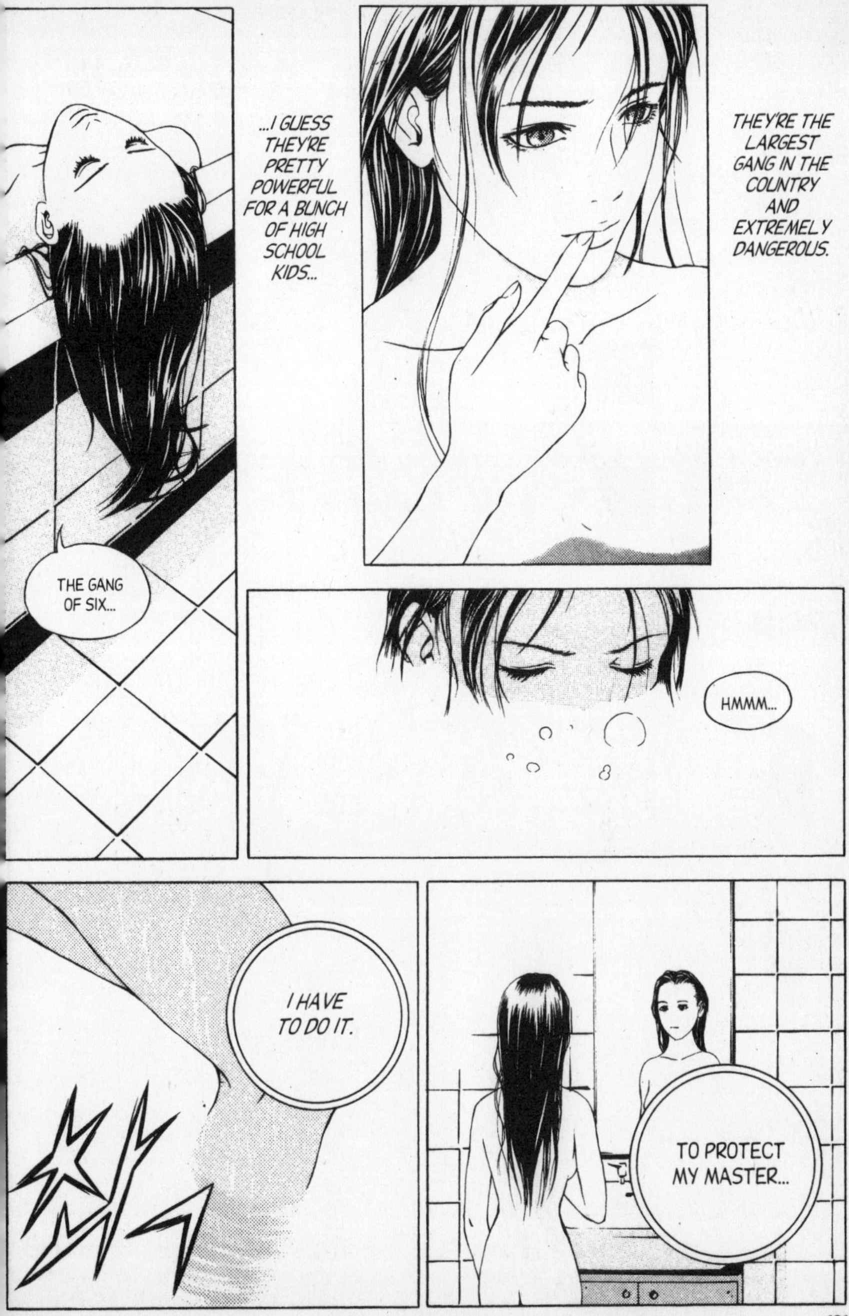
THE GANG OF SIX...
THEY'RE THE LARGEST GANG IN THE COUNTRY AND EXTREMELY DANGEROUS.
...I GUESS THEY'RE PRETTY POWERFUL FOR A BUNCH OF HIGH SCHOOL KIDS...
HMMM...
I HAVE TO DO IT.
TO PROTECT MY MASTER...

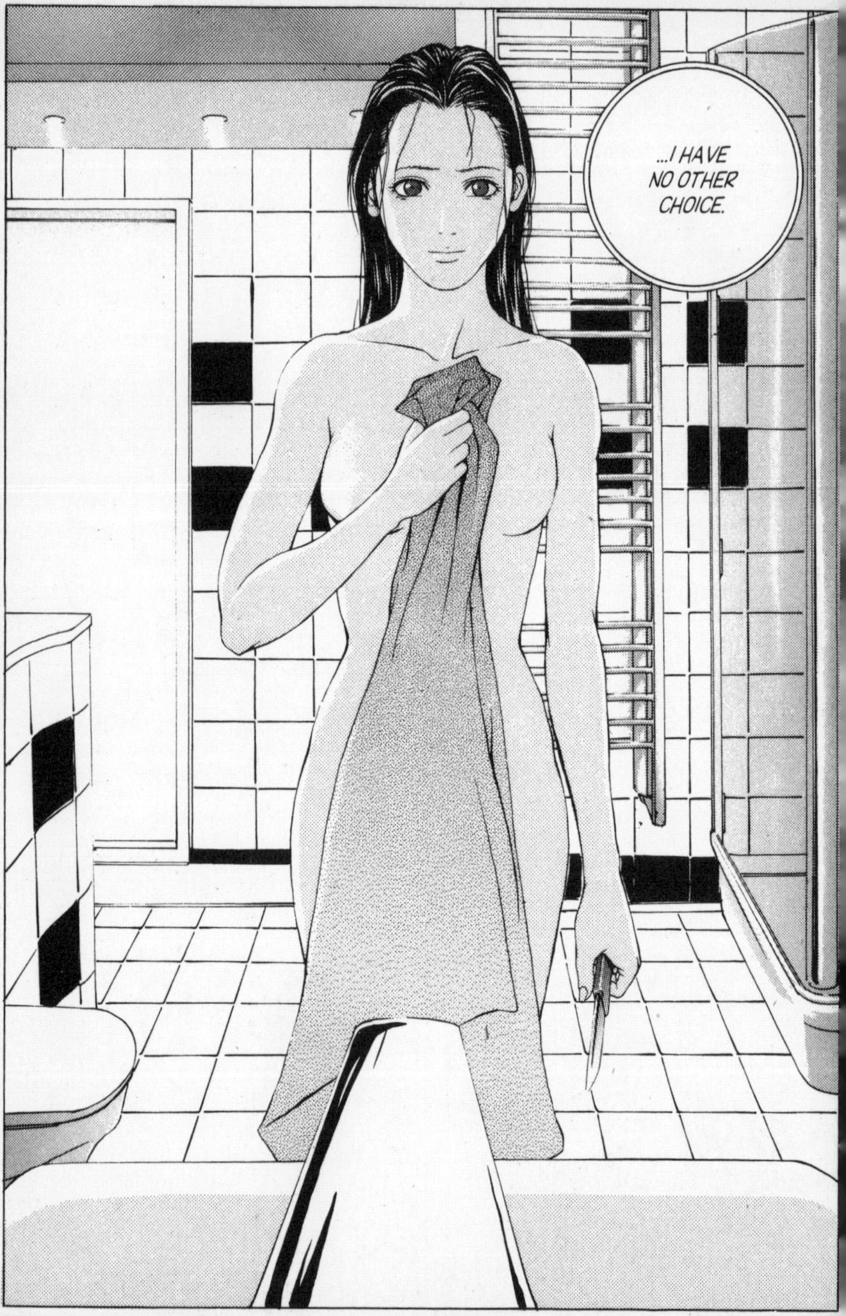
...I HAVE NO OTHER CHOICE.

#19. THE POWER OF THE NAME JOJO

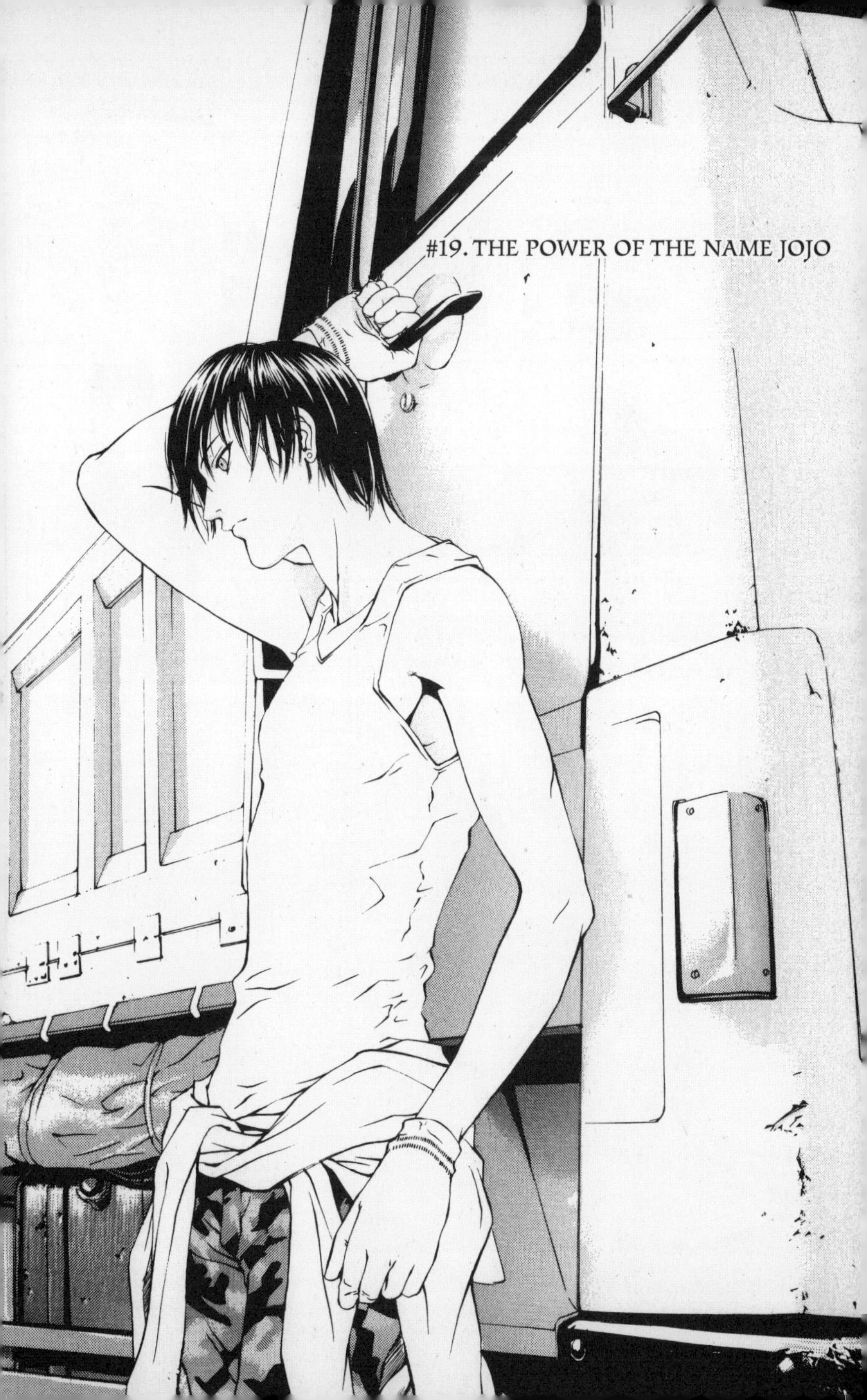

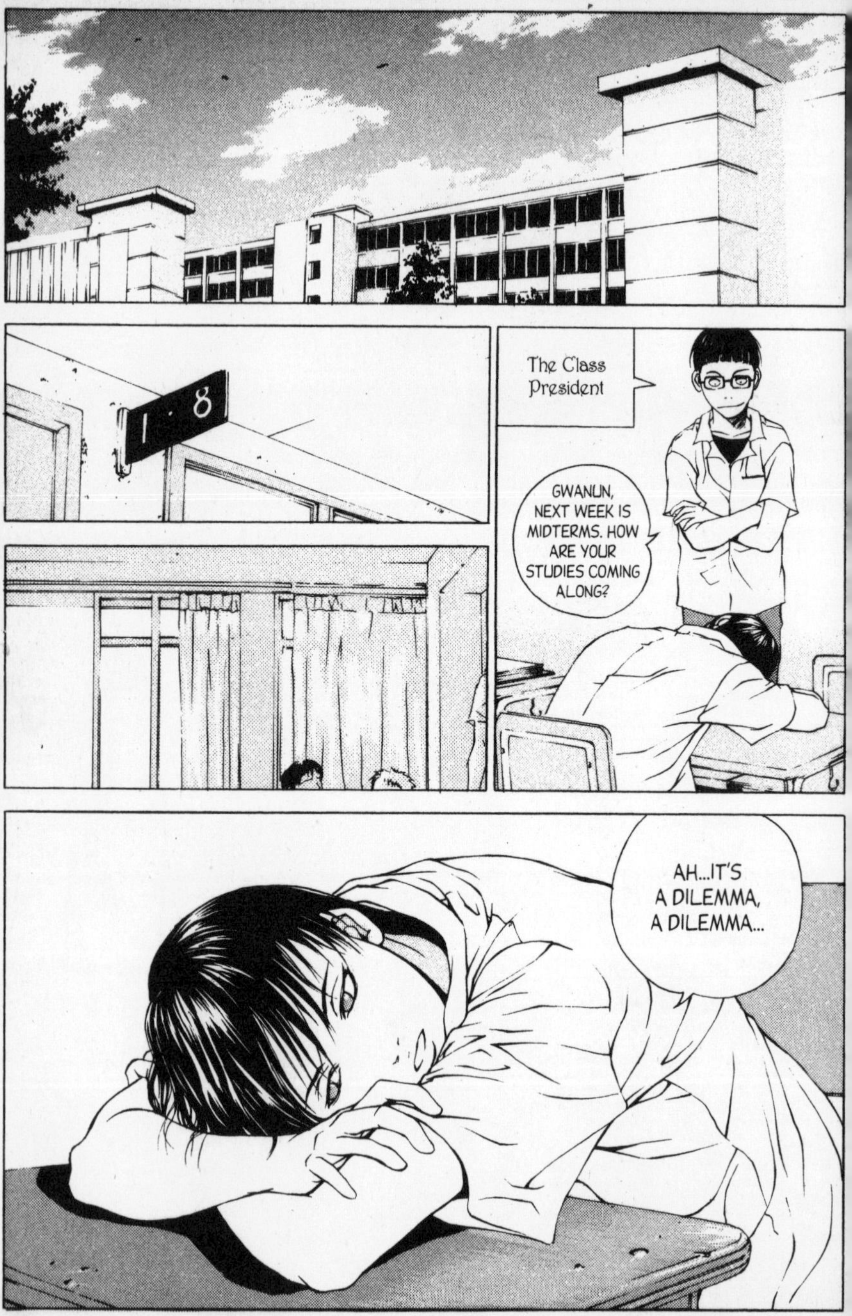
1 · 8
The Class President
GWANUN, NEXT WEEK IS MIDTERMS. HOW ARE YOUR STUDIES COMING ALONG?
AH...IT'S A DILEMMA, A DILEMMA...

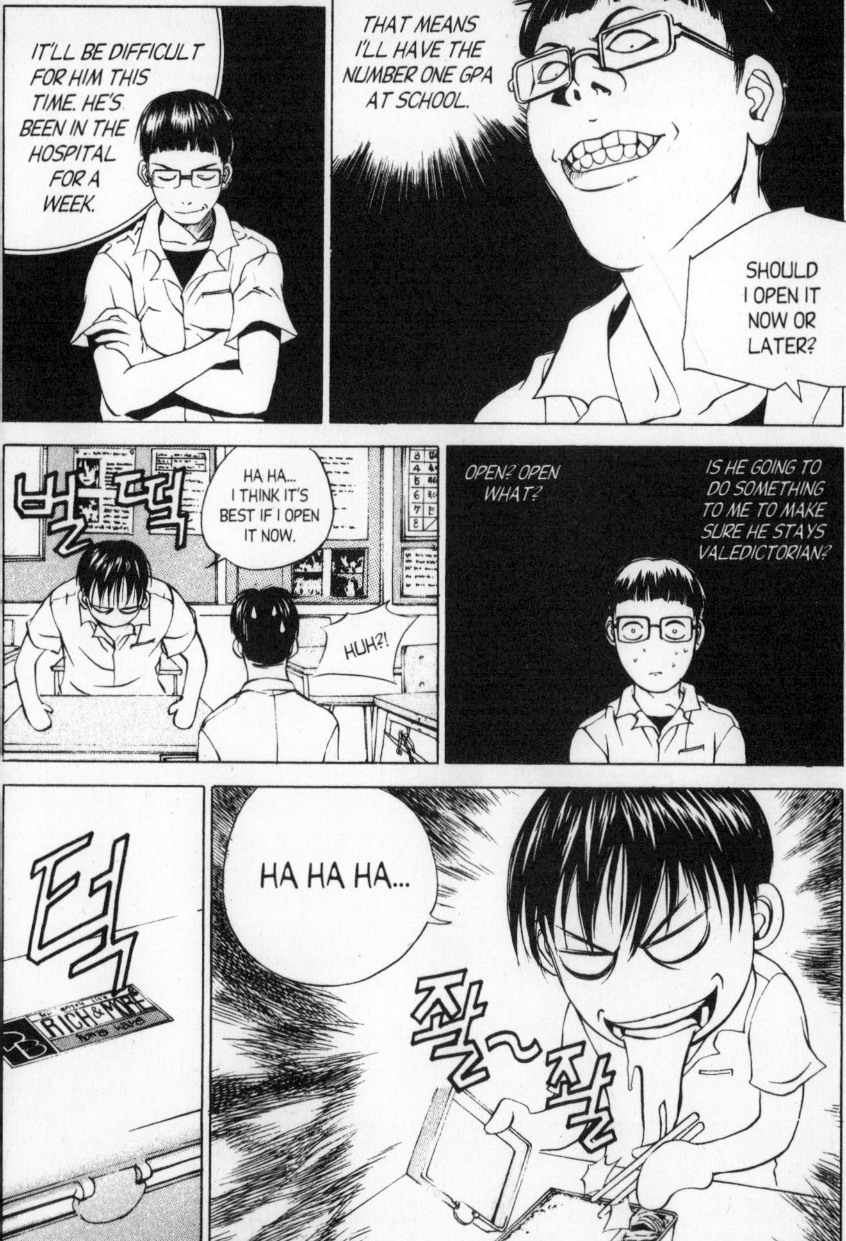
IT'LL BE DIFFICULT FOR HIM THIS TIME. HE'S BEEN IN THE HOSPITAL FOR A WEEK.
THAT MEANS I'LL HAVE THE NUMBER ONE GPA AT SCHOOL.
SHOULD I OPEN IT NOW OR LATER?
벌떡
HA HA... I THINK IT'S BEST IF I OPEN IT NOW.
HUH?!
OPEN? OPEN WHAT?
IS HE GOING TO DO SOMETHING TO ME TO MAKE SURE HE STAYS VALEDICTORIAN?
턱
RICH&MORE
HA HA HA...
좔~좔

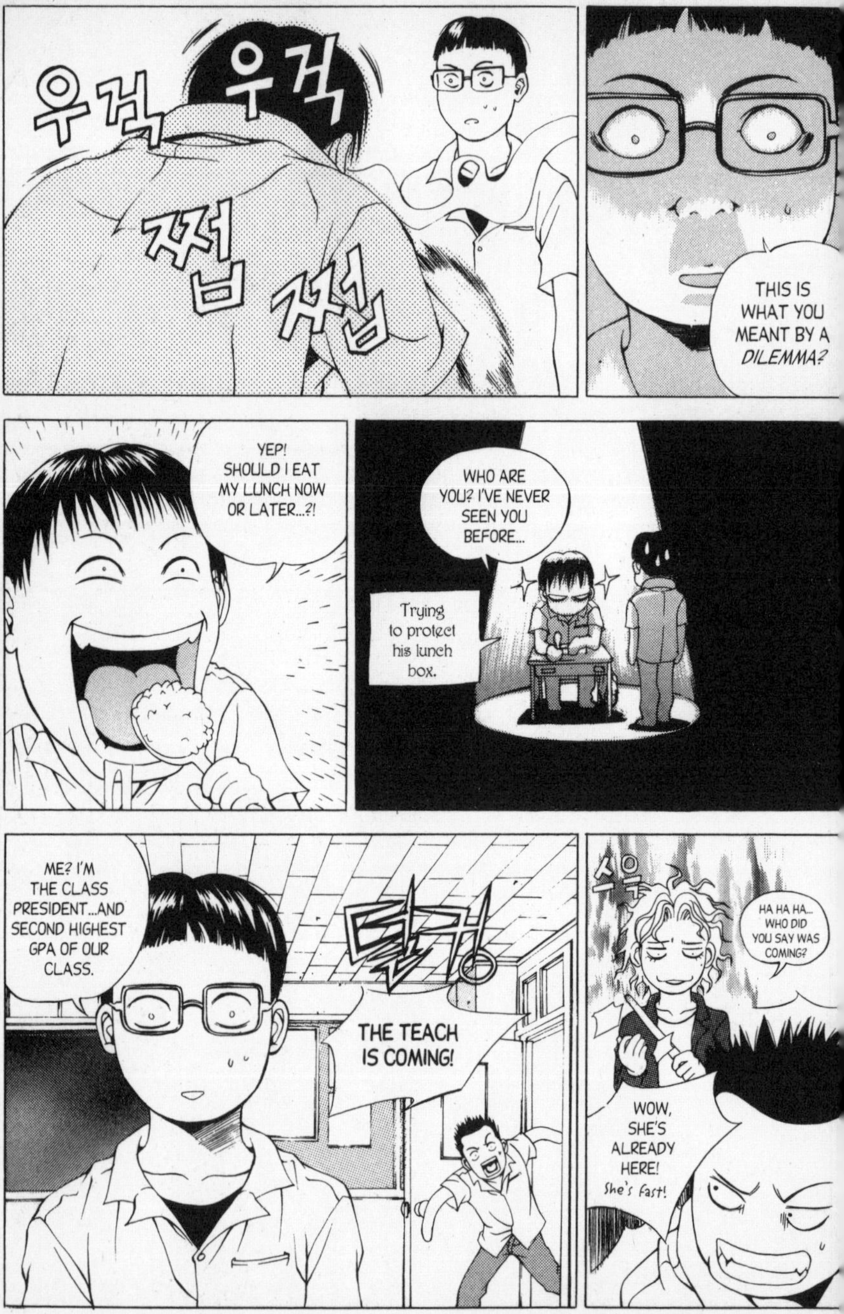
우걱 우걱
쩝 쩝
THIS IS WHAT YOU MEANT BY A *DILEMMA?*
YEP! SHOULD I EAT MY LUNCH NOW OR LATER...?!
WHO ARE YOU? I'VE NEVER SEEN YOU BEFORE...
Trying to protect his lunch box.
ME? I'M THE CLASS PRESIDENT...AND SECOND HIGHEST GPA OF OUR CLASS.
THE TEACH IS COMING!
HA HA HA... WHO DID YOU SAY WAS COMING?
WOW, SHE'S ALREADY HERE!
She's fast!

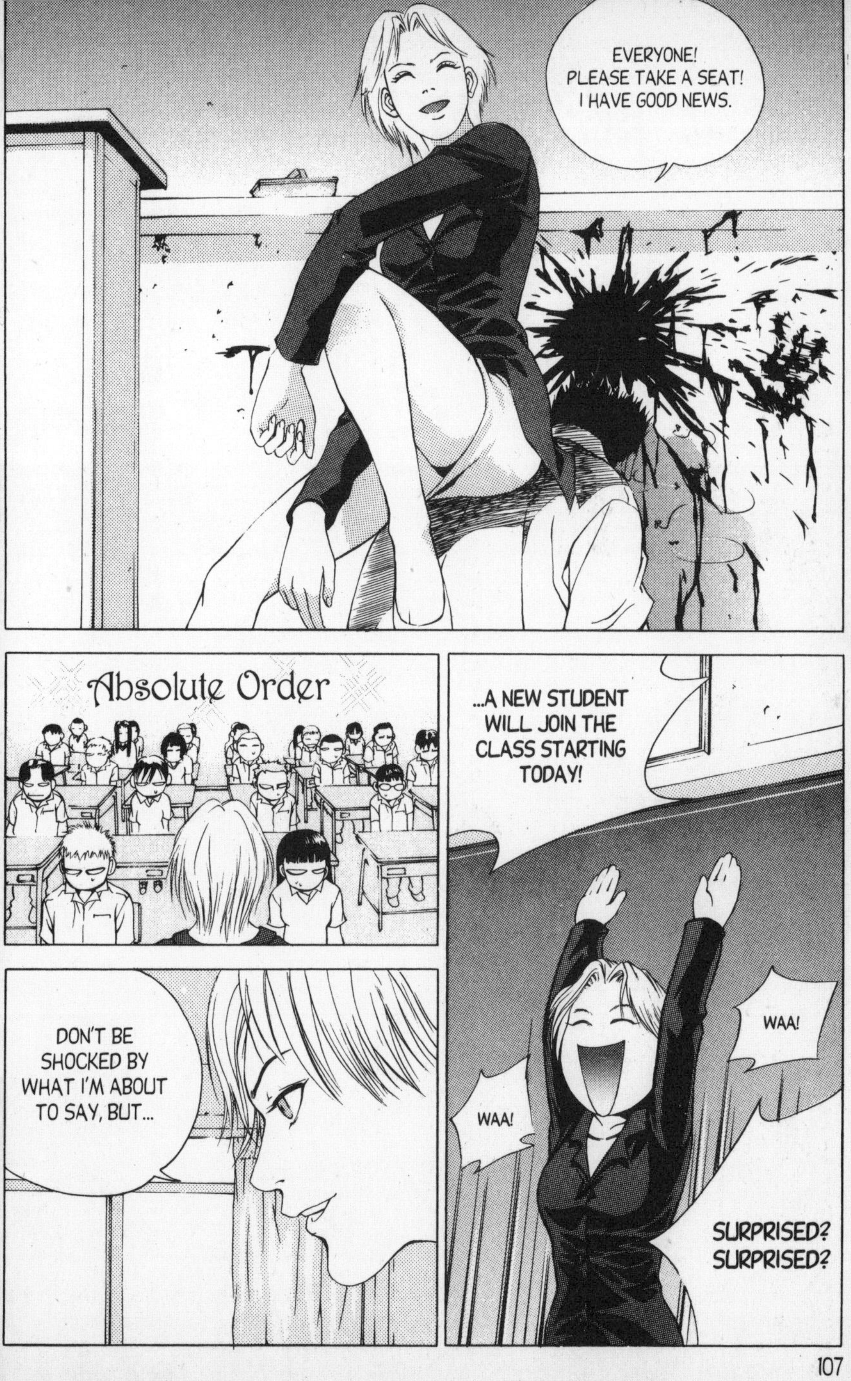
EVERYONE! PLEASE TAKE A SEAT! I HAVE GOOD NEWS.
Absolute Order
DON'T BE SHOCKED BY WHAT I'M ABOUT TO SAY, BUT...
...A NEW STUDENT WILL JOIN THE CLASS STARTING TODAY!
WAA!
WAA!
SURPRISED? SURPRISED?

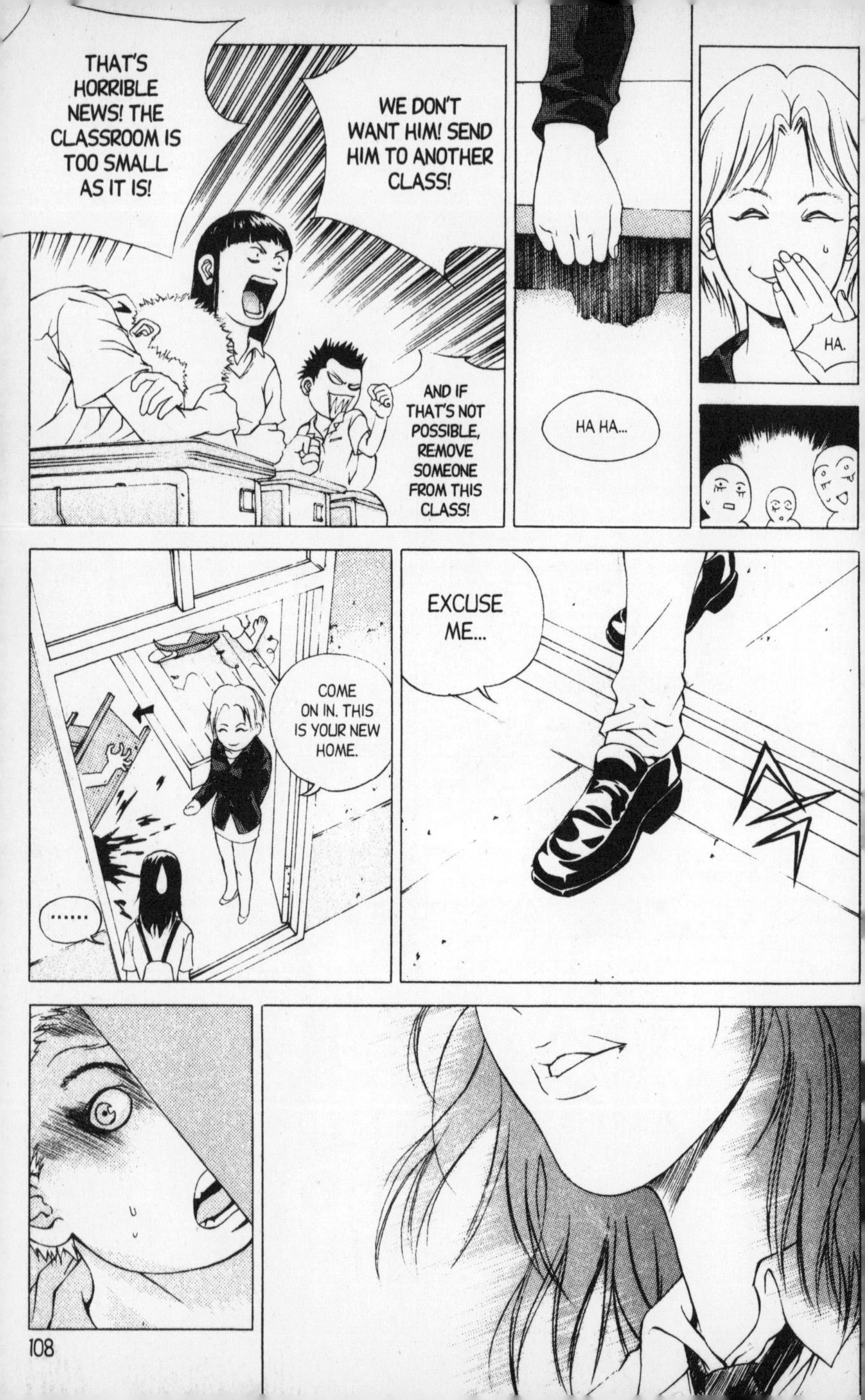
HA.
HA HA...
WE DON'T WANT HIM! SEND HIM TO ANOTHER CLASS!
THAT'S HORRIBLE NEWS! THE CLASSROOM IS TOO SMALL AS IT IS!
AND IF THAT'S NOT POSSIBLE, REMOVE SOMEONE FROM THIS CLASS!
EXCUSE ME...
COME ON IN. THIS IS YOUR NEW HOME.
......

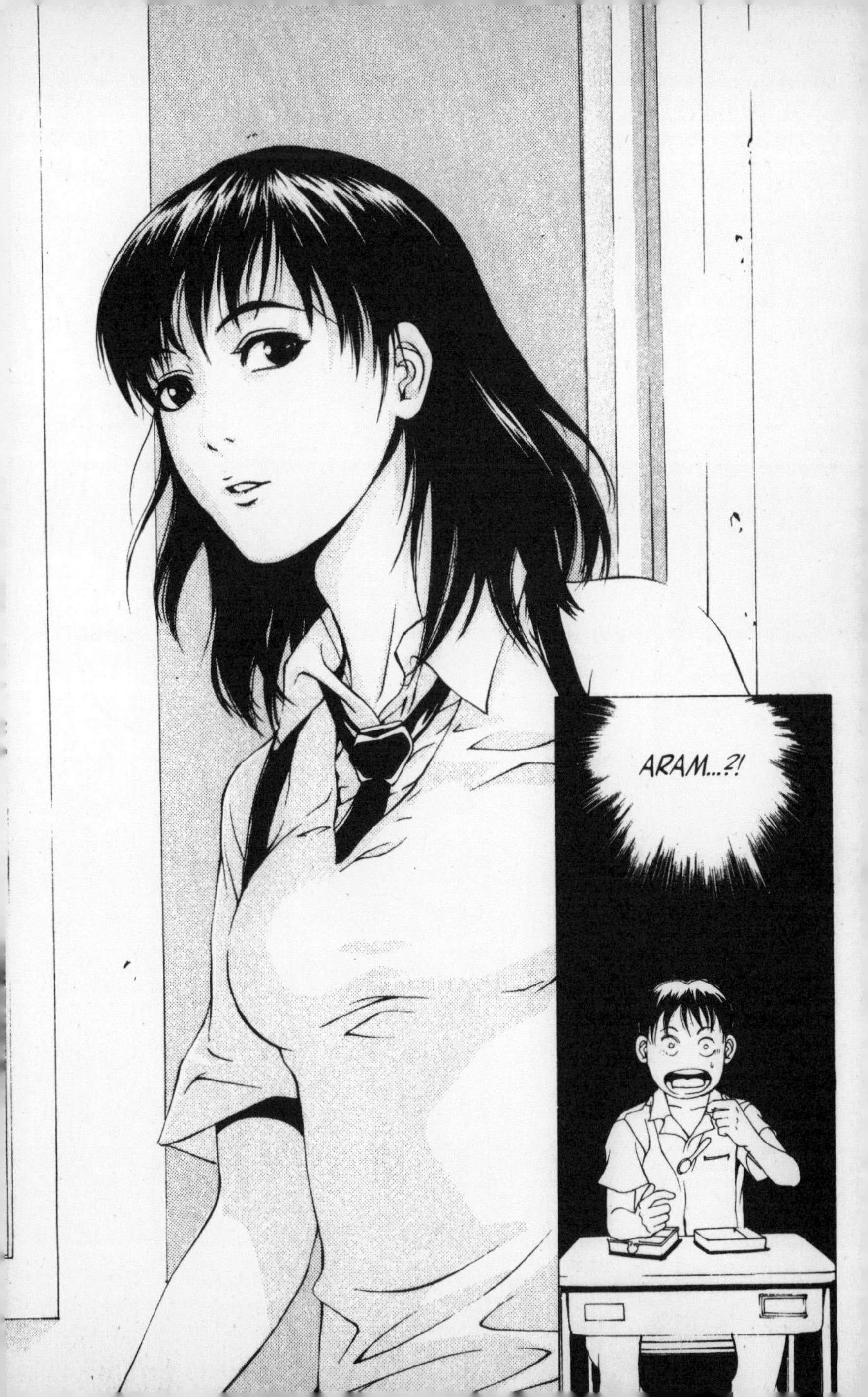
ARAM...?!

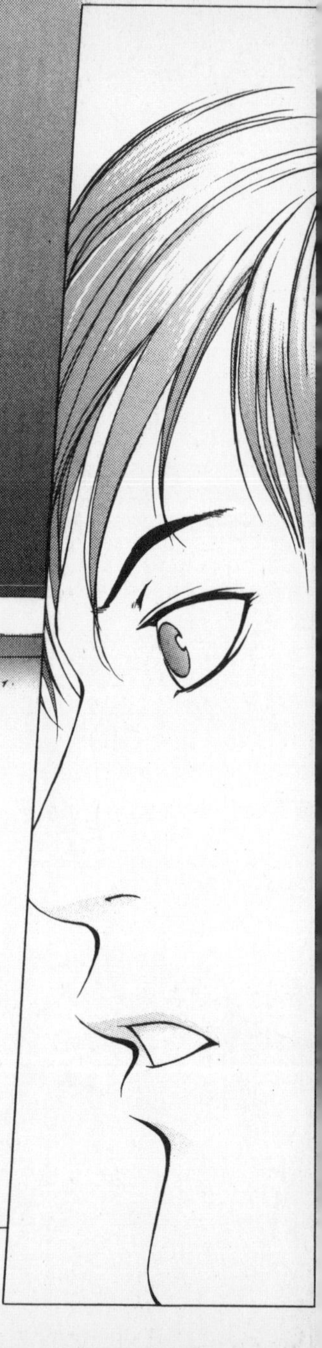
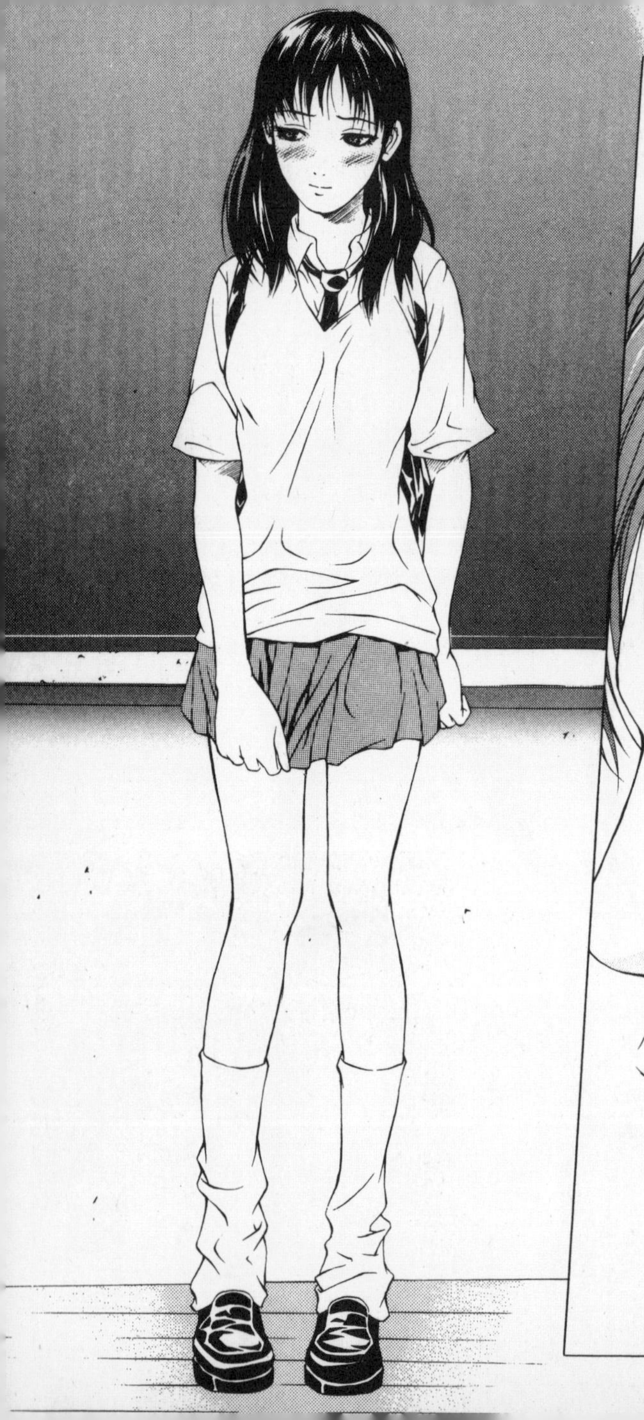

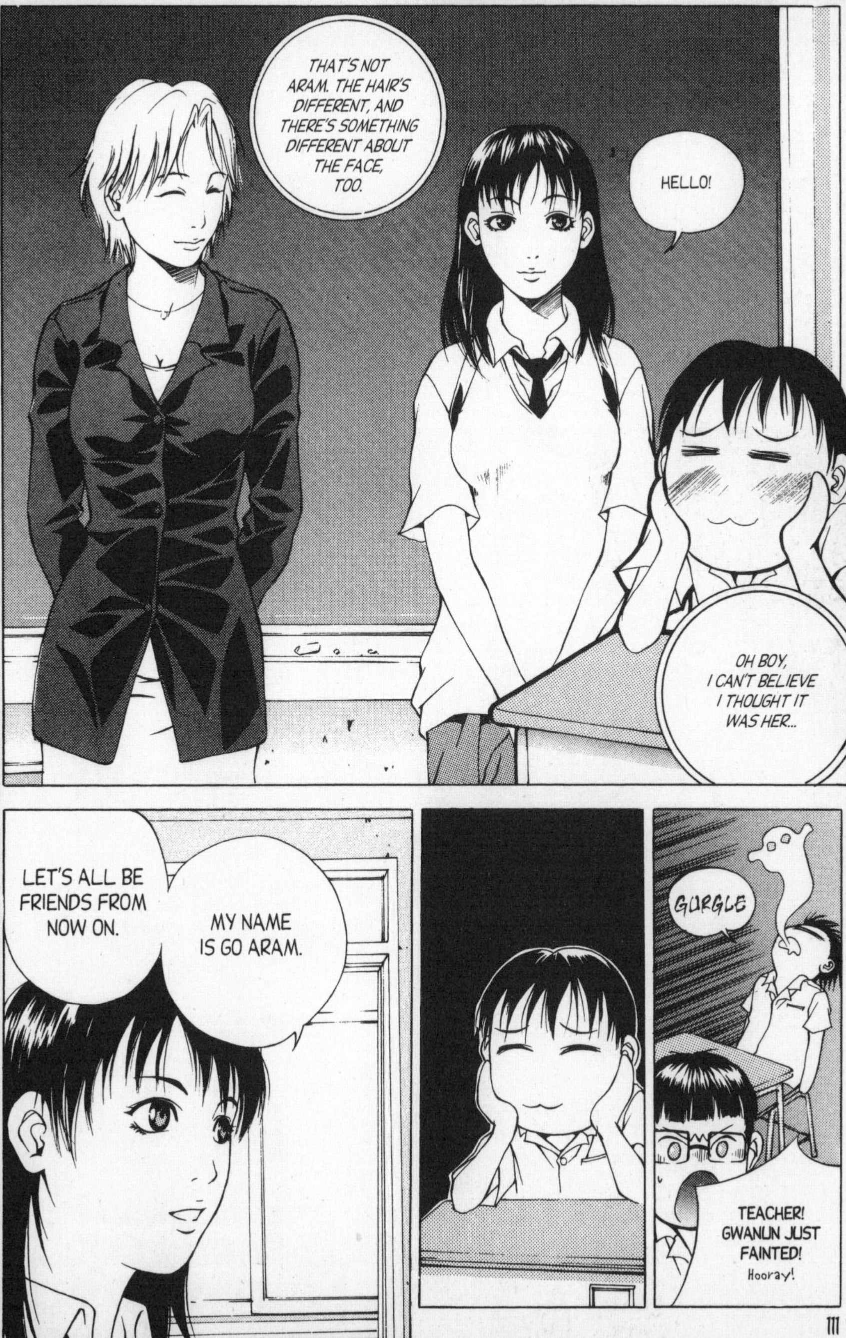
THAT'S NOT ARAM. THE HAIR'S DIFFERENT, AND THERE'S SOMETHING DIFFERENT ABOUT THE FACE, TOO.
HELLO!
OH BOY, I CAN'T BELIEVE I THOUGHT IT WAS HER...
MY NAME IS GO ARAM.
LET'S ALL BE FRIENDS FROM NOW ON.
GURGLE
TEACHER! GWANUN JUST FAINTED!
Hooray!

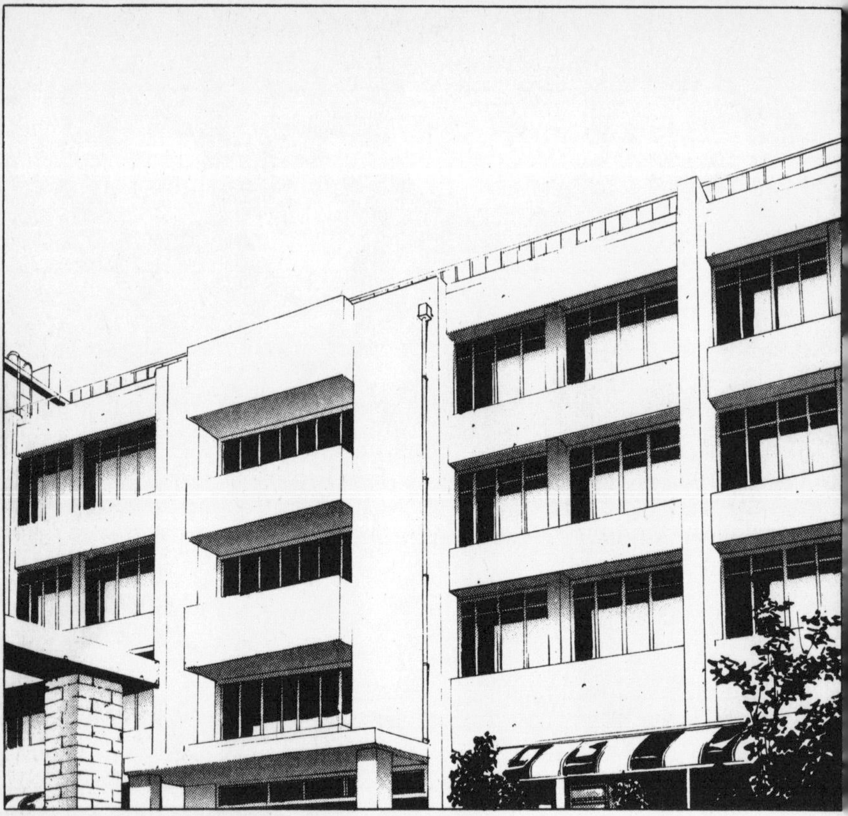

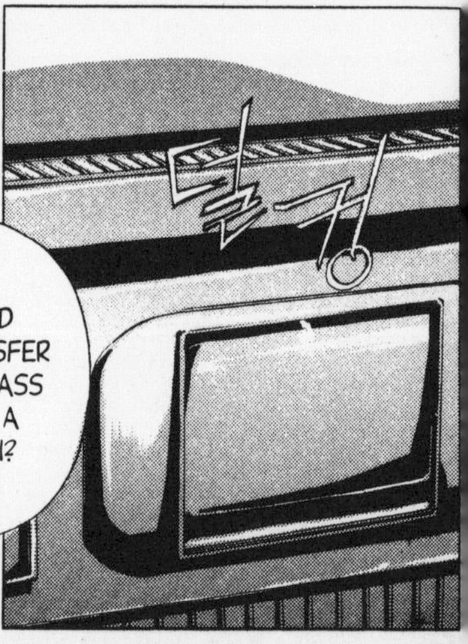
덜컹

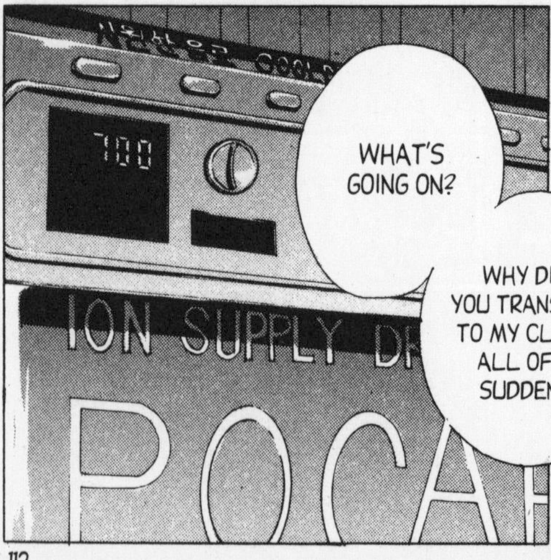
WHAT'S GOING ON?
WHY DID YOU TRANSFER TO MY CLASS ALL OF A SUDDEN?

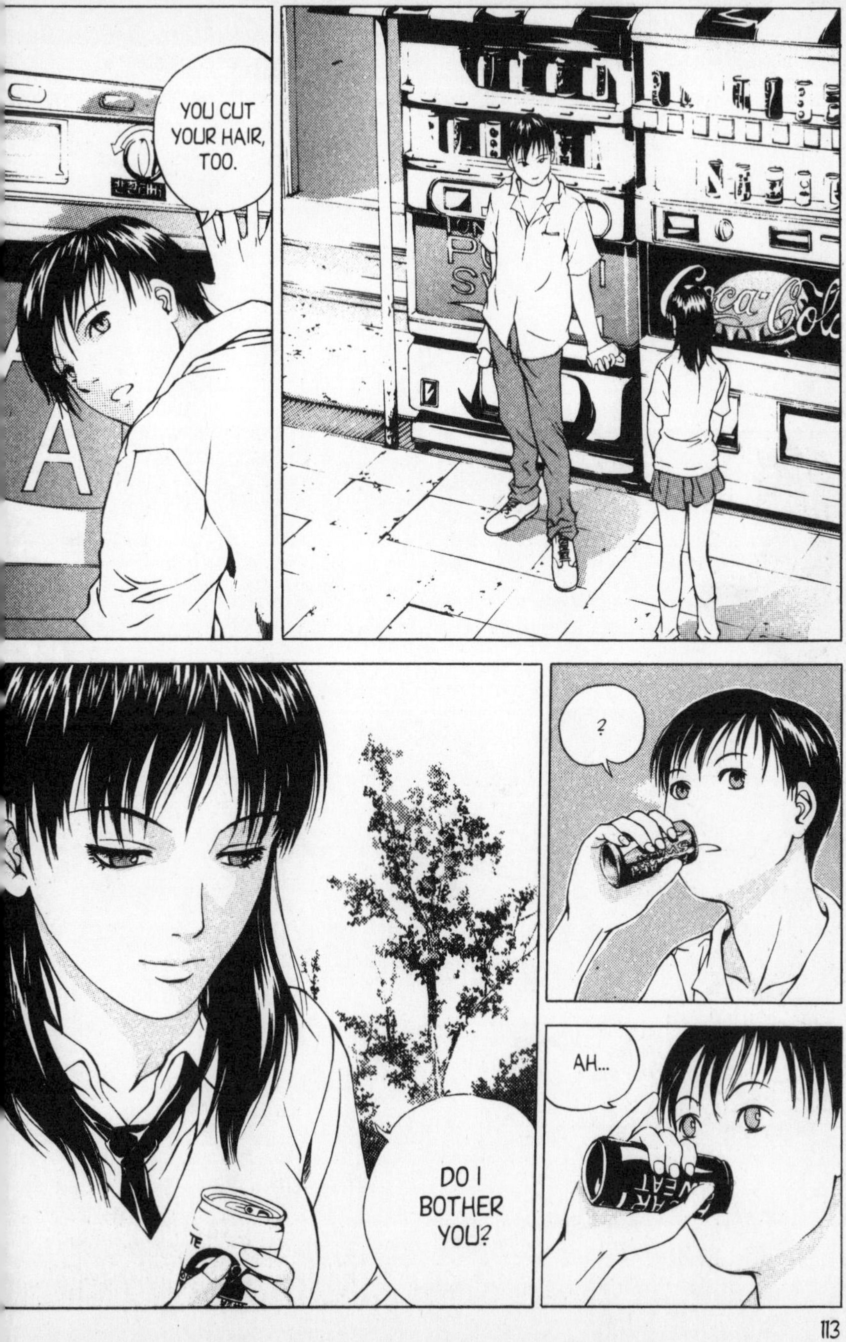
Coca-Cola
YOU CUT YOUR HAIR, TOO.
?
AH...
DO I BOTHER YOU?

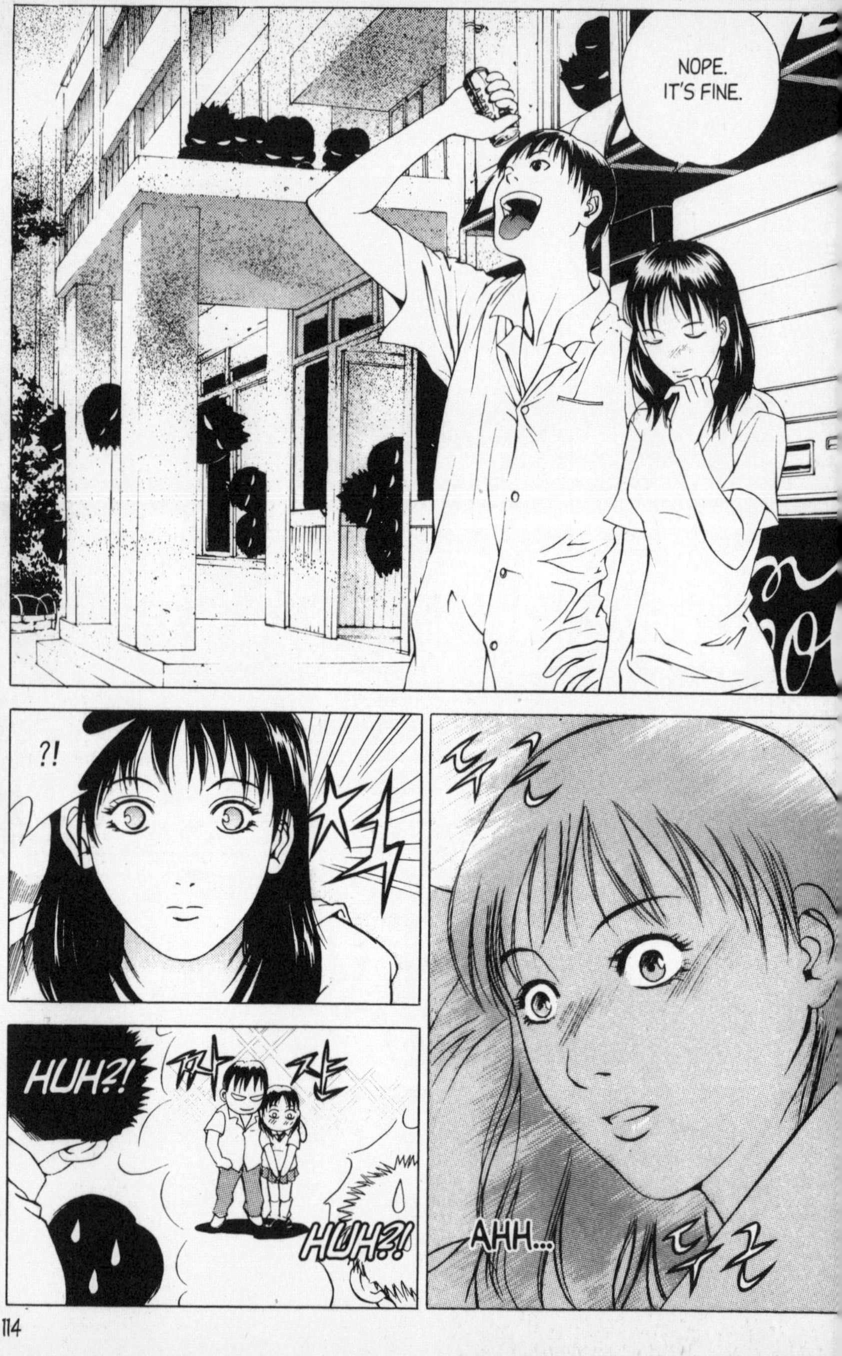
NOPE.
IT'S FINE.
?!
두근
AHH...
두근
짜잔
HUH?!
HUH?!

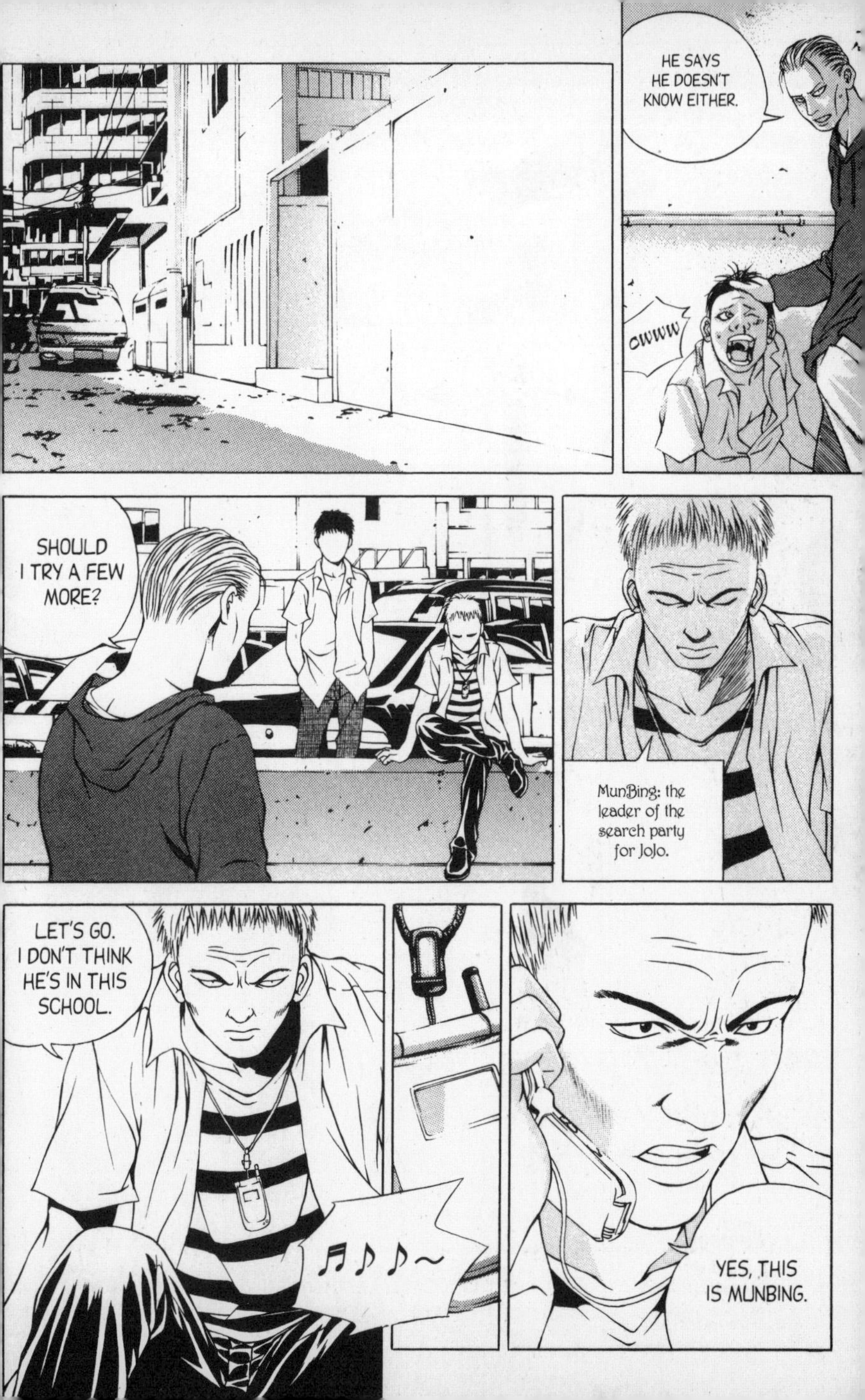
HE SAYS HE DOESN'T KNOW EITHER.
OWWW
SHOULD I TRY A FEW MORE?
MunBing: the leader of the search party for JoJo.
LET'S GO. I DON'T THINK HE'S IN THIS SCHOOL.
♬♪♪~
YES, THIS IS MUNBING.

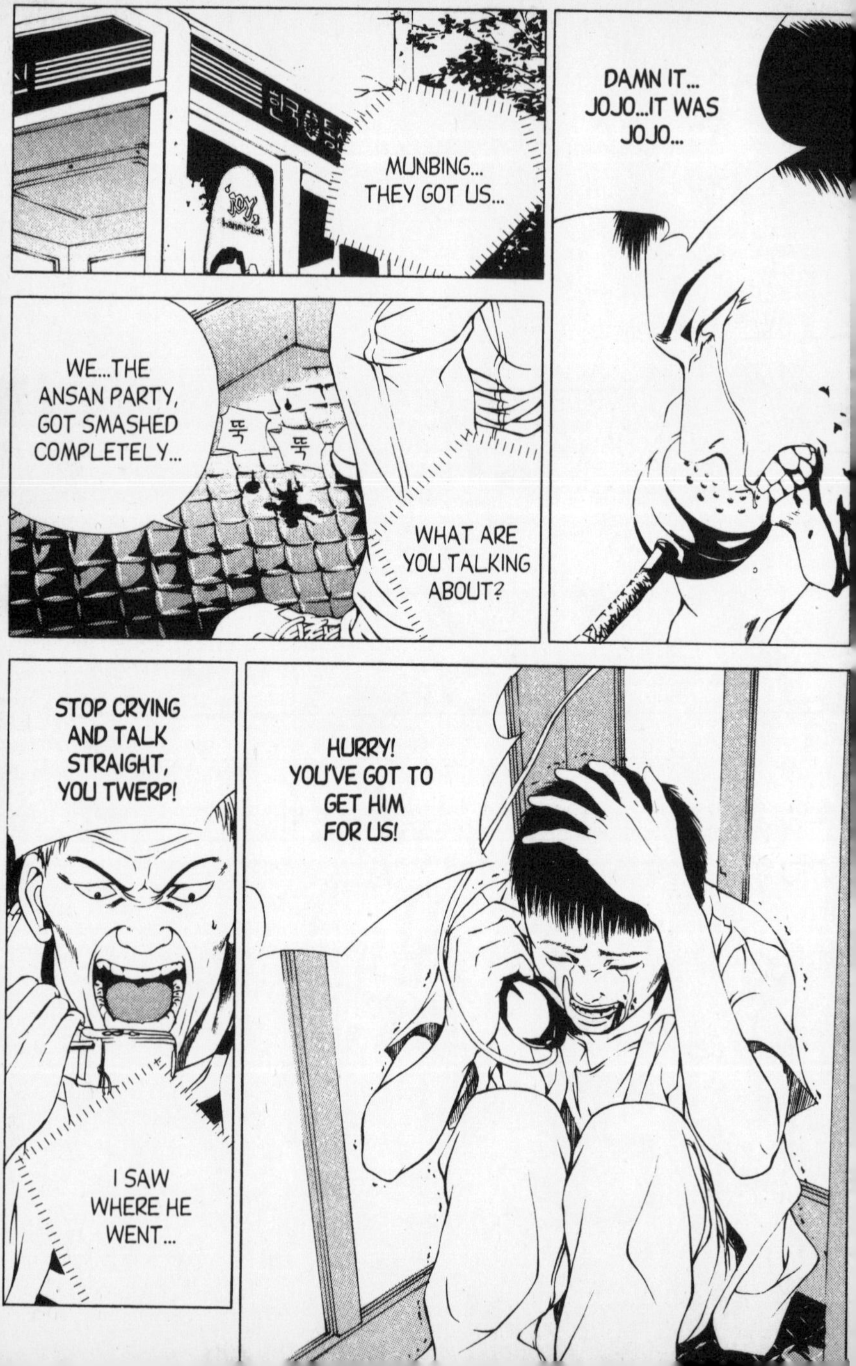
MUNBING... THEY GOT US...
DAMN IT... JOJO...IT WAS JOJO...
WE...THE ANSAN PARTY, GOT SMASHED COMPLETELY...
뚝
뚝
WHAT ARE YOU TALKING ABOUT?
STOP CRYING AND TALK STRAIGHT, YOU TWERP!
I SAW WHERE HE WENT...
HURRY! YOU'VE GOT TO GET HIM FOR US!

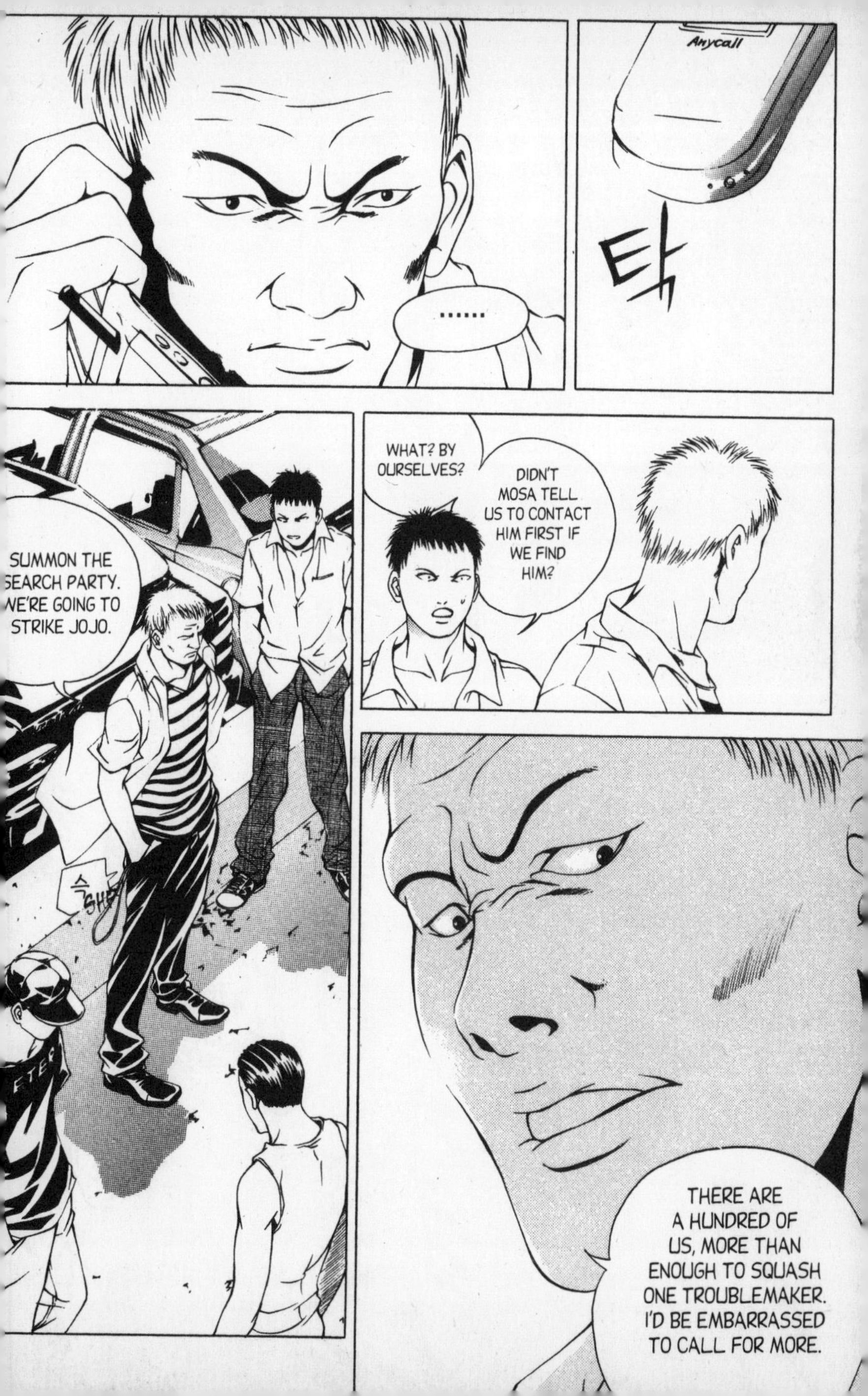

......
Anycall
탁
SUMMON THE SEARCH PARTY. WE'RE GOING TO STRIKE JOJO.
스
WHAT? BY OURSELVES?
DIDN'T MOSA TELL US TO CONTACT HIM FIRST IF WE FIND HIM?
THERE ARE A HUNDRED OF US, MORE THAN ENOUGH TO SQUASH ONE TROUBLEMAKER. I'D BE EMBARRASSED TO CALL FOR MORE.

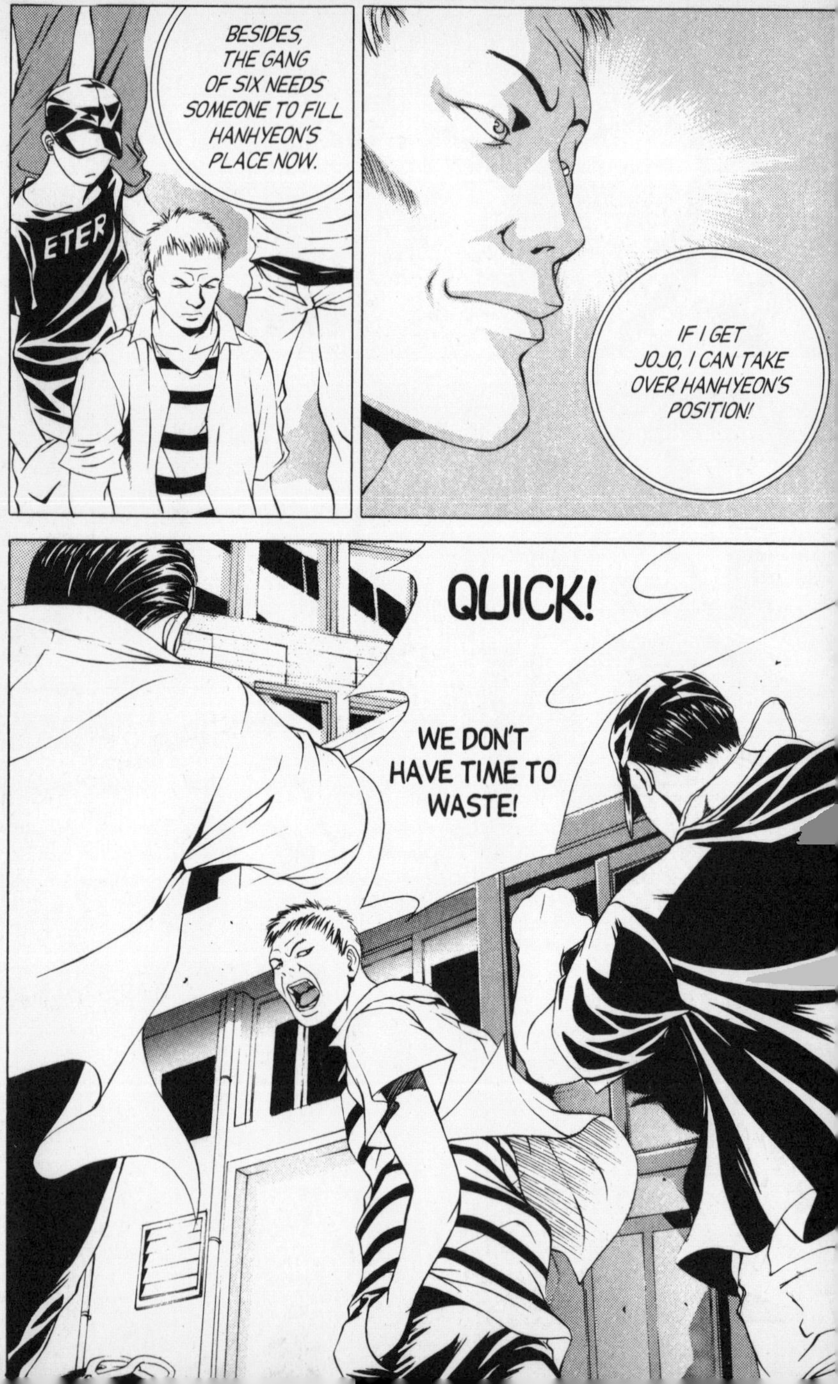
BESIDES, THE GANG OF SIX NEEDS SOMEONE TO FILL HANHYEON'S PLACE NOW.
IF I GET JOJO, I CAN TAKE OVER HANHYEON'S POSITION!
QUICK!
WE DON'T HAVE TIME TO WASTE!

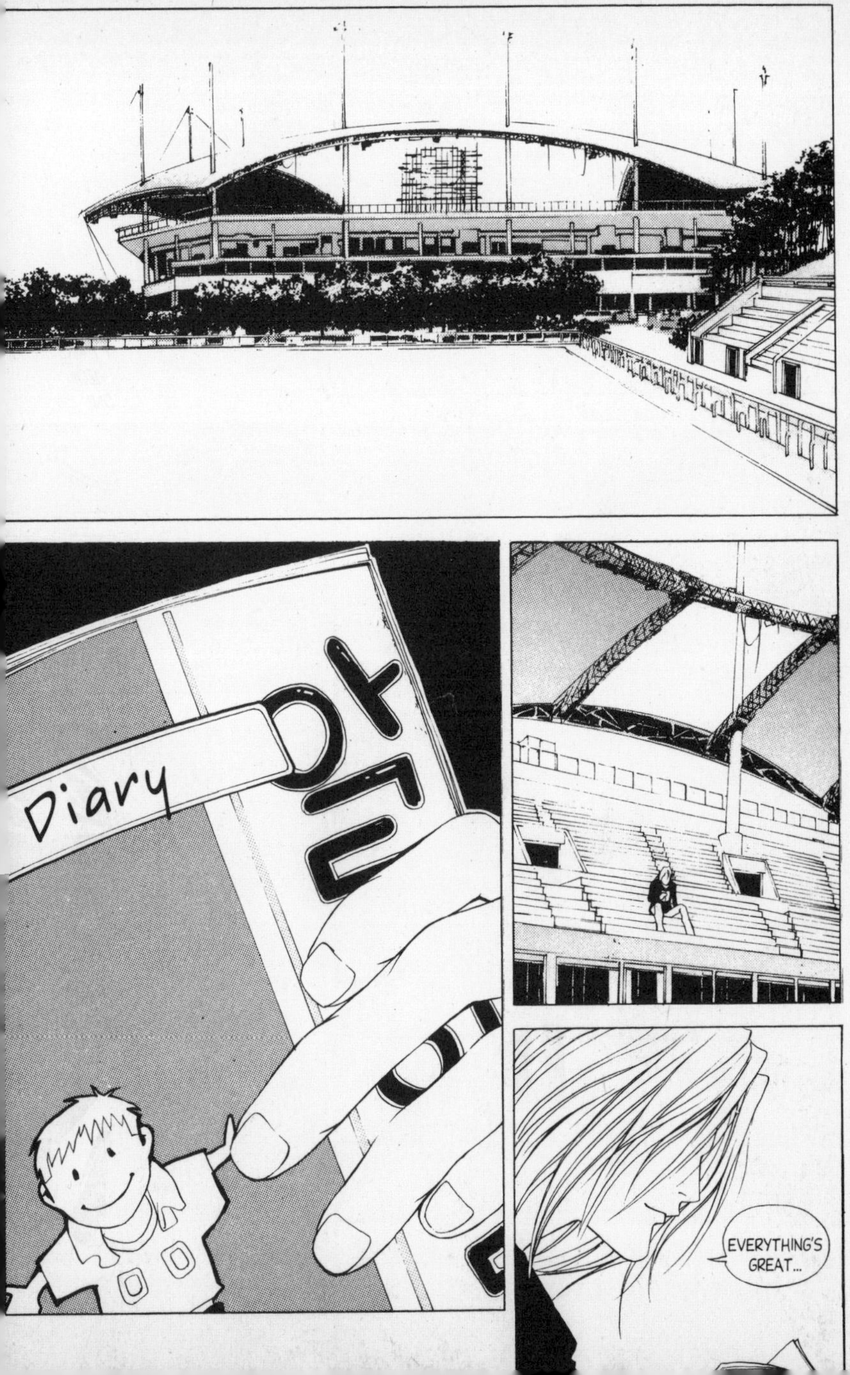
Diary
EVERYTHING'S GREAT...

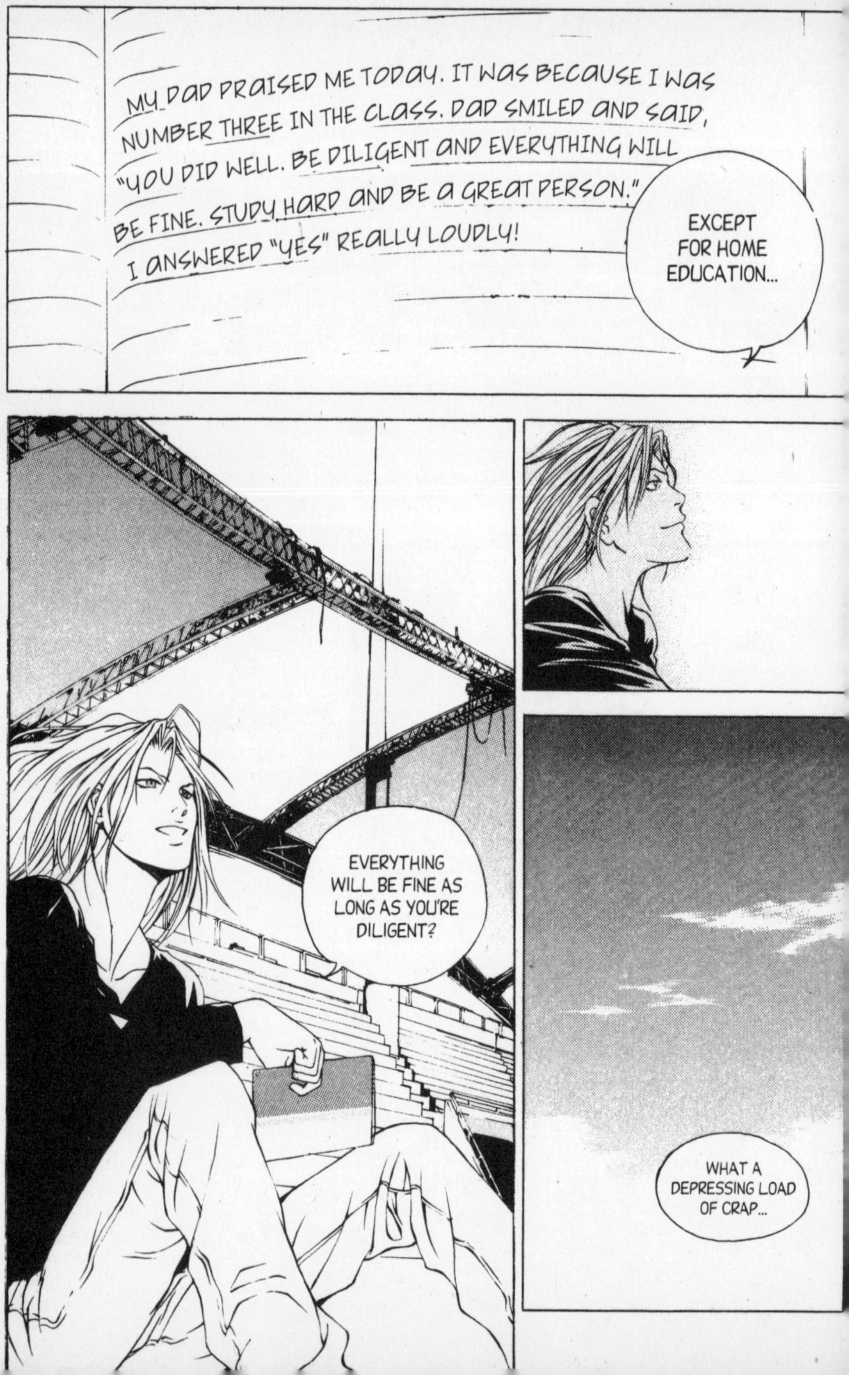
MY DAD PRAISED ME TODAY. IT WAS BECAUSE I WAS NUMBER THREE IN THE CLASS. DAD SMILED AND SAID, "YOU DID WELL. BE DILIGENT AND EVERYTHING WILL BE FINE. STUDY HARD AND BE A GREAT PERSON." I ANSWERED "YES" REALLY LOUDLY!
EXCEPT FOR HOME EDUCATION...
EVERYTHING WILL BE FINE AS LONG AS YOU'RE DILIGENT?
WHAT A DEPRESSING LOAD OF CRAP...

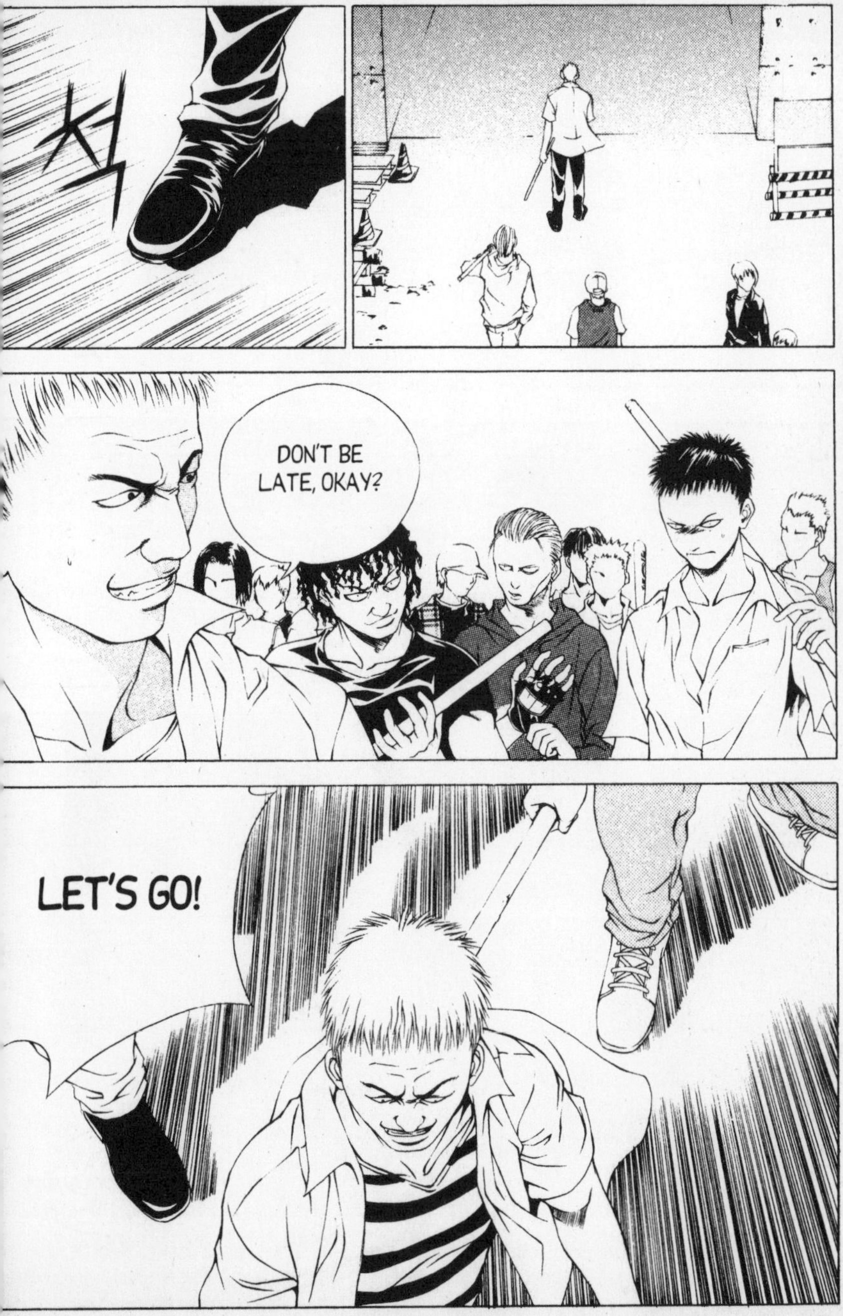
척
DON'T BE LATE, OKAY?
LET'S GO!

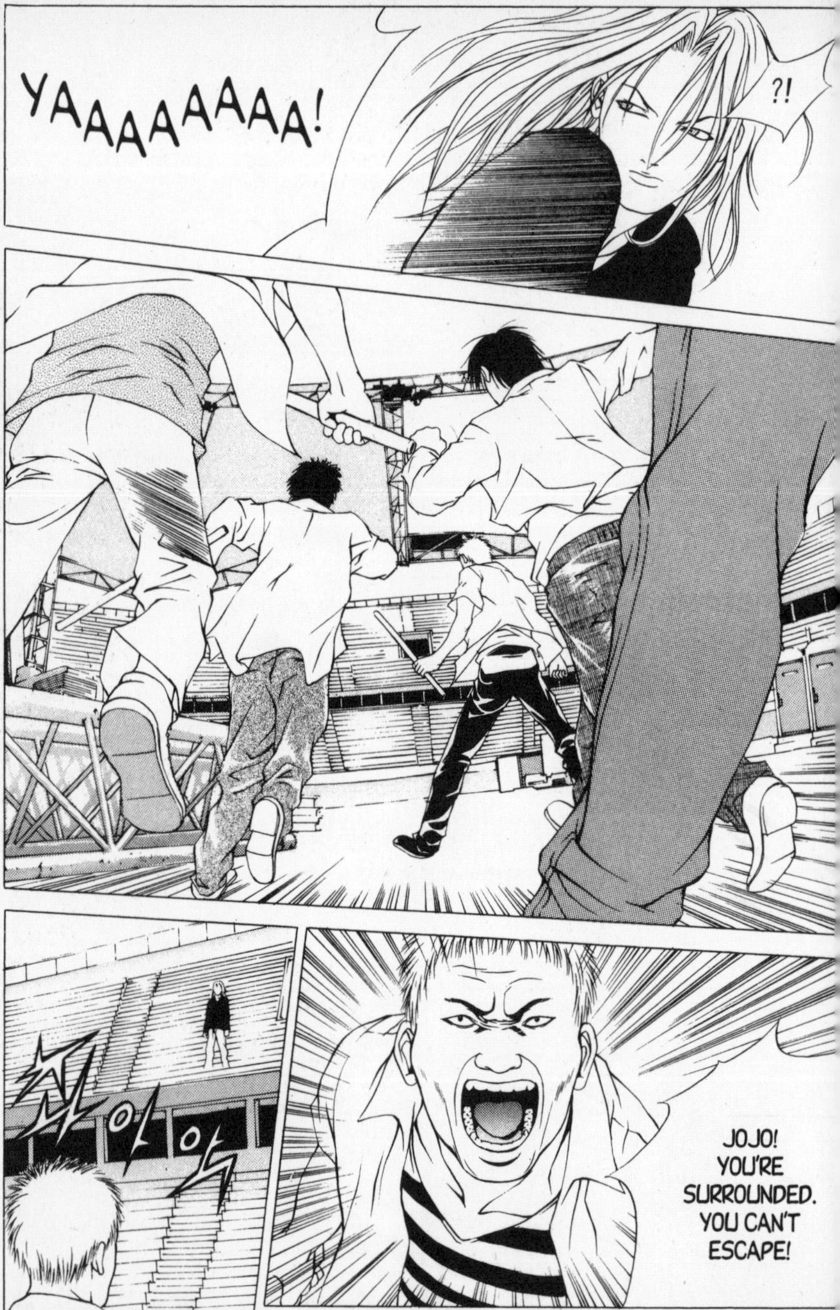
?!
YAAAAAAAA!
JOJO! YOU'RE SURROUNDED. YOU CAN'T ESCAPE!

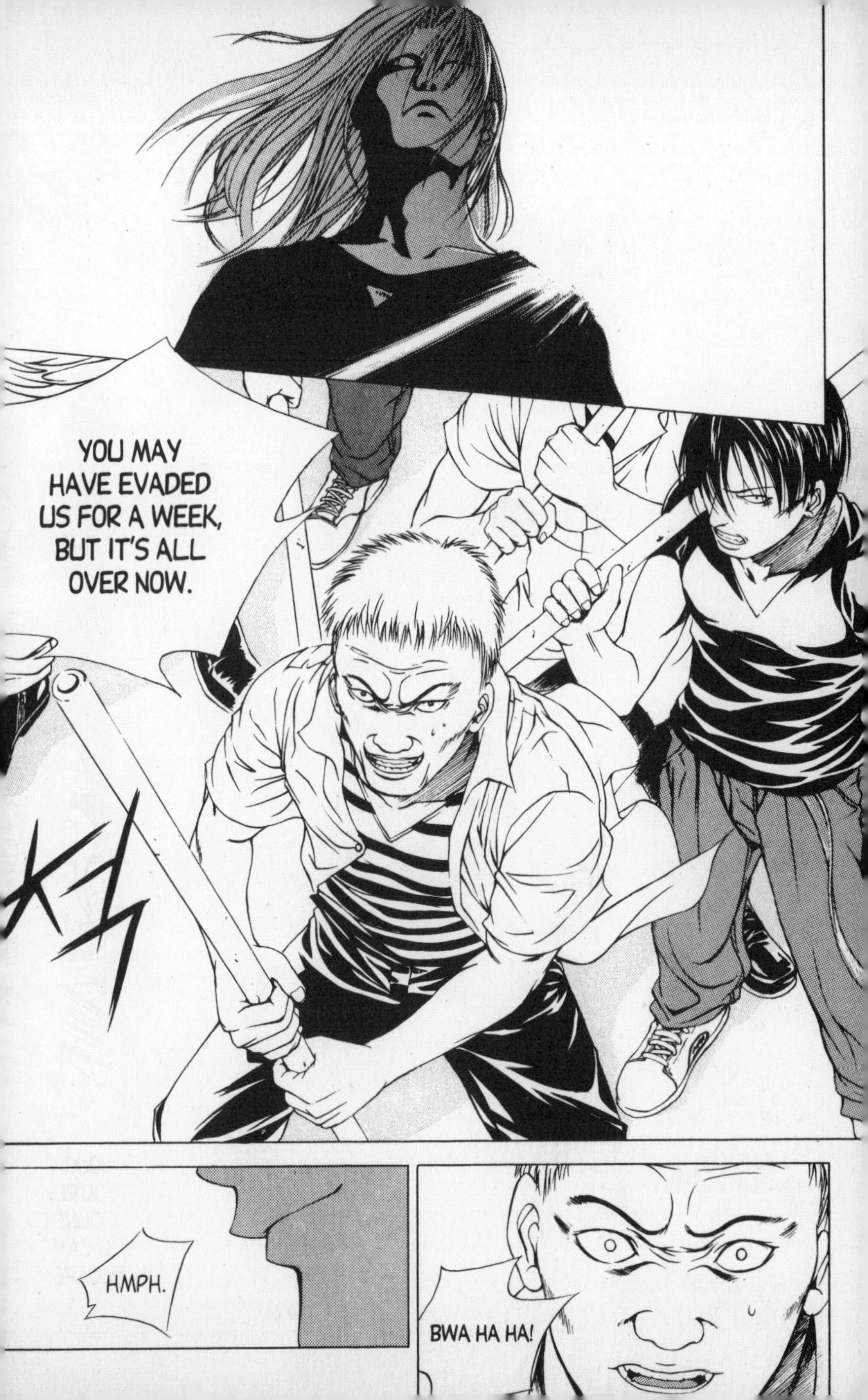
YOU MAY HAVE EVADED US FOR A WEEK, BUT IT'S ALL OVER NOW.
BWA HA HA!
HMPH.

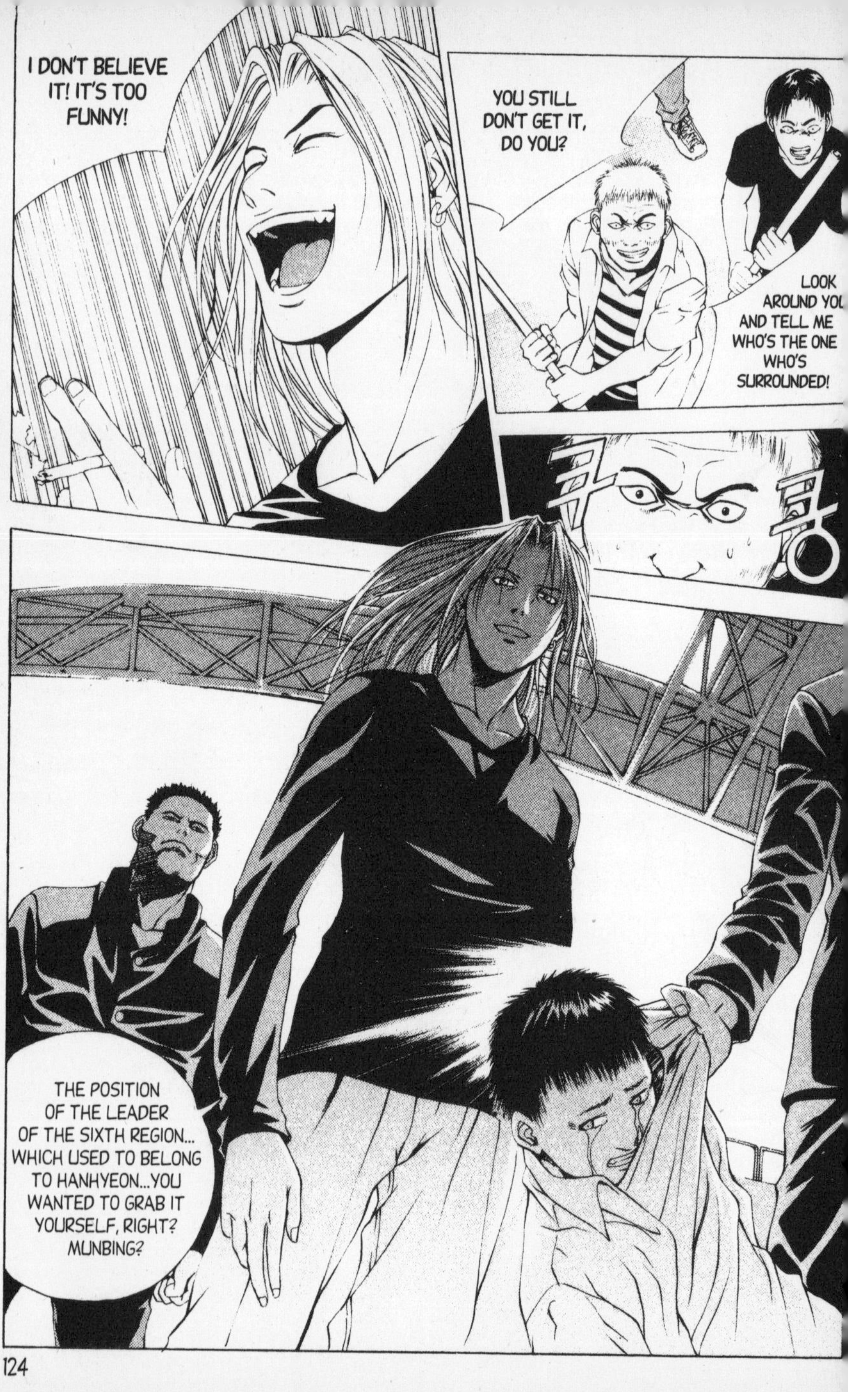
I DON'T BELIEVE IT! IT'S TOO FUNNY!
YOU STILL DON'T GET IT, DO YOU?
LOOK AROUND YOU AND TELL ME WHO'S THE ONE WHO'S SURROUNDED!
THE POSITION OF THE LEADER OF THE SIXTH REGION... WHICH USED TO BELONG TO HANHYEON...YOU WANTED TO GRAB IT YOURSELF, RIGHT? MUNBING?

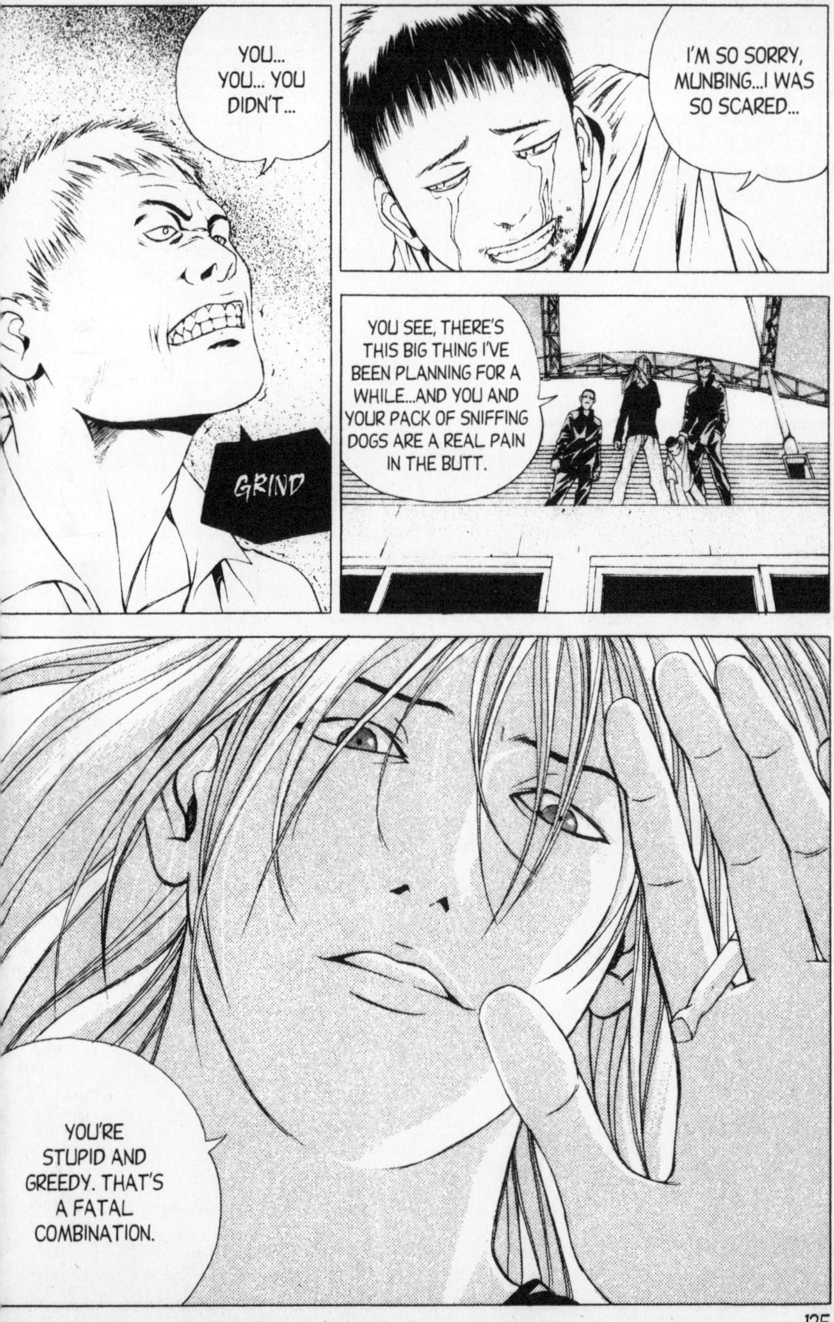
YOU... YOU... YOU DIDN'T...
GRIND
I'M SO SORRY, MUNBING...I WAS SO SCARED...
YOU SEE, THERE'S THIS BIG THING I'VE BEEN PLANNING FOR A WHILE...AND YOU AND YOUR PACK OF SNIFFING DOGS ARE A REAL PAIN IN THE BUTT.
YOU'RE STUPID AND GREEDY. THAT'S A FATAL COMBINATION.

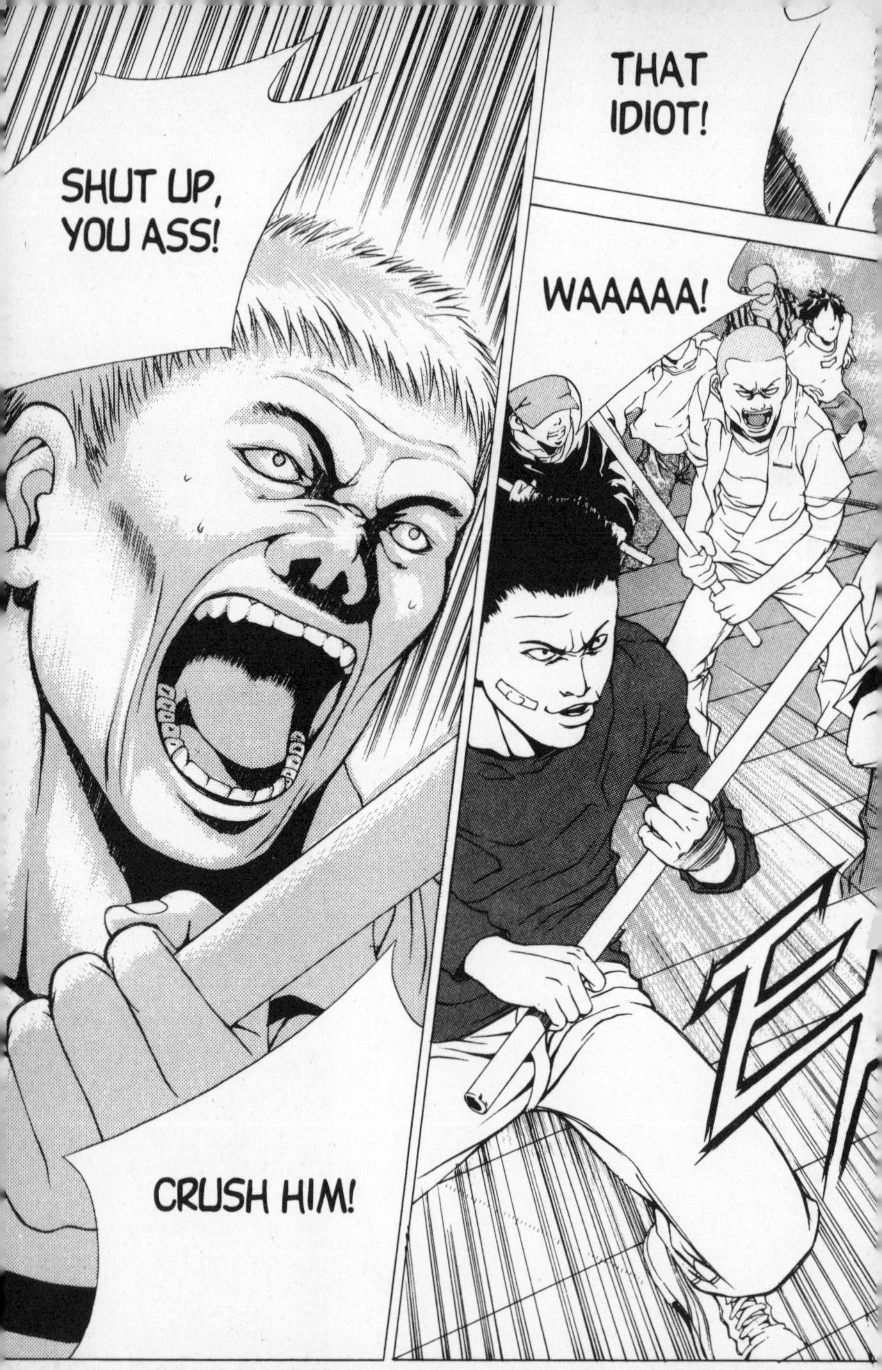
THAT IDIOT!
WAAAAA!
SHUT UP, YOU ASS!
CRUSH HIM!

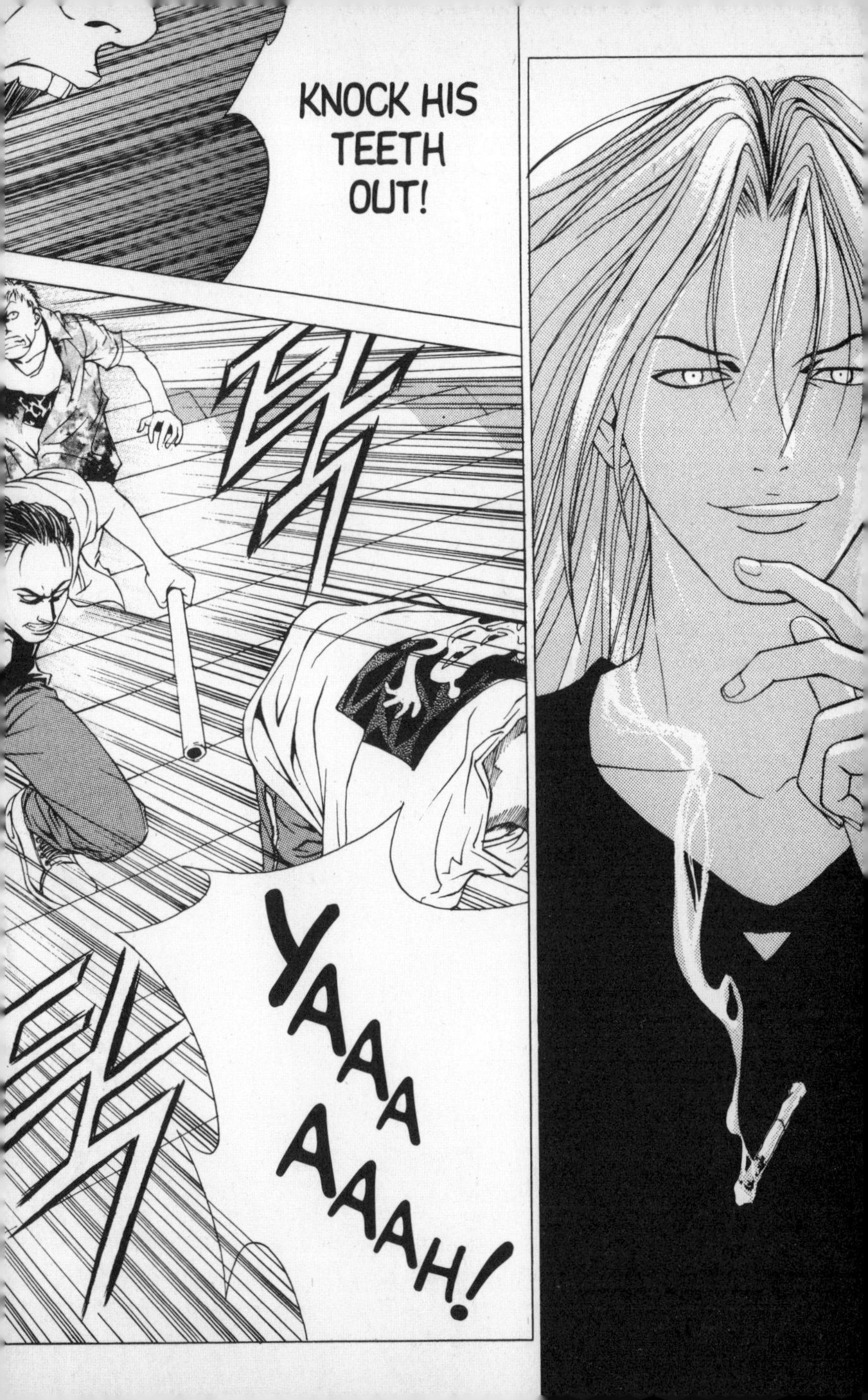
KNOCK HIS TEETH OUT!
YAAAAAAAH!

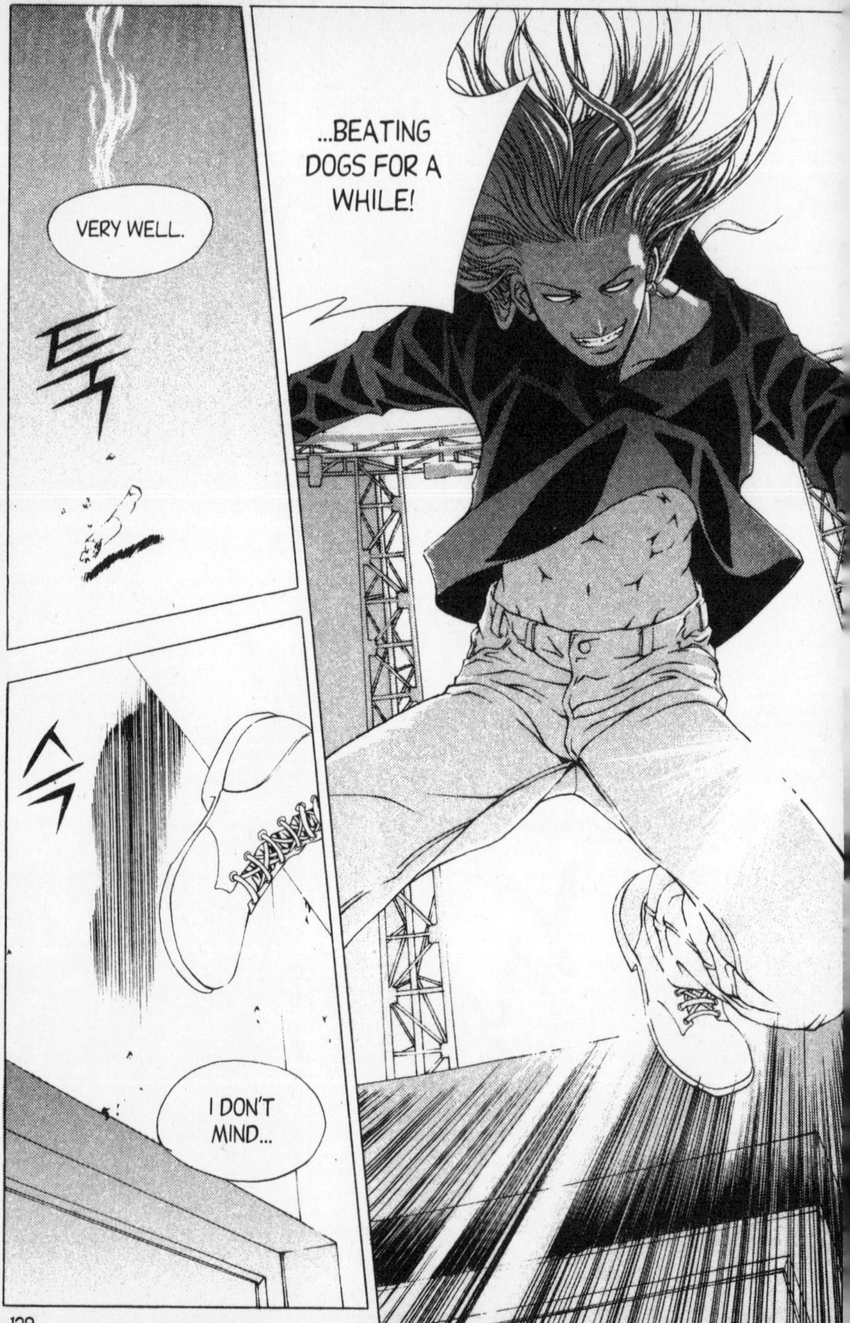
VERY WELL.
I DON'T MIND...
...BEATING DOGS FOR A WHILE!

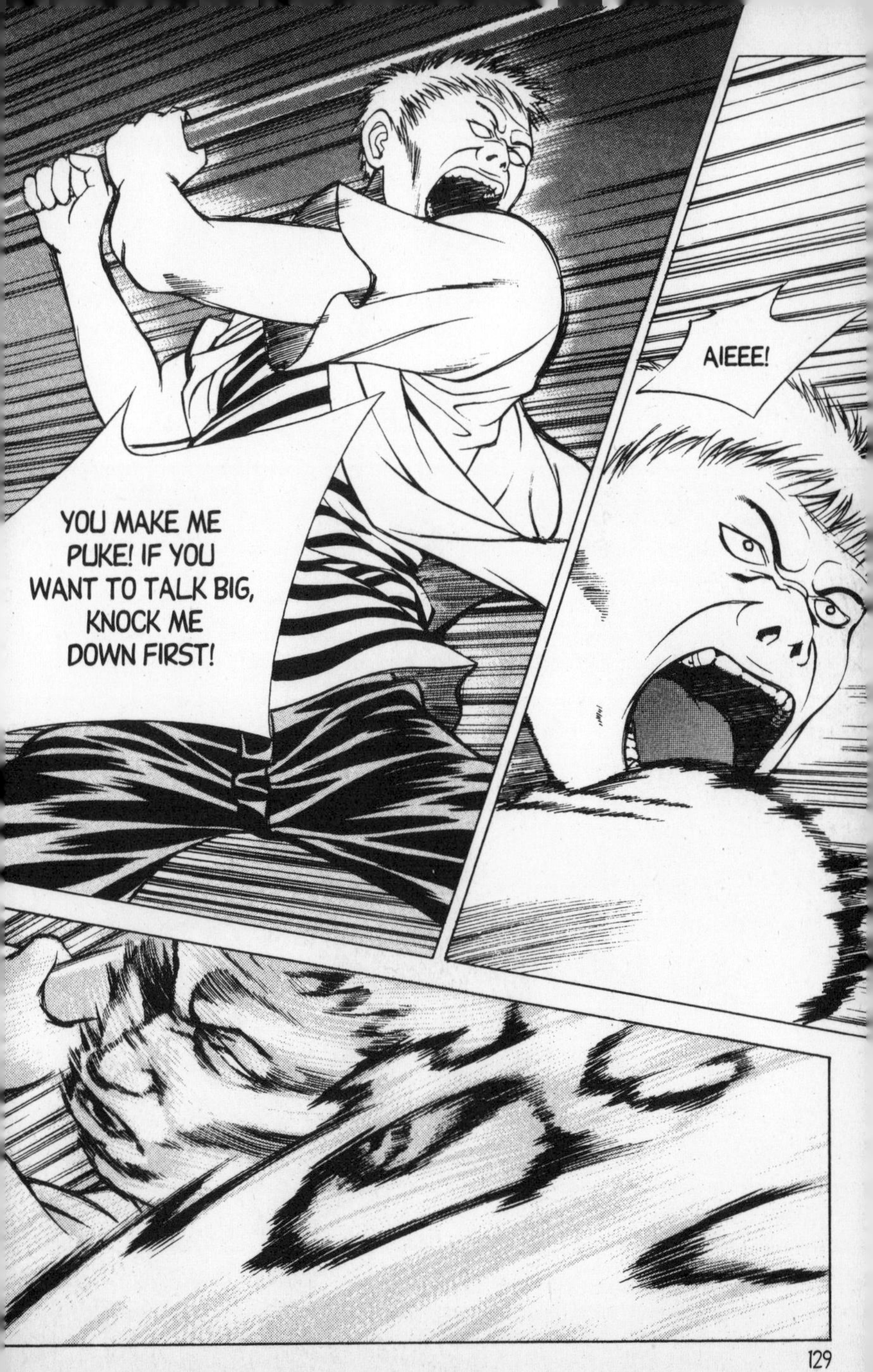
AIEEE!
YOU MAKE ME PUKE! IF YOU WANT TO TALK BIG, KNOCK ME DOWN FIRST!

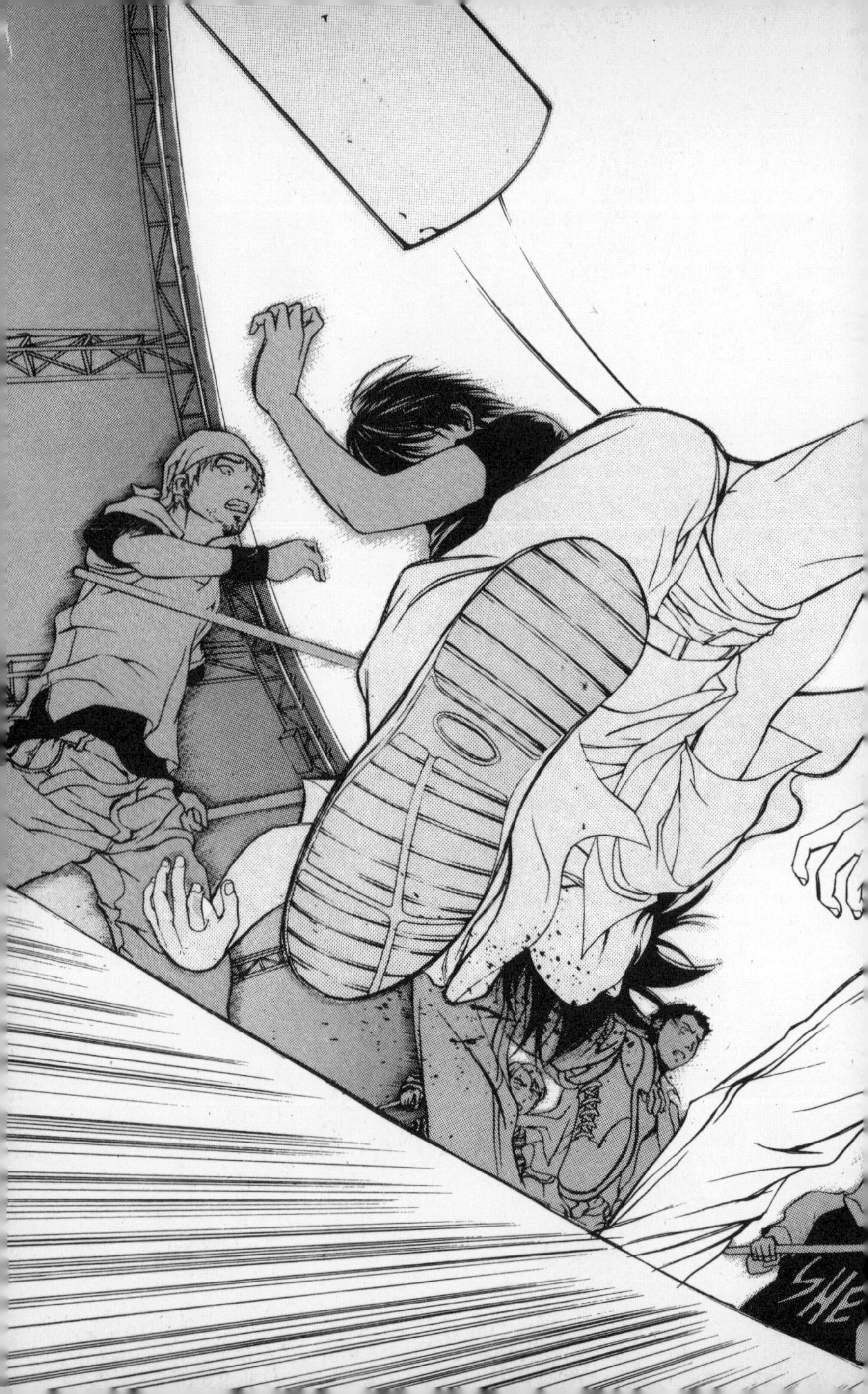
SHE

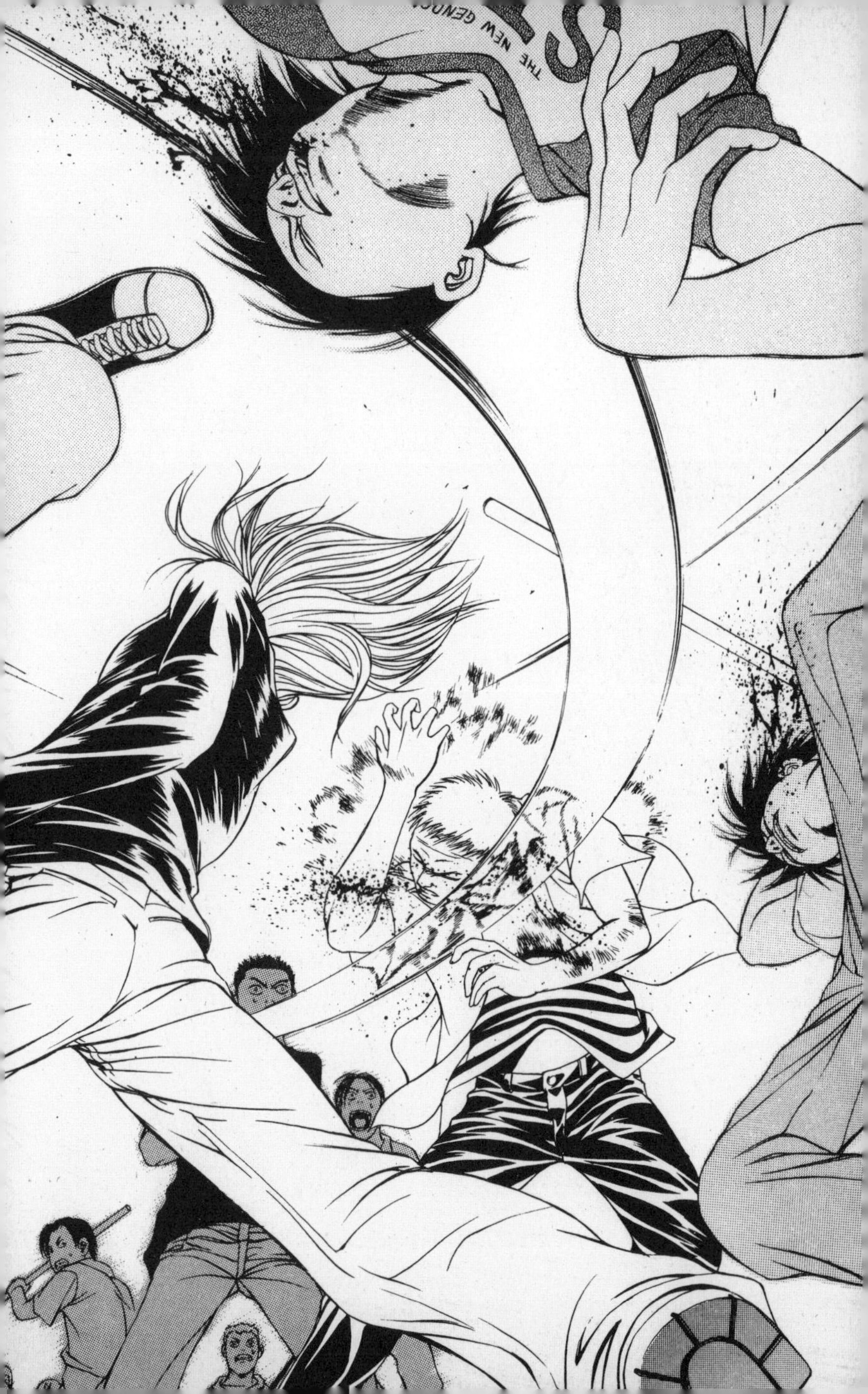

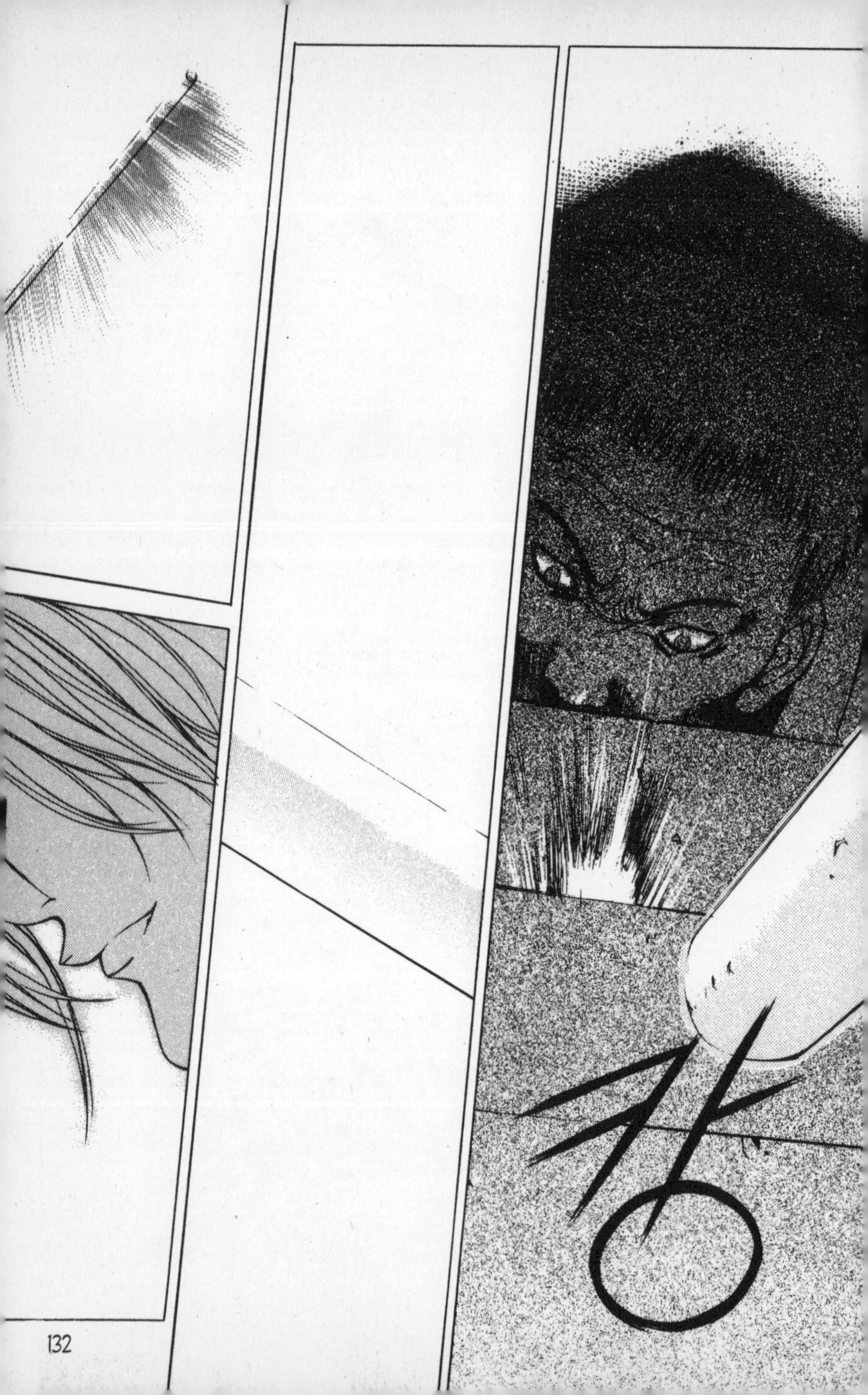

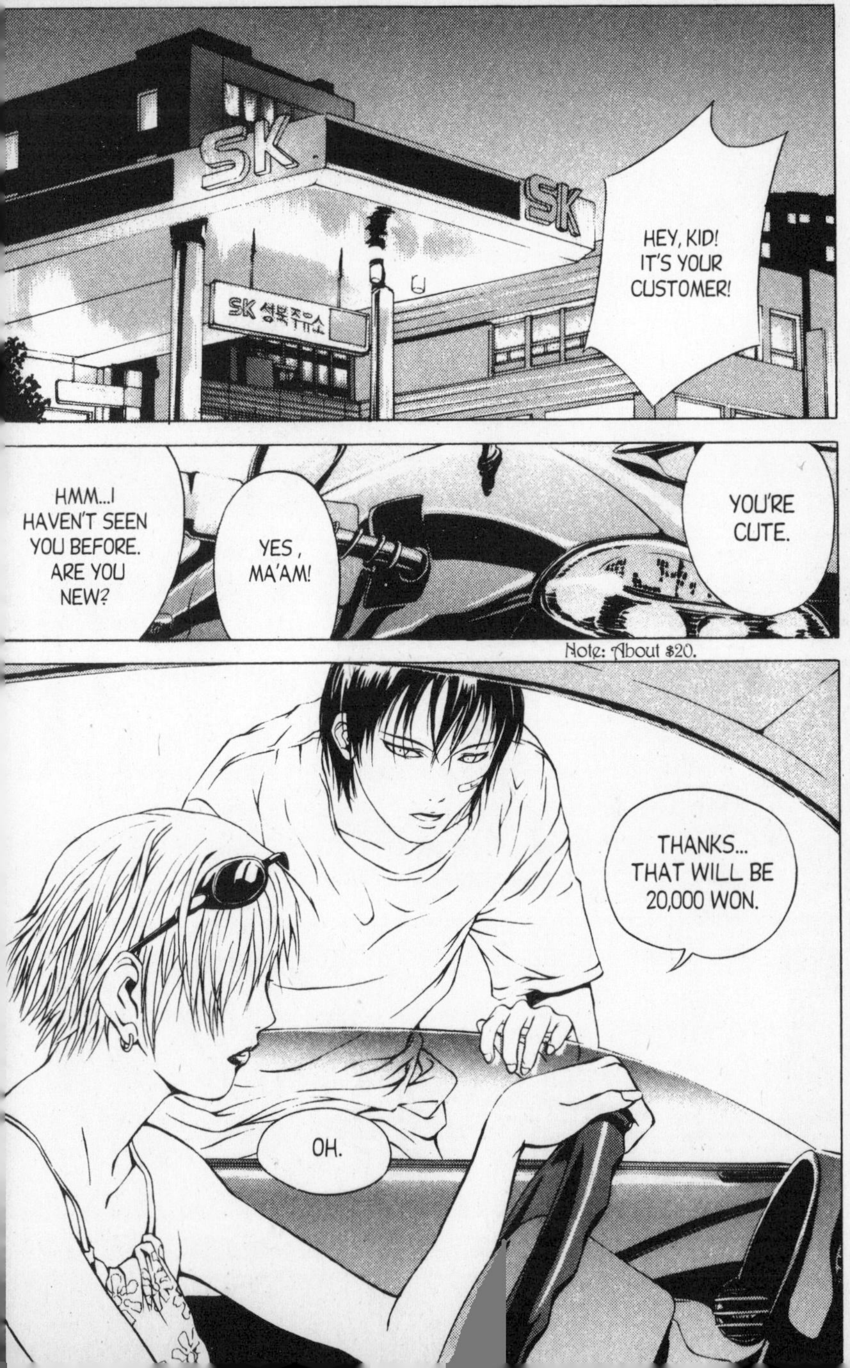
SK
SK
SK 성북주유소
HEY, KID! IT'S YOUR CUSTOMER!
HMM...I HAVEN'T SEEN YOU BEFORE. ARE YOU NEW?
YES , MA'AM!
YOU'RE CUTE.
THANKS... THAT WILL BE 20,000 WON.
OH.

Note: About $20.

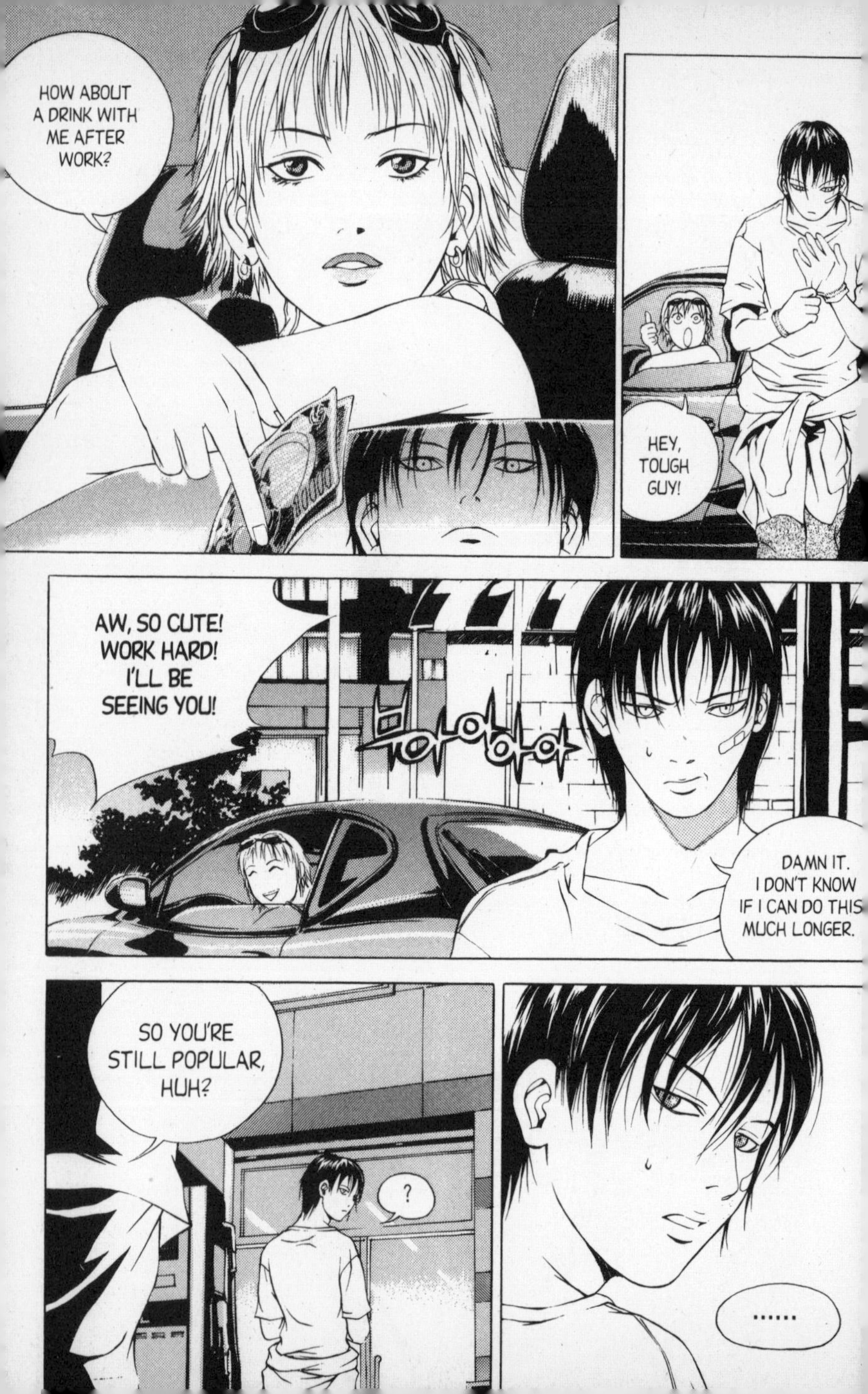
HOW ABOUT A DRINK WITH ME AFTER WORK?
HEY, TOUGH GUY!
AW, SO CUTE! WORK HARD! I'LL BE SEEING YOU!
DAMN IT. I DON'T KNOW IF I CAN DO THIS MUCH LONGER.
SO YOU'RE STILL POPULAR, HUH?
?
......

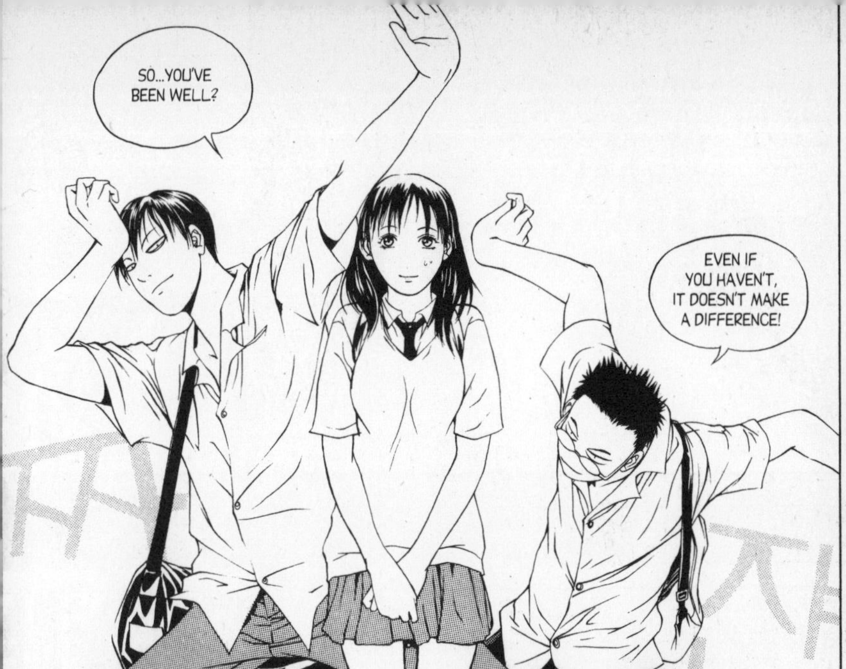
SO...YOU'VE BEEN WELL?
EVEN IF YOU HAVEN'T, IT DOESN'T MAKE A DIFFERENCE!
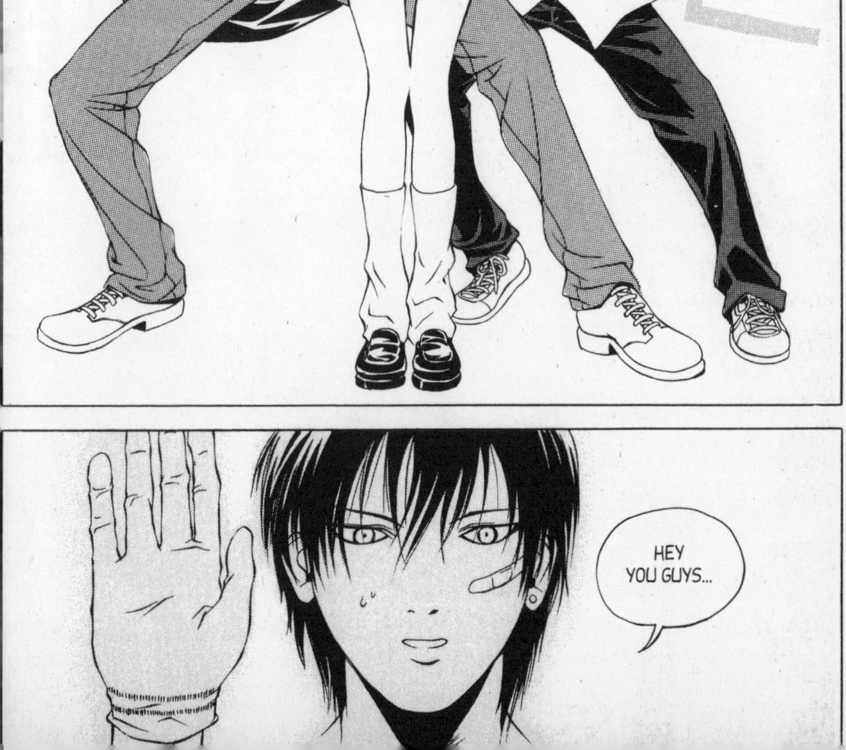
HEY YOU GUYS...

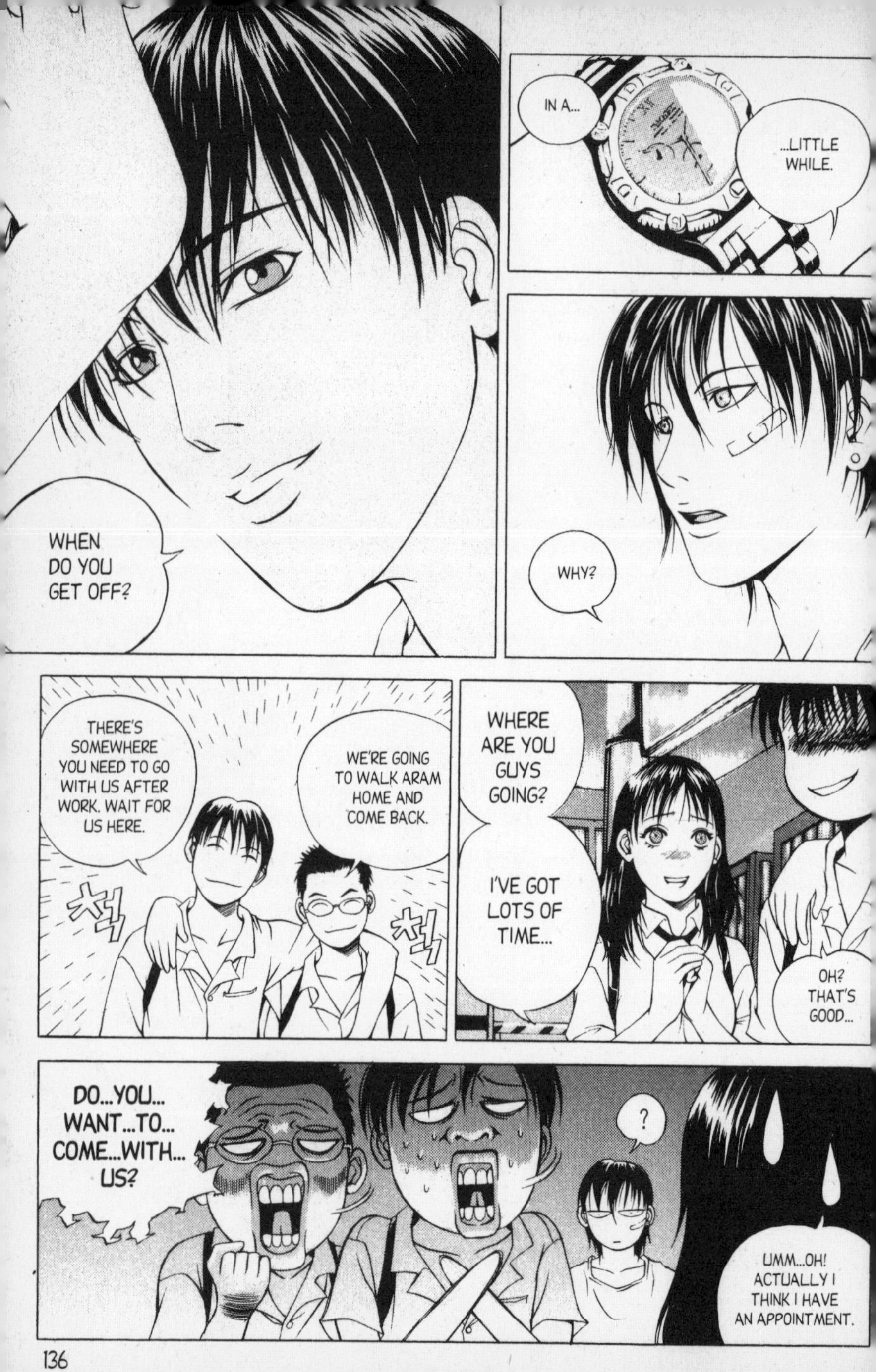
WHEN DO YOU GET OFF?
IN A...
...LITTLE WHILE.
WHY?
THERE'S SOMEWHERE YOU NEED TO GO WITH US AFTER WORK. WAIT FOR US HERE.
WE'RE GOING TO WALK ARAM HOME AND COME BACK.
척
척
WHERE ARE YOU GUYS GOING?
I'VE GOT LOTS OF TIME...
OH? THAT'S GOOD...
DO...YOU... WANT...TO... COME...WITH... US?
?
UMM...OH! ACTUALLY I THINK I HAVE AN APPOINTMENT.

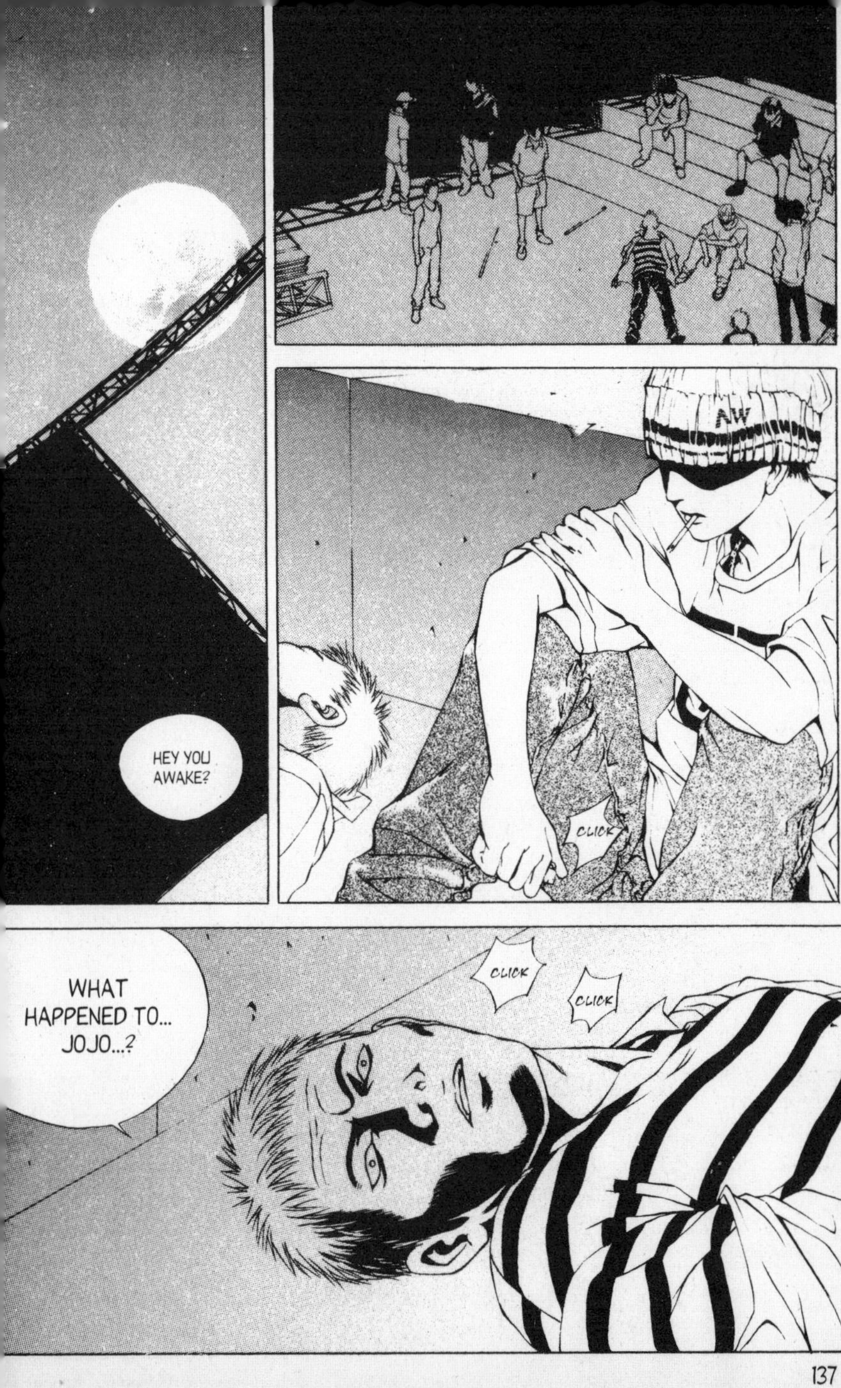
CLICK
HEY YOU AWAKE?
WHAT HAPPENED TO... JOJO...?
CLICK
CLICK

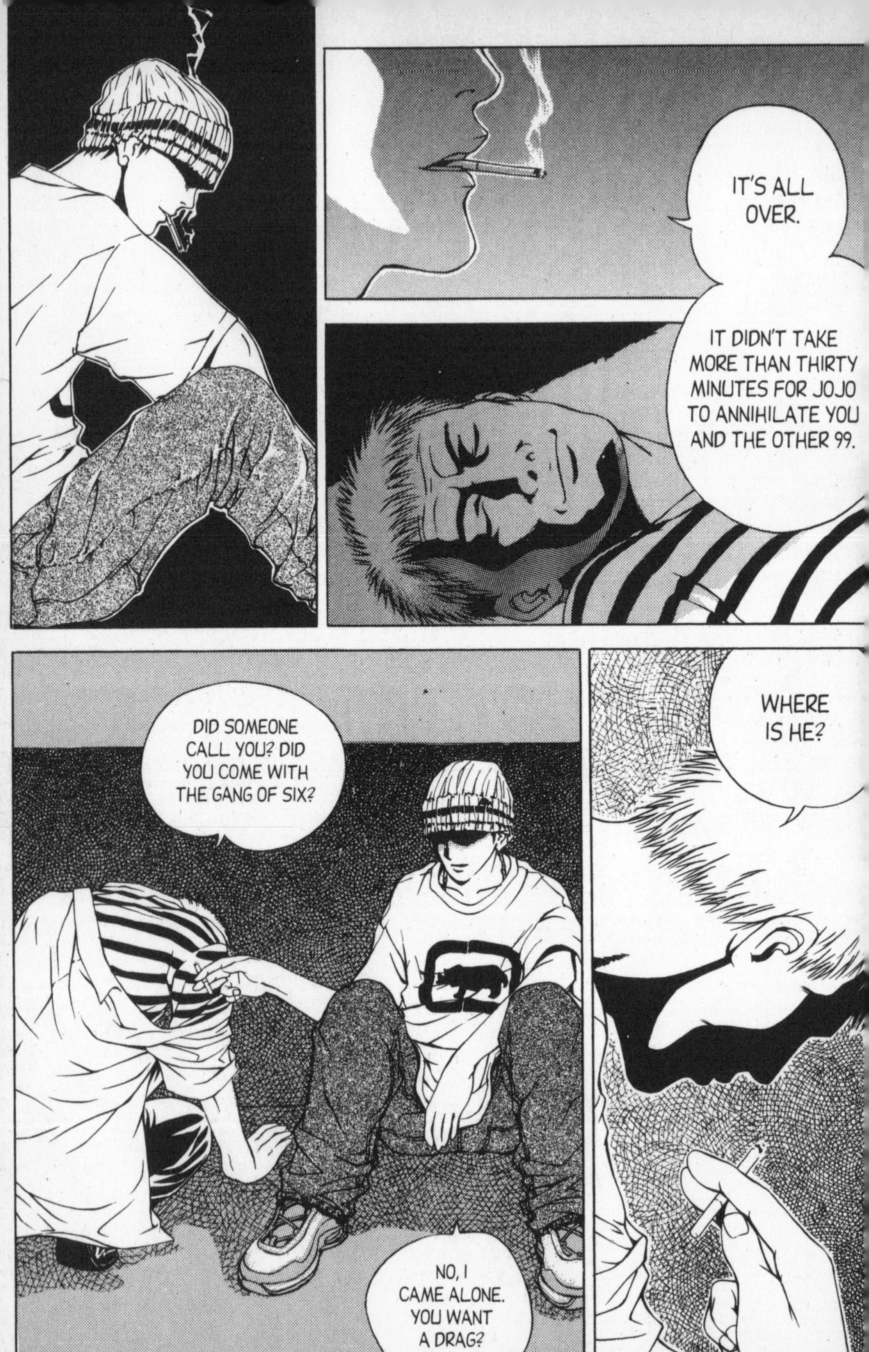
IT'S ALL OVER.
IT DIDN'T TAKE MORE THAN THIRTY MINUTES FOR JOJO TO ANNIHILATE YOU AND THE OTHER 99.
WHERE IS HE?
DID SOMEONE CALL YOU? DID YOU COME WITH THE GANG OF SIX?
NO, I CAME ALONE. YOU WANT A DRAG?

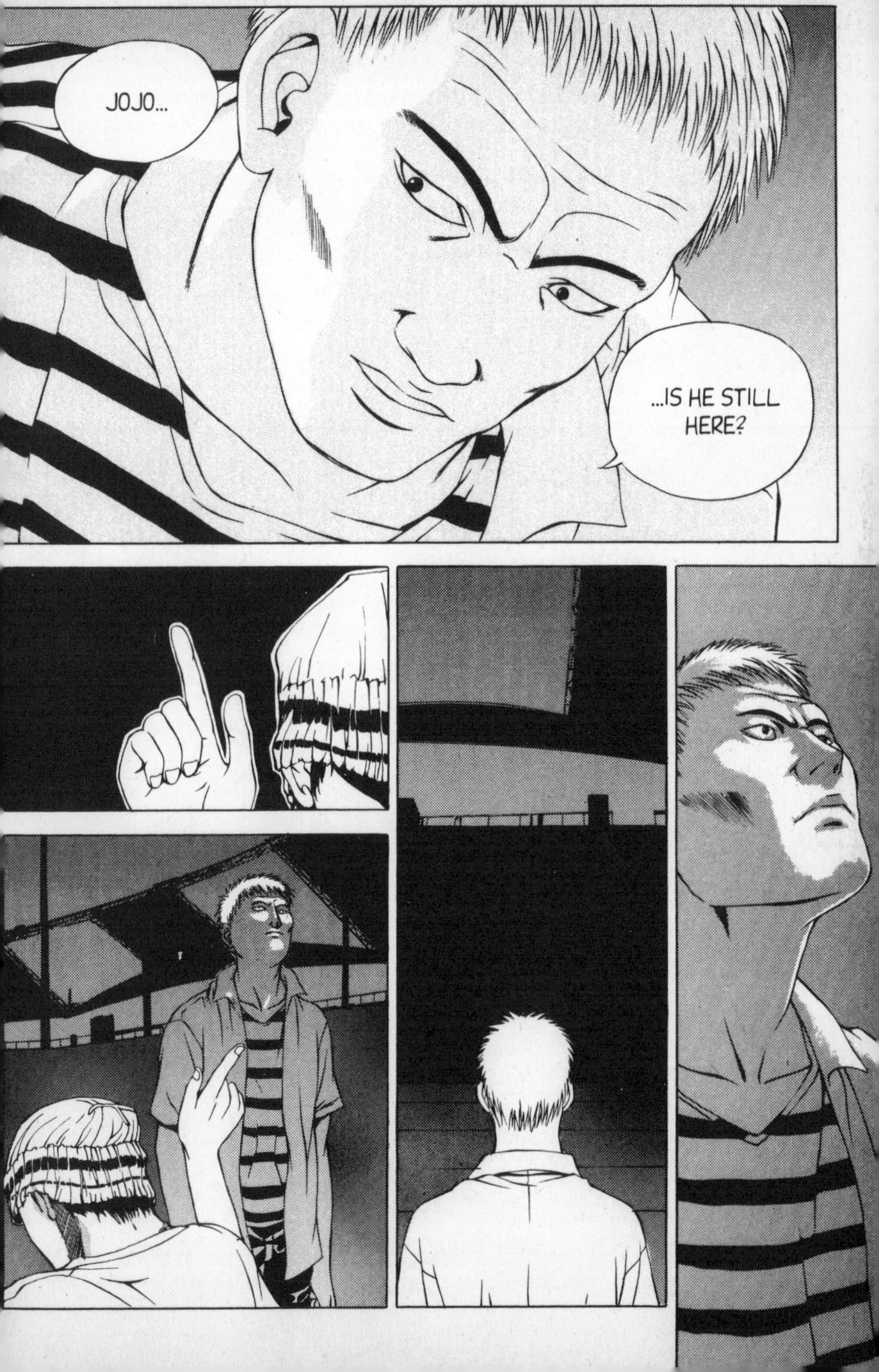
JOJO...
...IS HE STILL HERE?

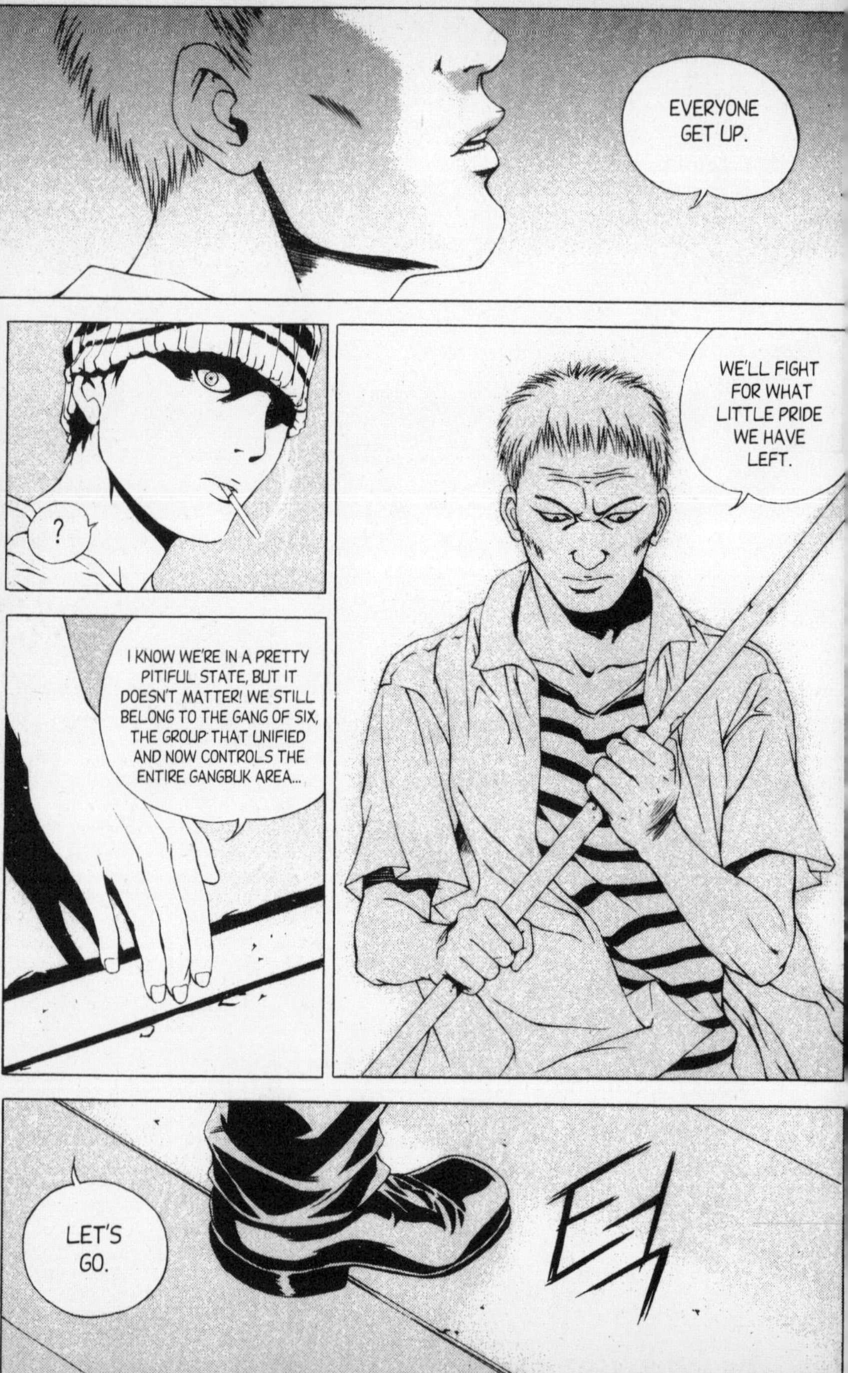
EVERYONE GET UP.
?
I KNOW WE'RE IN A PRETTY PITIFUL STATE, BUT IT DOESN'T MATTER! WE STILL BELONG TO THE GANG OF SIX, THE GROUP THAT UNIFIED AND NOW CONTROLS THE ENTIRE GANGBUK AREA...
WE'LL FIGHT FOR WHAT LITTLE PRIDE WE HAVE LEFT.
LET'S GO.

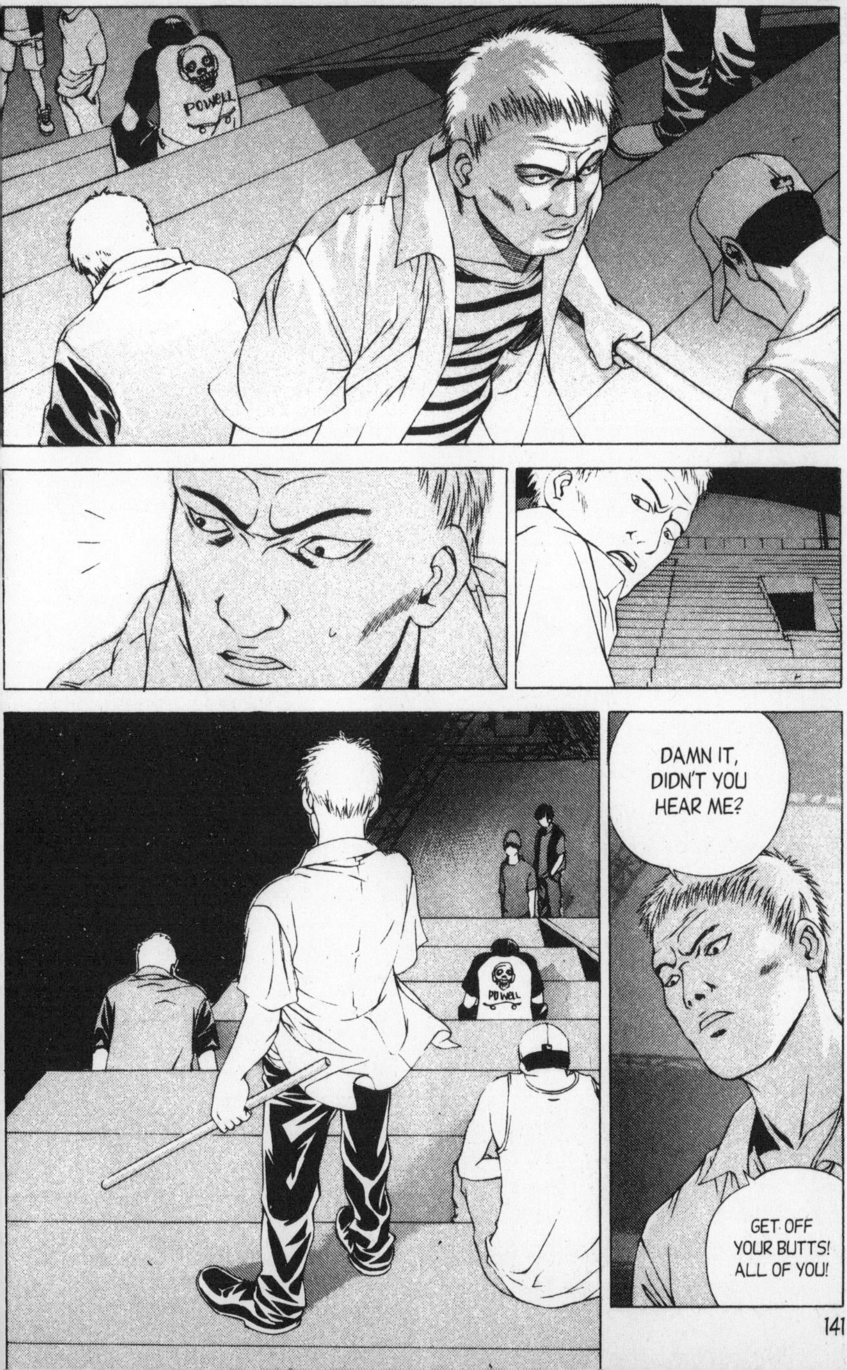
POWELL
POWELL
DAMN IT, DIDN'T YOU HEAR ME?
GET OFF YOUR BUTTS! ALL OF YOU!

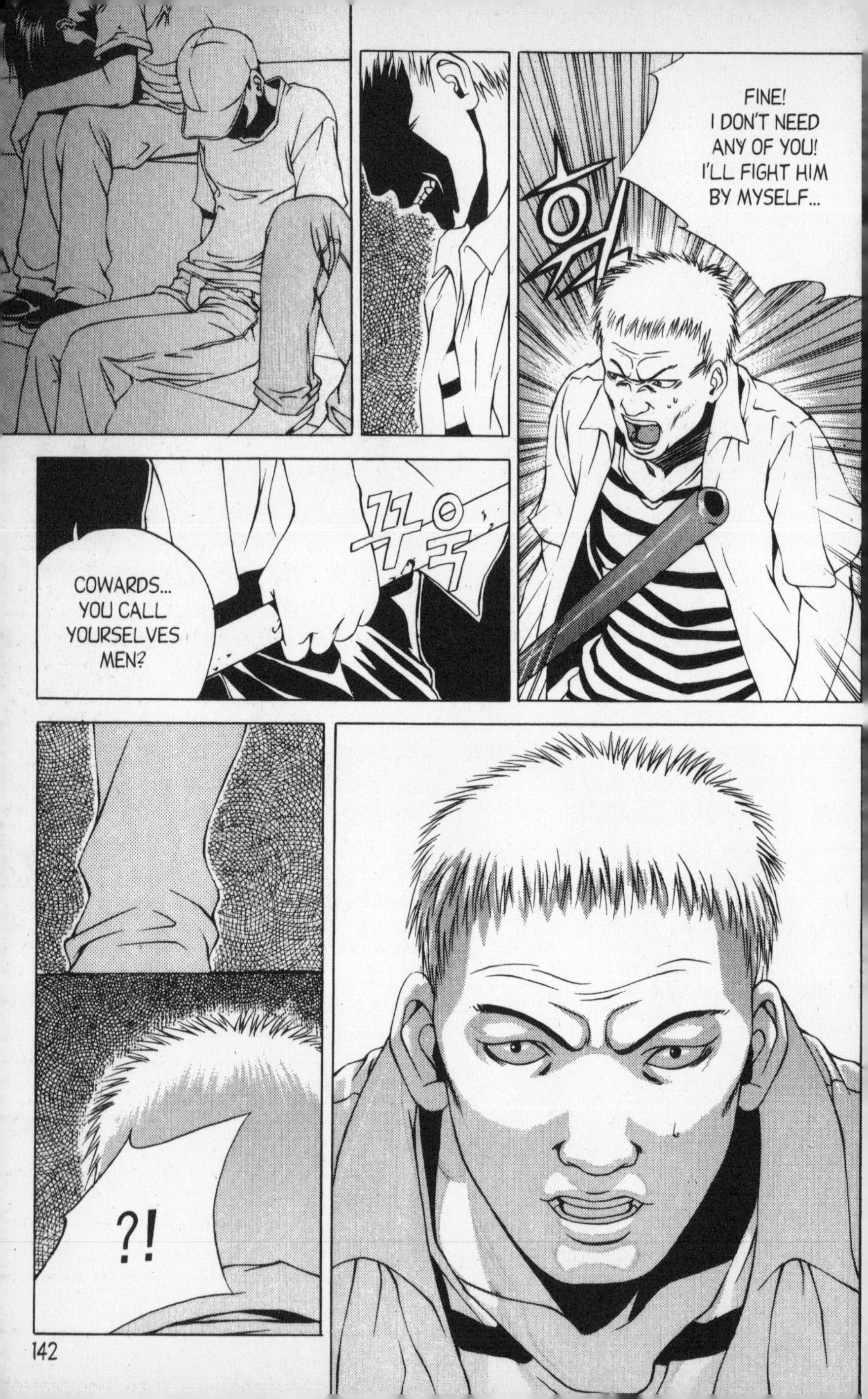
FINE!
I DON'T NEED
ANY OF YOU!
I'LL FIGHT HIM
BY MYSELF...
COWARDS...
YOU CALL
YOURSELVES
MEN?
?!

#20. A PICKPOCKET GIRL

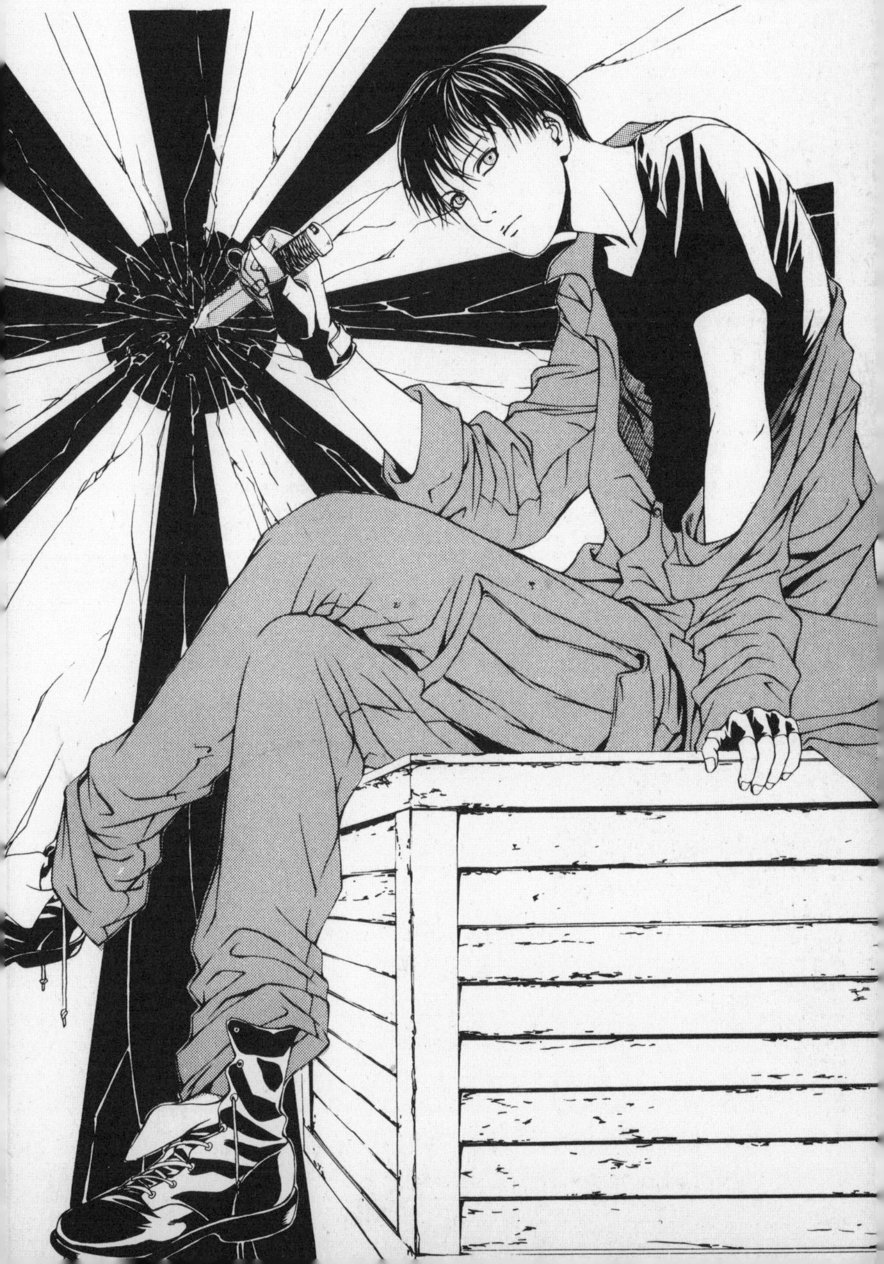

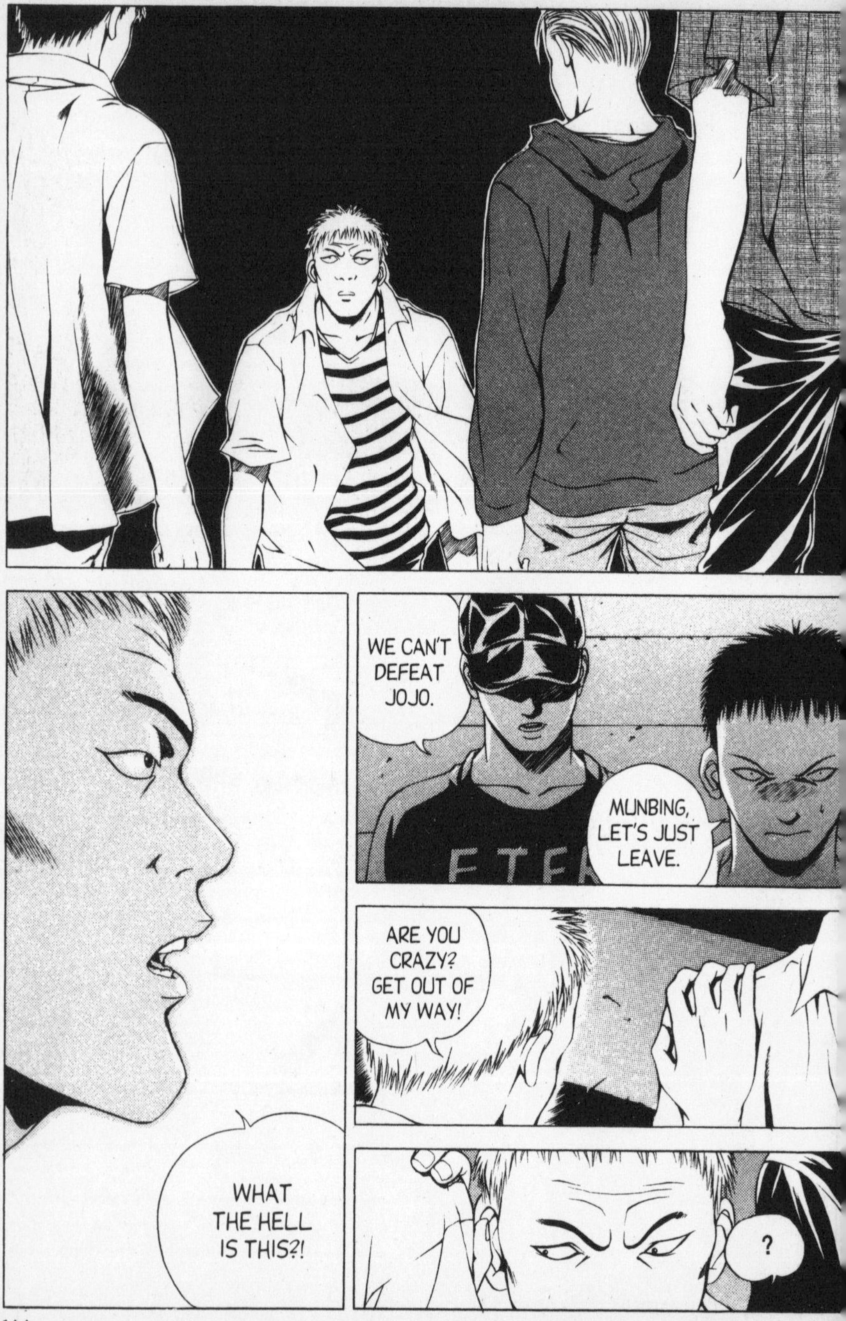
WE CAN'T DEFEAT JOJO.
MUNBING, LET'S JUST LEAVE.
ARE YOU CRAZY? GET OUT OF MY WAY!
?
WHAT THE HELL IS THIS?!

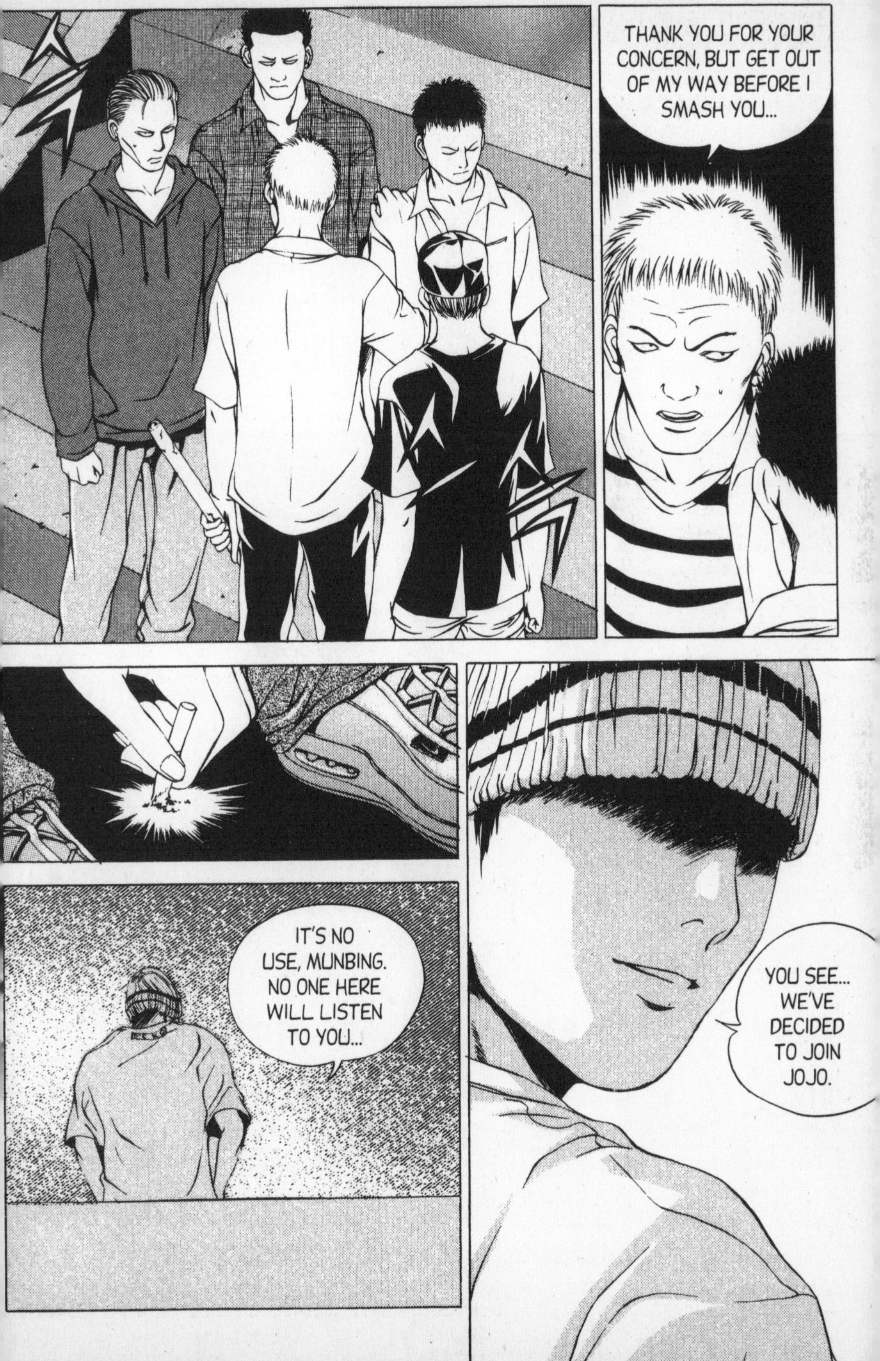
THANK YOU FOR YOUR CONCERN, BUT GET OUT OF MY WAY BEFORE I SMASH YOU...
IT'S NO USE, MUNBING. NO ONE HERE WILL LISTEN TO YOU...
YOU SEE... WE'VE DECIDED TO JOIN JOJO.

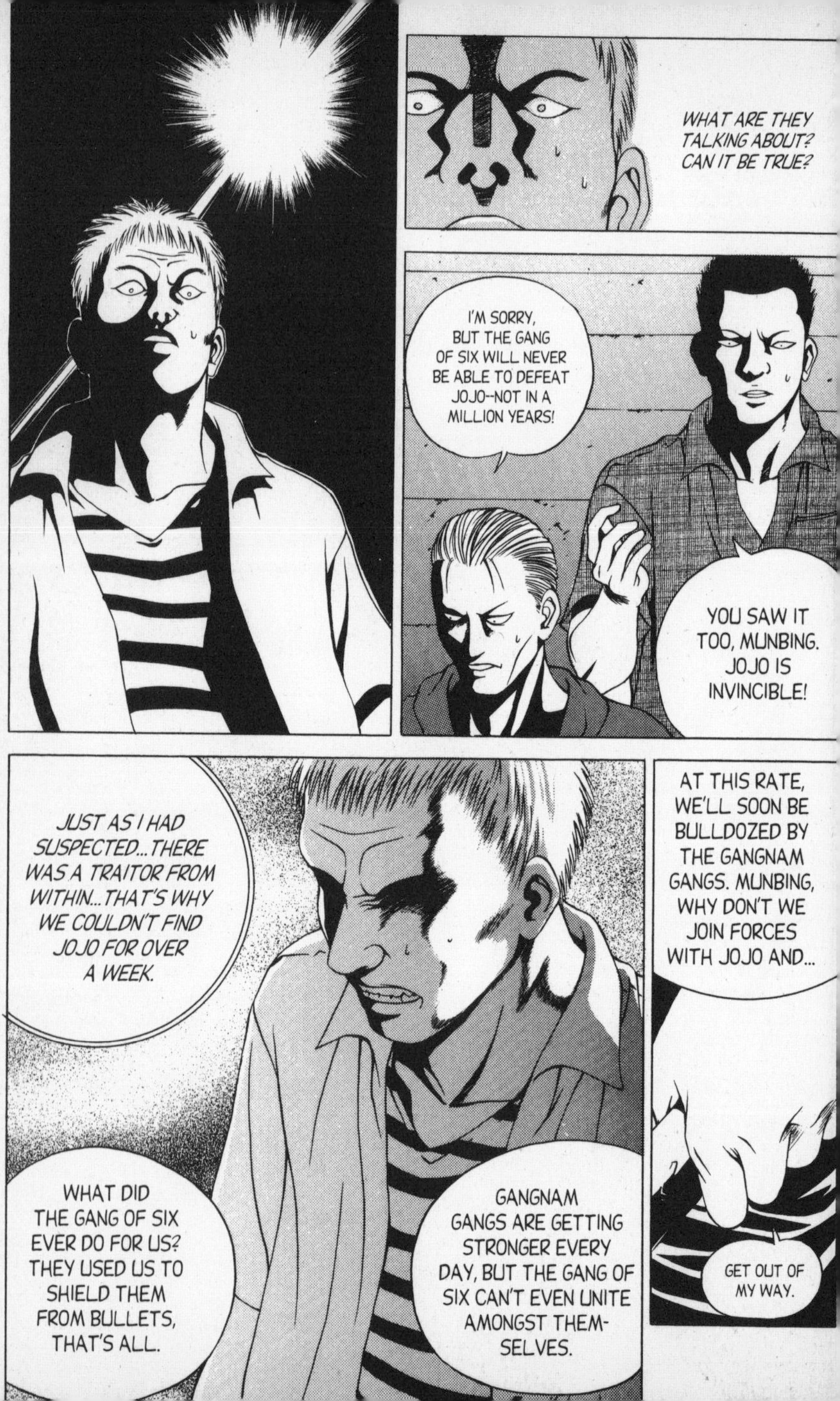
WHAT ARE THEY TALKING ABOUT? CAN IT BE TRUE?
I'M SORRY, BUT THE GANG OF SIX WILL NEVER BE ABLE TO DEFEAT JOJO--NOT IN A MILLION YEARS!
YOU SAW IT TOO, MUNBING. JOJO IS INVINCIBLE!
JUST AS I HAD SUSPECTED...THERE WAS A TRAITOR FROM WITHIN...THAT'S WHY WE COULDN'T FIND JOJO FOR OVER A WEEK.
WHAT DID THE GANG OF SIX EVER DO FOR US? THEY USED US TO SHIELD THEM FROM BULLETS, THAT'S ALL.
GANGNAM GANGS ARE GETTING STRONGER EVERY DAY, BUT THE GANG OF SIX CAN'T EVEN UNITE AMONGST THEM-SELVES.
AT THIS RATE, WE'LL SOON BE BULLDOZED BY THE GANGNAM GANGS. MUNBING, WHY DON'T WE JOIN FORCES WITH JOJO AND...
GET OUT OF MY WAY.

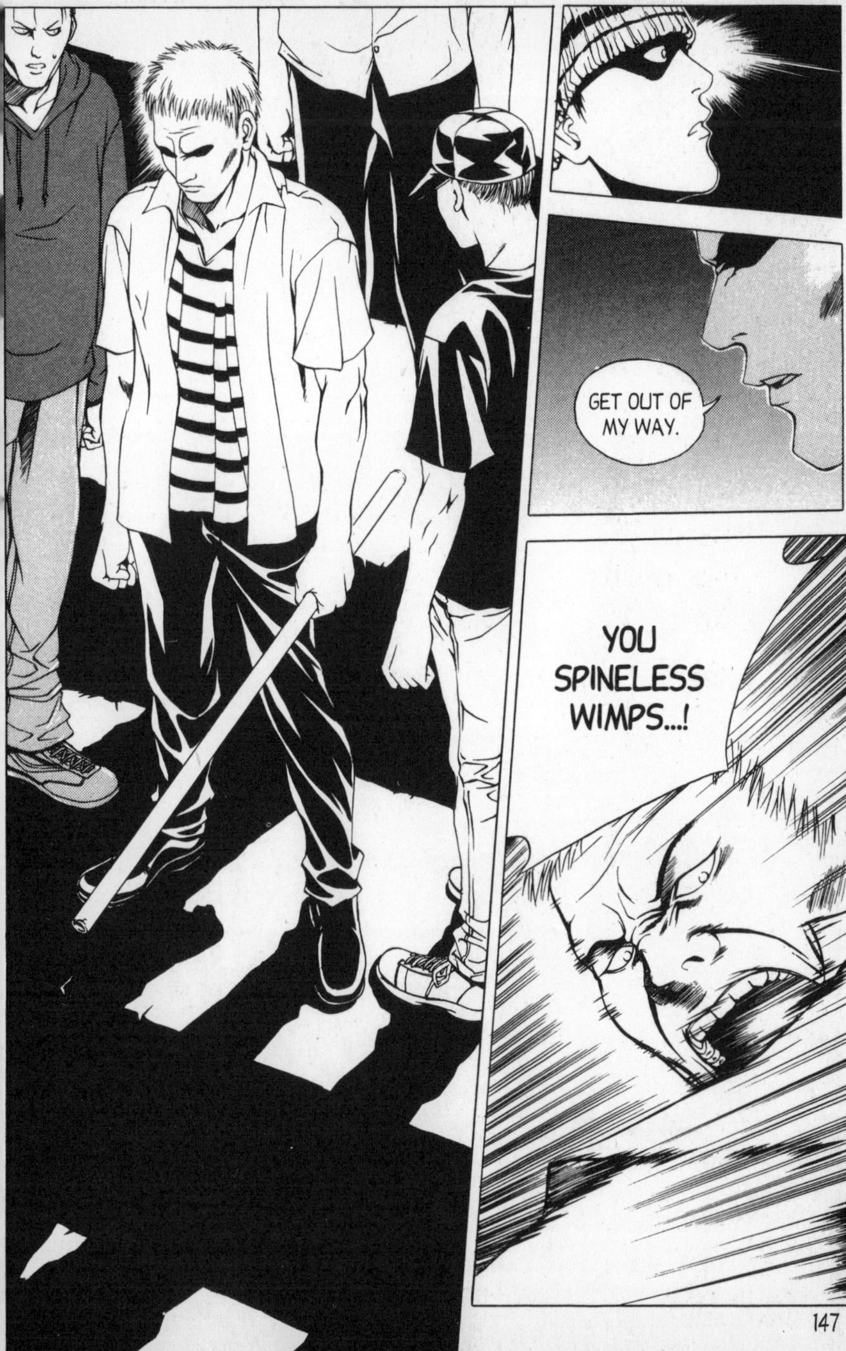
GET OUT OF MY WAY.
YOU SPINELESS WIMPS...!

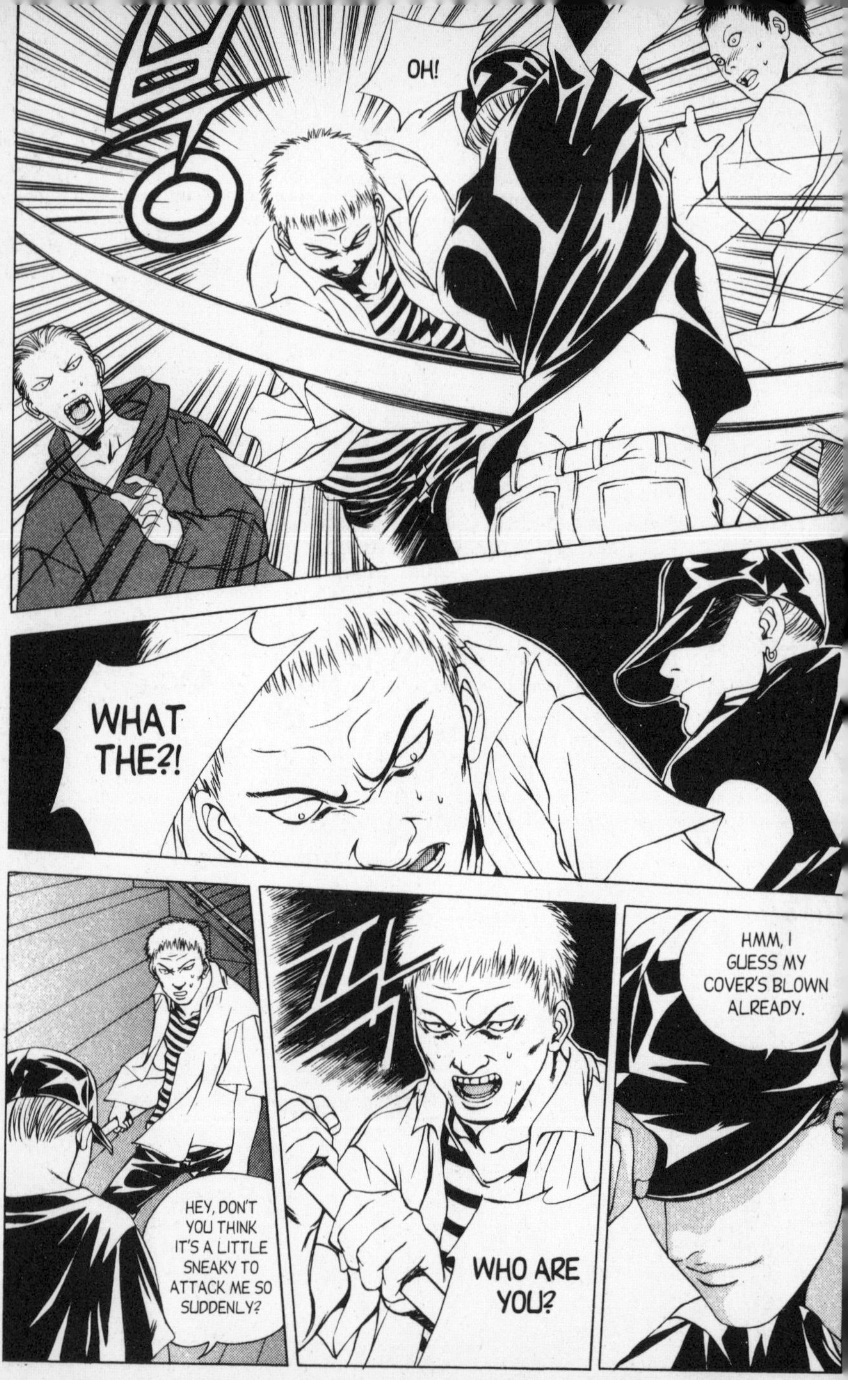
OH!
WHAT THE?!
HMM, I GUESS MY COVER'S BLOWN ALREADY.
WHO ARE YOU?
HEY, DON'T YOU THINK IT'S A LITTLE SNEAKY TO ATTACK ME SO SUDDENLY?

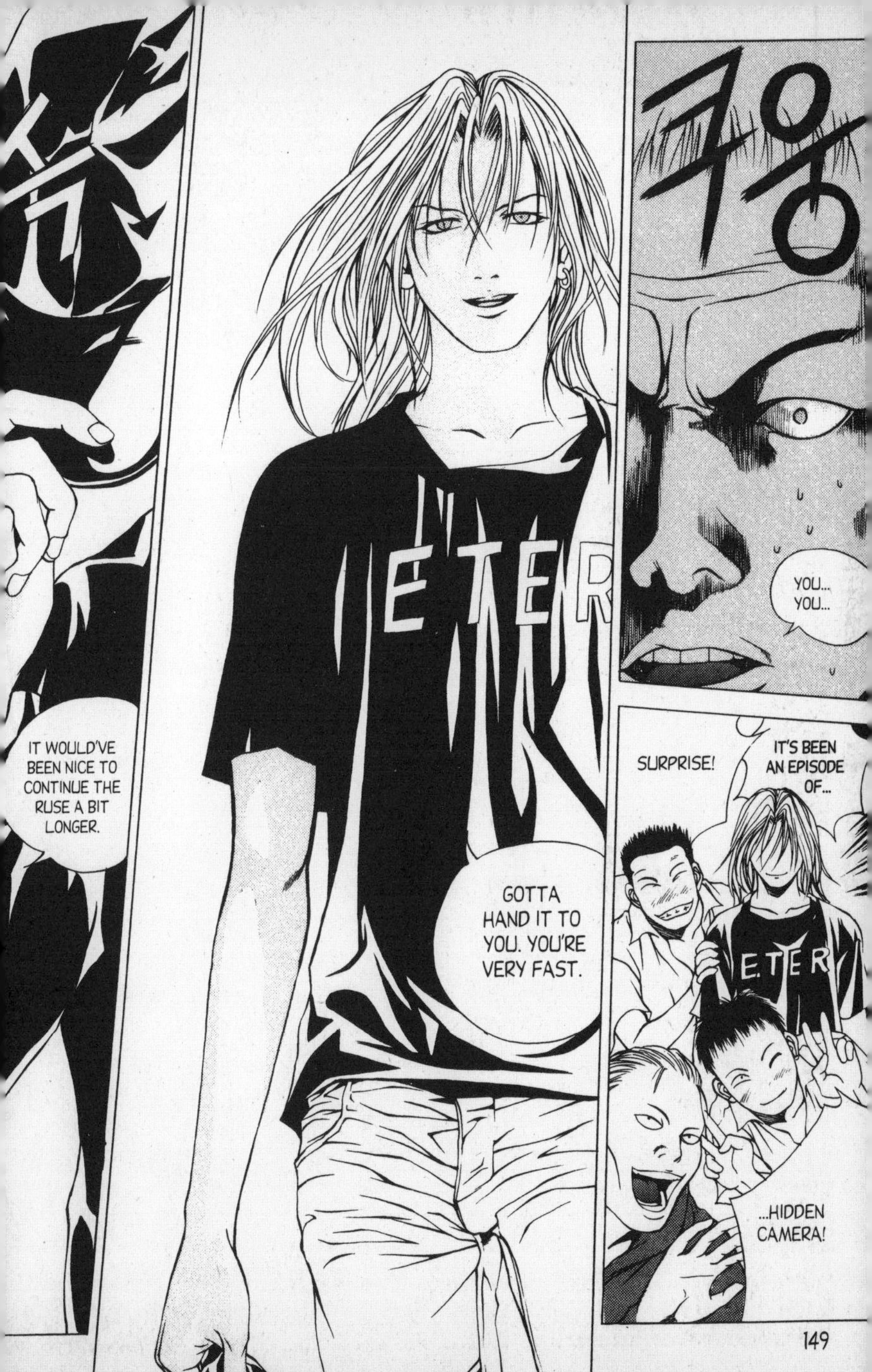
쿠웅
YOU... YOU...
SURPRISE!
IT'S BEEN AN EPISODE OF...
...HIDDEN CAMERA!
GOTTA HAND IT TO YOU. YOU'RE VERY FAST.
IT WOULD'VE BEEN NICE TO CONTINUE THE RUSE A BIT LONGER.

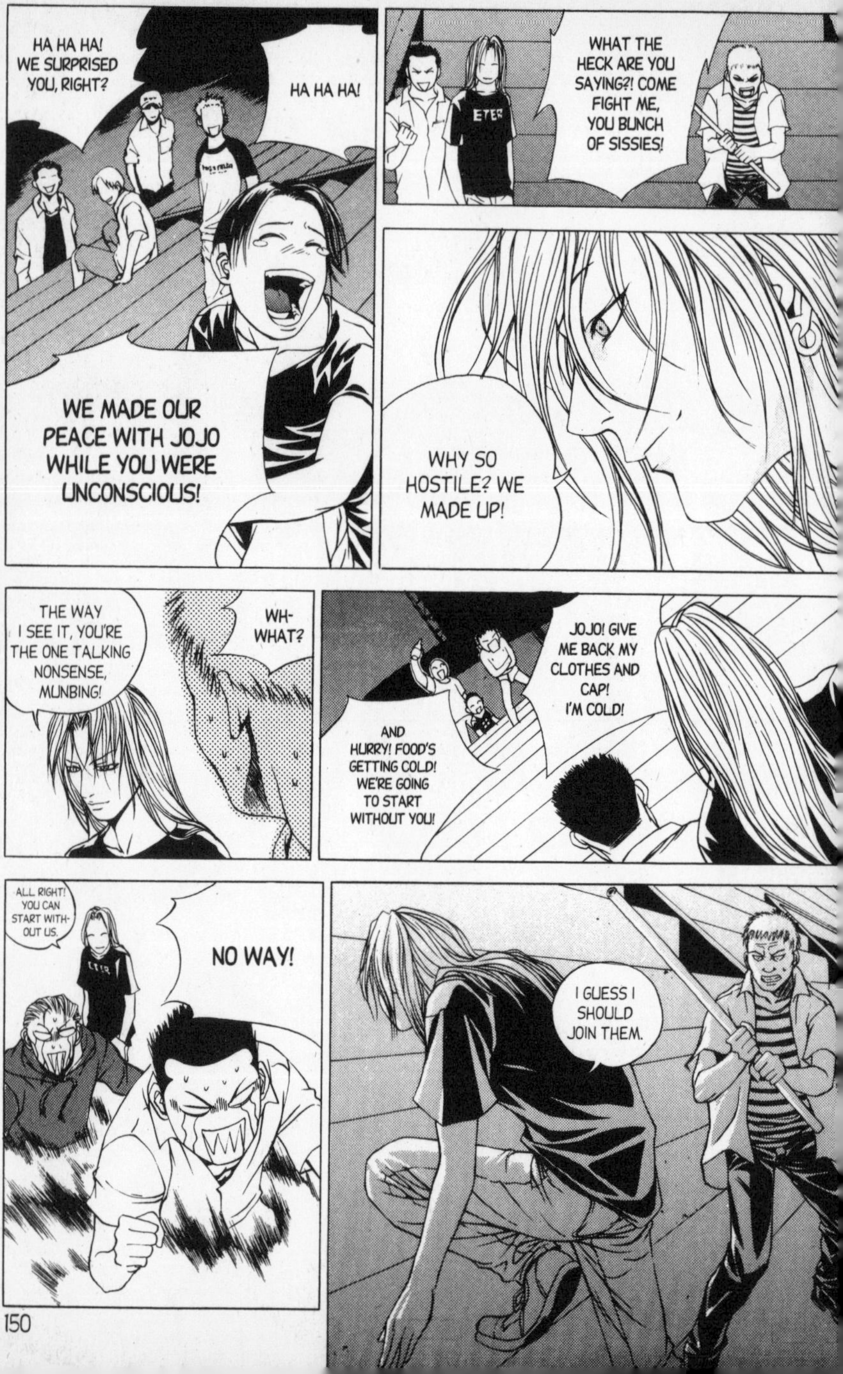
HA HA HA! WE SURPRISED YOU, RIGHT?
HA HA HA!
WE MADE OUR PEACE WITH JOJO WHILE YOU WERE UNCONSCIOUS!
WHAT THE HECK ARE YOU SAYING?! COME FIGHT ME, YOU BUNCH OF SISSIES!
WHY SO HOSTILE? WE MADE UP!
THE WAY I SEE IT, YOU'RE THE ONE TALKING NONSENSE, MUNBING!
WH- WHAT?
JOJO! GIVE ME BACK MY CLOTHES AND CAP! I'M COLD!
AND HURRY! FOOD'S GETTING COLD! WE'RE GOING TO START WITHOUT YOU!
ALL RIGHT! YOU CAN START WITH- OUT US.
NO WAY!
I GUESS I SHOULD JOIN THEM.

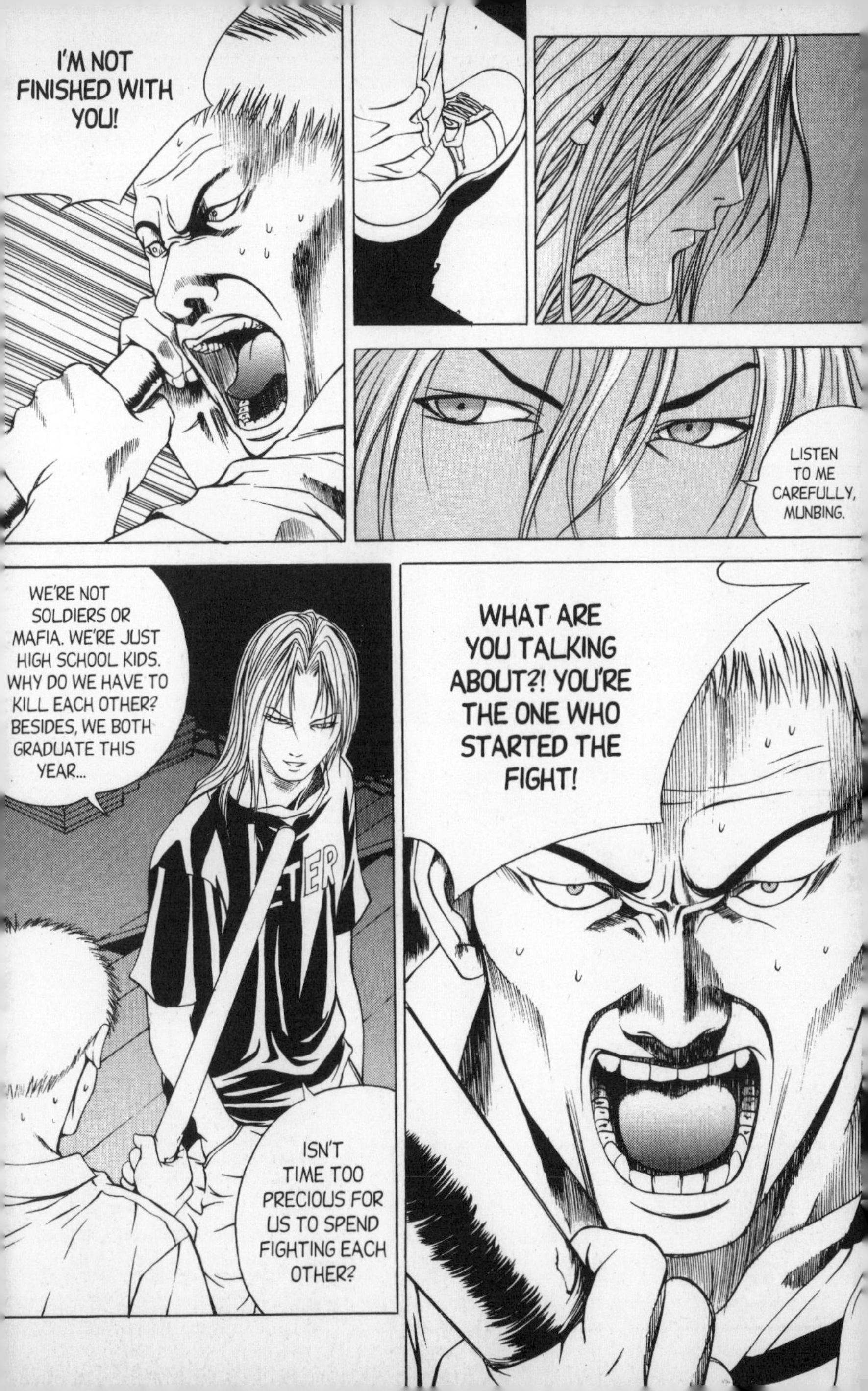
I'M NOT FINISHED WITH YOU!
LISTEN TO ME CAREFULLY, MUNBING.
WE'RE NOT SOLDIERS OR MAFIA. WE'RE JUST HIGH SCHOOL KIDS. WHY DO WE HAVE TO KILL EACH OTHER? BESIDES, WE BOTH GRADUATE THIS YEAR...
ISN'T TIME TOO PRECIOUS FOR US TO SPEND FIGHTING EACH OTHER?
WHAT ARE YOU TALKING ABOUT?! YOU'RE THE ONE WHO STARTED THE FIGHT!

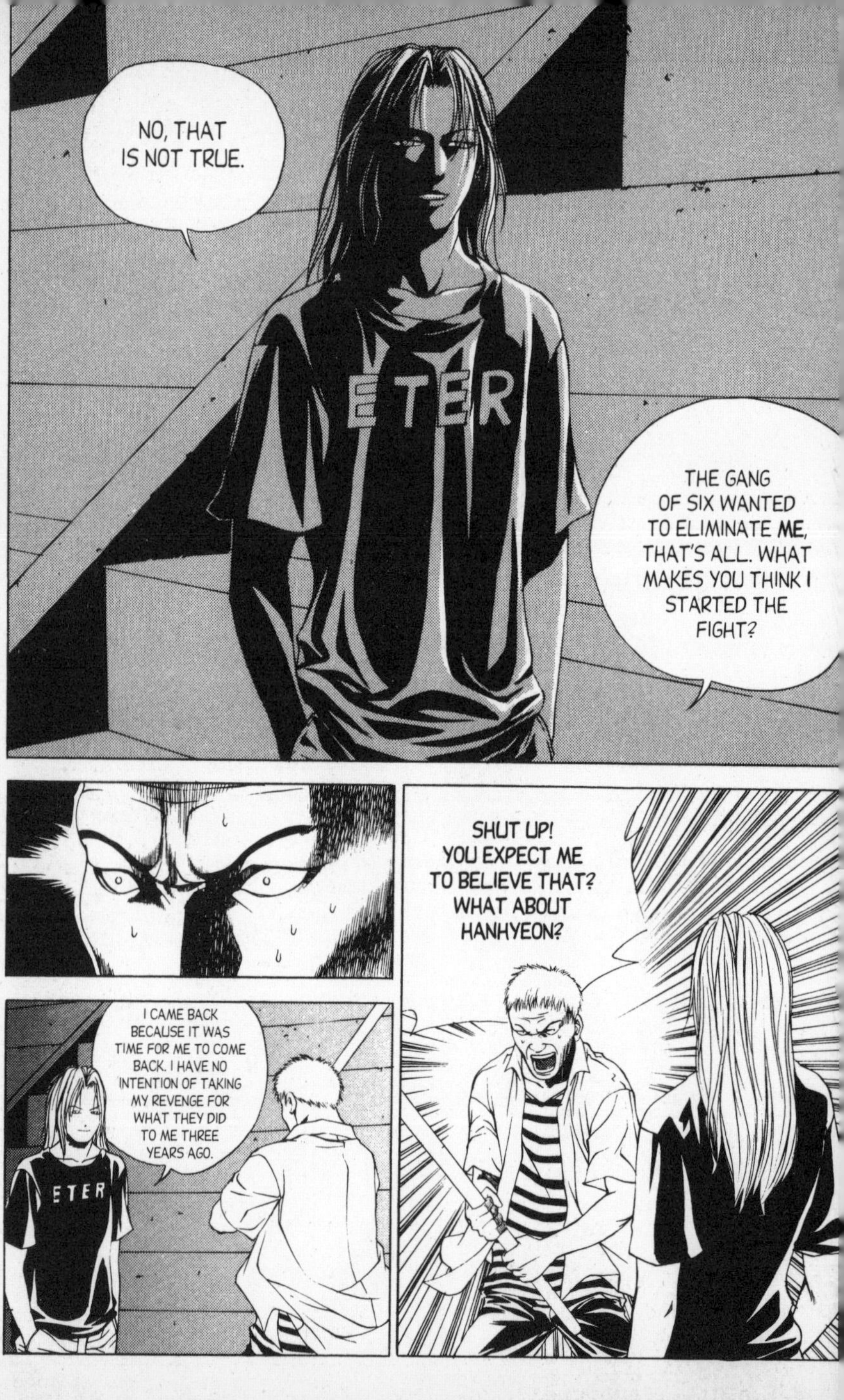
NO, THAT IS NOT TRUE.
THE GANG OF SIX WANTED TO ELIMINATE ME, THAT'S ALL. WHAT MAKES YOU THINK I STARTED THE FIGHT?
I CAME BACK BECAUSE IT WAS TIME FOR ME TO COME BACK. I HAVE NO INTENTION OF TAKING MY REVENGE FOR WHAT THEY DID TO ME THREE YEARS AGO.
SHUT UP! YOU EXPECT ME TO BELIEVE THAT? WHAT ABOUT HANHYEON?

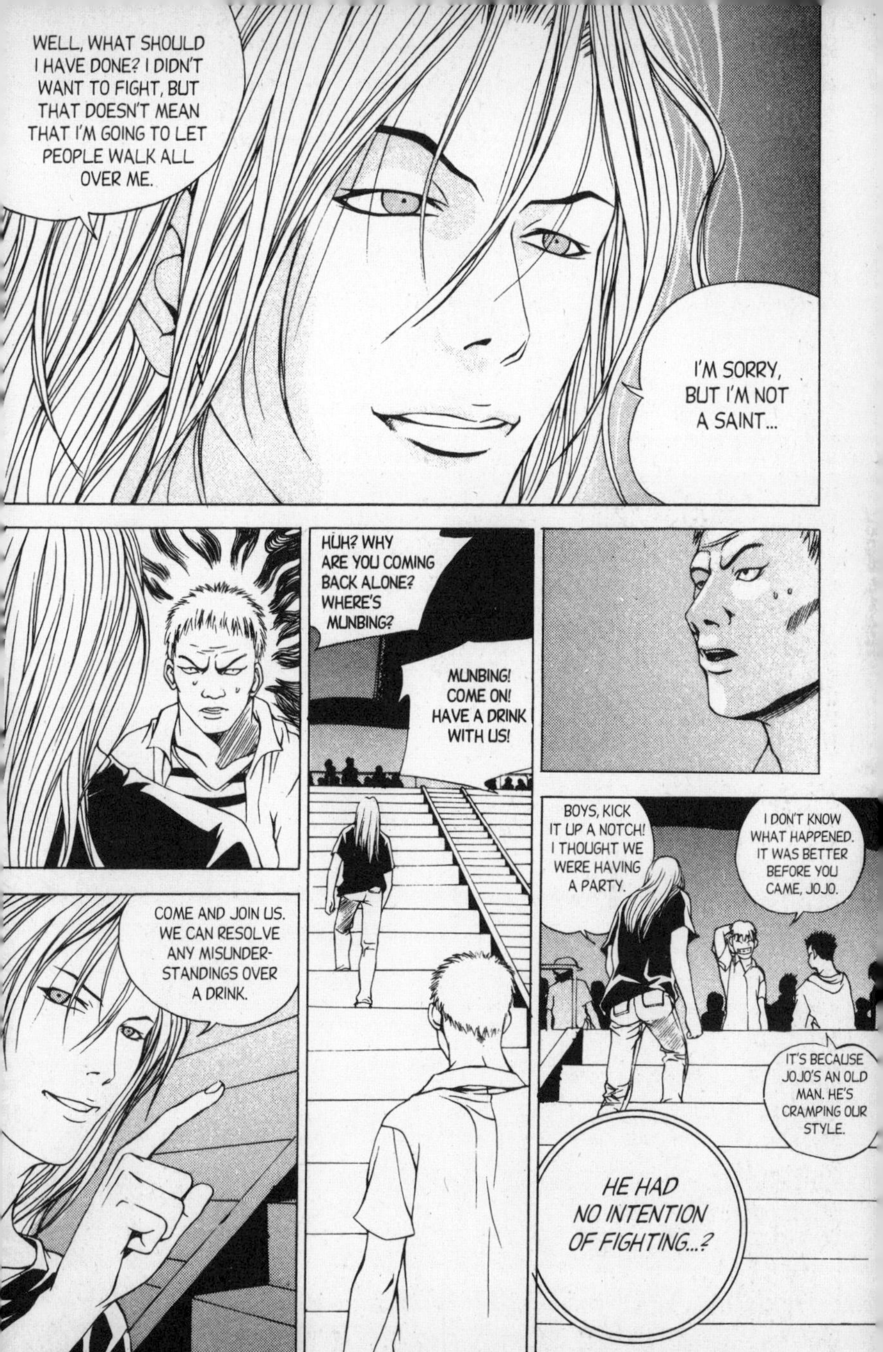
WELL, WHAT SHOULD I HAVE DONE? I DIDN'T WANT TO FIGHT, BUT THAT DOESN'T MEAN THAT I'M GOING TO LET PEOPLE WALK ALL OVER ME.
I'M SORRY, BUT I'M NOT A SAINT...
COME AND JOIN US. WE CAN RESOLVE ANY MISUNDER-STANDINGS OVER A DRINK.
HUH? WHY ARE YOU COMING BACK ALONE? WHERE'S MUNBING?
MUNBING! COME ON! HAVE A DRINK WITH US!
BOYS, KICK IT UP A NOTCH! I THOUGHT WE WERE HAVING A PARTY.
I DON'T KNOW WHAT HAPPENED. IT WAS BETTER BEFORE YOU CAME, JOJO.
IT'S BECAUSE JOJO'S AN OLD MAN. HE'S CRAMPING OUR STYLE.
HE HAD NO INTENTION OF FIGHTING...?

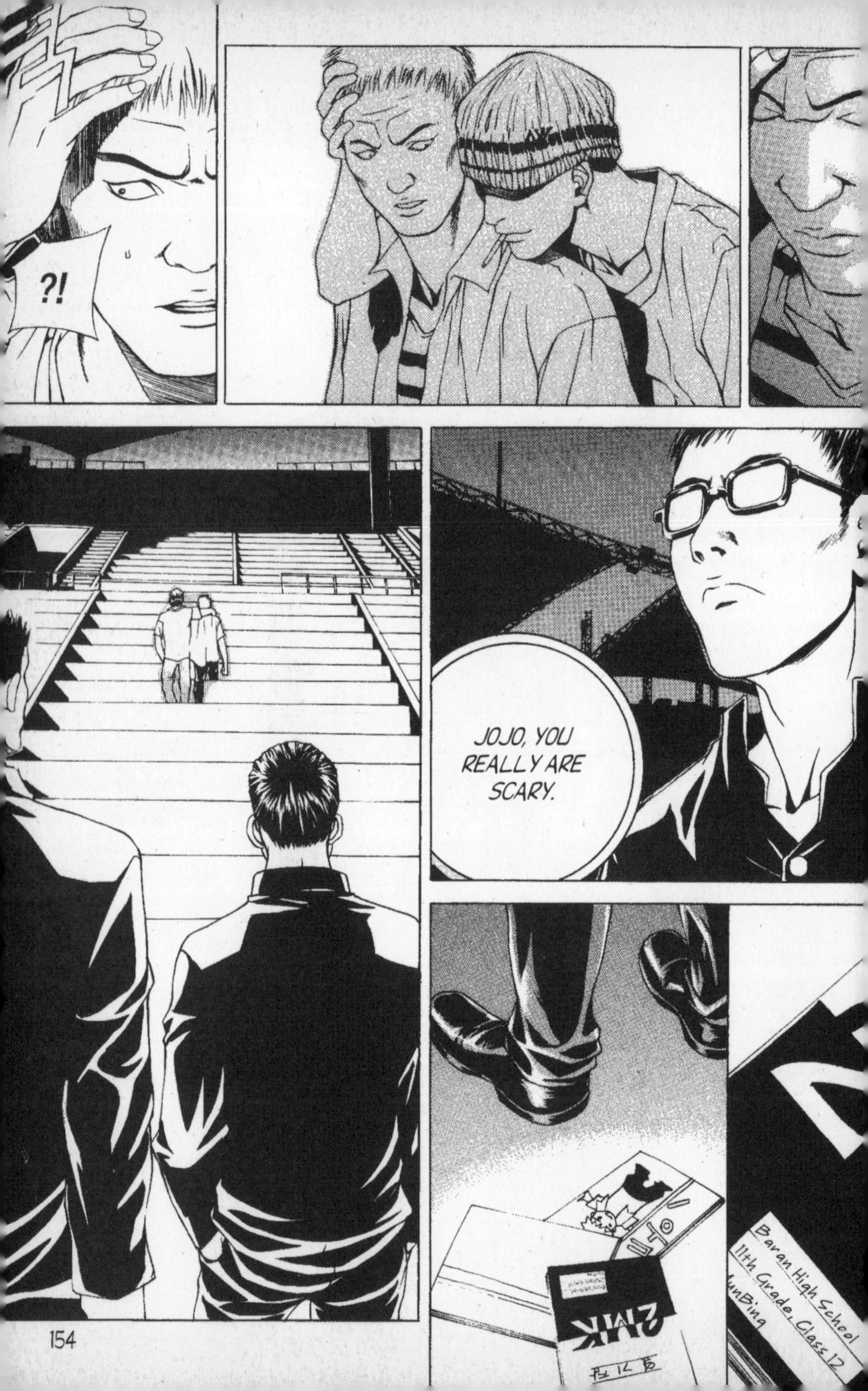
?!
JOJO, YOU REALLY ARE SCARY.
Baran High School
11th Grade, Class 12

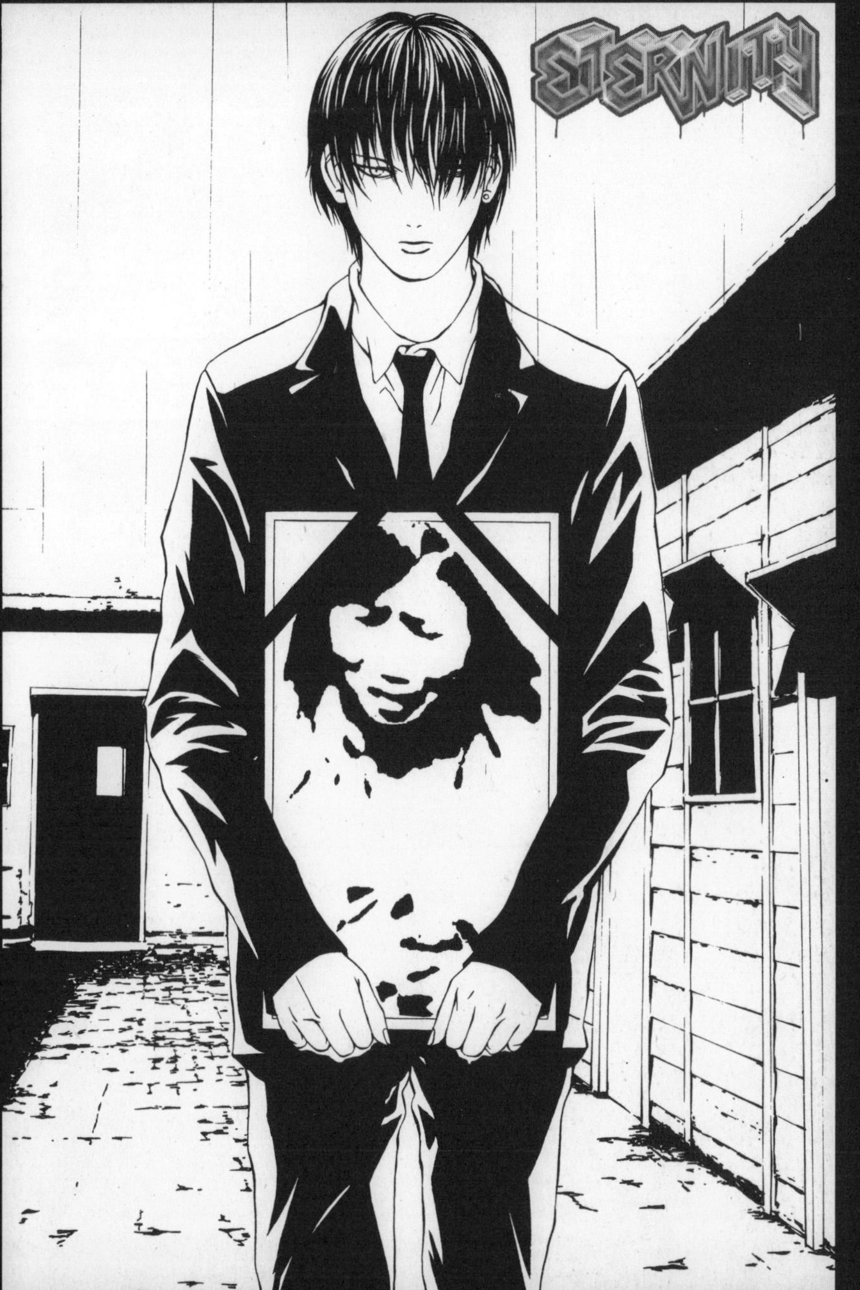
ETERNITY

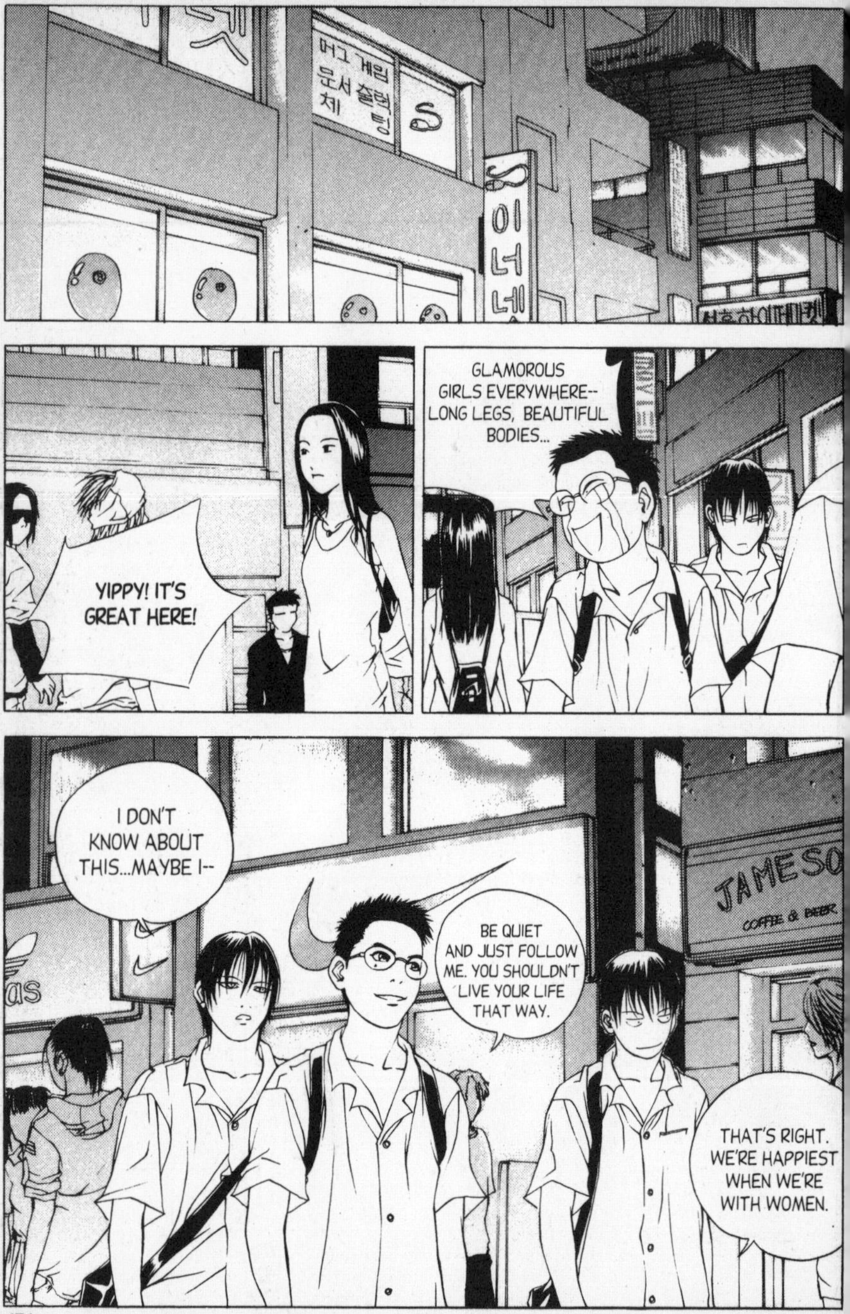
YIPPY! IT'S GREAT HERE!
GLAMOROUS GIRLS EVERYWHERE-- LONG LEGS, BEAUTIFUL BODIES...
I DON'T KNOW ABOUT THIS...MAYBE I--
BE QUIET AND JUST FOLLOW ME. YOU SHOULDN'T LIVE YOUR LIFE THAT WAY.
JAMESO
COFFE & BEER
THAT'S RIGHT. WE'RE HAPPIEST WHEN WE'RE WITH WOMEN.

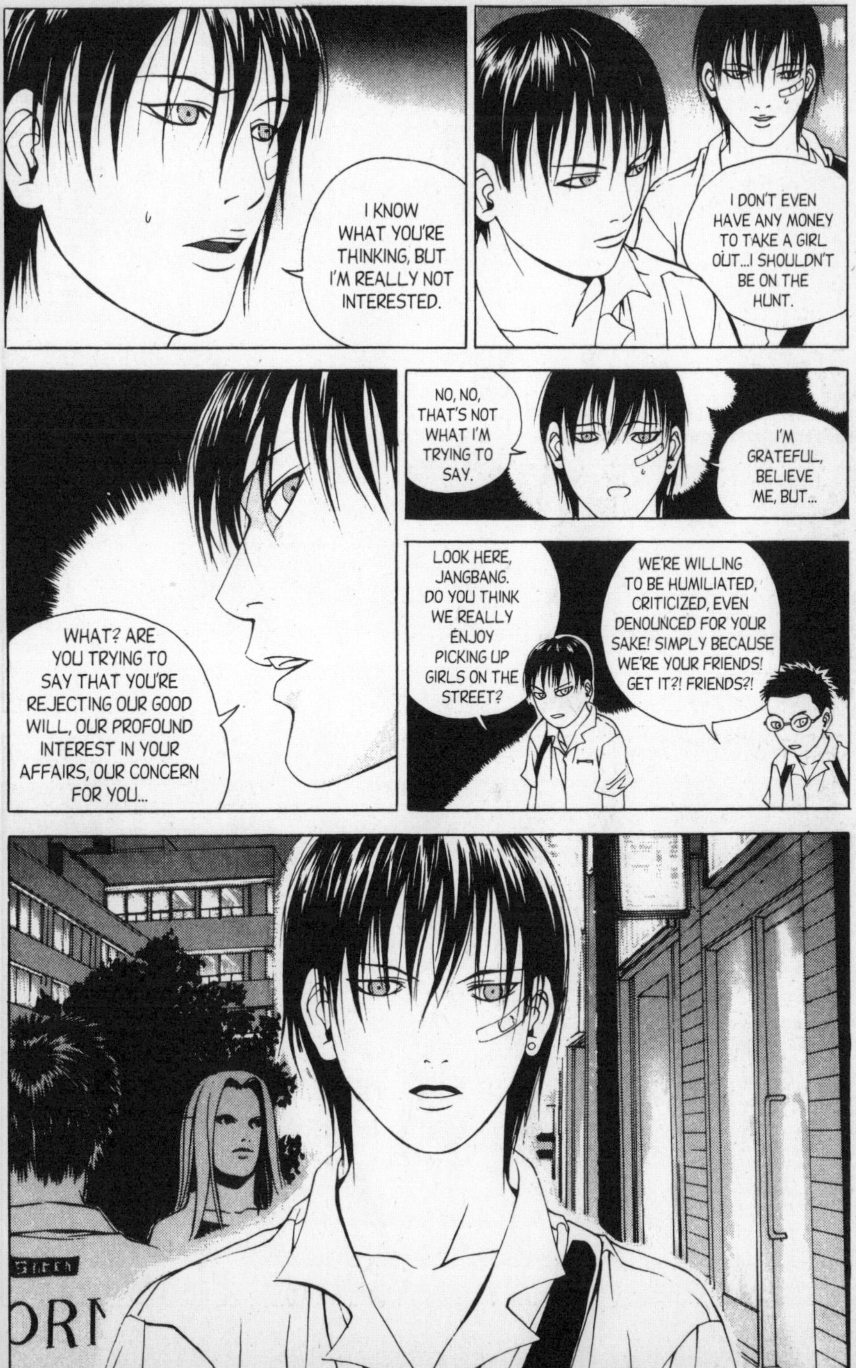
I KNOW WHAT YOU'RE THINKING, BUT I'M REALLY NOT INTERESTED.
I DON'T EVEN HAVE ANY MONEY TO TAKE A GIRL OUT...I SHOULDN'T BE ON THE HUNT.
WHAT? ARE YOU TRYING TO SAY THAT YOU'RE REJECTING OUR GOOD WILL, OUR PROFOUND INTEREST IN YOUR AFFAIRS, OUR CONCERN FOR YOU...
NO, NO, THAT'S NOT WHAT I'M TRYING TO SAY.
I'M GRATEFUL, BELIEVE ME, BUT...
LOOK HERE, JANGBANG. DO YOU THINK WE REALLY ENJOY PICKING UP GIRLS ON THE STREET?
WE'RE WILLING TO BE HUMILIATED, CRITICIZED, EVEN DENOUNCED FOR YOUR SAKE! SIMPLY BECAUSE WE'RE YOUR FRIENDS! GET IT?! FRIENDS?!

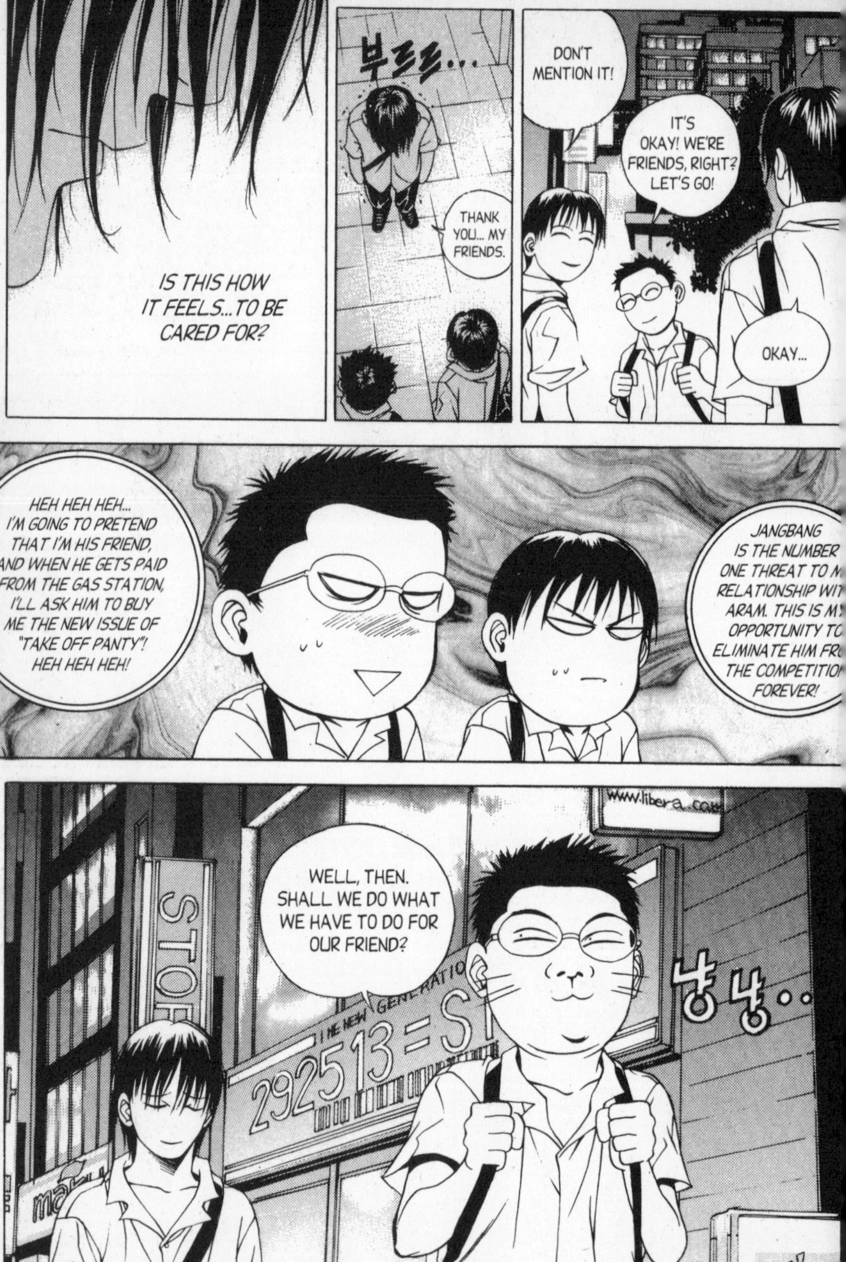
IS THIS HOW IT FEELS...TO BE CARED FOR?
부르르...
THANK YOU... MY FRIENDS.
DON'T MENTION IT!
IT'S OKAY! WE'RE FRIENDS, RIGHT? LET'S GO!
OKAY...
HEH HEH HEH... I'M GOING TO PRETEND THAT I'M HIS FRIEND, AND WHEN HE GETS PAID FROM THE GAS STATION, I'LL ASK HIM TO BUY ME THE NEW ISSUE OF "TAKE OFF PANTY"! HEH HEH HEH!
JANGBANG IS THE NUMBER ONE THREAT TO M RELATIONSHIP WIT ARAM. THIS IS M OPPORTUNITY TO ELIMINATE HIM FR THE COMPETITIO FOREVER!
WELL, THEN. SHALL WE DO WHAT WE HAVE TO DO FOR OUR FRIEND?
낭낭..

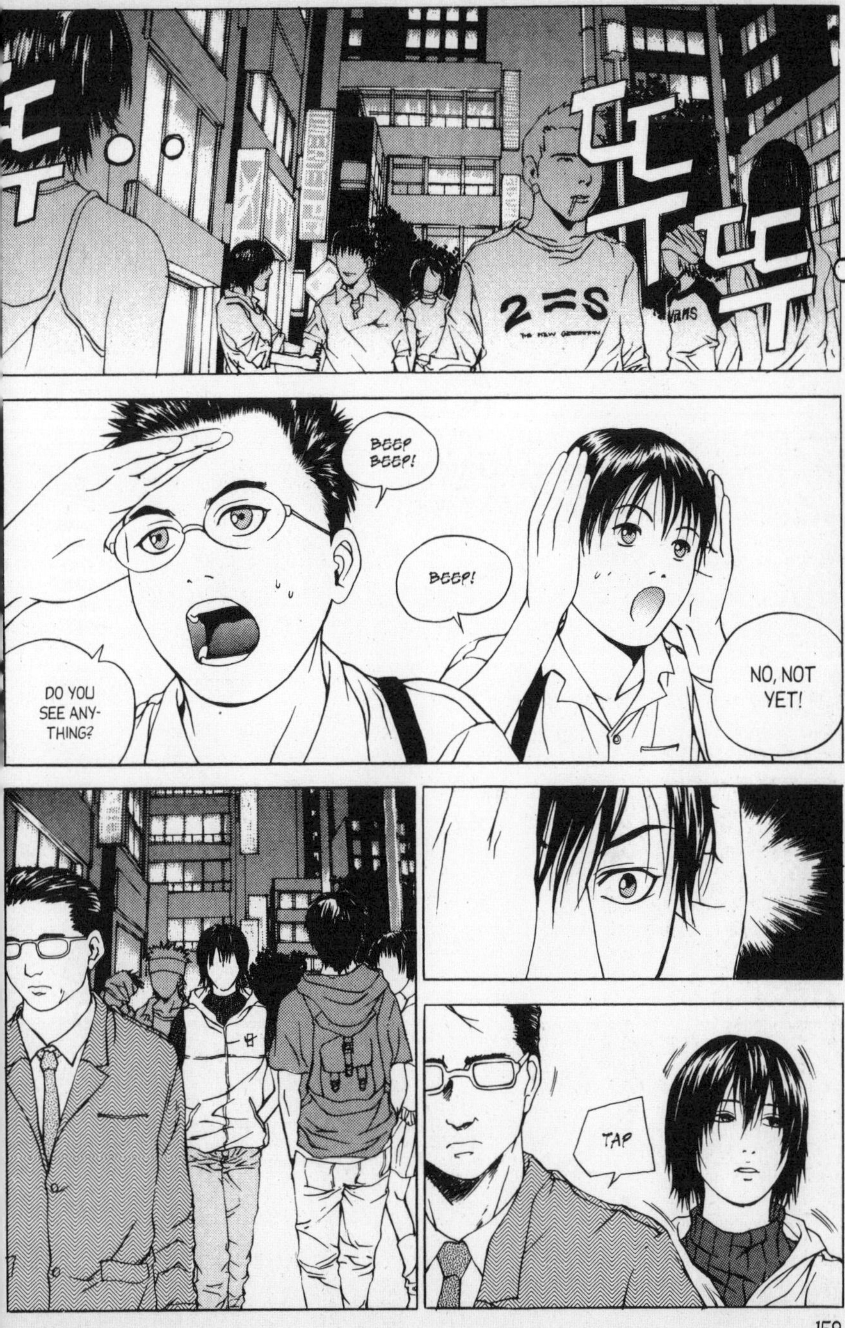
BEEP BEEP!
BEEP!
DO YOU SEE ANY-THING?
NO, NOT YET!
TAP

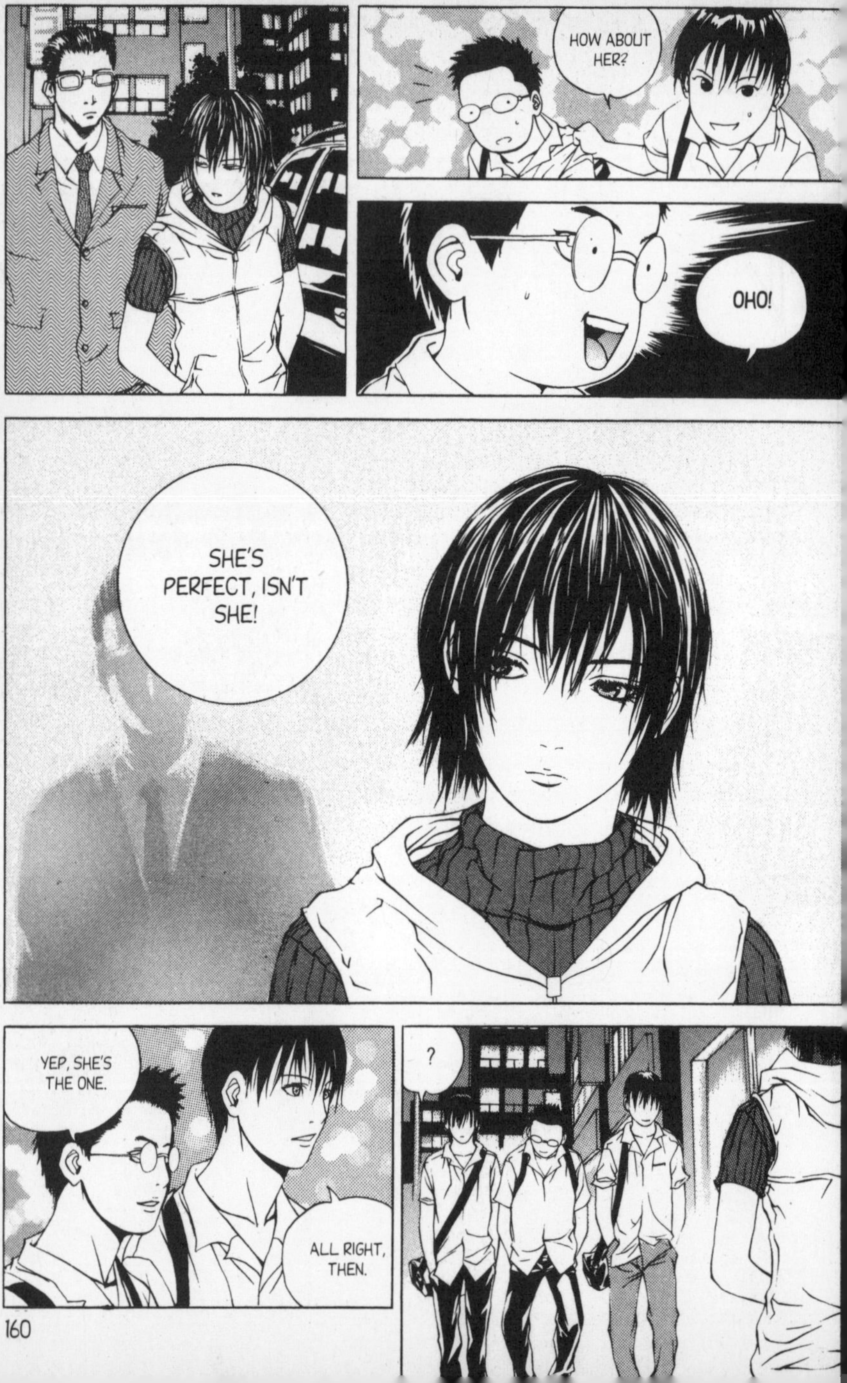

HOW ABOUT HER?
OHO!
SHE'S PERFECT, ISN'T SHE!
?
YEP, SHE'S THE ONE.
ALL RIGHT, THEN.

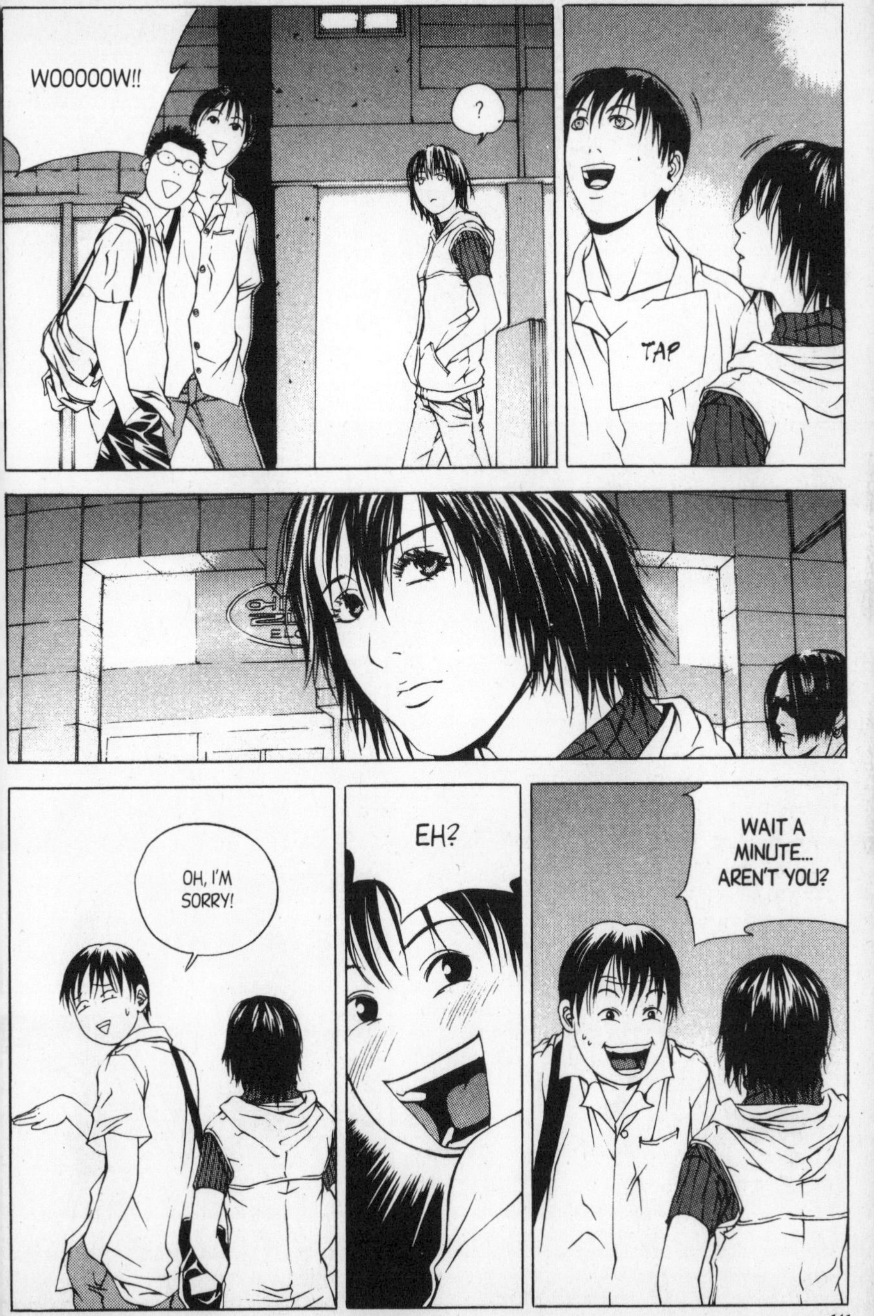
TAP
?
WOOOOOW!!
WAIT A MINUTE... AREN'T YOU?
EH?
OH, I'M SORRY!

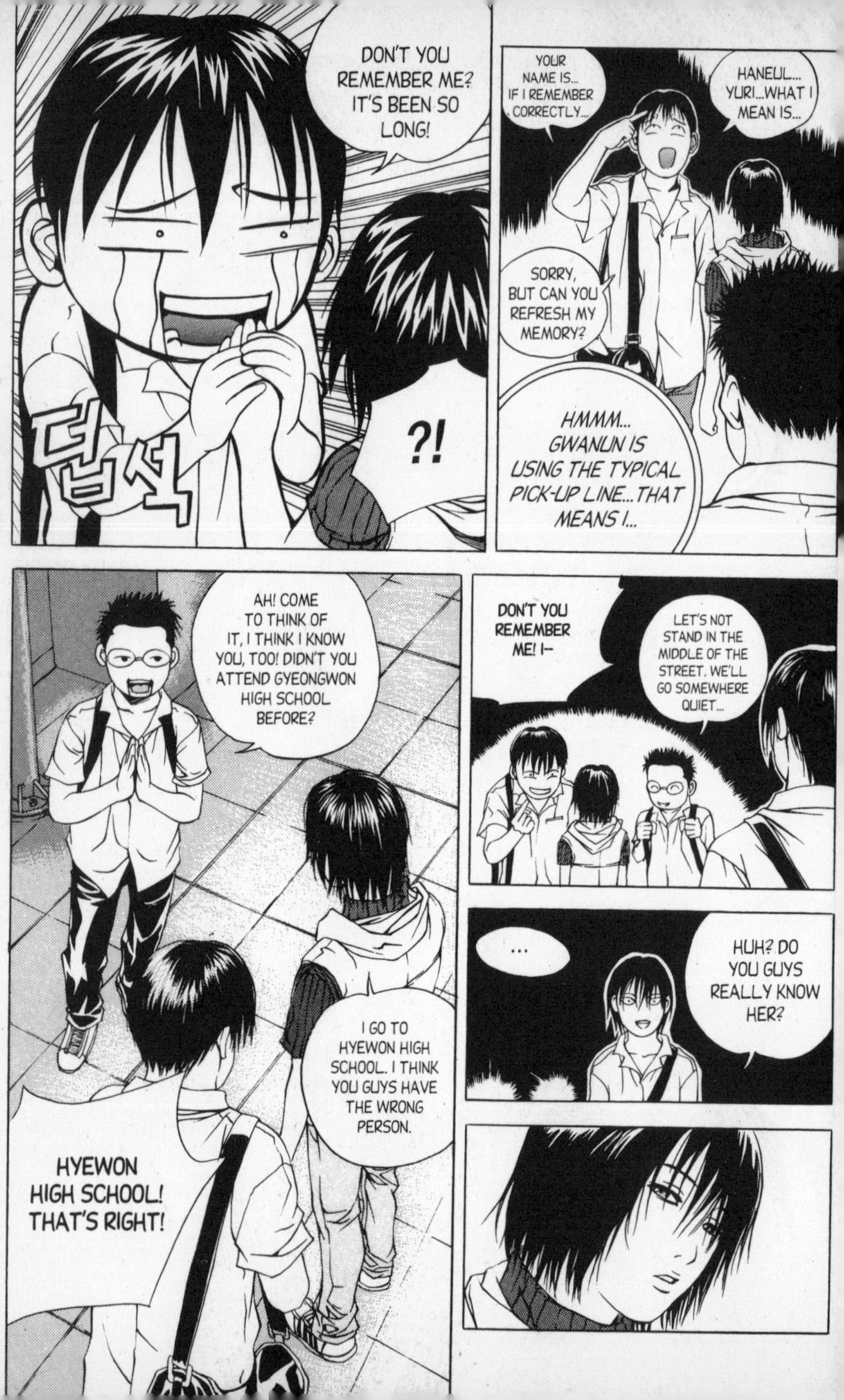
DON'T YOU REMEMBER ME? IT'S BEEN SO LONG!
덥석
?!
YOUR NAME IS... IF I REMEMBER CORRECTLY...
HANEUL... YURI...WHAT I MEAN IS...
SORRY, BUT CAN YOU REFRESH MY MEMORY?
HMMM... GWANUN IS USING THE TYPICAL PICK-UP LINE...THAT MEANS I...
AH! COME TO THINK OF IT, I THINK I KNOW YOU, TOO! DIDN'T YOU ATTEND GYEONGWON HIGH SCHOOL BEFORE?
I GO TO HYEWON HIGH SCHOOL. I THINK YOU GUYS HAVE THE WRONG PERSON.
HYEWON HIGH SCHOOL! THAT'S RIGHT!
DON'T YOU REMEMBER ME! I—
LET'S NOT STAND IN THE MIDDLE OF THE STREET. WE'LL GO SOMEWHERE QUIET...
...
HUH? DO YOU GUYS REALLY KNOW HER?

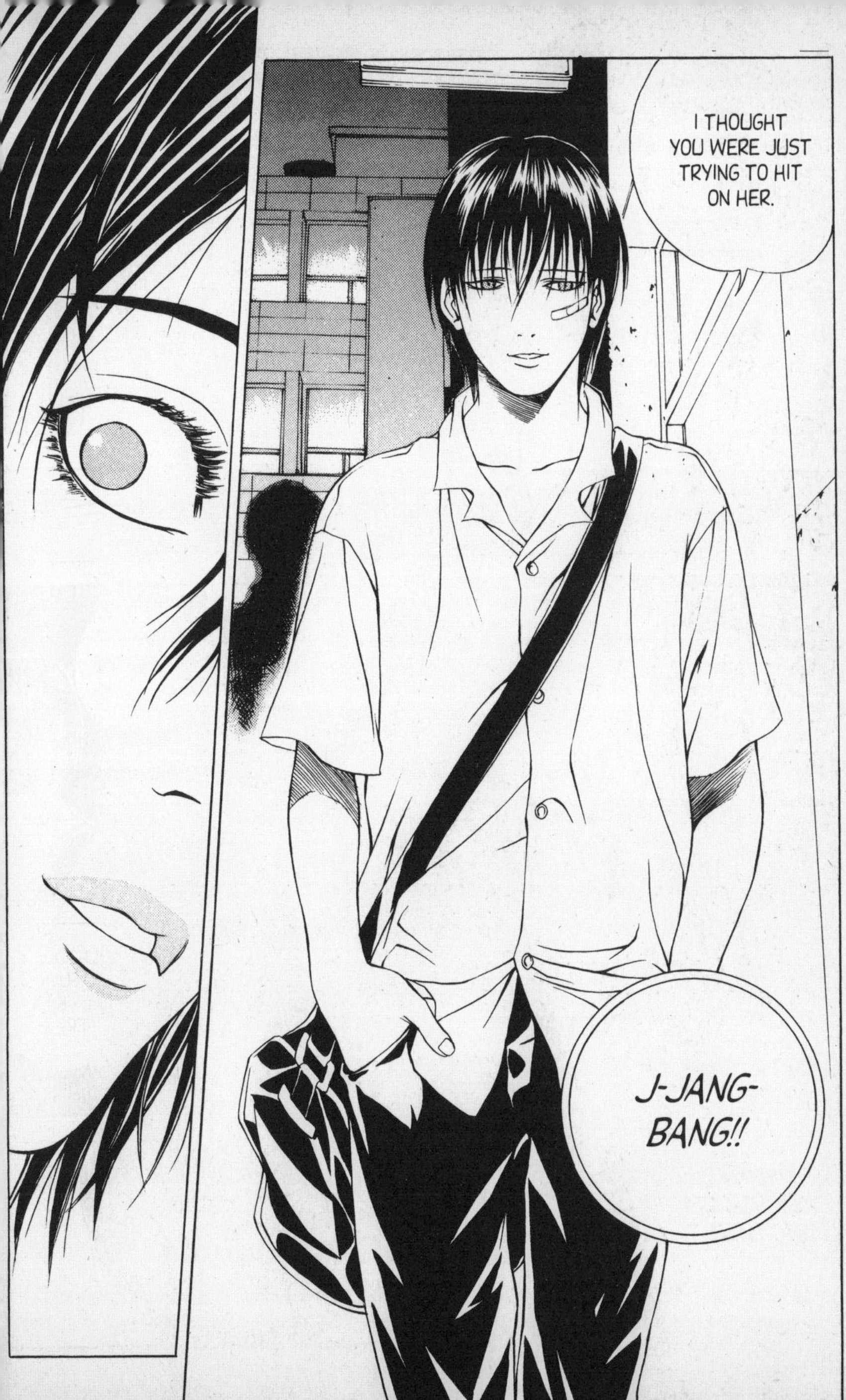
I THOUGHT YOU WERE JUST TRYING TO HIT ON HER.
J-JANG-BANG!!

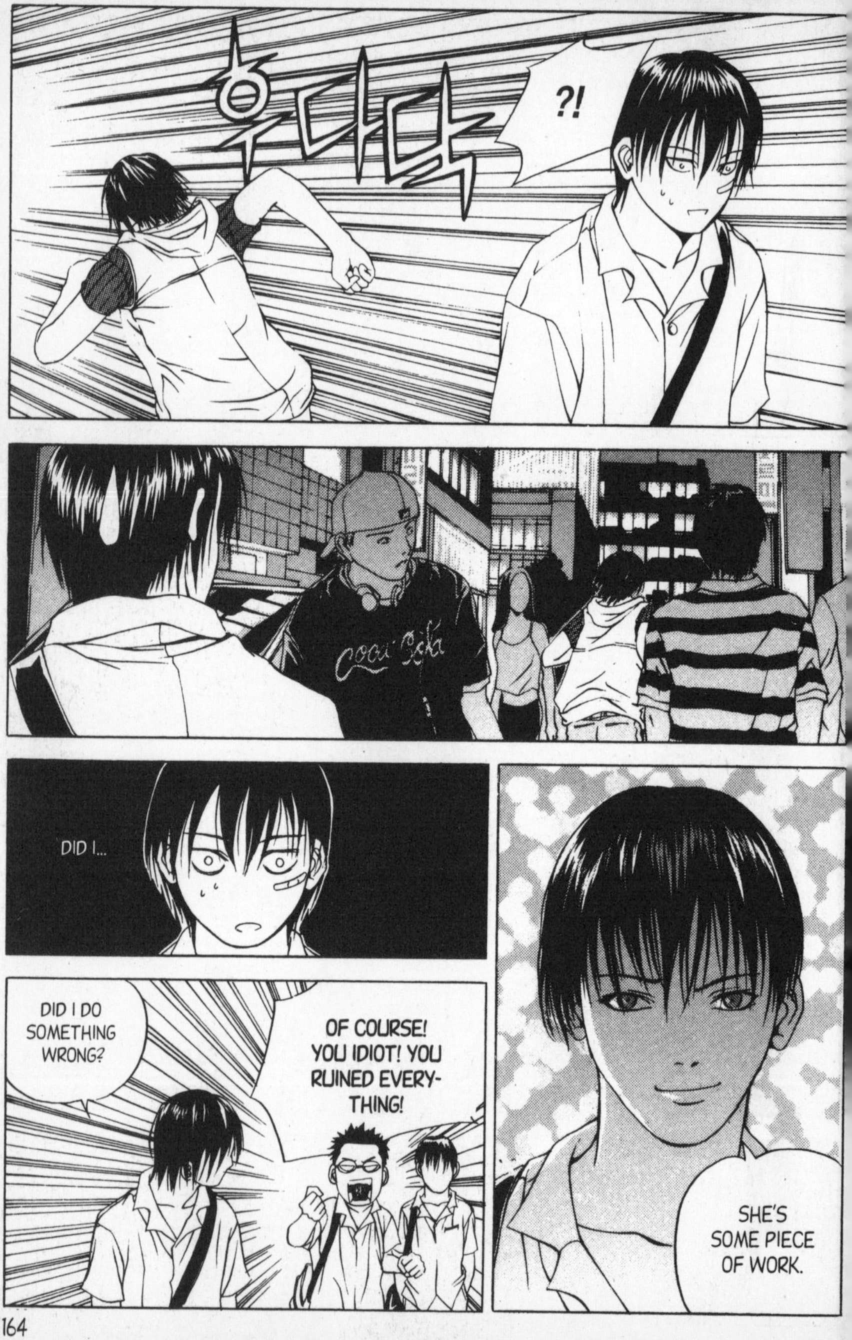

후다닥
?!
DID I...
DID I DO SOMETHING WRONG?
OF COURSE! YOU IDIOT! YOU RUINED EVERY-THING!
SHE'S SOME PIECE OF WORK.

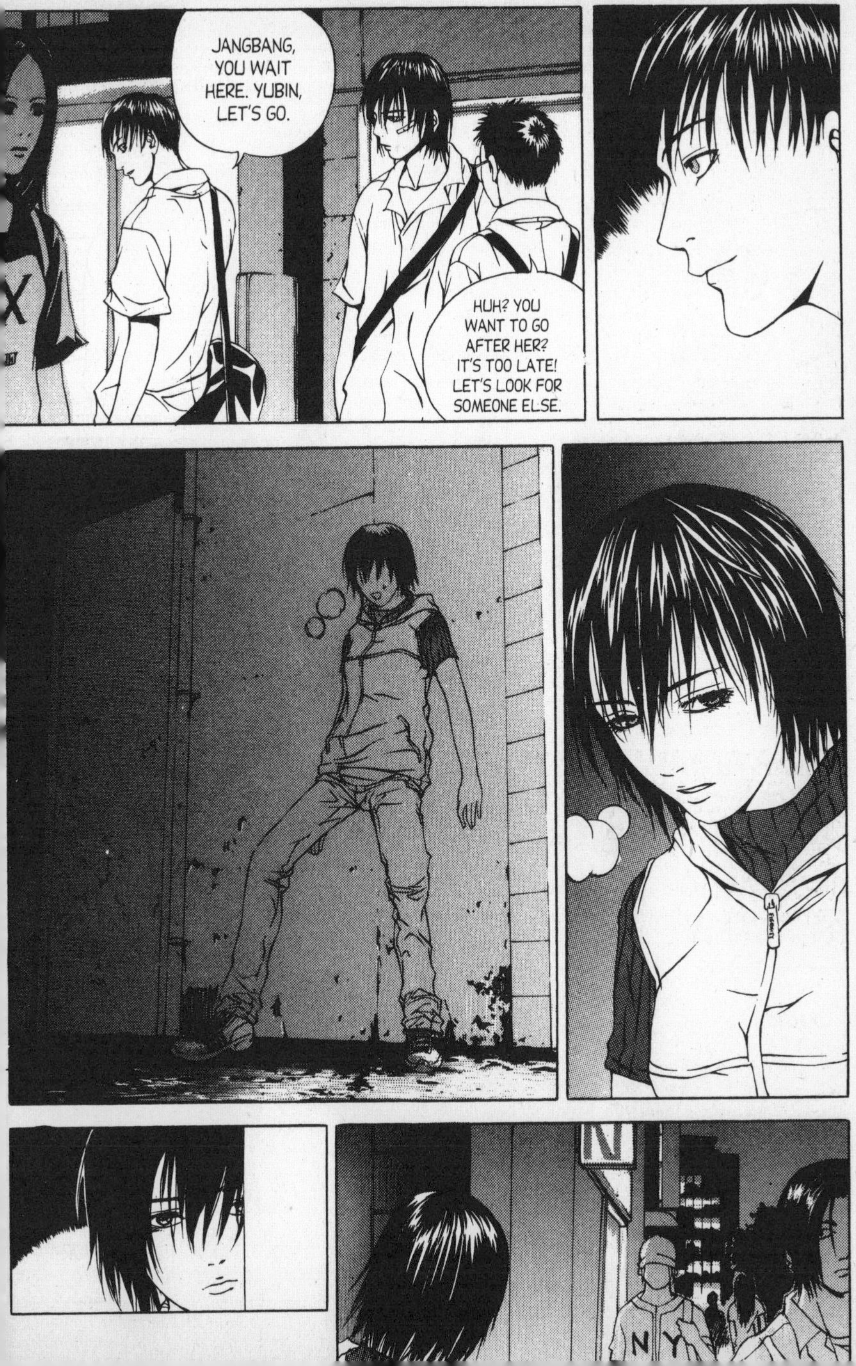
JANGBANG, YOU WAIT HERE. YUBIN, LET'S GO.
HUH? YOU WANT TO GO AFTER HER? IT'S TOO LATE! LET'S LOOK FOR SOMEONE ELSE.

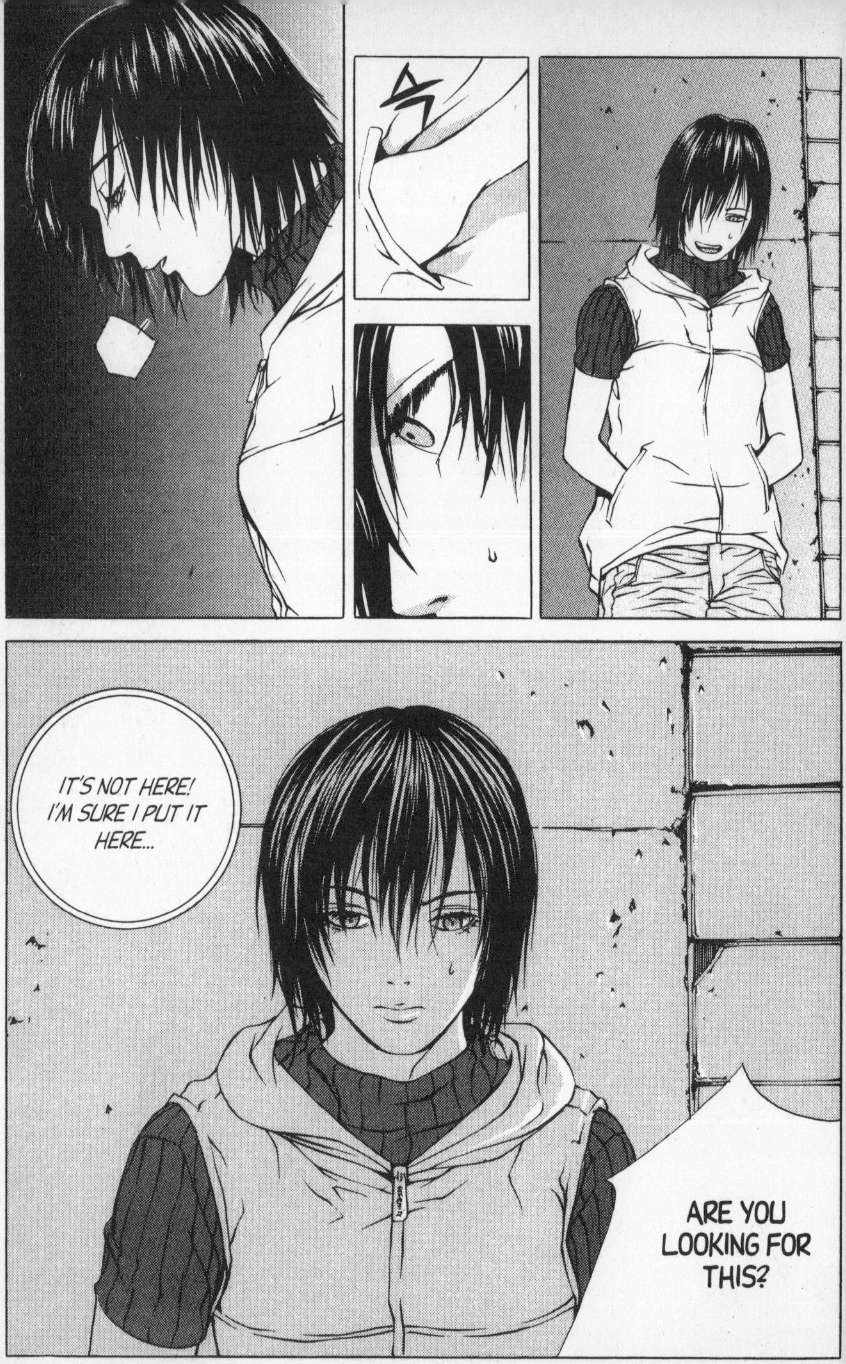
IT'S NOT HERE! I'M SURE I PUT IT HERE...
ARE YOU LOOKING FOR THIS?

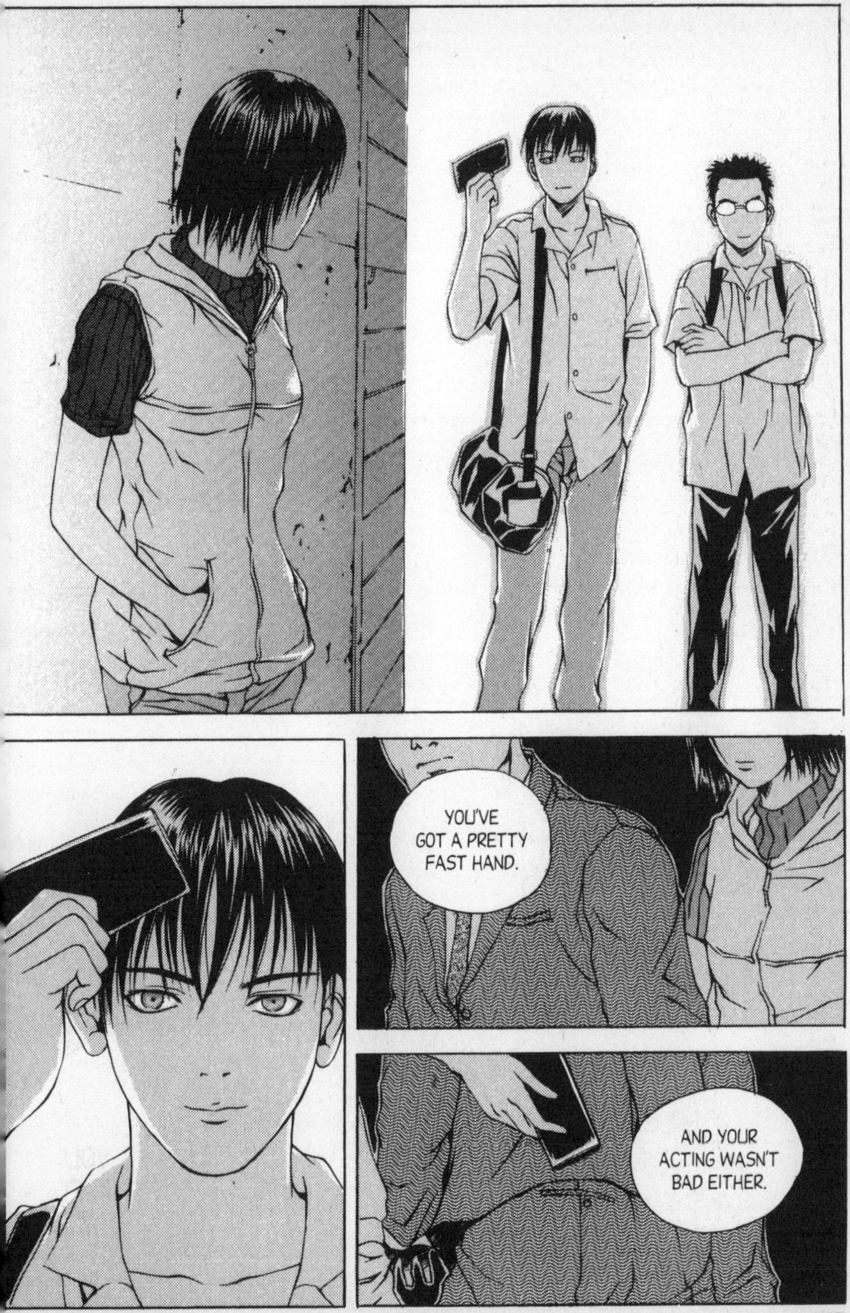
YOU'VE GOT A PRETTY FAST HAND.
AND YOUR ACTING WASN'T BAD EITHER.

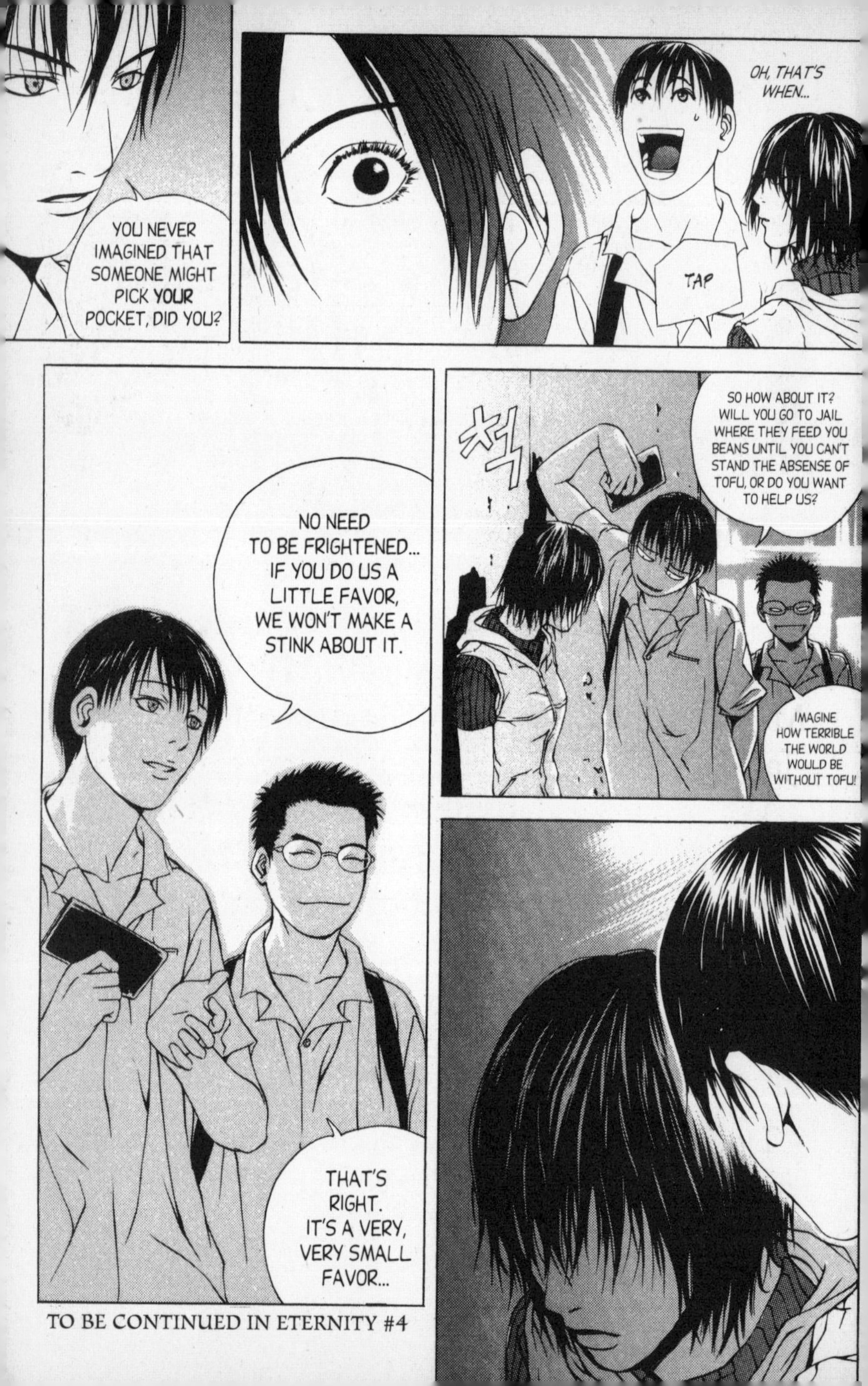
OH, THAT'S WHEN...
TAP
YOU NEVER IMAGINED THAT SOMEONE MIGHT PICK **YOUR** POCKET, DID YOU?
SO HOW ABOUT IT? WILL YOU GO TO JAIL WHERE THEY FEED YOU BEANS UNTIL YOU CAN'T STAND THE ABSENSE OF TOFU, OR DO YOU WANT TO HELP US?
IMAGINE HOW TERRIBLE THE WORLD WOULD BE WITHOUT TOFU!
NO NEED TO BE FRIGHTENED... IF YOU DO US A LITTLE FAVOR, WE WON'T MAKE A STINK ABOUT IT.
THAT'S RIGHT. IT'S A VERY, VERY SMALL FAVOR...

TO BE CONTINUED IN ETERNITY #4

IN THE NEXT VOLUME OF

ETERNITY

It looks like Jangbang is falling in love...but can you ever really trust a thief? Meanwhile, Mosa and the Gang of Six are still targeting Jangbang in an attempt to bring down Jojo. When they take Yubin hostage, it's up to Jangbang to rescue his friend. However, provoking Jangbang might ultimately open up a can of whoop-ass, the likes of which hasn't been seen in nearly 2,000 years! Be careful what you wish for, Mosa!

Timeless intrigue and action continues in ETERNITY volume 4!

ALSO AVAILABLE FROM 🐧 TOKYOPOP®

MANGA

.HACK//LEGEND OF THE TWILIGHT
@LARGE
ABENOBASHI: MAGICAL SHOPPING ARCADE
A.I. LOVE YOU
AI YORI AOSHI
ALICHINO
ANGELIC LAYER
ARM OF KANNON
BABY BIRTH
BATTLE ROYALE
BATTLE VIXENS
BOYS BE...
BRAIN POWERED
BRIGADOON
B'TX
CANDIDATE FOR GODDESS, THE
CARDCAPTOR SAKURA
CARDCAPTOR SAKURA - MASTER OF THE CLOW
CHOBITS
CHRONICLES OF THE CURSED SWORD
CLAMP SCHOOL DETECTIVES
CLOVER
COMIC PARTY
CONFIDENTIAL CONFESSIONS
CORRECTOR YUI
COWBOY BEBOP
COWBOY BEBOP: SHOOTING STAR
CRAZY LOVE STORY
CRESCENT MOON
CROSS
CULDCEPT
CYBORG 009
D•N•ANGEL
DEARS
DEMON DIARY
DEMON ORORON, THE
DEUS VITAE
DIABOLO
DIGIMON
DIGIMON TAMERS
DIGIMON ZERO TWO
DOLL
DRAGON HUNTER
DRAGON KNIGHTS
DRAGON VOICE
DREAM SAGA
DUKLYON: CLAMP SCHOOL DEFENDERS
EERIE QUEERIE!
ERICA SAKURAZAWA: COLLECTED WORKS
ET CETERA
ETERNITY
EVIL'S RETURN
FAERIES' LANDING
FAKE
FLCL
FLOWER OF THE DEEP SLEEP
FORBIDDEN DANCE
FRUITS BASKET
G GUNDAM
GATEKEEPERS
GETBACKERS

GIRL GOT GAME
GRAVITATION
GTO
GUNDAM SEED ASTRAY
GUNDAM SEED ASTRAY R
GUNDAM WING
GUNDAM WING: BATTLEFIELD OF PACIFISTS
GUNDAM WING: ENDLESS WALTZ
GUNDAM WING: THE LAST OUTPOST (G-UNIT)
HANDS OFF!
HAPPY MANIA
HARLEM BEAT
HYPER POLICE
HYPER RUNE
I.N.V.U.
IMMORTAL RAIN
INITIAL D
INSTANT TEEN: JUST ADD NUTS
ISLAND
JING: KING OF BANDITS
JING: KING OF BANDITS - TWILIGHT TALES
JULINE
KARE KANO
KILL ME, KISS ME
KINDAICHI CASE FILES, THE
KING OF HELL
KODOCHA: SANA'S STAGE
LAGOON ENGINE
LAMENT OF THE LAMB
LEGAL DRUG
LEGEND OF CHUN HYANG, THE
LES BIJOUX
LILING-PO
LOVE HINA
LOVE OR MONEY
LUPIN III
LUPIN III: WORLD'S MOST WANTED
MAGIC KNIGHT RAYEARTH I
MAGIC KNIGHT RAYEARTH II
MAHOROMATIC: AUTOMATIC MAIDEN
MAN OF MANY FACES
MARMALADE BOY
MARS
MARS: HORSE WITH NO NAME
MINK
MIRACLE GIRLS
MIYUKI-CHAN IN WONDERLAND
MODEL
MOURYOU KIDEN: LEGEND OF THE NYMPH
NECK AND NECK
ONE
ONE I LOVE, THE
PARADISE KISS
PARASYTE
PASSION FRUIT
PEACH FUZZ
PEACH GIRL
PEACH GIRL: CHANGE OF HEART
PET SHOP OF HORRORS
PHD: PHANTASY DEGREE
PITA-TEN
PLANET BLOOD
PLANET LADDER

10.19.04T

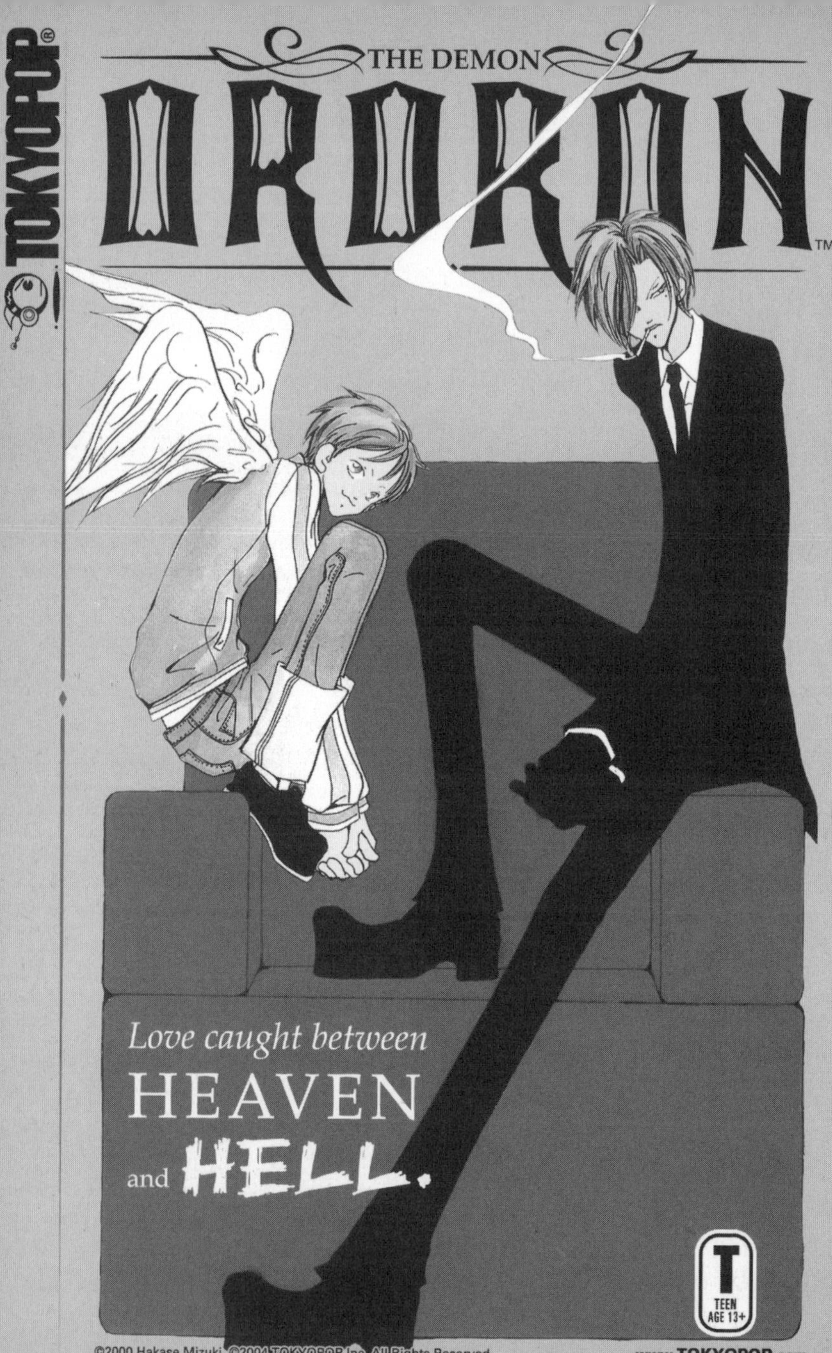
TOKYOPOP®
THE DEMON
ORORON
TM
Love caught between
HEAVEN
and HELL.
T
TEEN
AGE 13+

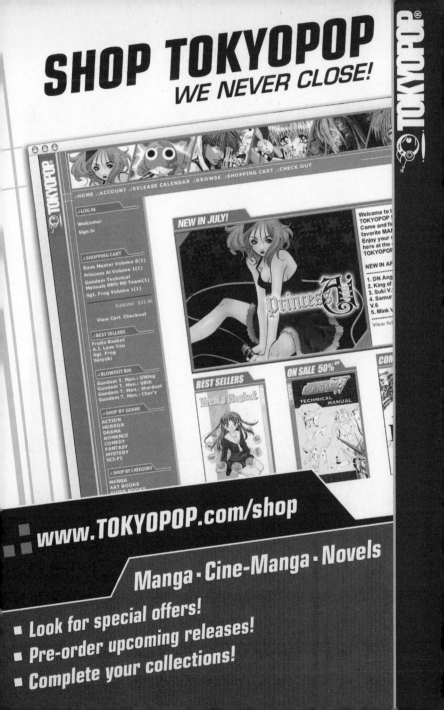

BOYS BE

A GUY'S GUIDE TO GIRLS

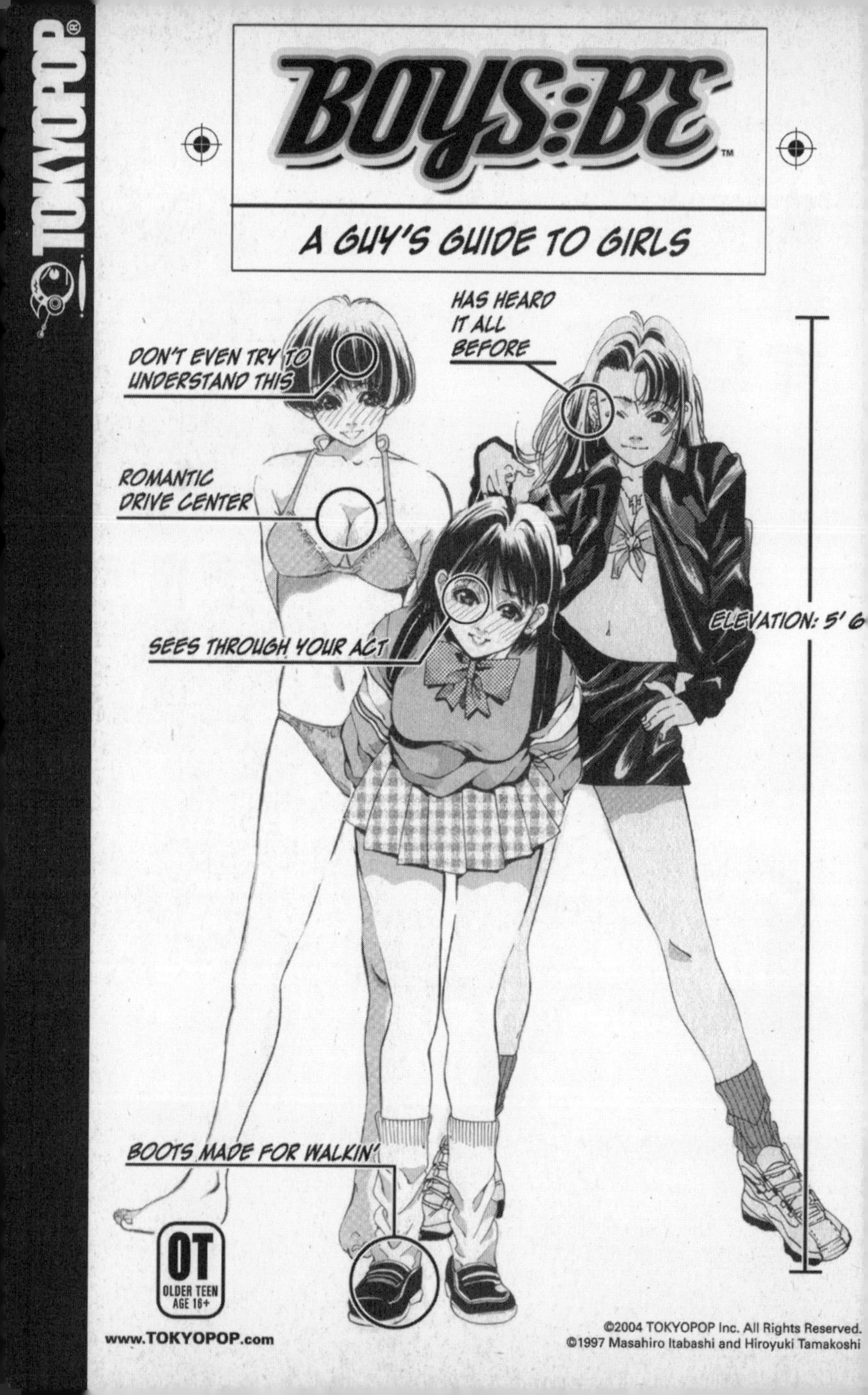
HAS HEARD IT ALL BEFORE
DON'T EVEN TRY TO UNDERSTAND THIS
ROMANTIC DRIVE CENTER
SEES THROUGH YOUR ACT
ELEVATION: 5' 6
BOOTS MADE FOR WALKIN'

OT OLDER TEEN AGE 16+